AU-18
Space Primer

Prepared by

AIR COMMAND AND STAFF COLLEGE
SPACE RESEARCH ELECTIVES SEMINARS

Air University Press
Air Force Research Institute
Maxwell Air Force Base, Alabama

September 2009

ISBN 978-1-58566-194-7

First Printing June 2010

Disclaimer

Air University Press
Air Force Research Institute
155 N. Twining Street
Maxwell AFB AL 36112-6026
http://aupress.au.af.mil

Contents

CONTENTS

Chapter		Page

Foreword

The US National Space Policy released by the president in 2006 states that the US government should "develop space professionals." As an integral part of that endeavor, AU-18, *Space Primer*, provides to the joint war fighter an unclassified resource for understanding the capabilities, organizations, and operations of space forces.

Historically, the United States has been a world leader in space exploration and use. In 2001, the Commission to Assess United States National Security Space Management and Organization unanimously concluded "that the security and well being of the United States, its allies, and friends depend on the nation's ability to operate in space."[1] Recent conflicts and world events continuously demonstrate the importance of space assets and capabilities to our security functions. Our navigation satellites provide instant pinpoint positional and targeting information to aircraft, ground forces, ships, and command centers. These same satellites provide a precise timing source around the world that is critical to maintaining infrastructures, including financial institutions, power grids, cell phones, and even our cable and satellite TV. Communications satellites provide global connectivity between all levels of our national security infrastructure. Weather satellites report meteorological data, better than ever before, in near real time directly to forces in theater. Early warning satellites detect and report missile launches and serve as both strategic and tactical theater warning. These same early warning satellites serve to cue the integrated missile defense system. Finally, the US government conducts satellite photo reconnaissance that includes near-real-time capability, overhead signals intelligence collection, and overhead measurement and signature intelligence collection, which contribute directly to the success of our war fighters.

This primer is a useful tool both for individuals who are not "space aware"—unacquainted with space capabilities, organizations, and operations—and for those who are "space aware," especially individuals associated with the space community, but not familiar with space capabilities, organizations, and operations outside their particular areas of expertise. It is your guide and your invitation to all the excitement and opportunity of space.

Last published in 1993, this updated version of the *Space Primer* has been made possible by combined efforts of the Air Command and Staff College's academic year 2008 "Jointspacemindedness" and "Operational Space" research seminars, as well as select members of the academic year 2009 "Advanced Space" research seminar.

ALLEN G. PECK
Lieutenant General, USAF
Commander, Air University

FOREWORD

Note

1. Commission to Assess US National Security Space Management and Organization, *Report of the Commission*, 11 January 2001.

Preface

This is a new beginning. It was 1993 when the predecessor to this document was last published, and much has changed. When we were asked to take on the challenge of updating and preparing the *Space Primer* for publication, we, in retrospect, did not fully understand what we were agreeing to. I, for one, certainly have a newfound respect for published authors. This product is the culmination of literally thousands of hours of work by many Air Command and Staff College (ACSC) students, ACSC faculty members, and the team at Air University Press working directly on this project, as well as many others who helped in some way or another. I am very proud of the dedicated team that contributed so much to making this project happen. They deserve the credit for all that is good in this *Space Primer*.

The purpose of the AU-18 *Space Primer* is to provide an unclassified "one-stop shopping" resource for the space professional and the joint war fighter to better understand the capabilities, organizations, and operations of space forces. We certainly hope you will find this product useful, and where you find errors, we ask that you will both forgive us and help us make this product better during the next revision. There is, no doubt, room for improvement. There was certainly much discussion on what should be included and who the target audience would be. Often it was quite difficult for our team to agree. Imagine trying to write an "air primer" that includes flight dynamics, physics, fighters, bombers, ISR, acquisitions, law, and so forth. That is what we were asked to do with this *Space Primer*, while making it useful for both the "credentialed space professional" and the joint war fighter. For those readers who find fault with the design, scope, or some other area of this product, it may be tempting to think, "I could have done better." I sincerely hope you do. If the best thing that comes from this publication is a new and better future version of the *Space Primer*, then we, the team that put this version together, will be very pleased. I do hope that it won't be another 16 years before the next version is published.

This product is in print due to the dedicated efforts of many people who deserve thanks! We greatly appreciate the support of the following organizations and the many fine individuals who assisted us in these organizations: Air Command and Staff College, Air University Press, the National Space Studies Center, and Air Force Space Command. I want to specifically thank my Air University Press editor, Ms. Demorah Hayes, for her patient guidance and tireless efforts. Without her, this project would likely not have been completed.

For my part, I would like to thank Col Jim Forsyth, USAF, retired, PhD, and Lt Col Jim Parco, USAF, PhD, for their patience and mentoring. During our tenure together at ACSC, they were very generous with their time, despite their many duties and commitments. They instilled in me a passion for education, both teaching and learning. To both of you, I am grateful and hope to continue on the journey you have helped me to begin.

I also wish to thank my wife, Jennifer, for her patience and understanding while I spent many hours working on this project at home, because I couldn't find the time while at work. To any organizations or persons I have inadvertently left out, that responsibility is mine alone; please accept my apologies and my thanks.

If you wish to comment on the *Space Primer* or suggest revisions for future editions, please send your feedback to AU18-updates@afspc.af.mil.

BRIAN C. TICHENOR
Lieutenant Colonel, USAF
Director, Advanced Space Research
Air Command and Staff College

List of Contributors

Air Command and Staff College

Academic Year 2008 Students

Maj Burton "Ernie" Catledge, USAF — Space and Missile Operations
Maj Edward "Ed" Chatters IV, USAF — Space Developmental Engineer
Maj Brian "Flash" Crothers, USAF — Space Developmental Engineer
Maj Bryan "Troll" Eberhardt, USAF — Communications and Information
Maj Brian Garino, USAF — Intelligence
Maj Jane Gibson, USAF — Space and Missile Operations
MAJ Kenneth "Ken" Kemmerly, USA — Communications and Information
Maj Christopher "Chris" King, USAF — Space and Missile Operations
Maj Jeffrey "Jefe" Lanphear, USAF — Space and Missile Operations
Maj Gabriel "Gabe" Medina, Dominican Republic Air Force — Mobility Pilot
LCDR Jeremy Powell, USN — Surface Warfare
MAJ Dillard "Wes" Young, USA — Armor/Cavalry

Academic Year 2009 Students

Maj Edward Byrne, USAF*+ — Space Developmental Engineer
Maj Paul "PK" Konyha III, USAF* — Space Developmental Engineer
Maj Jennifer Krolikowski, USAF — Space Developmental Engineer
Maj Michael Warner, USAF — Space Developmental Engineer

* Assistant Editor
+ Graphics Editor

ACSC Faculty Support

Lt Col Brian Tichenor — Research Director and Faculty Editor
Lt Col Winston "Pumbaa" Gould — Research Advisor
Lt Col Jonathon "J-Lo" Lowe — Research Advisor
Lt Col Bert Sparrow — Research Advisor
Maj Sean "Smokin" Boles — Faculty Editor
Lt Col Christine Weaver — Faculty Editor

About the Contributors

Maj Sean P. Boles (BS, aerospace engineering, US Naval Academy, Annapolis, MD; MBA, aeronautical and aviation business management, Embry-Riddle Aeronautical University, Daytona Beach, FL) is a faculty instructor and advisor on US armed forces, joint campaign planning and execution, air operations centers, and the Defense Intelligence Agency at Air Command and Staff College (ACSC), Air University. He instructs select international and US field grade officers and DOD civilians in the operational art of applying contemporary air and space power in support of US national objectives. Major Boles enlisted in the Navy and completed Machinist Mate "A" School, Naval Nuclear Power School, and the Navy Nuclear Power Prototype School, receiving top honors in 1989. After being assigned to the ballistic nuclear submarine, USS *Henry M. Jackson* (Fleet Ballistic Missile Submarine 736), Bangor, WA, he attended the Naval Academy. Upon graduation, Major Boles was commissioned in the Air Force on 29 May 1996 by an interservice exchange program. His career includes assignments as space and missile officer for Peacekeeper Intercontinental Ballistic Missile (ICBM) system, a mission planner and flight commander for the Defense Meteorological Satellite Program, and the project manager of proof-of-concept WindSat Coriolis Satellite Program for the National Polar-Orbiting Environmental Satellite System (NPOESS) Integrated Program Office. He was a core member of the Commander's Action Group, which included the Twentieth Air Force commander's executive officer, the chief, Current Operations, and deputy chief, Missile Operations at Headquarters (HQ) Twentieth Air Force. Major Boles is also a graduate of the Squadron Officer School (SOS) and ACSC.

Maj Edward P. Byrne (BS, aerospace engineering, State University of New York at Buffalo; MBA, Webster University, Los Angeles AFB, CA; master of military operational art and science [MMOAS], ACSC, Maxwell AFB, AL) was commissioned through Officer Training School (OTS) in May 1996. Major Byrne currently serves as flight commander for radar development and integration, Hanscom AFB, MA. His career includes assignments as chief, Satellite Command and Control Systems Modification Branch, Space and Missile Systems Center, Operating Location AO at Onizuka AFS, CA; flight commander and chief, Spacecraft Systems Branch, Operating Division 4 at Onizuka AFS, CA; chief, Delta II Mission Management, Space and Missile Systems Center at Los Angeles AFB, CA; and chief, Space and Launch Development Segment at the National Reconnaissance Office, Chantilly, VA. Major Byrne is also a resident graduate of SOS and ACSC.

Maj Burton H. Catledge (BA, speech communications, University of Northern Colorado, Greeley; MS, human resource management, Troy University, Malmstrom AFB, MT) is currently a student at ACSC. Major Catledge entered the Air Force in 1995. His career includes assignments as an ICBM crew commander, missile warning flight commander, 35th Fighter Wing chief of operational plans, and Pacific Air Forces chief of special technical operations. Major Catledge is also a resident graduate of SOS and the Air Force Weapons School.

Maj Edward P. Chatters IV (BS, aerospace and astronautical engineering, Auburn University, AL; MS, computer information systems, University of Phoenix, AZ) is currently the military assistant to the deputy assistant secretary of the Air Force for science, technology, and engineering at HQ US Air Force, Washington, DC. Major Chatters enlisted in the Marine Corps as an infantryman in 1993, received a commission in

1996, and served as a field artillery officer with the 1st Battalion, 10th Marine Regiment, 2nd Marine Division and subsequently as the operations officer of HQ and Support Battalion, Marine Corps Base, Camp Lejeune, NC. He transferred to the Air Force in November 2000 to work as a developmental engineer at the Air Force Research Laboratory (AFRL), Space Vehicles Directorate at Kirtland AFB, NM. Major Chatters' career includes assignments as an artillery platoon commander, target information officer for the 24th Marine Expeditionary Unit, battalion operations officer, lead engineer for spacecraft component technology team, deputy chief of the Space-Based Infrared Technology Branch, executive officer of AFRL Phillips Research Site, and orbital analyst and flight commander for the 1st Space Control Squadron, Cheyenne Mountain AFS, CO. Major Chatters is also a resident graduate of SOS and ACSC.

Maj Brian J. Crothers (BS, electrical engineering, Virginia Military Institute, Lexington; MS, electrical engineering, Air Force Institute of Technology (AFIT), Wright-Patterson AFB, OH) is currently a faculty instructor at ACSC, following his graduation as a student at the school. Major Crothers was commissioned in the Air Force in 1995. He has served previously as chief engineer for 25th Space Control and Tactics Squadron. Prior to that assignment he was a flight commander in the 36th Electronic Warfare Squadron, responsible for the electronic warfare reprogramming of F-16 and A-10 electronic warfare equipment. Before that he was flight commander, Test Support Flight, in the 346th Test Squadron, Air Force Information Warfare Center. There he supported electronic warfare effectiveness assessments for Compass Call and EA-6B Prowlers during Red Flag/Green Flag exercises and provided radio frequency vulnerability and emissions control assessments for a variety of other customers. Major Crothers was selected to attend the in-residence engineering program at AFIT as a 4IBY (specializing in electromagnetic field theory). His initial assignment was as a human factors engineer working on helmet-mounted cueing systems.

Maj Bryan T. Eberhardt (BS, computer science, Virginia Military Institute, Lexington; MA, international relations, Oklahoma University, Ramstein AB, Germany) is the commander of the 8th Communications Squadron, Kunsan AB, Republic of Korea. Major Eberhardt entered the Air Force in 1996. His career includes assignments as a program control manager for the Global Air Transportation and Execution System for Air Mobility Command's Computer Systems Squadron; an executive officer for the 631st Air Mobility Support Squadron; command and control systems flight commander for the 751st Communications Squadron at Osan AB, Republic of Korea; a current operations cell chief, war planner, and career field manager for the US Air Forces in Europe Communications and Information Directorate at Ramstein AB, Germany; and a network services flight commander and deputy commander in the 1st Communications Squadron at Langley AFB, VA. He has deployed as chief of current operations for the Combined Air Forces-North Communications and Information Directorate at Incirlik AB, Turkey, during Operation Iraqi Freedom (OIF) and was an infrastructure planner for Combined Joint Task Force 76 at Bagram AF, Afghanistan, in support of Operation Enduring Freedom (OEF). Major Eberhardt is also a resident graduate of SOS and ACSC.

Maj Brian W. Garino (BS, aviation management, flight technology, Florida Institute of Technology, Melbourne; MAS, aeronautical science, Embry Riddle Aeronautical University) is director of operations, 314th Training Squadron, Monterey, CA. Major Garino was commissioned via OTS in 1996. His career includes assignments as a squadron intelligence officer for a KC-135 squadron, counterterrorism officer at USCENTCOM, wing intelligence officer at McChord AFB, and executive officer for the J2 at US Joint Forces Command. Additionally, he completed an internship at the Defense Research Project Agency in 2006. He has deployed numerous times in support of Operations Northern Watch, Southern Watch, Allied Force, Enduring Freedom, and Iraqi Freedom.

Maj Jane E. Gibson (BS, biology, Air Force Academy, Colorado Springs, CO; MMOAS, ACSC, Maxwell AFB, AL) is the deputy, Operational Support and Sustainment Division SY/OS, Space Superiority Systems Wing, Space and Missile Systems Center, Los Angeles AFB, CA. The Space Superiority Systems Wing is responsible for equipping the joint war fighter with unrivaled offensive and defensive counterspace, space situation awareness, and special access required (SAR) capabilities required to gain, maintain, and exploit space superiority. Major Gibson entered the Air Force in 1994. Her career includes assignments as a deputy missile combat crew commander, missile combat crew commander and chief, Weapons and Tactics Codes Training at Malmstrom AFB, MT; orbital analyst and space control analyst at Cheyenne Mountain AFS, CO; and counterspace threat analyst and HQ squadron section commander at the National Air and Space Intelligence Center, Wright-Patterson AFB, OH. Major Gibson is a resident graduate of SOS and ACSC.

Lt Col Winston Gould (BS, business administration, Baptist College at Charleston, SC; MAS, aviation operations and management, Embry-Riddle Aeronautical University, Malmstrom AFB, MT; MMOAS, ACSC, Maxwell AFB, AL) currently serves as an airborne strike advisor, US Strategic Command (USSTRATCOM) Airborne Command Post, J317, Offutt AFB, NE. He previously served as the director of staff for the Department of International Security and Military Studies at ACSC. His deployment experience includes an assignment as a strategic policy planner with the Strategic Plans and Policy Directorate, Combined Forces Command—Afghanistan, in Kabul (OEF). Prior to his assignment to ACSC, he served as an airborne launch control system/intelligence planner instructor/evaluator aboard the E-6B Mercury aircraft. He has also served as the course chairman for the Information Warfare Applications Course, as an emergency war order planner for the 341st Missile Wing, and in various crewmember assignments, including senior instructor crew commander for the Minuteman III/CDB (Deuce) weapon system. Lieutenant Colonel Gould is a command ICBM operator with 168 Minuteman III/CDB alerts, 24 USSTRATCOM ground alerts, and 1,300 hours in the E-6B Mercury airframe. He is also a resident graduate of SOS and ACSC and a nonresident graduate of Air War College.

MAJ Kenneth G. Kemmerly (BA, criminology, Saint Leo University, Saint Leo, FL; MS, information technology management, Touro University International, Los Alamitos, CA; MMOAS, ACSC, Maxwell AFB, AL) is the J6, Joint Task Force Paladin, Joint Improvised Explosive Device Defeat Organization (JIEDDO), Afghanistan. Major Kemmerly is an Army signal officer who was commissioned by the Officer Candidate School in 1994. His career includes assignments as a signal platoon leader, signal company commander, brigade S6, observer controller/trainer, and command, control, communications, computers, and intelligence (C4I) combat developer for the Army's Future Combat Systems program. Major Kemmerly's military education includes Signal Officer Basic and Advanced Courses, Branch Automation Course, Airborne School, Combined Arms and Services Staff School, and ACSC.

Maj Paul P. Konyha III (BS, mechanical engineering, Louisiana Tech University, Ruston; MS, space studies, University of North Dakota, Grand Forks; MMOAS, ACSC, Maxwell AFB, AL) was commissioned through the Air Force Reserve Officer Training Corps in May 1996. Major Konyha currently serves as chief, Atlas V Engineering Division, Space and Missile Systems Center, Los Angeles AFB, CA. His career includes assignments as a Peacekeeper ICBM combat crew member and instructor at F. E. Warren AFB, WY; chief advanced communications systems engineer, Electronic Systems Center, Hanscom AFB, MA; operations flight commander, chief spacecraft engineer, and operations support officer, Operating Division Four, Onizuka AFS, CA; and chief of operations and executive officer, Signals Intelligence Systems Acquisition Directorate, National Reconnaissance Office, Chantilly, VA. Major Konyha is also a resident graduate of SOS and ACSC.

Maj Jennifer Krolikowski (bachelor of mechanical engineering, University of Dayton, OH; master of aeronautical engineering, Air Force Institute of Technology, Wright-Patterson AFB, OH) recently graduated from ACSC. Major Krolikowski's career includes assignments in a variety of engineering and acquisition positions in both the air and space communities. Her assignments include tours in the Air Force Research Lab and 49th Test Squadron conducting operational tests on the B-52. She then transitioned to space acquisition at the Space and Missile Systems Center in the Global Positioning System Program Office. Major Krolikowski was lead engineer for the Nuclear Detonation Detection System (NDS), GPS executive officer, GPS III Acquisition Integration Branch chief, and program executive office staff director for GPS while in Los Angeles. From there she was handpicked to be a course director and instructor for acquisitions and GPS at the newly established National Security Space Institute in Colorado Springs, CO. Prior to being selected for ACSC in residence, Major Krolikowski was the chief of Space-Based Infrared System (SBIRS) requirements at HQ Air Force Space Command (AFSPC).

Maj Jeffrey D. Lanphear (BS, sociology, University of the State of New York, Albany; MS, international management, Troy State University, Troy, AL; MMOAS, ACSC, Maxwell AFB, AL) is the operations officer of the National Reconnaissance Office Operations Squadron, Schriever AFB, CO. Major Lanphear entered the Air Force in 1985 as a Spanish cryptologic linguist. He was commissioned through OTS in June 1996. His career includes assignments as a missileer instructor/evaluator at Malmstrom AFB, MT; flight commander and executive officer at Onizuka AFS, CA; and orbital analyst, weapons and tactics chief, and operations support officer at Cheyenne Mountain AFS, CO. He has deployed to Afghanistan as the lead space weapons officer in support of OEF. Major Lanphear is also a resident graduate of SOS, the Air Force Weapons School, and ACSC.

Maj Jonathan E. Lowe (BA, international relations, Syracuse University, Syracuse, NY; MS, management, Lesley University, Cambridge, MA) is a senior space and missile operations officer currently serving as an academic instructor at ACSC. Prior to this, Major Lowe served on staff at Fourteenth Air Force as the chief of global exercise integration. Additionally, he was a flight commander for combat plans and senior space duty officer for the Joint Space Operations Center. Prior to the Fourteenth Air Force, Major Lowe also served as a space surveillance/missile warning officer and operations flight commander at the 10th Space Warning Squadron, Cavalier AFS, ND. Prior to his 10th Space Warning Squadron assignment, Major Lowe was assigned to the 392nd Training Squadron as a missile crew duty classroom/simulator instructor. Major Lowe was also a missile combat crew commander/instructor (classroom/simulator) at the 400th Missile Squadron/90th Operations Support Squadron, F. E. Warren AFB, WY. He is a resident graduate of SOS and a nonresident graduate of ACSC.

Maj Gabriel A. Medina (Dominican Republic) (MMOAS, ACSC, Maxwell AFB, AL) has been a member of the Dominican Air Force since 1 February 1994. After graduating from the Military Academy of the Dominican Armed Forces as an infantry officer, he was granted the Aviation Leadership Program scholarship by the US Air Force and earned his pilot wings at Laughlin AFB, TX, in 1998. His first assignment was with the Dominican Air Force Fighter Squadron where he worked as the operations officer, followed by the Air Transport Squadron working as the standardization and evaluation officer. Other assignments include operations officer and standardization and evaluation officer for the Dominican Air Force Flight School, flight and ground instructor, simulator and ground instructor for the instruments course, and test pilot for the maintenance command. Major Medina was also briefly assigned as the liaison officer between the US Military Assistance Advisory Group at the US Embassy in the Dominican Republic and the Dominican Air Force. He has flown over 4,100 hours in military and civilian aircraft. Major Medina is also a resident graduate of the Squadron Commander Course at the Inter American Air Forces Academy at Lackland AFB, TX, and ACSC.

LCDR Jeremy C. Powell (BS, secondary education, Indiana University, Bloomington; MBA, Webster University, Jacksonville, FL) is currently serving as the Navy Training with Industry Fellow at Home Depot's headquarters. LCDR Powell entered the Navy in 1997. His career includes sea assignments as a disbursing/sales officer on the USS Boone (Guided Missile Frigate 28) and supply officer on the USS Ross (Guided Missile Destroyer 71). His shore assignments include assistant supply officer/material officer at NAS Jacksonville and food service officer at NS Mayport. LCDR Powell is also a resident graduate of ACSC at Maxwell AFB, AL.

Lt Col Bert Sparrow (BS, business administration, University of Nebraska; MS, computer science, Lesley University, Cambridge, MA; MMAOS, ACSC, Maxwell AFB, AL) currently serves as the deputy chair of the International Security and Applied Warfare Studies Department, ACSC, Maxwell AFB, AL, where he supervises 35 academic professionals in developing three ACSC in-residence courses. Lieutenant Colonel Sparrow is a career space and missile officer. His career includes an ICBM assignment as senior standards/evaluation flight commander, F. E. Warren AFB, WY; a military satellite communications (MILSATCOM) assignment as flight commander, 3rd Space Operations Squadron, Schriever AFB, CO; a space intelligence assignment as collection manager, National Air Intelligence Center, Wright-Patterson AFB, OH, where he deployed to classified locations in support of OEF; an HQ, AFSPC staff assignment as space-lift range command lead, Peterson AFB, CO; and a joint staff officer assignment as space campaign planner, HQ USSTRATCOM/J5, Offutt AFB, NE. Lieutenant Colonel Sparrow is also a resident graduate of SOS, ACSC, and Joint Forces Staff College.

Lt Col Brian C. Tichenor (BS, business finance, Montana State University; MBA, aviation and aerospace administration, Embry Riddle Aeronautical University) is a member of the ACSC faculty and serves as the director, Advanced Space Research Elective and the director of staff for the Strategy and Leadership Department. Lieutenant Colonel Tichenor is a career space and missile officer who entered the Air Force in 1992 as a Minuteman III crewmember at Minot AFB, ND. Other assignments include

341st Logistics Group executive officer; chief, Space Warning Certification; chief, Strategic and Theater Missile Warning Certification; and flight commander and orbital analyst for the 1st Space Control Squadron in the Cheyenne Mountain Operations Center. Lieutenant Colonel Tichenor is a resident graduate of SOS and a nonresident graduate of both ACSC and AWC. His next assignment will be as the Space 300 course director at the National Security Space Institute in Colorado Springs, CO.

Maj Michael S. Warner (bachelor of aerospace engineering, Georgia Institute of Technology; MS, astronautics, The George Washington University; PhD, aerospace engineering, Georgia Institute of Technology) was an academic year 2009 student at ACSC. Major Warner is a developmental engineer who joined the Air Force in 1997 as a space systems analyst, National Air Intelligence Center, Wright-Patterson AFB, OH. Other assignments include assistant professor and executive officer, Department of Astronautics, US Air Force Academy, CO, and deputy branch chief and executive officer, Space Vehicles Directorate, AFRL, Kirtland AFB, NM. Major Warner is a residence graduate of SOS and ACSC. His next assignment will be as the Air Force military liaison to the National Science Board at the Pentagon.

Lt Col Christine M. Weaver (BS, biology, University of Portland, OR; MS, health care administration, Central Michigan University, Minot AFB, ND; MMOAS, ACSC, Maxwell AFB, AL) is a member of the ACSC faculty and serves as the Leadership and Warfare deputy course director in the Strategy and Leadership Department. Lieutenant Colonel Weaver entered the Air Force in 1992 as a Minuteman III crewmember at Minot AFB, ND. Other assignments include Western Range Delta II launch operations, Space Control Center operations in the Cheyenne Mountain Operations Center, and deputy director of protocol for AFSPC. She deployed as the chief of protocol for Central Command Forward during OIF in 2003. Lieutenant Colonel Weaver is a resident graduate of SOS and ACSC.

MAJ Dillard W. Young (BS, history, US Military Academy, West Point, NY; MPA, public administration, John Jay College of Criminal Justice, NY) is an Army functional area 40 space operations officer. Following the Joint and Combined Warfare School and the Army Space Operations Officer Qualification Course, he will be assigned to the NORAD Cheyenne Mountain Operations Center. Major Young entered the Army as an armor officer in 1996 upon graduation from West Point. His career includes assignments as a tank platoon leader, brigade reconnaissance troop executive officer, battalion operations officer, and heavy cavalry troop commander in a divisional cavalry squadron. His most recent assignment was as the Armor Branch representative and instructor of combined arms warfare at the US Military Academy. He has deployed in support of Operations Joint Guard (Bosnia), Joint Guardian (Kosovo), and Iraqi Freedom. Major Young is a graduate of the Armor Officer Basic Course, Scout Platoon Leader's Course, Armor Captain's Career Course, Combined Arms and Services Staff School, and ACSC.

Chapter 1

Space History

Maj Burton "Ernie" Catledge, USAF; and LCDR Jeremy Powell, USN

Control of space means control of the world, far more certainly, far more totally than any control that has been achieved by weapons or troops of occupation. Space is the ultimate position, the position of total control over Earth.

—Pres. Lyndon Johnson

Few events in our history have been more significant than the dawn of the space age. This chapter will discuss early space pioneers, the space race, manned space programs, the formation of the National Aeronautics and Space Administration (NASA), and a brief history of the US military in space.

Early Developments in Rocketry

Although we do not know for certain, most historians agree that the Chinese were the first to produce a rocket around 1212 AD, essentially a solid fuel arrow powered by gunpowder. These very early rockets contained black powder or something similar as the propellant (fuel). According to legend, a man named Wan Hu made the first attempt to build a rocket-powered vehicle in the early 1500s. He attached 47 rockets to a cart, and at a given signal, 47 workers simultaneously lit all of the rockets. In the ensuing explosion, the entire vehicle and Wan Hu disappeared in a cloud of smoke.[1]

The principles by which rockets operated were not understood until the late 1800s, when some men began thinking about using rockets for the transportation of people. Up to this point, the use of rockets in warfare had been very limited. For example, the British used Congreve rockets during the shelling of Fort McHenry in the War of 1812 (thus, "the rockets' red glare" in what became the US national anthem).[2] Yet even in warfare, the rocket's potential went unrecognized. Major advances in rocket technology did not occur until the early 1900s.

Events in America

Dr. Robert Goddard, commonly referred to as "the father of modern rocketry," is responsible for the advent of space exploration in the United States. He achieved most of the American accomplishments in rocket science in a somewhat autonomous effort. In 1909 he began his study of liquid-propellant rockets, and in 1912 he proved that rockets would work in a vacuum such as exists in space. The year 1919 brought an end to World War I as well as the publication of Dr. Goddard's book *A Method of Attaining Extreme Altitude*. This text laid the theoretical foundation for future American rocket developments such as staging that would be critical for the quest to land on the moon.[3]

On 16 March 1926 in Auburn, Massachusetts, Dr. Goddard made history as the first person to launch a liquid-fueled rocket. The strange-looking vehicle covered a ground distance of 184 feet in 2.5 seconds and rose to an altitude of 41 feet while achieving a speed of 60 miles per hour (mph).[4] In 1929 Goddard launched an improved version that was the first rocket to contain weather instruments. This vehicle rose to an altitude of 90 feet and provided some of the earliest weather readings from "on-board" sensors.[5]

Goddard and Rocket Technology in New Mexico

In 1930, with financial backing from Charles Lindbergh and the Guggenheim Foundation, Dr. Goddard moved his operation to New Mexico, where he continued his work until his death in 1945. His work centered on a number of improvements to his rockets, which resulted in a number of "firsts" in rocket science and technology. For example, Dr. Goddard was the first to develop a gyro-control guidance system, gimbaled nozzles, small high-speed centrifugal pumps, and variable-thrust rocket engines.[6] Today's modern rockets use all of these technologies.

Dr. Goddard's rocket project was a privately funded effort with absolutely no government funding, aid of any sort, or interest in his work. Notwithstanding, his accomplishments in rocketry were truly extraordinary. Meanwhile, a team of German scientists also interested in rocket development proved that rocket technology could have a devastating effect upon the world.

Events in Germany

The German rocket-development effort occurred in two phases. Phase one, 1923–31, involved Herman Oberth, Walter Hohmann, Johannes Winkler, and the Society for Space Travel. Phase two, 1932–45, involved the accomplishments of only one man—Wernher von Braun.

Phase One. Although he never actually built any rockets, Herman Oberth inspired others in Germany and other countries to do so (e.g., Dr. Goddard). He accomplished this through his 1923 publication on space and upper-atmosphere exploration. His book *The Rocket into Planetary Space* laid the foundation for the German rocket-development effort.[7] Oberth suggested that if a rocket could develop enough thrust, it could deliver a payload into orbit. Many people thought this impossible. However, Oberth's work inspired Johannes Winkler in 1927 to form the Society for Space Travel, of which Oberth later became president.[8] This society became the spawning ground for the most significant breakthroughs in space technology. Members of the organization would later include rocket pioneers such as Dr. von Braun.

In 1925 Walter Hohmann published his book *The Attainability of Celestial Bodies*, in which he defined the principles of rocket travel in space, including how to get into geosynchronous orbit.[9] In recognition of Hohmann and his work in rocketry, the orbital transfer technique used to move payloads between two coplanar circular orbits is called the Hohmann Transfer.

Johannes Winkler invented the first liquid-propellant rocket in Europe, the HW-1. The first launch attempt was a failure, but the second launch was successful in 1931, earning him the distinction of being the first person in Europe to launch a liquid-fueled rocket.[10]

Phase Two. In 1932 the National Socialist dictator Adolf Hitler rose to power in Germany and directed the German army to pressure Dr. von Braun to develop rockets for use in warfare. Hitler used the resulting rocket technology to terrorize London during World War II. Ironically, the rocket technology that resulted from Dr. von Braun's early work would eventually enable the United States to send a man to the moon.

Under direction of the German army, Dr. von Braun began experimenting with liquid-fuel rockets, leading to the development of the aggregate or "A" series. The Germans abandoned the A-1 after a number of launch failures, and development turned to the A-2. The A-2 achieved two successful launches in two days in December 1934, thus opening the door for the development of even larger rockets.[11]

In 1937 Gen Walter R. Dornberger, the head of the German army's rocket-development effort; Dr. von Braun; and their development team moved to a peninsula in northern Germany called Peenemünde. After two failures, predominately in the guidance systems, the A-4 was successfully launched in October 1942, becoming the first man-made object to reach the edge of space.[12] Research and development continued until 8 September 1944, when the first Vengeance weapon, the V-2 rocket (fig. 1-1), boosted a 2,000-pound (lb.) warhead to 3,500 mph and burned out, with the warhead continuing on a ballistic trajectory to a range of 200 miles, literally "falling" on Paris.[13]

Figure 1-1. V-2 rocket. (National Oceanic and Atmospheric Administration photo)

Events in the Soviet Union

Many historians say that the space age was born in the home of Russian schoolmaster Konstantin Eduardovich Tsiolkovsky. In 1883 he was one of the first to explain how it would be possible for a rocket to fly in space. Keep in mind that at this time most people did not believe man would ever fly. Consequently, Russians simply considered Tsiolkovsky eccentric. In 1898 he wrote the article "Investigating Space with Rocket Devices" for the Russian magazine *Science Review.* When it was finally published in 1903, it laid the framework for orbital spaceflight using rockets based on years of his calculations.[14]

Tsiolkovsky had a unique depth of understanding. He was the first to recommend the use of liquid propellants because they performed better and were easier to control than solid propellants. His notebooks contain many ideas and concepts that rocket engineers use today. His works also include detailed sketches of spaceship fuel tanks containing liquid oxygen and hydrogen (the same fuel used in the *Saturn V* rocket). Tsiolkovsky further recommended controlling a rocket's flight by inserting rudders in the exhaust or by tilting the exhaust nozzle, just as Dr. Goddard would suggest some 30 years later.

Tsiolkovsky determined a way of controlling the flow of liquid propellants with mixing valves and advocated cooling the combustion chamber by flowing one of the liquids around it in a double-walled jacket, as seen in the space shuttle engines of today. His spaceship cabin designs included life-support systems for absorption of carbon dioxide and proposed reclining the crew with their backs to the engines throughout the acceleration phase, as is currently done. Tsiolkovsky further suggested building the outer wall of spaceships with a double layer to provide better protection against meteors and increased temperature. Tsiolkovsky foresaw the use of an airlock for space-suited men to leave their ship and suggested that gyro-stabilization as well as multiple-stage boosters were the only way to attain the velocities required for space flight. Finally, he anticipated the assembly of space stations in orbit with food and oxygen supplied by vegetation growing within.[15]

Tsiolkovsky designed extensive calculations to ensure all his proposals were mathematically possible, but without funding, he was unable to perform any meaningful experimentation. Because of his considerable technical foresight and realistic approach to space problems, Tsiolkovsky is widely acknowledged as the father of space travel.

Rocket Development after World War II

This section will address booster and missile development in the Soviet Union (USSR) and the United States between 1945 and the early 1960s. The space race was a crucial component of the Cold War, as both nations strived to gain an advantage in rocket development, nuclear weapons delivery, and satellite technology.

Soviet Efforts

Immediately after World War II the Soviets and Americans raced to recover German rocket scientists and hardware. When the Red Army captured the major rocketry center of Peenemünde in May 1945, they found that most of the important personnel and documents were gone, already en route to America. The Soviets ended up with a majority of the hardware but only a few remaining scientists and technicians.[16]

In 1946 Stalin was not satisfied with the progress of the Soviet rocket effort at Peenemünde, so he ordered it moved to the Soviet Union. There, like in America, the expatriated German scientists and technicians worked with Soviet rocket scientists in an effort to improve the basic V-2 design. However, the Soviet team decided to take over primary control of the program and relegated the German team to a support role.[17] By the end of 1953, the USSR returned all the expatriated German rocket team to Germany.

Intercontinental Ballistic Missile. The United States was well ahead of the Soviet Union in nuclear technology and possessed the most powerful bomber force in the world. This unnerved the Russians and caused them to probe for an equalizer. In their search for this weapon, the Soviets began to realize the potential of the intercontinental ballistic missile (ICBM) for striking over long distances. The Soviets envisioned a missile capable of striking the United States from the Soviet Union. This thinking dominated all of Soviet rocket research, and by the end of 1947, the consensus in the Soviet Union was to build an ICBM with this capability. In their quest to build an ICBM, the Soviets developed a whole family of short- and medium-range ballistic missiles, the most important of which was the Shyster medium-range ballistic missile (MRBM), which became the world's first operational nuclear-tipped MRBM in 1956.[18]

In 1951 biological experiments with dogs convinced Soviet scientists that manned rocket flights were possible.[19] They were also convinced that they would soon have the capability to place large payloads into orbit. Thus, along with the development of the ICBM emerged the idea of space flight, which included the beginning of research into space suits, life support systems, and emergency escape systems for manned flights.

While Soviet scientists contemplated putting things into space, the vehicles required to accomplish this were being developed at an astonishing rate. The Soviet missile program was well on its way to becoming reality. In 1953 two more missiles entered the development phase: the SS-4 Sandal and the SS-6 Sapwood.

SS-4 (R-12) Sandal. The SS-4 was required to carry a one-megaton (MT) warhead across more than 1,118 miles. It used storable propellants that improved its launch rate capability and had an autonomous guidance system.[20] The SS-4 became operational in 1959 and remained in use for two decades. The SS-4 was the weapon at the heart of the Cuban missile crisis, when the Soviet Union deployed ICBM missiles to the island of Cuba in 1962.[21]

SS-6 (R-7) Sapwood. The SS-6 was still under development in 1956, but the Soviets were so sure of its success that they began discussing its use as a launcher for an artificial satellite. The Soviets announced to the world that they would launch a satellite into Earth orbit as part of International Geophysical Year (IGY) activities. The Western world did not take this proclamation seriously, oblivious to the great strides that the Soviets had made in rocketry.

The SS-6 (fig. 1-2) was ready for its first test launch in May 1957.[22] The Soviets traded stylish design for brute strength. They had not yet built powerful rocket engines,

Figure 1-2. SS-6 Sapwood. (NASA photo)

so they used more engines to compensate for the lack of powerful engines. The SS-6 was a single-stage missile with clustered engines and had twice the power of the US Atlas or Titan ICBMs. To avoid making the missile in several stages, the Soviets opted to go with a centralized cluster of motors. Ejection of these clusters occurred after they had used up their fuel, while the central core motor continued to burn.[23] By October 1957, the Soviets were ready to prove to the West that their missile capabilities were more than just a proclamation.

Sputnik. On 4 October 1957, the Soviets used their SS-6 Sapwood ICBM to launch the world's first artificial satellite—*Sputnik 1* (fig. 1-3).[24] On 3 November 1957, *Sputnik 2* entered space with Layka, a Soviet research dog, on board.[25] At this point, the Soviet Union had become the first nation to enter outer space with a biological life form.

US Efforts

While the Soviets had a well-coordinated rocket program, the United States did not. After the Soviets exploded their first hydrogen bomb (H-bomb) on 12 August 1953, the US armed services began to concentrate on missile development.[26] Around this time, the Air Force began work on its Atlas ICBM.

Air Force ICBM Program. Due to the Soviet's H-bomb capability, in 1955 President Eisenhower

Figure 1-3. *Sputnik 1*. (NASA History Office photo)

directed that the Atlas ICBM project become the nation's number one priority.[27] The Atlas was a 1.5-stage missile with external boosters that separated after burnout. Powered by liquid oxygen and kerosene, it required fueling prior to launch. Test launches had taken place by mid-1955, and by August 1959, the system had gained approval for use.[28] During the development of the Atlas, the Air Force was also working on another ICBM called the Titan.

The Titan I was a two-stage missile powered by oxygen and kerosene, also requiring fueling prior to launch. This fueling operation did not allow for a quick response if the United States were to come under attack.[29] This deficiency led to the development of the Titan II.

The Titan II was much more powerful than the Titan I and could stand alert fully fueled and ready to launch. Although the Titan II stayed in the inventory until 1987, these liquid giants were expensive to build and maintain, leading to the development of the Minuteman solid-fuel ICBM.

Work on the solid-fueled Minuteman ICBM began in 1957.[30] These missiles were lighter, smaller, and more easily stored. The fact that these systems could be built in larger numbers and their warheads improved accuracy offset their reduced payload capacity. The Minuteman met all test objectives by 1961 and entered service in 1962.[31]

Army Missile Program. Near the end of World War II, the US Seventh Army captured many intact German V-2 rockets along with Dr. von Braun and his rocket team.[32] This team was brought to the United States as part of Operation Paperclip, an Air Force program to bring German scientists to America after the war.[33] In 1945, the Army began moving the scientists to Fort Bliss, Texas, to establish a guided-missile program that began with the test firing of the captured V-2s (A-4). When asked about the design of their V-2, the Germans said they replicated the rocket Dr. Goddard flew in 1939. In January 1947 the A-4 Upper Atmosphere Research Panel stood up to coordinate tests of converted captured V-2s being used to carry various scientific instruments. This panel became the Upper Atmosphere Rocket Research Panel in 1948 and the Satellite Research Panel in 1957.[34]

In 1950 the Army moved its missile development group to Redstone Arsenal in Huntsville, Alabama. After the Korean War, the Army was looking for a missile with a range of about 500 miles, leading to the development of the Redstone missile (fig. 1-4). First fired on 20 August 1953, with many additional test firings through 1958, the Redstone entered service with Army units stationed in Germany in 1958.[35]

The Redstone was designed and developed between 1952 and 1954. This proved critical to the history of the entire US missile program, as this missile became the foundation for all future US missiles. The Army also ventured into a joint missile project with the Navy, referred to as the Jupiter missile program.

The Jupiter missile made use of Redstone missile technology, thereby saving time and money. In fact, Redstone missiles were used to

Figure 1-4. Redstone missile. (US Army photo)

6

test Jupiter nose cones. As the project progressed, the Navy lost interest because it wanted a small solid-fuel missile for submarine use, and the Jupiter was shaping up to be a large liquid-fueled missile. The Navy thus broke away to develop the Polaris missile.

The first Jupiter launch occurred in 1957, but the range was only 60 miles. By the third flight, developments improved the missile, and its range had increased to 1,600 miles, making it the first successful American intermediate-range ballistic missile (IRBM).[36] The Army Ballistic Missile Agency delivered its first Jupiter to the Air Force in 1958, and more than 60 missiles saw active service with Air Force units based in Italy and Turkey.

Navy Efforts. The Navy's rocket-development project revolved around three different missiles: the Aerobee sounding rocket, the Viking sounding rocket, and the Polaris submarine-launched ballistic missile (SLBM). The Aerobee project was initially designed to develop a missile capable of carrying a 100 lb. payload to an altitude of 75 miles. It consisted of two levels, the lower being solid fuel and the upper using liquid fuel. The first flight of the Aerobee took place in November 1947; since then it has served all three branches of the military.[37]

Seeking the ability to take accurate measurements, the Navy began looking into a missile program to assure a stable launch to extreme altitudes. This resulted in the development of the Viking sounding rocket, primarily based upon the V-2 design. Engine tests began in 1947, with the first Viking delivered for testing in 1949. In May 1949 the Viking had its successful maiden flight.[38] To evaluate the concept of launching rockets and missiles from ships at sea, the USS *Norton Sound* launched a test Viking.[39]

In September 1958, the Navy began to seriously consider launching missiles from ships. The Polaris project resulted. The first Polarises had a range of 1,500 miles, but that figure increased as the system reached maturity in 1963.[40] At the start of the project, it became apparent that a special vessel would be required to handle this missile, leading to the development of the Polaris submarine (fig. 1-5). By 1958, approval for the first three Polaris submarines was granted and construction began.

The first Polaris submarine was the USS *George Washington*—completed in June 1959 and commissioned in December 1959.[41] The USS *George Washington* participated in actual test firings of the Polaris missile in July 1960 (fig. 1-6), and in November of that same year, the new weapon system became operational.[42]

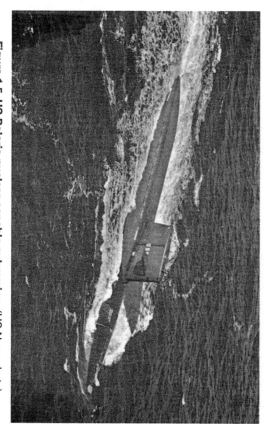

Figure 1-5. US Polaris nuclear-capable submarine. (US Navy photo)

Rocket development was not limited to military aspects. To support President Eisenhower's "Space for Peace" policy, the government was also investigating booster development to send satellites into orbit.

US Booster Development and the IGY. The original US military services' appraisals concerning the possibility of developing an effective ICBM were rather discouraging, as nuclear weapons of the day were large and bulky. At the time, the US nuclear deterrence capability rested on the back of the bomber force, since bomber aircraft were the only delivery systems that could carry these large weapons. However, the situation soon changed because:

- The Soviets demonstrated that they were serious about missile development.
- The Atomic Energy Commission announced the development of the hydrogen bomb.
- Nuclear weapons were getting smaller.
- The Soviets obtained a hydrogen bomb of their own.
- The Sputnik satellites were launched.

This series of events was enough to alert the US government to turn its efforts towards large-scale rocket development. The hope of closing the gap in the missile race lay in the development of military missiles. However, President Eisenhower was determined to separate the military programs from the IGY program in order to support his peaceful intentions for space policy.[43] The Redstone, Jupiter C, and Atlas missiles were ready to launch as early as September 1956, but a different decision was made. Our nonmilitary satellite program for IGY would be the Vanguard project.

Vanguard Project. Vanguard was designed to have as few links to the military as possible. Although an honorable idea, it was not practical because the military had the money, scientists, and hardware to get the job done. Funding for the project came from the National Science Foundation. The program was plagued with problems from the start, such as inexperienced contractors, tensions of the space race, and trying to get a configuration that worked. Nevertheless, President Eisenhower insisted that Vanguard become the space launch vehicle for US satellites.

Three Vanguard launches were conducted at the end of 1956 and into 1957 to test different aspects of the launch mission. However, in response to the Sputnik launch the decision was made to launch a satellite on the next scheduled Vanguard mission. On 6 December 1957, the United States attempted to launch its first satellite, which resulted in disaster.[44] After lifting several feet off the ground, the booster lost power and fell back, bursting into flames. Five days later, President Eisenhower approved a satellite launch using a modified Jupiter rocket, now called the Juno (Project Orbiter).

Figure 1-6. Polaris missile test. (US Navy photo)

The Juno booster/lift vehicle was launched, and the first US satellite, *Explorer I* (fig. 1-7), a 30 lb. cylinder, went into orbit on 31 January 1958.[45] Although the United States did not launch the world's first artificial satellite, the nation did discover the **Van Allen radiation belts, which may have been the most important discovery of the IGY.**[46] *Explorer I* transmitted until 23 May 1958.

Figure 1-7. *Explorer I* **satellite.** (NASA History Office photo)

Vanguard finally did succeed in getting off the ground on 17 March 1958, but this success was short-lived, as only two of the 11 total launch attempts between December 1957 and September 1959 were successful.[47]

Early US booster types emulated IRBM first stages rather than ICBM first stages. These new boosters were known as the Juno 2, Thor Able, Thor Delta, Thor Epsilon, and Thor Agena. The Thor boosters later evolved into the successful Delta boosters. For the larger payloads, development began from boosters developed from the larger successful ICBMs; these boosters were based upon the first stages of Atlas and Titan II development. The Atlas- and Titan II-derived boosters have launched many US satellites. With all of this space activity, the government decided it needed a civilian agency to coordinate and give direction to the US space effort.

NASA. President Eisenhower's administration came up with the concept of a coherent space effort. To help support this concept, Eisenhower appointed James R. Killian, president of the Massachusetts Institute of Technology, to be his scientific advisor. The military lobbied to maintain control of managing the national space effort. However, President Eisenhower was committed to his "Space for Peace" policy, and civilian control of the space program was essential to that concept. This civilian agency would handle all aspects of research and development, with scientists playing the leading role in guiding the space program.

While red tape tied up plans for this new agency, the president could not let time and events override our space program. He established the Advanced Research Projects Agency (ARPA) and quickly approved its plans for space exploration.[48] Although short-lived, ARPA was essentially the first official US space agency.

At this time, much maneuvering was occurring in Congress by various agencies who aspired to take control of the space program. One of these agencies, and the leading contender, was the National Advisory Committee on Aeronautics (NACA). At the time, no other agency could rival NACA's expertise in the field of aeronautics, and NACA felt that space would be a logical extension of its duties. However, Eisenhower was against this idea because he felt that NACA was, at times, too autonomous. Dr. Killian came to the rescue by proposing the National Aeronautics and Space Act, which was adopted on 1 October 1958, officially creating the National Aeronautics and Space Administration (NASA).[49] This plan created a broad charter for *civilian* aeronautical and space research, allowing the administration to absorb NACA. The core of NASA's facilities came from NACA. Within a few years, NASA obtained the organization and equipment to carry out the nation's space program.

Satellite Programs

This section will address some of the early satellite programs, of which there are four types: communication, weather, data collection, and exploration.

Communication Satellites

One of the most important and profound aspects of space utilization has been in the area of communication satellites. The use of communication satellites has brought the world's nations closer together. In May 1945 Arthur C. Clarke proposed that three satellites placed above the earth's equator at a distance of approximately 22,000 miles would maintain a constant position over that point and give total communication coverage.[50] This position is called a geosynchronous, geostationary, or Clarke's orbit. Today, most of the world's communication satellites reside in this type of orbit.

Project Score. The first voice returned from space was President Eisenhower's in 1958 under Project Score.[51] An Atlas ICBM with a tape-recorded Christmas message from the president to the world placed the satellite in orbit. It was the first prototype military communications satellite.

10

Echo. Echo was a 1960 NASA project consisting of a 100-foot-diameter plastic balloon with an aluminum coating, which passively reflected radio signals transmitted from a huge Earth antenna. A number of projects were attempted using balloons, but this proved to be somewhat impractical, and by 1963 civilian communications satellites with active transmitters were in orbit.[52]

Telstar. Telstar was the free world's first commercially funded communication satellite. AT&T financed the project, which launched on 10 July 1962.[53] Telstar's orbit was low Earth, but when in sight of its ground station, it did provide communications among the United States, the United Kingdom, and France. Telstar proved that the use of satellites as communications devices across vast distances was possible.

Syncom. Syncom, another NASA project launched in 1963, was the first communications satellite in geosynchronous orbit.[54] Used for many experiments, it also transmitted television broadcasts of the Tokyo Olympic Games in 1964.

Molniya. Launched in 1968, the Molniya was the first of many Soviet communication satellites using high-altitude, elliptical orbits that positioned the satellite over the entire Soviet Union during the day.[55]

International Telecommunications Satellite. The International Telecommunications Satellite (INTELSAT) Organization provided nations with a way of sharing the cost of satellite communications, based on the amount of use.

INTELSAT 1, or *Early Bird*, was the first of the series and became operational on 28 June 1965 with 240 telephone circuits. Designed to last 1.5 years, it provided service for four years.[56] *INTELSAT 2*, launched in 1967, provided an additional 240 circuits with a design life of three years.[57]

INTELSAT 3, launched in 1968, increased service by 1,500 circuits and improved its design life to five years.[58] Launched in 1971, *INTELSAT 4* contained 4,000 circuits plus two color TV channels and spot beams to increase broadcast efficiency. Its design life increased to seven years.[59] *INTELSAT 5* was launched in 1980 and is three-axis stabilized versus spin stabilized. It has 12,000 circuits and two TV channels.[60]

Westar. Launched in April 1974, Westar was a Western Union project and the United States' first domestic satellite. The first set, made up of *Westar I, II,* and *III,* was comprised of 12-transponder satellites with a capacity of 7,000 two-way voice circuits or 12 simultaneous color TV channels.[61] Design lifetime in orbit for the satellite was seven years.

Weather Satellites

Weather satellites show weather patterns that are obscured from the ground. There are two types of weather satellites: polar orbiting satellites and geostationary satellites. Each satellite is equipped with light and heat sensors, recorders, radio receivers and transmitters, and other recording instruments to create a picture of Earth weather. This section discusses some of the satellite systems that originate these pictures.

Television Infrared Operational Satellite. The television infrared operational satellite (TIROS) (fig. 1-8) was the first weather satellite program undertaken by the United States. Its objective was to test the feasibility of obtaining weather observations from space. Launched in April 1960 into a polar orbit, *TIROS-1* achieved all of its objectives.[62] It was operational for only 78 days but proved that satellites could be a useful tool for surveying global weather conditions from space. Nine additional TIROSs were launched.

Environmental Science Service Administration. Based on the success of the TIROS program, a fully operational version of the same satellite, called the TIROS

Operational System (TOS), was introduced in 1966.[63] The system used a pair of Environmental Science Service Administration (ESSA) satellites and provided uninterrupted worldwide observations.

Nimbus. Given the success of the TIROS program, the primary objective of the Nimbus program was to develop a satellite system capable of meeting the needs of the world's atmospheric science research community.[64] The Nimbus system, originally designed as a replacement for TIROS, became the means to test new remote sensing techniques as well as a means to sense the radiative properties of the earth's landmasses, oceans, and atmosphere. Other goals of the program included the development of new Earth surface-mapping techniques, new ground data-processing techniques, and the capability to sense atmospheric variables in the vertical (soundings).

Improved TIROS Operational Satellite. With the launch of the Improved TIROS Operational Satellite (*ITOS-1*) in 1970, a second generation of meteorological satellites came into being. The primary objective of the ITOS program was to combine the capabilities of ESSA's operational satellites and the knowledge gained from the ongoing Nimbus program into one operational program. The ITOS program served as the second generation of US operational weather satellites, eventually becoming the series we now know as the National Oceanic and Atmospheric Administration (NOAA) satellites.[65]

TIROS-N. Following the ITOS series of weather satellites, a third-generation series came into service and provided global observation service from 1978 through 1985.[66] These satellites employed advanced data-collection instruments. Included on the payload package was a very high-resolution radiometer that improved sea surface temperature mapping, for locating snow and sea ice as well as conducting night and day imaging.

Figure 1-8. TIROS weather satellite. (NASA image)

Data Collection Satellites

Since the TIROS weather satellites proved their worth by collecting data on weather patterns, after the first astronauts made detailed observations of the earth, scientists began to consider using satellites to collect data on the earth's land and water resources.

Land Satellites. In the early 1970's, the land satellite (LANDSAT) series (fig. 1-9) of data-collection satellites were employed. This series, because of its infrared microwave and imagery capability, opened up new areas of research never before explored in such detail. The first LANDSAT, originally called the Earth Resources Technology Satellite (ERTS), was developed and launched by NASA on 23 July 1972, on a Delta rocket from Vandenberg AFB, California.[67]

Figure 1-9. LANDSAT. (NASA image)

The satellite carried a television camera and an experimental sensor called the multispectral scanner. The utility of the synoptic, digital, multispectral scanner images was recognized rapidly and proved so valuable that a version of the sensor was flown on each of the subsequent four LANDSAT satellites (NASA changed the name of ERTS to LANDSAT 1 in 1975). By the time LANDSAT 1 was retired in 1978, its multispectral scanner had acquired over 300,000 images, providing repeated coverage of the global land surfaces.[68] The quality and impact of the resulting information exceeded all expectations.

SEASAT 1. Based on the LANDSAT series, NASA launched SEASAT 1 in 1978. Using microwave instruments, SEASAT 1 measured surface temperatures to within two degrees centigrade, wind speed, and direction and provided all-weather pictures of waves, ice phenomena, cloud patterns, storm surges, and temperature patterns of the ocean currents.[69]

Terrestrial and Extraterrestrial Exploration Satellites

The final type of early satellites includes the exploration satellites, designed to observe phenomenon in space and probe planets and other bodies in our solar system.

Explorer. The largest and oldest US exploration satellite program was the Explorer series. This particular group of satellites studied a wide range of space activities from Earth radiation to solar wind. Approximately 74 satellites in this series were launched, the first of which, Explorer 1, discovered the Van Allen radiation belts in 1958.[70]

US Planetary Probes. The United States has launched more than 24 planetary probe satellites, visiting most of the planets in our solar system. Numerous probes have launched to Venus, Mars, Jupiter, and Saturn. These probes were of the Mariner, Pioneer, Viking, and Voyager types. Remarkably, the two Voyager spacecraft, both launched in 1977, are still operational and continue to send back valuable information from the edge of the solar system. Voyager 2 is the farthest manmade object from Earth (10.16 billion miles as of January 2009).[71] More recent launches include Galileo in 1984 to Jupiter, Mars Climate Orbiter, Mars Global Surveyor, Mars Odyssey, Mars Pathfinder, and a recently launched first-ever probe (New Horizons) dedicated to the study of Pluto.

Hubble Space Telescope. The idea for the Hubble Space Telescope (HST) was conceived back in the 1940s, but work on the telescope did not start until the 1970s and 1980s.[72] The telescope did not become operational until the 1990s. The HST program is a cooperative program between NASA and the European Space Agency (ESA). The program objective is to operate a long-lived space-based observatory for astronomical observation. The HST is the largest on-orbit observatory ever built and is capable of imaging objects up to 14 billion light years away. The resolution of the HST is seven to 10 times greater than Earth-based telescopes. Ground-based telescopes can seldom provide resolution better than 1.0 arc-seconds, except momentarily under the very best observing conditions. The HST's resolution is, depending on conditions, 0.1 arc-seconds, which is 10 times better than ground-based telescopes.

Originally planned for 1979, the Large Space Telescope program called for the satellite to return to Earth every five years for refurbishment and on-orbit servicing every 2.5 years. Contamination as well as structural concerns negated the concept of ground return for the project. NASA then decided that a three-year cycle of on-orbit servicing would work out just as well as the first plan. The three HST servicing missions in December 1993, February 1997, and mid-1999 were enormous successes.

USSR Space Probes. The Soviets, while launching more planetary probes than any other country, have confined themselves to Mars, Venus, the moon, and the sun. Most of their initial attempts to send probes to Venus and Mars failed. These probes were of the Venera, Mars, Cosmos, Zond, and Vega series. An ambitious probe named *Mars-96* was launched in 1996 but failed to escape Earth orbit.[74]

Both the United States and the Russians are planning future probe missions back to Mars, Venus, the moons of Jupiter, and other interesting places within the solar system. As time has passed, more countries have entered the space exploration business (China, Japan, Germany, France, etc.) by sending probes into the cosmos.

Manned Space Exploration by the United States and USSR since 1960

Pres. George W. Bush said, "To leave behind Earth and air and gravity is an ancient dream of humanity. . . . This cause of exploration and discovery is not an option we choose; it is a desire written in the human heart. We are that part of creation which seeks to understand all creation. We find the best among us, send them forth into unmapped darkness, and pray they will return. They go in peace for all mankind, and all mankind is in their debt."[75]

Space Race

The United States had placed its prospects for getting into space first in Project Vanguard. However, the Russians entered orbit first, resulting in a public outcry among Americans. Sen. Lyndon Johnson (later to become president) of the Armed Forces Subcommittee recommended that a national space program be established. The consensus was that the United States needed a consolidated national space program to coordinate and guide its space efforts. Thus, NASA was formed in 1958. The space program would consist of two parts: the military functions under the control of the Department of Defense and the civilian functions under the control of NASA.

With the USSR's launch of Sputnik in 1957, the United States and the Soviet Union were firmly entrenched in the space race, which was an extension of the Cold War. The Soviet Union had beaten the United States in the unmanned space race, and the same would occur in the manned race. On 12 April 1961, the Soviets shocked the world again when Yuri Gagarin became the first person to orbit the earth.[76] Public outcry was not as strong as when Sputnik went up, but presidential concern was. President Kennedy addressed Congress and committed the nation to a project that by the end of the decade would land a man on the moon and return him safely. The president's decision to undertake this task was endorsed virtually without dissent.

The space race led to a number of programs, both American and Soviet, which greatly advanced our understanding of space and our capacities for manned space exploration.

Mercury (US): 1961–1963

In addition to sending a man into space, Mercury was designed to further our knowledge of man's capabilities in space. The Soviets had already proven that man could survive reentry. Mercury had a number of objectives, the most important of which were putting a man in orbit and devising a stepping-stone for an eventual journey to the moon. In the Mercury capsule, all systems were redundant, control was manual or automatic, and the control system technology was new.

The main objective of the Mercury project was to investigate man's ability to function in the space environment.[77] Mercury gained valuable information for the building and flying of more complex spacecraft, such as the Gemini and Apollo. The milestones began with the chimpanzee "Ham" flying in a capsule on 31 January 1961, followed by Alan Shepard's suborbital flight on 5 May 1961. Then on 20 February 1962, John Glenn became the first American to achieve Earth orbit, completing three revolutions.[78]

Vostok (USSR)

Unlike the Mercury capsule, the Vostok capsule was composed of two parts: the round-shaped manned section and the lower equipment bay located underneath the manned section. Vostok crew recovery was also different. With Mercury, the astronaut and capsule parachuted into the ocean, while the Soviet cosmonaut ejected from the capsule and was recovered on land. Vostok led the space race by carrying the first man into space in 1961 (Yuri Gagarin), putting the first woman in orbit in 1963 (Valentine Tereshkova), supporting the first dual-flight mission, and setting flight endurance records.[79]

Gemini (US): 1962-1966

The Gemini capsule was designed to carry two astronauts and had two sections—the upper or manned section and a lower equipment section. Because of the greater lift needed, the Titan II ICBM was used instead of the Atlas. The objectives of the Gemini program included developing procedures for practicing maneuvers critical to a moon landing: rendezvous, docking, and extravehicular activity (EVA).[80] Gemini also allowed astronauts to gain experience in longer missions and perform complicated maneuvers.

All the objectives set by NASA for Gemini were met. However, some tasks, such as spacewalks, turned out to be more difficult than anticipated. Gene Cernan's exertion during the spacewalk portion of the *Gemini IX* mission overtaxed his suit system and fogged his helmet visor.[81] Cernan had to terminate his EVA early due to fatigue. The problem was not solved until the last flight, *Gemini XII*, in November 1966. Edwin "Buzz" Aldrin used footholds, Velcro-covered tools, and hand grabs to work in space with ease.[82]

The Gemini milestones were vast and diverse and included the first orbital plane change, the first US dual flight, and the first hard docking and one-orbit rendezvous. Gemini's success gave the United States confidence to press ahead with the Apollo program and in effect placed the United States ahead of the Russians in the race to the moon.

Voskhod (USSR)

The Voskhod capsule was a Vostok modified to accept three cosmonauts.[83] A terminal-thrust braking system was added to achieve a soft landing. The Voskhod program was a stopgap measure instituted by the Soviet Union to make up for the stalled Soyuz program. The objectives of the Voskhod program were the same as those of Gemini and resulted in some notable accomplishments, including the first three-man craft orbit, the first spacewalk, and the first emergency manual reentry.[84]

Apollo (US)

The Apollo program was the final step to the moon. The objective of the program was twofold. First, the program was to gather information needed for a lunar landing. Secondly, Apollo was to actually land on the moon.

A new "tear drop" capsule was used, thus departing from the traditional "bell" shape of the Mercury/Gemini capsules. The Apollo system consisted of three parts: the command module, the service module, and the lunar module (fig. 1-10).[85]

The booster for this program started from scratch. With the help of Dr. von Braun, the Saturn boosters emerged, which included the *Saturn 1B* and the *Saturn 5* (fig. 1-11).

The advent of Apollo, as in the tradition of Mercury and Gemini, was a step-by-step process. However, the United States suffered a tragic event on 27 January 1967 when Apollo I developed a fire in the capsule that cost the lives of three astronauts: "Gus" Grissom, Ed White, and Roger Chaffee.[86] The space program was halted while NASA investigated the accident. Within 19 months, the manned portion of the Apollo program was back on track with an altered Apollo capsule.

The program pressed ahead, testing docking maneuvers, lunar landing procedures, and a slew of other experiments designed to get us to the eventual landing. Then on 20 July 1969, *Apollo 11* was the first of the Apollo series to land on the moon.[87] Six more missions to the moon followed, culminating with *Apollo 17*. The only subsequent mission that did not land on the moon was *Apollo 13*, which aborted some 205,000 miles from Earth when an oxygen tank exploded.[88] An anxious world watched as NASA

LM ASCENT-CSM DOCKED

Figure 1-10. Apollo system. (NASA image)

Figure 1-11. *Saturn 5.* (NASA photo)

worked feverishly through one problem after another to bring the crew back alive. Their success in doing so was one of the agency's finer moments and inspired a 1995 feature film that ignited the interest of a new generation in the Apollo program.

The United States met President Kennedy's goal and proved man could react to and solve in-flight emergencies (*Apollo 13*). Although the Apollo moon program was concluded, an abundance of valuable scientific information had been obtained.

Soyuz (USSR)

Like the Apollo program, the Soviet Soyuz program began on a tragic note when the *Soyuz 1* reentry parachute failed to deploy properly and the capsule slammed into the ground, killing Col Vladimir Komarov in April 1967.[89] As a result of this crash, the Soyuz program was halted for 19 months while changes in design were made. On 29 October 1968, Soyuz made its first successful safe flight and began achieving its major objectives of maneuvering in group flights, docking, prolonged space flight, and development of new navigation and spacecraft control systems.[90]

After a series of launch and in-flight problems led to them being beaten to the moon in July 1969, the Soviets turned their emphasis towards manned space stations. The Soyuz was used as a ferry to the Salyut and Mir space stations and now ferries personnel to the International Space Station.

Follow-On Manned Programs

Space technology has continued to advance through several follow-on manned programs. Among them are the US space shuttle, the Russian Mir space station, and the International Space Station, the largest and most complex international scientific project in history.

Skylab. A *Saturn 5* launched from Kennedy Space Center on 14 May 1973 and placed Skylab (fig. 1-12) into orbit.[91] Skylab was partially made from a third-stage section of the *Saturn 5* and was to be used for a variety of experiments, such as the effects of long-term weightlessness and human adaptation to zero gravity. Skylab proved to be a successful program—information was learned about these areas as well as others. In all, 46,000 images were taken of the earth and 127,000 pictures of solar activity in addition to a list of other achievements.[92]

Figure 1-12. Skylab. (NASA artist's drawing)

Due to a number of factors, such as increased solar activity and delays in getting the shuttle off the ground (the shuttle was to boost the satellite into a higher orbit), Skylab's orbit continued to decay until it made its final plunge on 11 July 1979.[93]

Salyut. The Soviet space station program began in 1971 with the launch of *Salyut 1*, which gave the USSR another first in space.[94] *Soyuz 10* had difficulty docking with the station, but *Soyuz 11* was able to successfully dock in June. Tragically, the crew was killed while returning to Earth, and again the Soviet space program was plagued with setbacks.[95] The experience gained from Salyut would help the Soviets achieve a highlight in their exploration on space—Mir.

Apollo-Soyuz (July 1975). The primary objectives of the Apollo-Soyuz program were the development of a rescue system, docking procedures, and crew transfer between US and Soviet spacecraft. Additional objectives dealt with conducting astronomy, Earth studies, radiation, and biological experiments. NASA used its last remaining Apollo spacecraft for this mission, and the crew consisted of Apollo veteran Tom Stafford, Vance Brand, and astronaut office chief and original *Mercury 7* astronaut Deke Slayton.[96] Although there were not many gains in technology, this program was viewed as a political success.

Space Transportation System. The primary motivation for NASA's perseverance with the Space Transportation System (STS) was to find a cost-effective manned system. The current STS can trace its roots back to the lifting body research conducted at Edwards AFB. On 5 August 1975, an X-24B made a textbook landing after a powered flight to 60,000 feet.[97] The X-24B was America's last rocket research aircraft and concluded the manned lifting body program. The X-series research developed many concepts that would eventually be incorporated into the space shuttle, such as dead stick landings, flat bottoms, and others.

The actual conceptual design for the STS began in 1969 when President Nixon directed top Department of Defense and NASA scientists to devise a post-Apollo manned program.[98] The Space Shuttle Task Group was formed to study the problem, and they recommended the STS.

Due to its design philosophy, the STS looked promising and was approved by President Nixon. The system concept included the use of reusable components, autonomous operations, large payload, relatively simple on-board operation, a cargo compartment designed for a benign launch environment, throttleable engines, and on-orbit retrieval and repair of satellites.[99] This design scheme (fig. 1-13) would provide the United States with routine access to space.

Components of the STS include the orbiter, an external fuel tank, and two reusable solid-rocket motors. The first STS launch occurred on 12 April 1981, with landing on 14 April.[100] The astronauts for the mission were Robert Crippen and Gemini and Apollo veteran John Young.

After many successful missions, tragedy struck STS 33 on 22 January 1986 when the *Challenger*

Figure 1-13. STS. (NASA History Office photo)

18

exploded after lift-off because of a faulty solid-rocket motor pressure seal design that was "unacceptably sensitive to a number of factors."[101] As in 1967 with *Apollo 1*, NASA investigated the cause and made corrections, but this time the manned space program was halted for 32 months. It was not until 29 September 1988 that America reentered space with the launch of the *Discovery*.[102]

On 1 February 2003, tragedy again struck the shuttle program.[103] The space shuttle *Columbia* broke apart during reentry, and seven astronauts were lost. The cause of the accident occurred during liftoff when a piece of foam insulation broke free from the external fuel tank and punctured the leading edge of the left wing. During reentry superheated air was able to enter the internal compartments of the wing, leading to structural failure.

After this loss, the investigation board and NASA questioned the continued usefulness of the STS. In January 2004, President Bush announced that the STS would continue to be used to service and complete the International Space Station (ISS) but would be retired in 2010 when the ISS is completed.[104]

Mir. The Mir (loosely translated "peace," "world," or "commune") complex was described as a third-generation space station by the Russian space program. The Mir (fig. 1-14) was modular in design, which allowed different modules to be added and subtracted or moved from place to place, making the Mir very versatile. One of the most important features of Mir was that it was permanently manned, which was a giant step toward breaking earthly ties.[105] Mir was probably the most durable single achievement of the Russian/Soviet space program.

Figure 1-14. Mir space station. (NASA photo)

The Mir was the central portion of the space station and was the core module for the entire complex. Four other compartments completed the Mir complex: the transfer, working, intermediate, and assembly compartments. All compartments were pressurized except for the assembly compartment.

The usual missions began with a launch of either two or three crew members. It usually took about two days for the spacecraft to reach and dock with Mir. Docking always took place on an axial port. As a precautionary measure during docking, the crew that was occupying Mir put on activity suits and retreated to the resident *Soyuz-TM*, which was the capsule the cosmonauts rode to and from the Mir. The *Soyuz-TM* stayed attached so the crew could escape if necessary. When hatches were opened, both crews removed their suits and began changeover procedures, which took differing amounts of time depending on what needed to be accomplished. After changeover was complete, the crews put their suits back on and returned to the *Soyuz-TM*. The crew that had been there the longest got in the older of the two capsules, leaving the newer one for the new crew.

The Mir had its share of problems. Originally designed to last only five years, the Russian space station was continuously occupied from 1987 to 2000 (with the exception of two short periods).[106] NASA astronauts were a part of the crews aboard Mir. In 1997, two life-threatening incidents almost forced abandonment of the station. In February, a fire broke out, triggered by a chemical oxygen generator that filled the station with choking smoke and blocked one of the escape routes to a docked *Soyuz* capsule.[107] Although no major damage ensued, it was a frightening 14 minutes for the six men on board. In June, an unmanned *Progress* cargo ship collided with the *Spektr* module, and the ruptured module began to decompress.[108] The three-man crew sealed off the damaged module, but the power on the station was reduced by half.

Mir's 15-year life span was a monumental achievement. Mir circled the earth 86,331 times, and 104 individuals spent time on the station (42 were Russian and 44 were American).[109] Mir received 70 unmanned dockings and the space shuttle nine times.[110] The seven longest-flying Americans achieved their records on Mir—Shannon Lucid stayed in space for 188 days.[111] The Russians on Mir set incredible duration records: Sergei Avdeev, 742 days in space; Valeri Poliakov, 678 days in space; and the list goes on.[112] The volume of science carried out on Mir was enormous. Its remains crashed into the South Pacific on 23 March 2001.[113]

International Space Station. When the International Space Station (fig. 1-15) is complete, it will represent a move of unprecedented scale off of the home planet. Led by the United States, the International Space Station draws upon the scientific and technological resources of 16 nations: Canada, Japan, Russia, 11 nations of the European Space Agency, and Brazil.

More than four times as large as the Russian Mir space station, the completed International Space Station will have a mass of about 1,040,000 pounds.[114] It will measure 356 feet across and 290 feet in length, with almost an acre of solar panels to provide electrical power to six state-of-the-art laboratories.[115] The station is in an orbit with an altitude of 250 statute miles with an inclination of 51.6 degrees.[116] This orbit allows the station to be reached by the launch vehicles of all the international partners to provide a robust capability for the delivery of crews and supplies. The orbit also provides excellent observations of Earth with coverage of 85 percent of the globe and overflight of 95 percent of the population.

The ISS program began in 1994 and moved into the first stage in 1995.[117] Phase 1 was the joint Mir/shuttle rendezvous program. The main objective of this program was to provide operations experience to Americans, as the ISS is also using the basic schematics of the Mir space station. Countries all over the world are responsible for different parts of the space station. The United States is responsible for the building of the Unity structure, an 18-foot-long node that will serve as a hub for other nodes to be attached.[118] The United States is also responsible for the nearly 80,000 lb. of hardware that go along with the station. The United States is also contributing solar array panels, rack structures, and hatch assemblies. Canada built the mobile service system (MSS) that provides external station robotics.[119] The European Space Agency (ESA) is developing both a pressurized laboratory called the Columbus Orbital Facility (COF) and the automated transfer vehicle (ATV), which will be used for supplying logistics and propulsion.[120] Hauling the pieces and parts of the space station will require 45 space flights on five types of launch vehicles over a five-year period. The three launch vehicles are the US space shuttle, Russian *Proton* and *Soyuz* rockets, the ESA's *Ariane 5V* rocket, and Japan's *H-2A* rocket.[121] Launch of the space station began on 20 November 1998 (five months behind schedule) with the Russian *Zarya* control module.[122] Since then, many more modules have been attached including Spacehab, the Zenith-1 truss structure, the laboratory module Destiny, the joint airlock module Quest, the integrated truss structure, the mobile servicing system, and the American propulsion module.[123] The ISS is still being constructed and is scheduled to be complete in 2010.

Figure 1-15. International Space Station. (NASA photo)

Current Space Initiatives

In the post–Cold War world, space programs are no longer solely the initiatives of two superpowers in a race to control space. New players such as Iran and India are engaged in their own space research and development, even as the United States and Russia continue to pursue robust space programs.

United States

In January 2004 President Bush announced a new direction for NASA after the STS program draws to a close with the completion of the International Space Station in 2010. President Bush announced that NASA will return to the moon, this time no later than 2020.[124] Through an initiative named the Constellation Program, NASA hopes to return to the moon and establish a permanent colony on its way to manned exploration of Mars. Elements of this program are already in the testing phase, and the *Ares I* crew launch vehicle is scheduled to be test-fired in April 2009.[125]

In addition to government-sponsored efforts to continue space exploration, many private companies in America are trying to make space travel a reality for everyone. In 2004 the Ansari X prize was developed to spur private-company interest in space travel. The prize awarded $10 million to the first private team to build and launch a spacecraft capable of carrying three people 100 kilometers (km) above the earth's surface, twice within two weeks.[126] Aerospace designer Burt Rutan and financier Paul Allen won the prize on 4 October 2004 when *SpaceShipOne* rocketed to an altitude of over 328,000 feet for the second time in less than 10 days.[127] Since that time, several other X prizes have been offered, including a $30 million prize for the first team to design and soft-land a robotic probe on the moon.[128]

China

China is the third nation on Earth capable of independently launching its citizens into orbit. On 15 October 2003, Yang Liwei blasted off from a remote space base in the Gobi Desert atop a *Long March 2F* rocket and entered China into the exclusive club of nations capable of manned space missions.[129] On 27 September 2008, China continued its rapid push into space by completing the country's first spacewalk.

China is currently planning to land a robotic rover on the moon in 2010 or 2012 and follow this with a probe to bring back lunar rock samples by 2015.[130] If these efforts are successful, China hopes to land a man on the moon by 2020—interestingly, the same year by which the United States hopes to send another manned mission to the moon.

Japan

Despite a recent string of failures in the domestically made *H-2A* rocket, the Japan Aerospace Exploration Agency (JAXA) has tentative plans to send a manned spacecraft to the moon by 2025.[131] Over the next 10 years, Japan will try to develop nanotechnology and robots to explore the moon, as well as a rocket and vehicle to get astronauts there. After this 10-year period, JAXA will reevaluate its plans. Other projects under development include a passenger airliner capable of flying Mach 2, or twice the speed of sound.[132]

Russia

Russia regularly sends Soyuz spacecraft to the International Space Station to resupply and support crew change-outs. In addition, Russia continues to put military payloads into space, as well as satellites to complete their Globalnaya Navigatisionnaya

Sputnikovaya Sistema (GLONASS) navigation system.[133] Recently, Russia joined the race to the moon, announcing a joint program with the ESA to develop a rocket and capsule. Although no timeline has been announced, the design may be similar to NASA's Orion spacecraft, currently in development as part of the Constellation project.[134]

Europe

The ESA is one of the world's leading space programs. In 2007 the ESA launched six *Ariane 5* rockets, all delivering their satellite payloads into space.[135] The ESA is working with Russia on a collaborative mission to the moon and has primarily focused its efforts on the moon, Mars, and asteroids. These Aurora programs are designed to explore the universe, stimulate new technology, and inspire the young people of Europe to be interested in science and technology. NASA and the ESA are currently working on a joint program to bring Martian soil samples back to Earth for the first time in history.[136]

Iran

In February 2008 Iran announced the launch of its first research rocket and unveiled its new space center.[137] On 3 February 2009, Iran entered the global space race when it successfully launched its first domestic satellite, *Omid*.

India

The Indian Space Research Organization (ISRO) seeks to develop satellites, launch vehicles, and sounding rockets. These platforms are used primarily for telecommunications, television, meteorology, and disaster warning.[138] The ISRO also has two reliable launch vehicles that place payloads from other countries into orbit as well. In 2007 an Italian satellite was placed into orbit, and in early 2008 an Israeli satellite was successfully placed in orbit.[139]

Where We Have Been and Where We Are Going

Mankind has been trying to solve the mysteries of the heavens since the beginning of time. With the development of the first rockets, man took the first tentative steps on this journey of discovery. Early pioneers such as Herman Oberth, Konstantin Tsiolkovsky, and Robert Goddard began to make the dream of space exploration a reality, paving the way for Dr. von Braun and other leading scientists.

Undaunted by countless failures on the ground and in flight, mankind continued the relentless pursuit of space. As rockets gave way to missiles and satellites, manned spaceflight slowly became a reality. Since the launch of *Sputnik* in 1957, mankind has come almost full circle in space exploration. Whereas the 1960s saw the Soviet Union and United States race to become the first to the moon, today the world is once again trying to achieve this goal. Now many nations are working to visit the moon by 2020 and hope to see a human being set foot on Mars.

As many historians believe that mankind's first steps on the moon in 1969 were the defining moment of the last century, perhaps we who are living now will be fortunate enough to witness one of the most important achievements in the history of the world—manned exploration to Mars and beyond.

Notes

1. NASA Education Working Group, *Rockets: A Teacher's Guide with Activities in Science, Mathematics, and Technology,* http://store.aiaa.org/kidsplace/kidsplacepdfs/Rockets.pdf (accessed 10 January 2008).

2. Kelly King Howes, *War of 1812* (Detroit, MI: UXL, 2002), 116–17.

3. David O. Woodbury, *Outward Bound for Space* (Boston: Little, Brown & Co., 1961), 21–22.

4. Ibid., 24.

5. Ibid.

6. Ibid., 25.

7. Hellen B. Walters, *Herman Oberth: Father of Space Travel* (New York: Macmillan, 1962), 60–62.

8. Ibid., 63.

9. William I. McLaughlin, "Walter Hohmann's Roads in Space," *Journal of Space Mission Architecture,* issue 2 (Fall 2000): 2, http://www2.jpl.nasa.gov/csmad/journal/issue2/toc.pdf (accessed 10 January 2008).

10. Willy Ley, *Rockets, Missiles, and Men in Space* (New York: Viking Press, 1968), 134.

11. Michael J. Neufeld, *Von Braun: Dreamer of Space, Engineer of War* (New York: Alfred A. Knopf, 2007), 72–73.

12. Ibid., 132–37.

13. Ibid., 184.

14. Roger D. Launius, *Frontiers of Space Exploration* (Westport, CT: Greenwood Press, 1998), 91–92.

15. William Shelton, *Soviet Space Exploration: The First Decade* (New York: Washington Square Press, 1968), 20–22.

16. Asif A. Siddiqi, *Challenge to Apollo: The Soviet Union and the Space Race, 1945–1974,* NASA History Series (Washington, DC: NASA, 2000), 24–28.

17. Ibid., 82–84.

18. Ibid., 120–21.

19. Peter Smolders, *Soviets in Space* (New York: Taplinger Publishing Company, 1974), 60.

20. Siddiqi, *Challenge to Apollo,* 114.

21. Robert Weisbrot, *Maximum Danger: Kennedy, the Missiles, and the Crisis of American Confidence* (Chicago: Ivan R. Dee, 2001), 73.

22. Siddiqi, *Challenge to Apollo,* 158.

23. Ibid., 130–31.

24. Ibid., 166–67.

25. Ibid., 173–74.

26. Ibid., 128.

27. Jacob Neufeld, *Development of Ballistic Missiles in the United States Air Force, 1945–1960* (Washington, DC: Office of Air Force History, USAF, 1990), 134.

28. Ibid., 192.

29. Ibid., 213–14.

30. Ibid., 227.

31. Ibid., 237.

32. Ibid., 199–200.

33. Ley, *Rockets, Missiles, and Men,* 223.

34. Roger D. Launius, "The Satellite and Rocket Research Panel," NASA History Office home page, http://www.hq.nasa.gov/office/pao/history/index.html (accessed 16 January 2008).

35. Erik Bergaust, *Rocket City, U.S.A.: From Huntsville, Alabama to the Moon* (New York: Macmillan, 1963), 88.

36. Ibid., 89–90.

37. Smithsonian National Air and Space Museum, "Military Origins of the Space Race," http://www.nasm.si.edu/exhibitions/gal114/spacerace/sec200/sec231.htm (accessed 21 January 2008).

38. Milton W. Rosen, *The Viking Rocket Story* (New York: Harper, 1955), 92–93.

39. Ibid., 137–40.

40. James Baar and William E. Howard, *Polaris!* (New York: Harcourt, Brace, 1960), 75.

41. J. J. Dicerto, *Missile Base beneath the Sea: The Story of Polaris* (New York: St. Martin's Press, 1967), 21.

42. Ibid., 1–2.

43. Walter Sullivan, *Assault on the Unknown: The International Geophysical Year* (New York: McGraw-Hill, 1961), 88.

44. Constance Green and Milton Lomask, *Vanguard: A History*, NASA History Series (Washington, DC: NASA, 1970), 208–9.

45. Ibid., 215.

46. Sullivan, *Assault on the Unknown*, 126.

47. Ibid., 219-28.

48. NASA Historical Staff, *Historical Sketch of NASA* (Washington, DC: NASA, 1965), 6.

49. Ibid., 8.

50. Ibid., 41.

51. Ibid.

52. Lane E. Wallace, *Dreams, Hopes, Realities: NASA's Goddard Space Flight Center: The First Forty Years* (Washington, DC: NASA History Office, 1999), 27.

53. Ibid., 136.

54. Ibid., 135–36.

55. Donald H. Martin, *Communications Satellites, 1958–1995* (El Segundo, CA: Aerospace Press, 1996), 179–82.

56. Ibid., 49–50.

57. Ibid., 50–51.

58. Ibid., 52–53.

59. Ibid., 53–57.

60. Ibid., 58–66.

61. Ibid., 211.

62. Herbert J. Spiegel and Arnold Gruber, *From Weather Vanes to Satellites: An Introduction to Meteorology* (New York: John Wiley and Sons, 1983), 12.

63. Ibid., 12.

64. Ibid.

65. David Baker, ed., *Jane's Space Directory, 2003–2004* (Alexandria, VA: Jane's Information Group, 2003), 429.

66. Astronautix, "Advanced Tiros N," http://www.astronautix.com/craft/advirosn.htm (accessed 24 January 2008).

67. Baker, *Jane's Space Directory*, 425.

68. Ibid., 426.

69. General Accounting Office (GAO), *Seasat Project*, PSAD-76-76 (Procurement and Systems Acquisition Division) (Washington, DC: GAO, 25 February 1976), 1.

70. Baker, *Jane's Space Directory*, 469.

71. NASA Jet Propulsion Laboratory, "Voyager Mission Operations Status Report #2009-01-02," week ending 2 January 2009, http://voyager.jpl.nasa.gov/mission/weekly-reports/index.htm (accessed 10 February 2009).

72. Valerie Neal, *Exploring the Universe with the Hubble Space Telescope* (Washington, DC: NASA, 1990), 55.

73. Ibid., 52–53.

74. Baker, *Jane's Space Directory*, 489.

75. Pres. George W. Bush, "Remarks at a Memorial Service for the STS-107 Crew of the Space Shuttle Columbia in Houston, Texas," 4 February 2003 (Washington, DC: Government Printing Office, 2003), http://fdsys.gpo.gov/fdsys/pkg/WCPD-2003-02-10/pdf/WCPD-2003-02-10-Pg156.pdf (accessed 27 March 2009).

76. Brian Harvey, *Russia in Space: The Failed Frontier?* (Chichester, UK: Praxis Publishing, 2001), 5–6.

77. Launius, "Satellite and Rocket Research Panel." 8.

78. H. J. P. Arnold, ed., *Man in Space: An Illustrated History of Spaceflight* (New York: CLB Smithmark Publishing, 1993), 44–46.

79. Ibid., 28–30.

80. Ibid., 47.

81. Ibid., 55.

82. Ibid., 57–58.

83. Harvey, *Russia in Space*, 7.

84. Von Hardesty and Gene Eisman, *Epic Rivalry: The Inside Story of the Soviet and American Space Race* (Washington, DC: National Geographic Society, 2007), 178–84.

85. Arnold, *Man in Space*, 60.

86. Ibid., 64.

87. Launius, "Satellite and Rocket Research Panel," 9.

88. Ibid., 24.

89. Harvey, *Russia in Space*, 8–9.

90. Ibid., 8–10.

91. Hardesty and Eisman, *Epic Rivalry*, 245.

92. Arnold, *Man in Space*, 110–21.

93. Ibid., 122.

94. Harvey, *Russia in Space*, 14.

95. Ibid., 14–15.

96. Arnold, *Man in Space*, 125.

97. Dennis R. Jenkins, *Space Shuttle: The History of the National Space Transportation System: The First 100 Missions* (Cape Canaveral, FL: Dennis Jenkins Publishing, 2001), 39.

98. Ibid., 74.

99. David M. Harland, *The Story of the Space Shuttle* (Chichester, UK: Praxis Publishing, 2004), 5–7.

100. Ibid., 29.

101. Presidential Commission on the Space Shuttle Challenger Accident, *Report of the Presidential Commission*, http://history.nasa.gov/rogersrep/v1ch4.htm (accessed 12 February 2009).

102. Ibid., 286.

103. Harland, *Story of the Space Shuttle*, 359–62.

104. Ibid., 385.

105. Roger D. Launius, *Space Stations: Base Camps to the Stars* (Washington, DC: Smithsonian Books, 2003), 147–48.

106. Ibid., 148.

107. Ibid., 164.

108. Ibid., 167–69.

109. Ibid., 172.

110. Ibid., 285–95.

111. Ibid.

112. Ibid.

113. Harland, *Story of the Space Shuttle*, 288.

114. Peter Bond, *The Continuing Story of the International Space Station* (Chichester, UK: Praxis Publishing, 2002), 2.

115. Ibid.

116. Launius, *Space Stations*, 153.

117. Harland, *Story of the Space Shuttle*, 288.

118. Bond, *Continuing Story*, 3.

119. Ibid., 5.

120. Ibid., 9.

121. Ibid., 136–46.

122. Launius, *Space Stations*, 186.

123. Harland, *Story of the Space Shuttle*, 363–79.

124. Pres. George W. Bush, "A Renewed Spirit of Discovery," program announcement, 14 January 2004, http://georgewbush-whitehouse.archives.gov/space/renewed_spirit.html (accessed 30 March 2009).

125. NASA, "Constellation: America's Fleet of Next-Generation Launch Vehicles," NASA fact sheet, http://www.nasa.gov/mission_pages/constellation/ares/aresI.html (accessed 5 February 2008).

126. X Prize Foundation, "Ansari X Prize," http://www.xprize.org/x-prizes/ansari-x-prize (accessed 5 February 2008).

127. Scaled Composites, Web site, http://www.scaled.com/projects/tierone/ (accessed 5 February 2008).

128. Google Lunar X Prize, Web site, http://www.googlelunarxprize.org/lunar/competition/guidelines (accessed 5 February 2008).

129. Xinhua News Agency, "China Launches First Manned Spacecraft," China View/View China, http://news.xinhuanet.com/english/2003-10/15/content_1123817.htm (accessed 5 February 2008).

130. *Space Today Online*, "China's Moon Flights," http://www.spacetoday.org/China/ChinaMoonflight.html (accessed 5 February 2008).

131. Space.com, "Japan Announces Manned Moon Flight by 2025," http://www.space.com/missionlaunches/ap_050406_japan_moon.html (accessed 5 February 2008).

132. Ibid.

133. RussianSpaceWeb.com, "Back to Basics: Another Apollo Clone," http://www.russianspaceweb.com/ soyuz_acts_origin.html#2008 (accessed 6 February 2008).
134. Ibid.
135. European Space Agency, "Aurora Exploration Programme," http://www.esa.int/SPECIALS/Aurora/ SEMZOS39ZAD_0.html (accessed 6 February 2008).
136. Ibid.
137. Associated Press, "Iran Launches Research Rocket, Unveils Space Center," FOXNews.com, http:// www.foxnews.com/story/0.2933.327977,00.html (accessed 6 February 2008).
138. Ibid.
139. Indian Space Research Organization, Web site, http://www.isro.org/ (accessed 6 February 2008).

Chapter 2

Space Power Theory

Maj Burton "Ernie" Catledge, USAF; and LCDR Jeremy Powell, USN

The Soviet Union's launch of *Sputnik* in 1957 became the basis for space power theory, and international debate immediately emerged on potential applications of an enemy satellite orbiting the earth. Theories ranged from dropping nuclear weapons from space to peacefully overflying countries for treaty verification.[1] Half a century later, the United States is still asking, what does space power mean? Operations Desert Storm, Allied Force, Enduring Freedom, and Iraqi Freedom gave military theorists a glimpse into the application of space power; however, the validity of their theories has yet to be extensively tested. Theorists continue to search for strategies to interpret and employ space power.

Because law is one of the foundations for space power theory, this chapter begins by exploring air and sea precedents in developing space law. (Space law is discussed more fully in chapter 3.) Second, this chapter highlights the fallacy of assuming space power theory is an extension of air and sea theory. Finally, this chapter presents four leading space power theories and explains the evolution of space power thought.

Air and Sea Precedents in Developing Space Law

Law has provided the basis for air and sea power and is considered foundational in developing a space power theory. Given the short history of US space activities, Irvin White offers "a compelling case for the evolution of space law from a basis in international sea and air traditions."[2] Dr. Everett Dolman states in his book *Astropolitik: Classical Geopolitics in the Space Age* that "the bulk of air law, codified in the twentieth century in conjunction with rapid technological developments of the air, then jet plane, has developed primarily through bilateral treaties and multilateral conventions. Law of the sea, on the other hand, developed primarily by codifying existing customary and normative behaviors of seafaring states."[3] The major contentious issues in regards to air, space, and naval theory are delimitations, sovereignty, registration and liability, and innocent passage.[4]

Delimitation

Delimitation attempts to answer the question of where airspace ends and where space begins. According to Dolman, "The two most prevalent approaches for defining outer space have been spatial and functional. The spatial approach explains that space begins just below the lowest point at which an object can be maintained in orbit . . . about 52 miles."[5] The second approach to defining outer space is "the functional approach [that] is based on the propulsion systems of the air/spacecraft and is legally based in 1919 and 1944 International Air Conventions, which defined aircraft as 'any machine that can derive support from reactions of the air.' Under this definition, space begins just beyond the maximum height at which aerodynamic flight is possible."[6] An internationally recognized definition of where space begins has to be the first governing principle in establishing space law. Without this definition of space, the second question of sovereignty cannot be answered.

Sovereignty

In addition to delineation, sovereignty aids in developing a framework for space law. The "definition of air space is acceptable for aircraft, since, due to gravity and the relatively small altitudes concerned, the air space above the earth can be monitored and controlled. It can be possessed. There is a legally important distinction here: the air is not susceptible to sovereignty, but the air space is."[7] Having sovereignty in space does not mean having control of space due to the rotation of the earth. Therefore, basing space sovereignty on airspace law is problematic.[8]

While not without its limitations, sea law can aid in developing a working definition of space sovereignty:

Prior to 1958, the limit of territorial seas had been generally recognized as between 3 and 12 miles. The International Conventions on the Law of the Sea of 1958 and 1960 were unable to formalize a universal legal limit for territorial or contiguous seas, or for high seas. . . . Like the sea, outer space can be divided into subregions, usually defined by their distance from the earth. These distinctions, described in astropolitical terms, include near-Earth and geostationary space, cislunar and translunar space, deep space, etc., and are usually put forward by military or nationalist supporters who wish to derive maximum control of the commons for the benefit of their constituency.[9]

Dolman argues that "the only definition of sovereign space that may truly matter is one that incorporates the notion of a region that can be effectively defended."[10] The US Navy does not attempt to control the entire sea—only the portions that are in support of national interests. Establishing space superiority without first defining space sovereignty results in ineffective use of space resources.

Registration and Liability

The third issue regarding sea and airpower that has relevance for space power is registration and liability. The United Nations (UN) Convention on the Law of the Sea requires each nation to keep a registry of ships. Individual nations, however, may have their own rules and regulations for registration, safety, and related issues.[11] Dolman notes that "in contrast to sea law, aircraft have the additional requirement of *holding* the nationality of the state in which they are registered. . . . The requirements for registration of objects in space are stricter than those for sea or air, with the justification that such registration is necessary because of the greater potential for global physical and/or environmental damage. . . . The most compelling reason for registration of spacecraft, according to policy makers, is to enhance national security."[12] In reference to the 1967 Outer Space Treaty ratification, UN Ambassador Arthur Goldberg stated, "This is a matter of national security. We believe that when there is registration of launchings this gives us an opportunity to, and the world community to, check up on whether the launchings are, indeed, peaceful or whether they are for some other purposes."[13]

Innocent Passage

The final issue of air and sea law that provides a framework for space power theory is the issue of innocent passage. According to the definition of innocent passage for sea areas, "passage is innocent so long as it is not prejudicial to the peace, good order, or security of the coastal state. Innocent passage on the seas is far less strict than the air regime, and the space regime is the least constrained of all."[14] For example, the definition of innocent passage on the oceans permits photographic and other reconnaissance activities in which Soviet Union-equipped fishing trawlers with sophisticated surveillance equipment monitor US shores.[15] Innocent passage of the sea seems to be the most likely model for establishing a space framework for legal activities in space.

Limitations of Air and Sea Power Models

While sea and air models are instructional, the distinction between the mediums provides additional insight into why space power is unique. Lt Cdr John J. Klein's article "Corbett in Orbit: A Maritime Model for Strategic Space Theory" proposes that, given the lack of a comprehensive space theory, previous models should be used for development of a comprehensive theory to develop a space strategy. However, Klein correctly analyses the limitations of equating air and space power as aerospace power.[16] The assumption that air and space power are inextricably linked—that the same theories which apply to airpower also apply to space power—is faulty:

Early thinkers on space forces considered them simply "high-flying air forces." For example, U.S. Air Force space doctrine was first established merely by replacing the word "air" with the coinage "aerospace" in the literature. According to aerospace integrationists, space power is no different from airpower, because it delivers similar products to users. Consequently, in that view, no separate space power theory or definition is warranted, since aerospace power embraces space operations.[17]

The air and space power linkages begin to fray when one considers the activities US space operations support. Space operations can be categorized into civil, commercial, military, and intelligence. Airpower, on the other hand, focuses almost exclusively on the military aspect. According to Klein, "because of the diverse and pervasive nature of the space activities of the United States, its space operations have implications spanning all elements of national power—diplomatic, military, economic, technological, and information."[18]

Klein notes that "some strategists, pointing to the similarities between sea and space operations, suggest that the best possible space theory would be achieved by simply substituting 'space' for 'sea' in naval strategy."[19] Brentnall, Kohlhepp, Davenport, Cole, and others offered several sea-power analogies to explain space power. The following is a partial list of some of those analogies:

- US dependence on sea power (and now space power) for national growth, prosperity, and security.
- The need for a space battleship to control the "narrows" of the celestial seas.
- The concepts of sea (space) control and sea (space) supremacy.
- Global coverage (the ability to project power around the world).
- Free passage.

- Commercial possibilities.
- A force in being.
- Vehicular rather than positional sovereignty.[20]

However, naval power theory, Klein says, "deals with ships, shipbuilding, war at sea, and military forces associated with navies. Moreover, naval theory is primarily concerned with the means and methods of employing force at sea to achieve national goals while increasing national power and prestige. . . . Consequently, the applicability of the naval model to space is limited, since it does not adequately encompass the interaction and interdependence of other environments or military forces."[21]

Given the similarities and differences between the three domains, are air and sea models applicable for developing a space power theory? The answer is yes; however, the theorist must begin by approaching space as a unique environment rather than reversing the operation and making space fit into the sea and air theories. Adm Alfred Thayer Mahan admonishes "that while it is wise to observe the things that are alike, it is also wise to look for things that differ, for when the imagination is carried away by the detection of points of resemblance—one of the most pleasing of mental pursuits—it is apt to be impatient of any divergence in its new-found parallels, and so may overlook or refuse to recognize such."[22]

Characteristics and Definition of Space Power

Since space is a unique domain and air and sea models are lacking, a new strategy is required. With space law codified, the next step in developing a theory is to identify the characteristics and provide a definition of space power. Lt Col David E. Lupton, in his book *On Space Warfare: A Space Power Doctrine*, provides the framework, outlines the characteristics, and offers a definition of space power:

Space power, it follows, is the ability to use the space environment in pursuit of some national objective or purpose. Second, space power may be purely military, such as the collection of surveillance data, or nonmilitary, such as earth resource data collection or civilian communications. Third, all four elements of national power embody not just military forces but civilian capabilities as well. For instance, Gen H. H. "Hap" Arnold described air power as the total aeronautical capabilities of a nation. Admiral Mahan even included the nature of a country's political institutions as a determinant of a nation's sea power. By extension, the space shuttle, a civilian vehicle, along with the political structure that allowed its development, contributes to US space power. A definition that includes these three characteristics is that space power is the ability of a nation to exploit the space environment in pursuit of national goals and purposes and includes the entire astronautical capabilities of the nation. A nation with such capabilities is termed a space power.[23]

Lupton's Four Schools of Thought

Having defined space power, Lupton further discusses four schools of thought regarding space power theory. Particularly, he explores those differences in fundamental beliefs that impact the analysis of the four schools of doctrinal thought concerning the best way to employ space forces.[24] His discussion of the sanctuary, survivability, high-ground, and control schools provides the basis for the three remaining space theorists discussed.

Sanctuary School. The fear that space would be weaponized after the *Sputnik* launch resulted in a declaration that space must be reserved for peaceful purposes. The first school, the sanctuary school, was born out of this philosophy:

A fundamental tenet of this school is that the primary value of space forces is their capability to "see" within the boundaries of sovereign states. This value stems from the space vehicle's legal overflight characteristic. Proponents of sanctuary doctrine argue that past arms limitations treaties could not have been consummated without space systems that serve as the "national technical means of treaty verification. . . ."

The prospects for any future treaties would be extremely dim without the ability of space systems to fulfill President Eisenhower's dream of open skies. Thus, space systems have had a tremendous stabilizing influence on relations between the two superpowers. Finally, these advocates caution that overflight is a granted right that nations have not attempted to deny and that any proposed military use of space must be weighed against the possible loss of peaceful overflight. This train of thought leads to the conclusion that the only way to maintain the legal overflight characteristic is to designate space as a war-free sanctuary.[25]

Survivability School. The basic tenet of Lupton's survivability school is that "space systems are inherently less survivable than terrestrial forces." Several factors lead him to this conclusion:

First is the long-range weapon effects in the space environment, coupled with a belief that nuclear weapons are more likely to be used in the remoteness of space. Second, the quasipositional nature of space forces and their vehicular sovereignty imply that space forces cannot rely on maneuverability or terrestrial barriers to increase survivability. . . . Advocates of the survivability school . . . have serious reservations as to the military value of space forces. They agree that military forces can do certain military functions . . . more economically and efficiently in peacetime than other forces. They believe, however, that space forces must not be depended on for these functions in wartime because they will not survive.[26]

High-Ground School. The third school of thought, known as the high-ground school, believes the force that dominates space will have an asymmetric advantage over its opponent and thus be less vulnerable to attack:

[This] school harkens back to the old military axiom that domination of the high ground ensures domination of the lower lying areas. Disciples of this "high-ground" school advocate a space-based ballistic missile defense (BMD). They argue that the global-presence characteristic of space forces combined with either directed-energy or high-velocity-impact space weapons provide opportunities for radical new national strategies. In their view, space-based defensive forces can reverse the current stalemate caused by the preeminence of the offense and create either an offensive-defensive balance or a preferred defensive stalemate. This rebalancing would allow replacement of the flawed strategy of assured destruction with one of assured survival. . . . The high-ground school believes space forces will have a dominant influence.[27]

Control School. The final of Lupton's schools is the control school:

The control school declines to place an exact value on space forces and only suggests their value by using air power and sea power analogies. For example, according to Gen Thomas A. White, ". . . Whoever has the capacity to control space will likewise possess the capacity to exert control over the surface of the earth." Others argue that there are space lanes of communications like sea lanes of communications that must be controlled if a war is to be won in the terrestrial theaters. Control school advocates argue that the capability to deter war is enhanced by the ability to control space and that, in future wars, space control will be coequal with air and sea control.[28]

Given the four schools of thought, Lupton believes that the control school should be the basis for a space power strategy.

The recent Chinese and US antisatellite launches have nullified the sanctuary school as a viable basis for a space power theory. US reliance upon space services such as the global positioning system (GPS), satellite communications (SATCOM), missile warning, and space-based weather makes space a fundamental part of military as well as commercial operations. Given the reliance upon these services, the survivability school is no longer realistic. Given the proliferation of space weapons, the evolution of space power lies with the high-ground and control schools.

Oberg Space Power Theory

James Oberg picks up the space power theory discussion where Lupton leaves off and outlines four reasons for developing a space power theory. Oberg dismisses the sanctuary, survivability, and high-ground schools of thought and proposes further development of space power theory using the control school of thought.[30]

[First, space power theory] provides a foundation of appreciation of the unique nature of space. Space is not earth and terrestrial metaphors are not helpful and in fact are harmful. With a good space power theory, you can formulate innovative strategies and also make sure that you have all of them, because as we will see later on, many times you find that you didn't initially think of a solution that turns out to have been the best one; it wasn't thought of in time to choose it. The second point, which is an elaboration on the first, is that a good theory of space power protects workers and decision-makers from false analogies, the ultimate "high ground" self-delusion. Another elaboration on the first point is that because space is so unpredictable and unearthly, in the literal meaning of the word, things can be invented or done there, developed and deployed there, that catch people by surprise. The Sputnik shock of forty-five years ago is such a thing that many of us remember. It was one of the great surprises of the twentieth century. Other surprises like that could be out there if we lack an adequate space power theory. And lastly a good theory provides a criterion, a measure of "goodness," for selection among competing options.[31]

Oberg proposes the following foundations for a space power theory when developing a space policy:

- The primary attribute of current space systems lies in their extensive view of the earth.

- A corollary of this attribute is that a space vehicle is in sight of vast areas of Earth's surface.

- Space exists as a distinct medium.

- Space power alone is insufficient to control the outcome of terrestrial conflict or insure the attainment of terrestrial political objectives.

- Space power has developed, for the most part, without human presence in space, making it unique among all forms of national power.

- Situational awareness in space is a key to successful application of space power.

- At some time in the future, the physical presence of humans in space will be necessary to provide greater situational awareness.

- Technological competence is required to become a space power, and conversely, technological benefits are derived from being a space power.

- Control of space is the linchpin upon which a nation's space power depends.

- As with earthbound media, the weaponization of space is inevitable, though the manner and timing are not at all predictable.

- Scientific research and exploration pay off.

- Space operations have been and continue to be extremely capital intensive.

- There will be wild cards.[32]

The lack of accurate space power analogies has created a great deal of confusion. Oberg dismisses previous air and naval analogies and encourages theorists to view space as a separate environment with unique challenges and opportunities. The uniqueness of the environment should be the basis for space power theory rather than viewing space as an extension of the naval or air domain.

Astropolitik

Dr. Dolman, in his book *Astropolitik: Classical Geopolitics in the Space Age*, blends the high-ground and control schools and argues that a realist's view on developing space power theory is necessary. Dolman writes, "Strategy, grand strategy in particular, . . . is ultimately political in nature, that is to say the ends of national strategy are inextricably political, yet the means or dimensions of strategy are not limited."[33] Dolman proposes that the United States "seize control of outer space and become the shepherd (or perhaps watchdog) for all who would venture there, for if any one state must do so, it is the most likely to establish a benign hegemony."[34]

Dolman proposes three steps to implementing his plan. "First, the United States should declare that it is withdrawing from the current space regime and announce that it is establishing a principle of free-market sovereignty in space. . . . Second, by using its current and near-term capacities, the United States should endeavor at once to seize control of low-earth orbit."[35] According to Dolman, in 1961 Dandridge Cole polled 423 leaders in the astronautic community about his Panama hypothesis ("that there are strategic areas in space which may someday be as important to space transportation as the Panama Canal is to ocean transportation"),[36] Cole reported that about 80 percent agreed with this hypothesis. Dolman argues that US military control of "low-Earth orbit would be for all practical purposes a police blockade of all current space-ports, monitoring and controlling all traffic both in and out."[37] The third step in implementing Dolman's plan is establishing a national space coordination agency, which would "define, separate, and coordinate the efforts of commercial, civilian, and military space projects. . . . A complementary commercial space technology agency could be subordinated or separated from the coordination agency, to assist in the development of space exploitation programs at national universities and colleges, fund and guide commercial technology research, and generate wealth maximization and other economic strategies for space resources and manufacturing."[38]

Dolman's realist view of space power dismisses the notion that a nation should hold to a strategy hoping one's enemy won't challenge the status quo. Like Oberg, Dolman dismisses the sanctuary and survivability schools. He argues for a high-ground/control space power theory. Given the reliance upon space and the threats already posed in space, the United States should encourage free passage in space while having the capacity to prevent those who will disrupt this freedom.

Klein's Maritime Model

Most of the discussion of Klein's maritime model is reproduced directly from his article "Corbett in Orbit: A Maritime Model for Strategic Space Theory," *Naval War College Review* 57, no. 1 (Winter 2004): 59–74.

While air and naval theories offer insight into a space theory, neither air nor naval theories are capable of sufficiently addressing space:

Both air and naval models are relevant to space operations and activities, but neither possesses the breadth needed for a strategic space theory. The air model, in its aerospace variant, takes into account the interrelationships of other forces and environments, but it has a primarily military focus. The naval model includes national interests, such as prestige and power, but is focused on naval engagements alone and tends to exclude other operations or forces. Yet there is a theoretical model that incorporates other mediums and forces, as aerospace power does, while including broad national interests, as the naval model does.[39]

Maritime Model. Klein suggests the use of a maritime model for theorizing space power—maritime theory is much broader than naval theory and is more relevant to space operations than air theory: "The term 'maritime,' in contrast to 'naval,' connotes the whole range of activities and interests regarding the seas and oceans of the world, and their interrelationships: science, technology, cartography, industry, economics, trade, politics, international affairs, imperial expansion, communications, migration, international law, social affairs, and leadership."[40]

Among the most recognized maritime strategists is Sir Julian Stafford Corbett, whose work *Some Principles of Maritime Strategy*, can serve as the foundation for developing a space theory:

Sir Julian Stafford Corbett (1854–1922), acclaimed as Great Britain's greatest maritime strategist, is particularly renowned for his 1911 work *Some Principles of Maritime Strategy*, a "fusion of history and strategy." . . . Therefore, it is Corbett's ideas and principles, from *Some Principles of Maritime Strategy*, that we will use as a framework for deriving a strategic space theory.

Corbett wrote of the implications for national power of maritime operations in both peace and war. Like Carl von Clausewitz—whom he cites extensively—Corbett recognized that both land and sea operations are influenced by national politics and interests. The object of naval warfare being in his view to control maritime communications, including commercial and economic aspects, Corbett held that naval action can influence the balance of wealth and power among nations.

Nonetheless, Corbett acknowledged that sea and land operations are interdependent, that naval strategy and operations constitute only a subset of a nation's wartime operations. He repeatedly stated the necessity for the closest cooperation of ground and sea forces. In fact, in a departure from the conventional thought of his day, Corbett considered it of paramount importance that naval strategy work within the overall national strategy, since it is almost impossible for war to be decided by naval action alone (*Some Principles*, page 15). Therefore, the purpose of maritime strategy is to determine the "mutual relations of your army and navy in a plan of war" (page 16).

Another theme of Corbett's work is "command of the sea," which he considers different from the occupation of territory by an army, for the high seas cannot be subjected to political dominion or ownership. The inherent value of the sea, in his view, is as a means of communication. Consequently, Corbett defines command of the sea as the "control of maritime communications, whether for commercial or military purposes" (94). He explicitly states, however, that to command the sea is a relative advantage, not an absolute; it does not mean that the enemy cannot act, only that it cannot seriously interfere with one's actions. The normal state of affairs, Corbett observes, is not a commanded sea but an uncommanded one—that is, command of the sea is normally in dispute (91).

Maritime communications pertain to those routes by which the flow of "national life is maintained ashore"; therefore, they have a broader meaning than land lines of communication and are not analogous to those traditionally used by armies (93, 100). While maritime communications include supply and trade, they also include lines of communication that are of a strategic nature and are thus critical for a nation's survival. The objective of controlling maritime communications is protection of one's own commerce and interference with the enemy's economic interests, ultimately the defeat of the adversary's "power of resistance" (102). Corbett argues that the primary object of the fleet, therefore, is to secure sea lines of communication, putting the enemy's fleet out of action if it is in a position to render them unsafe (102).

For Corbett, offensive operations are called for when political objectives necessitate acquiring something from the enemy; as a more "effective" (his term) form of war than the defensive, offensive operations should be the preference of the stronger power (31). Notwithstanding the advantage of the offensive, however, even a superior naval force seeking a decisive victory will likely find the enemy in a position where he cannot easily be affected; throughout naval history fleets have been able to thwart attempts to force decisive battle by retiring to the safety of coasts and ports (158). Still, and despite this limitation, Corbett expressed concern that some naval professionals made a fetish of the offensive. Corbett argued that defensive operations should not be shunned or avoided; they are, he held, specifically called for when political objectives necessitate preventing the enemy from gaining something (32). Moreover, defensive objectives are the "stronger" form of war and, as a rule, should be resorted to by the weaker navy until it is strong enough to assume the offensive (310–11).

Like Clausewitz, Corbett classified wars according to whether the object is limited or unlimited. Because of the nonescalatory nature of truly limited warfare, a nation initiating a limited war needs the "power of isolation" to defend itself against an unlimited counterstroke. Such "isolation" could be achieved by commanding the sea to such a degree as to make it effectively an "insuperable physical obstacle." In such a case, "He that commands the sea is at great liberty and may take as much or as little of the war as he will."

Corbett envisioned several actions that may be taken by lesser naval powers to dispute command of the sea. A lesser naval force would be unlikely to win a decisive major fleet engagement, yet it could achieve significant results. Through minor naval actions—such as attacks on sea lanes and coastal raids (261–62)—it could contest a superior power's command of the sea and thereby accomplish at least limited political objectives. In such ways a lesser power could disturb enemy plans, regardless of its fleet's size, while strengthening its own national power and prestige (61).

A small navy could also effectively dispute command of the sea through the "fleet in being" concept (166). A decisive defeat at the hands of a more capable navy would make one's fleet unavailable should the situation later develop in one's favor (211). Consequently, keeping its fleet actively "in being"—not merely in existence but in active and vigorous life—constitutes a defensive strategy for a relatively small maritime power (214).

Corbett theorized that victory at sea is dependent upon the relative strength of one's force and the exploitation of one's "positions"—naval bases, commercial, and nearby focal areas where trade routes converge (106). If correctly exploited, strategic positions allow a naval force to restrict the size of any enemy force, thus creating favorable conditions for battle (72). Corbett specifically considered it more effective to control ports and maritime choke points, thereby threatening the enemy's commerce and potentially luring his fleet into battle on one's own terms, than to seek out the enemy's fleet for a decisive action (185).

Relatedly, Corbett envisioned blockades, of two types, "close" and "open." The former closes the enemy's commercial ports. "By closing [the enemy's] commercial ports we exercise the highest power of injuring him which the command of the sea can give us"—the enemy must either submit to the close blockade or fight to release himself (185). In contrast, in an open blockade a fleet occupies distant and common lines of communication—a means for a stronger navy to force the enemy out of its harbors. "It is better to sit upon his homeward bound trade routes, thus costing him his trade, or making his fleet come for a decisive battle," than repeatedly attempt to seek out an enemy who habitually retires to the safety of his ports (156–57).

The obverse of blocking maritime communications—in fact, the object of naval warfare, in Corbett's view—is protecting them. This was to be achieved by the "cruiser," a vessel of endurance and power sufficient for long, independent deployments on the sea lines of communication. Corbett considered the importance even of the battleship secondary to that of the cruiser (114). Because of the wide expanses of sea and the numerous maritime routes and coastlines involved, cruisers had to be built in significant numbers.

Finally, if cruisers were to be dispersed to distant operating areas, naval forces had also to be able to concentrate rapidly and decisively when needed (132). Such a strategic combination of concentration and dispersal in warfare, Corbett argues, allows a fleet to engage the enemy's central mass when needed but in the meantime to preserve the flexibility necessary to control maritime communications and to meet minor attacks in several areas at once (133).[41]

Deriving a Strategic Space Theory.

From Corbett's discussion of maritime theory, Klein proposes to "extrapolate and define" a theory of space operations, acknowledging the differences between maritime and space operations but contending that at the strategic and theoretical levels, they share many commonalities:

Maritime operations are not the same as space operations; environmental, technological, and physical factors are definitively different. Nevertheless, many of their strategic aspects are similar, and therefore they may be presumed to share certain theoretical principles. We may attempt, therefore, to derive objectively a space theory in strict keeping with Corbett's original context and strategic intent, verifying the applicability of its principles against contemporary literature.[42]

National Power Implications. Space operations and activities utilizing space-based assets have broad implications for national power in peace and war, implications that include diplomatic, military, economic, technological, and information elements. Furthermore, military operations in space are extensively interrelated with national and political interests, and any action in space, even minor ones, can impact the balance of wealth and power among nations.

Interdependence with Other Operations. Operations in space are interdependent with those on land, at sea, and in the air. Space warfare is just a subset of wartime strategy and operations; accordingly, space forces must operate in concert with other military forces. Moreover, space strategy should work within the overall national strategy, since it is next to impossible for space operations alone to decide a war's outcome.

Command of Space. Command of space is the control of space communications for civil, commercial, intelligence, and military purposes. The inherent value of space is as a means of communications; therefore, space warfare must work directly or indirectly toward either securing command of space or preventing the enemy from securing it. Command of space does not mean that one's adversary cannot act, only that he cannot seriously interfere in one's actions. Additionally, the command of space will normally be in dispute.

Space Communications. Space communications are those lines of communications by which the flow of national life is sustained in and through space. These include strategic lines of communication, critical to a nation's survival, that serve the movement of trade, materiel, supplies, and information. By attack upon space communications, a nation can adversely affect another's civil, commercial, intelligence, and military activities, thereby reducing that nation's will to resist. The primary purpose of space warfare is to secure space communications; enemy forces that are in a position to render them unsafe must be put out of action.

Strategy of the Offense. Offensive operations in space are called for when political objectives necessitate acquiring something from the adversary. Generally speaking, offensive operations in space are reserved to the stronger space power. However, an offensive force looking for a decisive victory will likely not find it, since the enemy will usually fall back to a position of safety. Offensive operations must be decided upon with caution; space assets can be thrown away on ill-considered attacks.

Strategy of the Defense. Despite the advantage of offensive space operations, the utility of defensive operations is substantial; offensive and defensive operations are mutually complementary, and any campaign must have characteristics of both. Defensive space operations are called for when political objectives necessitate preventing the enemy from achieving or gaining something. Defensive operations are inherently the stronger form of action and should be used extensively by lesser space forces until the offensive can be assumed.

The Power of Isolation. A nation wishing to initiate limited war in or through space requires a defensive capability adequate to protect itself against an unlimited counterattack. The "power of isolation" is made possible by commanding space and making it an insuperable physical obstacle, enabling one nation to attack another for limited political purposes without fear of a devastating counteroffensive. To paraphrase Corbett, "He that commands space is at great liberty and may take as much or as little of the war as he will."

Actions by Lesser Space Forces. Although a less capable space force is unlikely to win a decisive space engagement, it can still contest the command of space, thereby achieving limited political objectives. To this end the weaker force may seize local or temporary command in areas where the stronger force is not present. Additionally, lesser space forces can disrupt commercial or economic interests or interfere in minor ways with space-based systems. Both types of action are meant to disturb an enemy's plans while increasing the lesser nation's power.

Another effective method by which a lesser space force might dispute command is the "fleet in being" concept. It is important for relatively weak space forces to avoid decisive engagements with stronger ones, but they can be kept safe and active until the situation changes in their favor. Furthermore, while avoiding large-scale engagements with a superior space force, a lesser one can conduct minor attacks against space communications or space-related activities, thus preventing the stronger power from gaining general command of space.

Strategic Positions. Strategic positions include launch facilities, up-and-down link systems, space bases or stations, and focal areas where operations and activities tend to converge. If correctly exploited, strategic positions allow a space force to restrict the movement of the enemy forces or information, thus improving the conditions for military operations. Since it will prove difficult to force an adversary into a decisive engagement, it is better to control strategic positions and threaten commerce and operations, thereby forcing the enemy to action on favorable terms. By exploiting strategic positions through occupation of the enemy's space lanes of communication and closing points of distribution, we destroy elements of the enemy's "national life" in space.

Blockades. Closely related to strategic positions are the methods of blockades, whether close or open. The close blockade for space operations equates to preventing the deployment of systems from launch facilities and to interfering with communications in the vicinity of uplinks or downlinks, as well as impeding the movement of vehicles near space-based hubs. Close blockade may be achieved by physical systems or vehicles or interference measures. In Corbett's model, suppressing operations at these distribution points obliges the adversary either to submit or fight. In contrast, a more capable space power can impose an open blockade, occupying or interfering with the distant and common space lines of communication, to force an adversary into action. Like the close blockade, methods include both physical systems and interference.

Cruisers. The object of space warfare is to control space communications, and therefore a means of establishing this control is required. Consequently "cruisers" are needed in large numbers to defend the vast volumes occupied by space lines of communication. One possible implementation of the "cruiser" concept would be inexpensive micro-satellites designed to defend high-value space assets from attack or space-based interference. Space systems that perform purely offensive operations with negligible influence on space lines of communication are of secondary importance.

Dispersal of Forces. Space forces and systems should in general be dispersed to cover the widest possible area yet retain the ability to concentrate decisive force rapidly. Dispersal of forces will allow the protection of a nation's space assets and interests, thereby facilitating defensive operations or minor attacks wherever a nation's space interests are threatened. To defend against or neutralize a significant threat, however, space forces should quickly concentrate firepower or other destructive effects. This combination of dispersal and concentration preserves the flexibility needed to control space communications but allows an adversary's "central mass" to be engaged when necessary.[43]

Conclusion

Despite operating in space for 51 years, the United States still lacks a comprehensive space strategy. The lack of a space strategy stems from a mantra that space should not be weaponized and should only be used for peaceful purposes. While this is a noble position, the reality is that the United States faces a decision to either continue to ignore air and sea history or adopt a proactive policy, including a space strategy that is designed to control space. Theodore Roosevelt understood the implications of sea power and as assistant secretary of the navy and president, he advocated for a robust US Navy. Despite the protests that a more powerful Navy would heighten the risk of war, Roosevelt funded and built the Great White Fleet that sailed around the world. Roosevelt wrote, "Preparation for war is the surest guaranty for peace. Arbitration is an excellent thing, but ultimately those who wish to see this country at peace with foreign nations will be wise if they place reliance upon a first-class fleet of first-class battleships rather than on any arbitration treaty which the wit of man devise."[44] Roosevelt seized an opportunity to establish a credible military navy which secured the peace during his tenure as president.

The United States is once again at a critical juncture. Should we be naïve and believe that as long as we don't weaponize space our adversary won't? Or should the United States take advantage of the technology and opportunities, develop a comprehensive space power strategy, and preserve freedom of access in space?

Notes

1. Everett C. Dolman, *Astropolitik: Classical Geopolitics in the Space Age* (New York: Frank Cass Publishers, 2002), 94.

2. Dolman, 113. See Irvin White, *Decision-Making for Space: Law and Politics in Air, Sea and Outer Space* (West Lafayette, IN: Purdue University Press, 1971).

3. Dolman, *Astropolitik*, 113.

4. Ibid., 114.

5. Ibid., 115.

6. Ibid., 115–16. The definition of aircraft is found in Lincoln P. Bloomfield, "The Prospects for Law and Order," in *Outer Space: New Challenge to Law and Policy*, ed. J. E. S. Fawcett (Oxford: Clarendon Press, 1984), 156.

7. Dolman, *Astropolitik*, 117.

8. Ibid.

9. Ibid.

10. Ibid., 117–18.

11. White, *Decision-Making for Space*, 82.

12. Dolman, *Astropolitik*, 118–19.

13. Quoted in Dolman, *Astropolitik*, 119. See US Senate, *Ambassador Goldberg: Hearings before the Committee on Foreign Relations*, 90th Cong., 1st sess., 7 March 1967, 16.

14. Dolman, *Astropolitik*, 119.

15. Ibid., 120.

16. Lt Cdr John J. Klein, "Corbett in Orbit: A Maritime Model for Strategic Space Theory," *Naval War College Review* 57, no. 1 (Winter 2004): 61.

17. Klein, *Corbett in Orbit*, 61. See Gen Thomas White, USAF, "Air and Space Are Indivisible," *Air Force Magazine*, March 1958, 40–41; and M. V. Smith, "Ten Propositions Regarding Space Power" (thesis, Air University, Maxwell AFB, AL, June 2001), 109.

18. Klein, *Corbett in Orbit*, 60. See Joint Forces Command, "Joint Forces Command Glossary," www.jfcom.mil/about/glossary.htm.

19. Klein, *Corbett in Orbit*, 62. Klein references Lt Col David E. Lupton, *On Space Warfare: A Space Power Doctrine* (Maxwell AFB, AL: Air University Press, 1988), 65.

20. Judson J. Jussel, *Space Power Theory: A Rising Star* (Maxwell AFB, AL: Air University Press, 1998), 49.

21. Klein, *Corbett in Orbit*, 62.

22. Alfred Thayer Mahan, *The Influence of Sea Power upon History, 1660–1783* (New York: Hill and Wang, 1963), 2.

23. Lupton, *On Space Warfare*, 4. A collection of airpower definitions, including those by Gens Billy Mitchell and H. H. Arnold, is found in John Cobb Cooper, *Explorations in Aerospace Law: Selected Essays by John Cobb Cooper*, ed. Ivan Vlasic (Montreal: McGill University Press, 1968), 17–35. Mahan's elements of sea power are contained in Mahan, *Influence of Sea Power*, 22–77. For another comprehensive definition of sea power, see E. R. Potter and Chester W. Nimitz, eds., *Sea Power* (Englewood Cliffs, NJ: Prentice Hall, 1960), 19.

24. Lupton, *On Space Warfare*, 15.

25. Ibid., 35.

26. Ibid., 36.

27. Ibid., 36–37.

28. Ibid., 37.

29. Ibid., 86.

30. James E. Oberg, "Toward a Theory of Space Power: Defining Principles for U.S. Space Policy" (lecture, Army & Navy Club, Washington DC, 20 May 2003), www.marshall.org/pdf/materials/140.pdf (accessed 2 June 2009).

31. Oberg, 3.

32. Ibid., 15–16.

33. Dolman, *Astropolitik*, 143.

34. Ibid., 157.

35. Ibid.

36. Quoted in Dolman, *Astropolitik*, 149.

37. Dolman, *Astropolitik*, 157.

38. Ibid., 158.

39. Klein, *Corbett in Orbit*, 62.

40. Ibid. Klein references John B. Hattendorf, "The Uses of Maritime History in and for the Navy," *Naval War College Review* 56, no. 2 (Spring 2003): 19.

41. Klein, *Corbett in Orbit*, 63–66. Parenthetical references are to Julian S. Corbett, *Some Principles of Maritime Strategy*, introduction and notes by Eric J. Grove (Annapolis, MD: Naval Institute Press, 1988).

42. Klein, *Corbett in Orbit*, 66.

43. Ibid., 66–69.

44. Mario R. DiNunzio, *Theodore Roosevelt: An American Mind* (New York: Penguin, 1994), 174.

Chapter 3

Current Space Law And Policy

Maj Jane Gibson, USAF; and LCDR Jeremy Powell, USN

Space policy defines the overarching goals and principles of the US space program. International and domestic laws and regulations, national interests, and security objectives shape the US space program. This chapter examines the international and domestic legal parameters within which the United States conducts its space programs and outlines the basic tenets of US space policy. The laws governing the utilization of the space domain remain largely unchanged since the former Soviet Union and the United States entered the "space race" in the 1950s. This is of growing concern as the number of nations seeking access to space increases. Space policy formulation is a critical element of the US national planning process, as it governs all aspects of the US role in space. Furthermore, fiscal considerations both shape and constrain space policy. This chapter details Department of Defense (DOD), Army, Navy, and Air Force space policies, derived from the National Space Policy. It concludes with an analysis of the doctrinal principles that guide the conduct of military space activities.

International Space Law

The term *space law* refers to a body of law drawn from a variety of sources and consisting of two basic types of law governing space-related activities: international and domestic. The former refers to rights and obligations the United States has agreed to through multilateral or bilateral international treaties and agreements. The latter refers to domestic legislation by Congress and regulations promulgated by executive agencies of the US government.

Table 3-1, at the end of this chapter, summarizes key international treaties and agreements that affect the scope and character of US military space activities. The primary international forum for the development of laws and principles governing outer space is the United Nations Office for Outer Space Affairs (UNOOSA).[1] Though the term *outer space* has been used since 1967, the Legal Subcommittee of the United Nations Committee on the Peaceful Uses of Outer Space has not established the definition or delimitation of outer space, but rather leaves the definition to the member states. In recent years, this has repeatedly been a topic for discussion at each session. Jerry Sellers offers this definition from *Understanding Space:* "For awarding astronaut wings, NASA defines space at an altitude of 92.6 km (57.5 mi). For our purposes, space begins where satellites can maintain orbit—about 130 km (81 mi)."[2] Listed below are some of the more important basic principles and rules from the Treaty on Principles Governing the Activities of States in the Exploration and Use of Outer Space, including the Moon and Other Celestial Bodies, which was signed on 27 January 1967.[3]

International law applies to outer space. Such law includes the United Nations Charter, which requires all UN members to settle disputes by peaceful means and prohibits the threat to use, or actual use of, force against the territorial integrity or political independence of another state. The charter also recognizes a state's inherent right to act in individual or collective self-defense.

Outer space, the moon, and other celestial bodies are not subject to appropriation by claim of sovereignty, use, or occupation, or any other means. In 1976 eight equatorial countries claimed sovereignty over the geostationary orbital arc above their territory. Most other countries, including all major space powers, rejected the claim.

Outer space is free for use by all countries. This principle relates to the nonappropriation principle and is analogous to the right of innocent passage on the high seas.

Outer space will be used for peaceful purposes only. Most Western nations, including the United States, equate peaceful purposes with nonaggressive ones. Consequently, all nonaggressive military use of space is permissible, except for specific prohibitions of certain activities noted elsewhere in this section.

Astronauts are "peaceful envoys of mankind." If forced to make an emergency landing, they should not be harmed or held hostage, and they must be returned to the launching country as soon as possible. Upon request, the spacecraft also should be returned if possible, and the launching country will pay the costs involved.

Objects launched into space must be registered with the UN. Basic orbital parameters, launch origin, launch date, and a brief explanation of the purpose of the satellite are required, although the UN set no time limit for providing this information.

A country retains jurisdiction and control over its registered space objects. This rule applies regardless of the condition of the objects.

A country is responsible for regulating, and is ultimately liable for, the outer space activities of its citizens. In outer space, liability for damage is based on fault; therefore, assessing blame for objects colliding would be extremely difficult. The launching country is absolutely liable for damage caused on Earth.

Nuclear weapons tests and other nuclear explosions in outer space are prohibited. Before this prohibition, the United States conducted two atmospheric nuclear detonation tests. In 1958 the United States exploded three small nuclear devices in outer space in Project Argus.[4] The purpose of these tests was to assess the impact of an electromagnetic pulse caused by high-altitude nuclear explosions on radio transmissions and radar operations and to increase understanding of the geomagnetic field and the behavior of charged particles within.[5] In 1962 the United States planned to conduct further experiments with the ionosphere in Project Starfish. This project involved one device below the limit of outer space and two larger devices "at several hundred kilometers height."[6] Only one missile actually reached its projected altitude; the other two resulted in launch failures. The High-Frequency Active Auroral Research Program (HAARP) found this projection of the results: "In this experiment the inner Van Allen Belt will be practically destroyed for a period of time; particles from the belt will be transported to the atmosphere. It is anticipated that the earth's magnetic field will be disturbed over long distances for several hours, preventing radio communication. The explosion of the inner radiation belt will create an artificial dome of polar light that will be visible from Los Angeles."[7] The actual successful test did expand the belt formed by the Argus experiment.

Nuclear weapons and other weapons of mass destruction (such as chemical and biological weapons) may not be placed into orbit, installed on celestial bodies, or stationed in space in any other manner.

A country may not test any kind of weapon, nor establish military bases, installations, or fortifications, nor conduct military maneuvers on celestial bodies. The use of military personnel for scientific research or other peaceful purposes is permissible.

Interfering with national technical means of verification is prohibited provided such systems are operating in accordance with generally recognized principles of international law and are in fact being used to verify provisions of specific treaties.

The United States adheres to the premise in international law that any act not specifically prohibited is permissible. Thus, even though the list (see table 3-1 at the end of the chapter) of prohibited acts is sizable, there are few legal restrictions on the use of space for nonaggressive military purposes. As a result, international law implicitly permits the performance of such traditional military functions as surveillance, reconnaissance, navigation, meteorology, and communications. It permits the deployment of military space stations along with testing and deployment in Earth orbit of nonnuclear weapon systems. This includes antisatellite weapons, space-to-ground conventional weapons, the use of space for individual and collective self-defense, and any conceivable activity not specifically prohibited or otherwise constrained.

Another widely accepted premise is that treaties usually regulate activities between signatories only during peacetime. This rule holds true unless a treaty expressly states that its provisions apply or become operative during hostilities, or the signatories can deduce this from the nature of the treaty itself. In other words, countries presume that armed conflict will result in the suspension or termination of a treaty's provisions. Good examples are treaties whose purpose is to disarm or limit quantities of arms maintained by the signatories. Therefore, during hostilities, the scope of permissible military space activities may broaden significantly.

In the past, the only significant competitor to the United States was the former Soviet Union. Today, several nations have entered the space domain and have national legislation governing their space-related activities. Those countries include Argentina, Australia, Canada, Finland, France, Germany, Hungary, Indonesia, Japan, New Zealand, Philippines, Republic of Korea, Russian Federation, Slovakia, Sweden, South Africa, Tunisia, Ukraine, the United Kingdom, and the United States.[8]

Domestic Space Law

Domestic law has always shaped military space activities via the spending authorization and budget appropriation process. For example, in the mid-1980s, Congress deleted funding for further testing of the Air Force's direct-ascent antisatellite (ASAT) weapon, and the program was cancelled for lack of funds. In addition, a number of laws not designed solely to address space have applicability. For instance, under the Communications Act of 1934 (amended by the Telecommunications Act of 1996), the president has the authority to gain control of private communications assets owned by US corporations during times of crisis.[9] Since the 1960s, this authority has included both the ground and space segments of domestically owned communications satellites.

The Reagan administration placed emphasis on the creation of a third sector of space activity, commercial space, in addition to the traditional military and civil sectors. Congress passed the Commercial Space Launch Act of 1984 to facilitate the development of a commercial launch industry in the United States. From a DOD perspective, the importance of this legislation lay in its authorization for commercial customers to use DOD launch facilities on a reimbursable basis.[10] DOD is now overseeing commercial operations from its facilities and placing commercial payloads in the launch queue. The intertwining of the commercial space industry and DOD space programs whenever possible provides a benefit to both parties.

The Commercial Space Act of 1998 furthered this policy of getting the government out of the launch business and required a DOD study of the projected launch services through 2007.[11] It also called on the DOD to identify the "technical, structural, and legal impediments associated with making launch sites or test ranges in the United States viable and competitive." It also required the government to purchase space transportation services instead of building and operating its own vehicles, required NASA to privatize the space shuttle, and allowed excess intercontinental ballistic missiles (ICBM) to be used as low-cost space boosters. An amendment to the act was proposed in 2003, but it did not pass the House of Representatives. Results of the study mandated by the act are pending.

National Space Policy

A nation's space policy is extremely important, especially as it relates to space law and space doctrine. In order to understand present US space policy and attempt to predict its future, an examination of its evolution is necessary. While policy provides space goals and a national framework, national interests and national security objectives actually shape the policy. This framework will lead towards building and meeting future US requirements and subsequent national space strategies.

Early Policy

The launch of *Sputnik I* on 4 October 1957 had an immediate and dramatic impact on the formulation of US space policy. Although the military had expressed an interest in space technology as early as the mid-1940s, a viable program failed to emerge for several reasons: intense interservice rivalry, military preoccupation with the development of ballistic missiles, and national leadership that did not initially appreciate the strategic and international implications of emerging satellite technology. Once national leadership gained this appreciation, it became committed to an open and purely scientific space program.

The emergence of *Sputnik I* transposed this line of thought. Besides clearly demonstrating that the Soviets had the missile technology to deliver payloads at global ranges, *Sputnik* led to a much wider appreciation of orbital possibilities. The result was the first official US government statement that space was of military significance. This statement, issued on 26 March 1958 by Pres. Dwight D. Eisenhower's Science Advisory Committee, declared that the development of space technology and the maintenance of national prestige were important for the defense of the United States.[12]

The first official national space policy was the National Aeronautics and Space Act of 1958. This act stated that the policy of the United States was to devote space activities to peaceful purposes for the benefit of all humankind. It mandated separate civilian and national-security space programs and created a new agency, the National Aeronautics and Space Administration (NASA), to direct and control all US space activities, except those "peculiar to or primarily associated with the development of weapons systems, military operations, or the defense of the United States." The Department of Defense was to be responsible for these latter activities.[13]

The National Aeronautics and Space Act of 1958 established a mechanism for coordinating and integrating military and civilian research and development. It encouraged significant international cooperation in space and called for preserving the role of the United States as a leader in space technology and its application. Thus, the policy framework for a viable space program was in place. The principles enunciated by the act became basic tenets of the US space program. These tenets included peaceful focus on the use of space, separation of civilian and military space activities, emphasis on international cooperation, and preservation of a space role. All presidential space directives issued since 1958 have reaffirmed these basic tenets.

A space program of substance still did not exist however, and the Eisenhower administration's approach to implementing the new space policy was conservative, cautious, and constrained. The government consistently disapproved of the early DOD and NASA plans for manned space flight programs. Instead the administration preferred to concentrate on unmanned, largely scientific missions and to proceed with those missions at a measured pace. It was left to subsequent administrations to give the policy substance.

Intervening Years

Two presidential announcements, one by John F. Kennedy on 25 March 1961 and the second by Richard M. Nixon on 7 March 1970, were instrumental in providing the focus for the US space program. As the *Army Space Reference Text* notes,

The Kennedy statement came during a period of intense national introspection. The Soviet Union launched and successfully recovered the world's first cosmonaut. Although Yuri Gagarin spent just 89 minutes in orbit, his accomplishment electrified the world. This caused the United States to question its scientific and engineering skills as well as its entire educational system. The American response articulated by President Kennedy as a national challenge to land a man on the Moon and return him safely to Earth defined US space goals for the remainder of the decade.[14]

Prestige and international leadership were clearly the main objectives of the Kennedy space program. However, the generous funding that accompanied the Apollo program had important collateral benefits as well. It permitted the buildup of US space technology and the establishment of an across-the-board space capability that included planetary exploration, scientific endeavors, commercial applications, and military support systems.

President Johnson's years in office saw the commencement of work on nuclear ASATs and the cancellation of the DynaSoar (Dynamic Ascent and Soaring) Flight program. This program, which began in 1958, was a 35-foot glider with a small delta wing and was to be boosted into orbit by a *Titan III* rocket. The program was determined to be unnecessary in light of NASA's manned spacecraft program.

According to the *Army Space Reference Text*, "as the 1960s drew to a close, a combination of factors including domestic unrest, an unpopular foreign war and inflationary pressures forced the nation to reassess the importance of the space program. Against this backdrop, President Nixon made his long-awaited space policy announcement in March 1970. His announcement was a carefully considered and worded statement that was clearly aware of political realities and the mood of Congress and the public."[15] In part, it stated that "space expenditures must take their proper place within a rigorous system of national priorities. . . . Operations in space from here on in must become a normal and regular part of national life. Therefore, they must be planned in conjunction with all of the other undertakings important to us."[16]

The *Army Space Reference Text* continues, "Although spectacular lunar and planetary voyages continued until 1975 as a result of budgetary decisions made during the 1960s, the Nixon administration considered the space program of intermediate priority and could not justify increased investment or the initiation of large new projects. Space was viewed as a medium for exploiting and extending the previously realized technological and scientific gains. The emphasis was on practical space applications" to benefit American society.[17]

During the Nixon years, the space world saw three notable events:

- On 5 January 1972, Nixon approved the development of the space shuttle.
- The National Aeronautics and Space Council (started by the Space Act of 1958) was inactivated.
- The Gemini B/Manned Orbiting Laboratory (MOL) was shelved due to lack of urgency and funding.

Within the DOD, this accentuation on practicality translated into reduced emphasis on manned spaceflight but led to the initial operating capability for many of the space missions performed today. The Defense Satellite Communications System, Defense Support Program, Defense Meteorological Satellite Program (DMSP), and the Navy's Transit Navigation Satellite Program (later to evolve as the global positioning system) were all initial versions of the systems developed and fielded during this period.

One major new space initiative undertaken during the 1970s eventually had far greater impact on the national space program than planners had originally envisioned—the Space Transportation System (STS), or space shuttle. The shuttle's goal was routine and low-cost access to orbit for both civil and military sectors. However, as development progressed, the program experienced large cost and schedule overruns. These problems caused the US space program to lose much of its early momentum, as the high costs would adversely affect other space-development efforts, both civil and military. In addition, schedule slippage meant a complete absence of American astronauts in space for the remainder of the decade.

Carter Administration Space Policy

Pres. Jimmy Carter's administration conducted a series of interdepartmental studies to address the malaise that had befallen the nation's space effort. The studies addressed apparent fragmentation and possible redundancy among civil and national security sectors of the US space program. The administration also sought to develop a coherent recommendation for a new national space policy. These efforts resulted in two 1978 Presidential Directives (PD): PD-37, *National Space Policy,* and PD-42, *Civil Space Policy.*

PD-37 reaffirmed the basic policy principles contained in the National Aeronautics and Space Act of 1958. It identified the broad objectives of the US space program, including the specific guidelines governing civil and national security space activities.

PD-37 was important from a military perspective because it contained the initial tentative indications that a shift was occurring in the national security establishment's view on space. Traditionally, the military had seen space as a force enhancer, or an environment in which to deploy systems to increase the effectiveness of land, sea, and air forces. Although the focus of the Carter policy was clearly on restricting the use of weapons in space, PD-37 reflected an appreciation of the importance of space systems to national survival, a recognition of the Soviet threat to those systems, and a willingness to push ahead with development of an antisatellite capability in the absence of verifiable and comprehensive international agreements restricting such systems. In other words, the administration was beginning to view space as a potential war-fighting medium.

PD-42 was directed exclusively at the civil space sector to guide US efforts over the next decade. However, it was devoid of any long-term space goals, expecting the nation to pursue a balanced evolutionary strategy of space applications, space science, and exploration activities. The absence of a more visionary policy reflected the continuing developmental problems with the shuttle and the resulting commitment of larger-than-expected resources.

Reagan Administration Space Policy

Pres. Ronald Reagan's administration published comprehensive space policy statements in 1982 and 1988. The first policy statement, pronounced on 4 July 1982 and embodied in National Security Decision Directive (NSDD) 42, reaffirmed the basic tenets of previous (Carter) US space policy. It also placed considerable emphasis on the STS as the primary space launch system for both national security and civil government missions. In addition, it introduced the basic goals of promoting and expanding the investment and involvement of the private sector in space. Space-related activities comprise a third element of US space operations, which complement the national security and civil sectors.

The single statement of national policy from this period that most influenced military space activities and illuminated the transition to a potential space war-fighting framework is NSDD-85, dated 25 March 1983. Within this document, President Reagan stated his long-term objective to eliminate the threat of nuclear-armed ballistic missiles through the creation of strategic defensive forces. This NSDD coincided with the establishment of the Strategic Defense Initiative Organization (SDIO) and represented a significant step in the evolution of US space policy. Since 1958, the United States had, for a variety of reasons, refrained from crossing an imaginary line from space systems designed to operate as force enhancers to establishing a war-fighting capability in space. The ASAT initiative of the Carter administration was a narrow response to a specific Soviet threat. However, the Strategic Defense Initiative program represented a significant expansion in DOD's assigned role in the space arena.

The second comprehensive national space policy incorporated the results of a number of developments that had occurred since 1982, notably the US commitment in 1984 to build a space station and the space shuttle *Challenger*. For the first time, the national space program viewed the commercial space sector as equal to the traditional national security and civil space sectors. Moreover, the new policy dramatically retreated from its previous dependence on the STS and injected new life into expendable launch vehicle programs. In the national security sector, this policy was the first to address space control and force application at length, further developing the transition to war-fighting capabilities in space.

In 1988, the last year of the Reagan presidency, Congress passed a law allowing creation of a National Space Council (NSPC), a cabinet-level organization designed to coordinate national policy among the three space sectors. The incoming administration would officially establish and very effectively use the NSPC.

G. H. W. Bush Administration Space Policy

Released in November 1989 as National Security Directive (NSD) 30, and updated in a 5 September 1990 supplement, the Bush administration's national space policy retained the goals and emphasis of the final Reagan administration policy. The Bush policy resulted from an NSPC review to clarify, strengthen, and streamline space policy, and has been further enhanced by a series of National Space Policy Directives (NSPD) on various topics. Areas most affected by the body of Bush policy documentation included:

- US commercial space policy guidelines.
- Provision of a framework for the National Space Launch Strategy.
- LANDSAT Remote-Sensing Strategy.
- Space Exploration Initiative.
- Space-Based Global Change Observation System, a key component of the nation's overall approach to global stewardship and one of the nation's highest priority science programs.

The policy reaffirmed the organization of US space activities into three complementary sectors: civil, national security, and commercial.[18] The three sectors coordinate their activities to ensure maximum information exchange and minimum duplication of effort.

The Bush policy proceeded to detail specific policy, implementing guidelines and actions for each of the three space sectors and intersector activities. The civil sector was to engage in all manners of space-related scientific research, develop space-related technologies for government and commercial applications, and establish a permanent manned presence in space. NASA remained the lead civil space agency, with NASA and the Departments of Defense, Commerce, and Transportation working cooperatively with the commercial sector to make government facilities and hardware available on a reimbursable basis.

According to the Bush policy, the United States would conduct those activities in space that are necessary to national defense. Such activities contribute to security objectives by: (1) deterring or, if necessary, defending against enemy attack; (2) assuring that enemy forces cannot prevent our use of space; (3) negating, if necessary, hostile space systems; and (4) enhancing operations of US and allied forces. In order to accomplish these objectives, DOD would develop, operate, and maintain a robust space force structure capable of satisfying the mission requirements of space support, force enhancement, space control, and force application.[19]

Primarily directed at the civil and national security sectors, several policy requirements applied across sector divisions. These included such things as continuing the technology development and operational capabilities of remote-sensing systems, space transportation systems, and space-based communications systems and the need to minimize space debris.

Clinton Administration Space Policy

A repositioning of priorities in the Clinton administration was reflected by the decision in August 1993 to merge various White House science and technology councils into one National Science and Technology Council (NSTC), which would do most of the day-to-day work through permanent or ad hoc interagency working groups. The National Space Council was absorbed into the new NSTC, along with the National Critical Materials Council and the Federal Coordinating Council for Science, Engineering, and Technology.

The White House structure for articulating national policy for science and technology was put in place by the Presidential Review Directive (PRD)/NSTC series and the Presidential Decision Directive (PDD)/NSTC series as established by PDD/NSTC 1. Within four months during the summer of 1994, three additional policies were established articulating Clinton's space policy.

PDD/NSTC 2, "US Polar-Orbiting Operational Environmental Satellite Systems" (May 1994). PDD/NSTC 2 called for the Departments of Commerce and Defense "to integrate their programs into a single, converged, national polar-orbiting operational environmental weather satellite system."[20] This began occurring in 1997. The DMSP satellite program merged with the National Oceanic Atmospheric Administration (NOAA) satellite program in May 1998. The new system formed by the merger of the two programs was known as the Polar-Orbiting Environmental Satellite (POES) System.

PDD/NSTC 3, "LANDSAT Remote-Sensing Strategy" (May 1994). PDD/NSTC 3, replacing Bush's NSPD 5, assured the continuity of LANDSAT-type data of the same quality and reduced the risk of data gap, that is, loss of Earth-sensing data due to a lack of LANDSAT.

PDD/NSTC 4, "National Space Transportation Policy" (August 1994). PDD/NSTC 4 superseded all previous policies for US space transportation and "established national policy, guidelines, and implementation actions for the conduct of national space transportation programs."[21] It also allocated space transportation responsibilities among federal civil and military agencies.

PDD/NSTC 8, "National Space Policy" (May 1996). In September 1996, the Clinton administration released its National Space Policy (dated May 1996), which had five goals:

- Gain knowledge by exploration (1989).
- Maintain national security (1989).
- Enhance competitiveness and capabilities (new).
- Get private sector investment (1989).
- Promote international cooperation (1989).

These goals were very similar to those established in 1978 by President Carter, and their heritage went back as far as the 1958 National Aeronautics and Space Act under Eisenhower. For each major area of space covered in the 1996 National Space Policy (civil, defense, intelligence, commercial, and intersector), a set of guidelines similar to the ones in the 1989 National Space Policy was established.

G. W. Bush Administration Space Policy

President Bush declared his desire to restructure our defense and deterrence capabilities to correspond to emerging threats in NSPD-23, *National Missile Defense*. It stated that the deployment of missile defenses was an essential component of this broader effort.[22]

At the outset, the president directed his administration to examine the full range of available technologies and basing modes for missile defenses that could protect the United States, our deployed forces, and our friends and allies. Our policy was to develop and deploy, at the earliest possible date, ballistic missile defenses drawing on the best technologies available.

In August 2002 the administration proposed an evolutionary way ahead for the deployment of missile defenses. The capabilities planned for operational use in 2004 and 2005 included ground-based interceptors, sea-based interceptors, additional Patriot (PAC-3) units, and sensors based on land, at sea, and in space. In addition, the United States worked with allies to upgrade key early-warning radars as part of our capabilities. The Department of Defense began to implement this approach and moved forward with plans to deploy a set of initial missile defense capabilities beginning in 2004.

The US government began a broad review of US space policies in 2002 in order to adjust to the domestic and international developments in recent years that had affected US space capabilities. One important component of this review focused on the relationship between the United States government and the commercial remote-sensing industry. The last policy covering this area had been issued in 1994. Since that time, there had been significant changes to this critical area of US national and economic security. A new commercial remote-sensing space policy was the first product of the ongoing National Space Policy Review.

The fundamental goal of the US commercial remote-sensing space policy was "to advance and protect U.S. national security and foreign policy interests by maintaining the nation's leadership in remote-sensing space activities, and by sustaining and enhancing the U.S. remote sensing industry. Doing so will also foster economic growth, contribute to environmental stewardship, and enable scientific and technological excellence."[23]

To support this goal, the policy declared that the US government would do the following:

- Rely to the maximum practical extent on US commercial remote-sensing space capabilities for filling imagery and geospatial needs for military, intelligence, foreign policy, homeland security, and civil users;

- Focus US government remote-sensing space systems on meeting needs that cannot be effectively, affordably, and reliably satisfied by commercial providers because of economic factors, civil mission needs, national security concerns, or foreign policy concerns;

- Develop a long-term, sustainable relationship between the US government and the US commercial remote-sensing space industry;

- Provide a timely and responsive regulatory environment for licensing the operations and exports of commercial remote-sensing space systems; and

- Enable US industry to compete successfully as a provider of remote-sensing space capabilities for foreign governments and foreign commercial users, while ensuring appropriate measures are implemented to protect US national security and foreign policy interests.[24]

Current National Space Policy

The most current National Space Policy was signed in August 2006 and supersedes all previous policies. This policy recognizes the advantages that space has given the United States for nearly five decades, and it also recognizes the vulnerabilities of space and the need to protect our interests in this vital medium: "Those who effectively utilize space will enjoy added prosperity and security and will hold a substantial advantage over those who do not. Freedom of action in space is as important to the United States as air power and sea power. In order to increase knowledge, discovery, economic prosperity, and to enhance the national security, the United States must have robust, effective, and efficient space capabilities."[25] Solidifying US resolve to support international treaties regarding the use of space (see table 3-1 at the end of the chapter), the principles of the current space policy mirror those treaties.

The fundamental goals of this policy are to:

- Strengthen the nation's space leadership and ensure that space capabilities are available in time to further US national security, homeland security, and foreign policy objectives;

- Enable unhindered US operations in and through space to defend our interests there;

- Implement and sustain an innovative human and robotic exploration program with the objective of extending human presence across the solar system;

- Increase the benefits of civil exploration, scientific discovery, and environmental activities;

- Enable a dynamic, globally competitive domestic commercial space sector in order to promote innovation, strengthen US leadership, and protect national, homeland, and economic security;

- Enable a robust science and technology base supporting national security, homeland security, and civil space activities; and

- Encourage international cooperation with foreign nations and/or consortia on space activities that are of mutual benefit and that further the peaceful exploration and use of space, as well as to advance national security, homeland security, and foreign policy objectives.[26]

In general, the National Space Policy takes into account not only the engagement of the US military in activities worldwide for the past 15 years, but also recognizes the need to retain space superiority in the face of other nations' advancements in the space realm. The current policy clearly defines the roles of the secretary of defense and the director of national intelligence to achieve the military goals of the policy. It also provides guidelines for civil space activities by specifying the roles of the secretaries of commerce and interior and the administrator of NASA.

The utility of space has been proven both militarily and in the civil sector. Space assets have been crucial in recent years to domestic and international disaster relief efforts. The Bush administration clearly understood the need for space, and its policy emphasized the importance placed on this domain.

Department of Defense Space Policy

Though a new National Space Policy took effect in 2006, the current DOD Space Policy is dated 1999. On 9 July 1999 the secretary of defense released the most current revision to the DOD Space Policy; the previous one is dated 1987. This DOD Space Policy incorporates new policies and guidance promulgated since 1987 and includes the National Space Policy issued by President Clinton in October 1998. It sets the freedom of space as a vital area and establishes definitions of the four mission areas using the terms *space combat, combat support, service support,* and *space as a medium*—just like air, sea, and land.

Major changes address the transformation of the international security environment; the promulgation of new national security and national military strategies; changes in the resources allocated to national defense; changes in force structure; lessons learned from the operational employment of space forces; the global spread of space systems, technology, and information; advances in military and information technologies; the growth of commercial space activities; enhanced intersector cooperation; and increased international cooperation.

In addition, the DOD Space Policy establishes a comprehensive policy framework for the conduct of space and space-related activities. US Space Command is listed as the point of contact for DOD military space. The DOD policy also calls for integrating space into military operations doctrine. The DOD Space Policy is published as DOD Directive 3100.10, *Space Policy,* dated 9 July 1999.[27]

Army Space Policy

The Army space policy was approved in April 2003 and can be found in Field Manual (FM) 3-14, *Space Support to Army Operations,* which describes the Army's commitment to space capabilities:

The Army space policy clearly indicates the commitment to develop and use space, including the following:

- Operating space systems
- Providing space forces
- Developing and using equipment for space operations
- Executing terrestrial-based space control
- Providing appropriate doctrine and tactics, techniques, and procedures

The Army space policy confirms that Army access to, and use of, space capabilities is essential to operational success. Army space and space-related activities enhance operational support to warfighters and contribute to successful execution of Army missions.

It is clear that the national space policy, DoD space policy, and Army space policy reflect the critical importance of space for current and future U.S. military operations. Space is already an integral part of Army operations and will continue to contribute to the increasing effectiveness of the Army and joint land warfighting dominance. The Army's use of space and its effort to further develop space capabilities for land warfare has been very effective. The intent of this doctrine is to capture and codify the elements of that success and provide the basis for continuing success.[28]

Navy Space Policy

The US Navy defines its space policy in Secretary of the Navy (SECNAV) Instruction 5400.39C, *Department of the Navy Space Policy*. The policy was approved in 2004, and the implementation plan was sent to the force in May 2005. The policy describes the role of the Department of the Navy (DON) in integrating space capabilities into the Navy:

The United States Navy and Marine Corps must maintain their ability to tactically exploit the capabilities provided by space systems and participate in all appropriate aspects of the changed NSS [National Security Space] environment in order to function as an integrated member of the Nation's joint warfighting team. Consequently, the DON must continually reassess its approach and investment to ensure that naval forces receive the maximum benefit of space-based capabilities. The DON will: (1) integrate the essential capabilities provided by space systems at every appropriate level throughout the naval force; and (2) shape the outcome of joint deliberations on future space system capabilities to ensure the combat effectiveness of naval forces.[29]

Air Force Space Policy

The earliest recorded statement of Air Force policy regarding space occurred on 15 January 1948, when Gen Hoyt S. Vandenberg stated, "The USAF, as the service dealing primarily with air weapons, especially strategic, has logical responsibility for the satellite."[30] As reflected in General Vandenberg's statement, Air Force leaders have traditionally viewed space as an atmosphere in which the Air Force would have principal mission responsibilities. This view was perhaps best articulated by former Air Force chief of staff Gen Thomas D. White, when he coined the term *aerospace* during testimony before the House Committee on Science and Astronautics in February 1959: "Since there is no dividing line, no natural barrier separating these two areas (air and space), there can be no operational boundary between them. Thus, air and space comprise a single continuous operational field in which the Air Force must continue to function. The area is aerospace."[31]

Because of this early positioning, the Air Force assumed the predominant space role within DOD. Air Force space policy has evolved as that role expanded. However, the policy was not formally documented until 1988. In late 1987 and early 1988, the Air Force convened the Blue Ribbon Panel, a senior-level working group comprised of both space and aviation professionals who evaluated whether the service should continue to seek the leadership role for DOD space activities, and if so, how best to proceed.

The panel strongly affirmed the desirability of operating in space to accomplish Air Force missions and achieve wider national security objectives. It also developed a list of recommendations for making the most effective use of the space arena in future Air Force operations. On 2 December 1988, the Air Force formally adopted the Blue Ribbon Panel's fundamental assumptions and codified them in a new space policy document. With only a few minor modifications to accommodate organizational change within the service, this document remains the current statement of comprehensive Air Force space policy. The tenets of that policy are discussed below.

Space power will be as decisive in future combat as airpower is today. This long-term vision recognizes the inherent advantages that space operations bring to military endeavors and looks forward to a time when technology, experience, and widespread acceptance allow the United States to make full use of those advantages.

The United States must be prepared for the evolution of space power from combat support to the full spectrum of military capabilities. The Air Force believes that space is a military operating arena just as land, sea, and air are. Expansion of the space-control and force-application mission areas is necessary and desirable to take full advantage of space for effective accomplishment of national security objectives.

The Air Force will make a solid corporate commitment to integrate space throughout the Air Force. To use space effectively, the Air Force must fully institutionalize space operations. There can be no separation of a "space Air Force" and an "aviation Air Force." Combat power is greatest and most effective when operations in the two mediums are closely integrated. In an effort to accomplish this integration, the Air Force became devoted to incorporating space into its doctrine; normalizing space responsibilities within the Air Staff; instituting personnel cross-flow measures to expand space expertise throughout the service; encouraging space-related mission solutions and expertise at all major commands and air component commands; and consolidating space system requirements, advocacy, and operations in Air Force Space Command.

The United States, DOD, and Air Force all have a policy for the military space mission areas of space control, force application, force enhancement, and space support, with implementation guidelines for each area. Updated DOD and Air Force space policies are expected shortly in light of the new National Space Policy.

US national space policy has, for the most part, kept pace with the growth of its US space program and is now one of the most well-documented areas of government policy. It clearly articulates goals that are both challenging and within the realm of possibility.

Summary

According to Air Force Doctrine Document (AFDD) 2-2, *Space Operations*, "Our space forces perform functions that are critical for the joint force—intelligence, surveillance and reconnaissance; command and control; positioning, navigation, and timing; weather services; counterspace; communications; and spacelift. As our reliance on space increases, so too must our ability to integrate space capabilities throughout joint operations. To retain the US military's asymmetric advantage based on space superiority, our Air Force must fully exploit and defend the space domain."[32]

Our responsibilities in space include a large and growing number of functions that contribute to the defense of the United States. Space operations are important elements of a credible deterrent. They have proven their value in resolving conflicts on terms acceptable to the United States. We consider military operations in space as being among our prime national security responsibilities and conduct these operations according to the letter and spirit of existing treaties and international law. As our space program has matured over a period of nearly four decades, our policy and doctrine have reflected ever increasing roles and responsibilities and have particularly expanded their emphasis on space as a war-fighting medium.

56

Table 3-1. International treaties, agreements, and conventions that limit military activities in space[a]

Agreement	Principle/Constraint
United Nations Charter (1947)	Made applicable to space by the Outer Space Treaty of 1967
	Prohibits states from threatening to use, or actually using, force against the territorial integrity or political independence of another state (Article 2[4]).
	Recognizes a state's inherent right to act in individual or collective self-defense when attacked. Customary international law recognizes a broader right to self-defense, one that does not require a state to wait until it is actually attacked before responding. This right to act preemptively is known as the right of anticipatory self-defense (Article 51).
Limited Test Ban Treaty (1963)	Bans nuclear weapon tests in the atmosphere, in outer space, and underwater.
	States may not conduct nuclear weapon tests or other nuclear explosions (i.e., peaceful nuclear explosions) in outer space or assist or encourage others to conduct such tests or explosions (Article I).
Outer Space Treaty (1967)	Outer space, including the moon and other celestial bodies, is free for use by all states (Article I).
	Outer space and celestial bodies are not subject to national appropriation by claim of sovereignty, use, occupation, or other means (Article II).
	Space activities shall be conducted in accordance with international law, including the UN Charter (Article III).
	The moon and other celestial bodies are to be used exclusively for peaceful purposes (Article IV).
	Nuclear weapons and other weapons of mass destruction (such as chemical and biological weapons) may not be placed in orbit, installed on celestial bodies, or stationed in space in any other manner (Article IV).
	A state may not conduct military maneuvers; establish military bases, fortifications, or installations; or test any type of weapon on celestial bodies. Use of military personnel for scientific research or other peaceful purpose is permitted (Article IV).
	States are responsible for governmental and private space activities and must supervise and regulate private activities (Article VI).
	States are internationally liable for damage to another state (and its citizens) caused by its space objects (including privately owned ones) (Article VII).
	States retain jurisdiction and control over space objects while they are in space or on celestial bodies (Article VIII).
	States must conduct international consultations before proceeding with activities that would cause potentially harmful interference with activities of other parties (Article IX).
	States must carry out their use and exploration of space in such a way as to avoid harmful contamination of outer space, the moon, and other celestial bodies, as well as to avoid the introduction of extraterrestrial matter that could adversely affect the environment of the earth (Article IX).
	Stations, installations, equipment, and space vehicles on the moon and other celestial bodies are open to inspection by other countries on a basis of reciprocity (Article XII).
	Expands on the language of Article V of the Outer Space Treaty, which declares astronauts are to be regarded as "Envoys of Mankind" and be rendered "all possible assistance."
Agreement on the Rescue and Return of Astronauts and Objects Launched into Outer Space (1968)	Calls for a state in which a spacecraft crashes or a state operating in space that is in a position to assist astronauts in distress to conduct rescue operations (if it is a manned craft) and to speedily return astronauts to the launching state. Hardware need only be returned to the launching state upon request and need not be returned promptly.

Table 3-1. International treaties, agreements, and conventions that limit military activities in space[a] *(continued)*

Agreement	*Principle/Constraint*
Antiballistic Missile (ABM) Treaty between the United States and USSR (1972)	Prohibits development, testing, or deployment of space-based ABM systems or components (Article V).
	Prohibits deployment of ABM systems or components except as authorized in the treaty (Article I).
	Prohibits interference with the national technical means a party uses to verify compliance with the treaty (Article XII).
Liability Convention (1972)	A launching state is absolutely liable for damage by its space object to people or property on the earth or in its atmosphere (Article II).
	Liability for damage caused elsewhere than on Earth to another state's space object, or to persons or property on board such a space object, is determined by fault (Article III).
Convention on Registration (1974)	Requires a party to maintain a registry of objects it launches into Earth orbit or beyond (Article II).
	Information of each registered object must be furnished to the UN as soon as practical, including basic orbital parameters and general function of the object (Article IV).
Environmental Modification Convention (1980)	Prohibits military or other hostile use of environmental modification techniques as a means of destruction, damage, or injury to any other state if such use has widespread, long-lasting, or severe effects (Article I).

[a] The texts and information on these treaties and agreements can be found at www.un.org. See the section on international law—treaties at http://untreaty.un.org/English/treaty.asp. Another great reference is the Archimedes Space Law and Policy Library at http://www.permanent.com/archimedes/LawLibrary.html.

Notes

1. UNOOSA. "Space Law: Frequently Asked Questions," http://www.unoosa.org/oosa/en/FAQ/splawfaq.html (accessed 1 April 2009).

2. Jerry Jon Sellers, *Understanding Space: An Introduction to Astronautics*, 2nd ed. (Boston: McGraw Hill, 2004), 73.

3. "Treaty on Principles Governing the Activities of States in the Exploration and Use of Outer Space, Including the Moon and Other Celestial Bodies," 27 January 1967, available in UN Publication ST/SPACE/11 (New York: United Nations, 2002), http://www.unoosa.org/oosa/SpaceLaw/outerspt.html (accessed 2 April 2009).

4. Rosalie Bertell, "Background of the HAARP Project," http://www.earthpulse.com/src/subcategory.asp?catid=1&subcatid=1 (accessed 2 April 2009).

5. Ibid.

6. Ibid.

7. Ibid.

8. UNOOSA. "Space Law: Frequently Asked Questions."

9. *Communications Act of 1934 as Amended by the Telecommunications Act of 1996*, http://www.fcc.gov/Reports/1934new.pdf (accessed 22 May 2009).

10. Bonnie E. Fought, "Legal Aspects of the Commercialization of Space Transportation Systems," *Berkeley Technology Law Journal* 3, no. 2 (Spring 1988), http://www.law.berkeley.edu/journals/btlj/articles/vol3/fought.html (accessed 19 May 2009).

11. *Commercial Space Act of 1998*, Public Law 105-303, HR 1702 (28 October 1998), http://www.nasa.gov/offices/ogc/commercial/CommercialSpaceActof1998.html (accessed 2 April 2009).

12. President's Science Advisory Committee, "Introduction to Outer Space," NASA Historical Reference Collection, 26 March 1958, http://history.nasa.gov/sputnik/16.html (accessed 3 April 2009).

13. *National Aeronautics and Space Act*, Public Law 85-568, 72 Stat. 426 (29 July 1958), http://www.nasa.gov/offices/ogc/about/space_act1.html (accessed 3 April 2009).

14. Army, *Army Space Reference Text*, July 1993.

15. Ibid.

16. Richard M. Nixon, "Statement about the Future of the United States Space Program," 7 March 1970, http://www.nixonlibraryfoundation.org/index.php?src=gendocs&link=papers_1970 (accessed 2 April 2009).

17. Army, *Army Space Reference Text*.

18. Ibid.

19. White House, *National Space Policy Directives and Executive Charter*, 2 November 1989.

20. NOAA. "National Polar-Orbiting Operational Environment Satellite System (NPOESS)," updated August 2002, http://www.publicaffairs.noaa.gov/grounders/npoess.html (accessed 15 May 2009).

21. NASA. "Explanation of Executive Branch Policy Directives," http://www.au.af.mil/au/awc/awcgate/explain.htm (accessed 15 May 2009).

22. White House, National Security Presidential Directive (NSPD) 23, *Missile Defense Policy*, 17 December 2002.

23. White House, "US Commercial Remote Sensing Policy," 25 April 2003, 2.

24. Ibid.

25. White House, "US National Space Policy," 31 August 2006, 1.

26. Ibid., 2.

27. DOD Directive 3100.10, *Space Policy*, 9 July 1999, http://www.dtic.mil/whs/directives/corres/pdf/310010p.pdf (accessed 15 May 2009).

28. Army FM 3-14, *Space Support to Army Operations*, 18 May 2005, 15.

29. SECNAV Instruction 5400.39c, *Department of the Navy Space Policy*, 6 April 2004.

30. Quoted in Paul B. Stares, *Space Weapons and US Strategy* (London: Croom Helm, 1985), 28.

31. Delbert R. Terril, Jr., *Air Force Role in Developing International Outer Space Law* (Maxwell AFB, AL: Air University Press, 1999), 36.

32. AFDD 2-2, *Space Operations*, 27 November 2006, ii.

Chapter 4

Space Doctrine

Maj Christopher J. King, USAF; MAJ Dillard W. Young, USA;
Maj Edward P. Byrne, USAF; and Maj Paul P. Konyha III, USAF

Doctrine provides, in essence, a knowledge base for making strategy decisions. Doctrine is always somewhat abstract and thus provides the foundation from which to begin thinking when facing a concrete and specific decision. Without doctrine, strategists would have to make decisions without points of reference or guidance. They would continually be faced with the prospect of "reinventing the wheel" and repeating past mistakes. Superior doctrine should be the storehouse of analyzed experience and military wisdom and should be the strategist's fundamental guide in decisionmaking.

—Col Dennis M. Drew, USAF, Retired
and Dr. Donald M. Snow
Making Strategy: An Introduction to
National Security Process and Problems

The US National Space Policy Letter establishes the national space strategy and emphasizes the nation's reliance on space power. It codifies the space roles of the secretary of defense and the director of national intelligence in accomplishing space policy goals. The guidance for conducting space operations is published at both the joint and service levels. Air Force and Army service space doctrine is linked to national-level space strategy through joint space doctrine, Joint Publication (JP) 3-14, *Space Operations*. (Neither the Navy nor the Marine Corps has space doctrine.) This chapter summarizes the three primary doctrinal publications (joint, Air Force, and Army) that address military space operations and the relationships among them. If conflicts arise between JP 3-14 and individual service space doctrine, JP 3-14 takes precedence unless coordinated by the chairman of the Joint Chiefs of Staff (CJCS) and other members of the Joint Chiefs of Staff (JCS). If operating as part of a multinational force, commanders should follow multinational doctrine and procedures that have been ratified by the United States.

Joint Doctrine for Space Operations

Space capabilities continue to improve and evolve as new and better technologies are developed. As a result, space operations have become integrated into almost all aspects of joint military operations. To ensure these capabilities are efficiently and effectively integrated, it is essential that both the joint force commanders (JFC) and space operators have a mutual understanding of how and what space operations contribute to joint operations. JP 3-14 strives to achieve this objective by providing the guidelines for planning, executing, and assessing joint space operations.[1] This publication provides space doctrine fundamentals for all joint war fighters (air, land, sea, space, cyberspace, and special operations forces); describes the military operational principles associated with space operations support from, through, and in space; explains command relationships and responsibilities between the Joint Staff, combatant commands, US Strategic Command (USSTRATCOM), and USSTRATCOM functional and service components; and establishes a framework for the employment of space forces and space capabilities.[2] JP 3-14 describes the fundamentals of military space operations, the space mission areas, and command and control of space forces. It also outlines roles, responsibilities, and support to space planning.

Fundamentals of Military Space Operations

The section on fundamentals of military space operations includes discussions on the military space contribution to joint operations and on operational considerations for space.

Military Space Contributions to Joint Operations. Currently, space operations are viewed as a significant force multiplier when successfully integrated with joint military operations. To ensure the most effective allocation of space forces, it is necessary that all parties have a clear and common understanding of the available space capabilities (military, national, civil, commercial, and foreign) and the means to integrate these capabilities throughout the planning, execution, and assessment of joint mission operations.

The rapid advancement of new technologies has increased the application of space capabilities throughout the military, civil, and commercial sectors of the United States. As US reliance on space systems continues to increase, so does its potential vulnerability. Any intentional interference with these systems is viewed by the United States as an infringement on its rights. Commanders must anticipate hostile actions against space systems and take the necessary precautions to ensure their protection. The protection of military space capabilities also provides US forces the freedom to exploit space capabilities at a time and place of their choosing.

Space systems are unique in that they provide a truly global and responsive capability. Commanders must understand, however, that space systems are a limited resource. New requirements for space support can be satisfied by using deployed systems, which may take hours to days, or by developing and deploying new systems, which usually takes years.

Space forces employ the principles of joint operations and enable the application of these principles by other joint forces. Since the inception of joint doctrine, there have existed nine principles of war: objective, offensive, mass, economy of force, maneuver, unity of command, security, surprise, and simplicity. Three new principles—restraint, perseverance, and legitimacy—have been added to comprise the new 12 principles of joint operations. JP 3-0, *Joint Operations,* provides a detailed description on the purpose of these 12 principles. JP 3-14 provides a brief description of each of the 12 principles and also includes discussions on how each principle is employed and the outcome each enables, as it relates to space operations.

Operational Considerations for Space. Integration of space capabilities throughout the range of military operations provides the joint forces with numerous advantages necessary for mission success. The supported commander should integrate and synchronize these capabilities throughout all aspects and phases of the planning process. Both the supported and supporting commanders must coordinate the deployment and employment of required space forces. Coordination is sometimes difficult since space forces simultaneously support numerous global customers. It is the responsibility of the commander, USSTRATCOM (CDRUSSTRATCOM) to prioritize space capabilities and resources required to meet the supported commander's needs.

Commanders should take into account the following considerations when coordinating military operations. First, commanders should understand how others, including friends and adversaries, use space in support of military and civilian operations. Second, they must provide allies and coalition partners with the necessary access to resources and information. Third, commanders must establish the means to monitor the operational status of space systems. Fourth, they should understand the capabilities and limitations of space forces in relation to the mission at hand. Finally, commanders should understand the potential risks and impacts to space-based and ground-based systems and operations.

Commanders should also have an understanding of the unique characteristics of operating in the space environment as well as the advantages and disadvantages provided by space operations. Satellite orbits are chosen based on the mission they are designed to perform. Once in orbit, a satellite's motion is governed by physics and orbital mechanics. (See chapter 6 for more information regarding orbital mechanics.) Because a nation's sovereign territory does not extend into space, countries benefit from uninpeded satellite overflight of other nations. A major advantage of operating from space is that it provides direct line-of-sight to large areas of the earth's surface. Operating from space also has its disadvantages. Space is a harsh environment. Although systems are designed to survive in space, they are still susceptible to phenomena, such as space weather events or space debris, that have little or no impact to Earth-based systems. Space systems are also vulnerable to attacks. Today, many methods that can be used to disrupt or deny space capabilities are inexpensive, unsophisticated, and easily acquired by adversaries.

Space Mission Areas

JP 3-14 identifies four mission areas in US military space operations: space force enhancement, space support, space control, and space force application.[3]

Space Force Enhancement. Space force-enhancement operations multiply joint force effectiveness by increasing the combat potential and operational awareness and providing needed joint force support. There are five force-enhancement functions: (1) intelligence, surveillance, and reconnaissance (ISR); (2) missile warning; (3) environmental monitoring; (4) satellite communications; and (5) space-based positioning, navigation, and timing.[4] For detailed information regarding the five force-enhancement functions, refer to JP 3-14, appendices A–E.

Space Support. According to JP 3-14, "space support includes space lift operations (launching and deploying satellites), satellite operations (maintaining, sustaining, and rendezvous and proximity operations), and reconstitution of space forces (replenishing lost or diminished satellites)."[5]

Space Control. The space control mission area includes "offensive space control (OSC), defensive space control (DSC), and space situational awareness (SSA). OSC is used to deny adversary freedom of action in space and is based on negation and offensive prevention measures. DSC is used to protect space capabilities and is based on protection and defensive prevention measures. SSA involves characterizing the space capabilities operating within the terrestrial environment and space domain."[6]

Space Force Application. "Space force application operations consist of attacks against terrestrial-based targets carried out by military weapons systems operating in or through space."[7] Specific responsibilities for the force-application mission can be found in DOD Instruction (DODI) 3100.13, *Space Force Application*.

Command and Control of Space Forces

Command relationships are necessary to generate and maintain unity of command, effort, and purpose in achieving joint force and national security objectives. For space operations, CDRUSSTRATCOM is responsible for promoting, planning, prioritizing, deconflicting, integrating, synchronizing, and executing military space operations.

Command Relationships. CDRUSSTRATCOM is charged with conducting the military space operations mission. The commander, Joint Functional Component Command for Space (CDR JFCC Space) is the primary point of contact for military space operations. The responsibility for managing day-to-day space operations has been delegated to CDR JFCC Space by CDRUSSTRATCOM. CDRUSSTRATCOM has also delegated coordinating authority for space operations planning and execution, operational control (OPCON) of designated space and missile-warning forces, and management of the theater event system to CDR JFCC Space.

It is the nature of space operations that space assets provide simultaneous support to multiple global customers. Therefore, these forces normally remain attached to CDRUSSTRATCOM. Situations may arise, however, that require the transfer of space forces to a specific combatant commander (CCDR).

Responsibilities. CCDRs are responsible for prioritizing their requirements for space operations support and providing them to CDRUSSTRATCOM. CCDRs should also establish guidance and objectives for joint forces, identify OSC and DSC objectives that must be met, and if necessary, consider designating a space coordinating authority (SCA).

Space Coordinating Authority. The SCA is responsible for planning, coordinating, and integrating space capabilities and operations within the joint force. The SCA can either be retained by the JFC or designated to a component commander. The SCA collects requirements and determines if they can be satisfied by space capabilities. If so, the SCA plans and conducts space operations within established processes. Once coordinated, the SCA provides a prioritized list of requirements to the JFC for approval. The SCA also monitors theater space operations and events and ensures their respective commanders are aware of all coordination activities.

Role of Non-Department of Defense Capabilities. Space systems are a limited resource. Often DOD space systems cannot satisfy all CCDR requirements and must be augmented by civil, commercial, international, allied, or other US government agency systems. USSTRATCOM is the primary organization responsible for coordinating non-DOD space support to fulfill CCDR requirements.

Roles and Responsibilities

According to JP 3-14, "The joint force achieves maximum utility from space forces when they are organized and employed effectively. While some command and support relationships are enduring, others may vary for operations of different scopes and purposes. The joint force allocates space forces in the joint operations planning process."[8]

Chairman of the Joint Chiefs of Staff. The CJCS establishes a standardized system for assessing each combatant command's and combat support agency's readiness to employ space forces. The CJCS is also responsible for developing joint doctrine for the exploitation of space capabilities, developing joint space training and military education, integrating space forces and their industrial base into the Joint Strategic Capabilities Plan, and establishing policies for the integration of the National Guard and Reserve forces. Finally, the CJCS provides direction to CCDRs for the exploitation of space capabilities throughout the joint operation planning process.

Combatant Commanders. CCDRs are responsible for satisfying mission needs and must consider all available options, including space operations. When space forces are required, the CCDR is responsible for prioritizing requirements and submitting them to CDRUSSTRATCOM. Once approved, CCDRs ensure space capabilities are integrated into joint mission plans. Depending on the complexity and scale of the effort, CCDRs may need to employ staff elements or component commands to assist with the space mission. CCDRs are also responsible for responding to Joint Staff inquiries regarding the coordination, readiness, and protection of space forces.

US Strategic Command. The Unified Command Plan assigns USSTRATCOM the responsibility for the space operations mission. This responsibility includes planning, directing, coordinating, and controlling space assets and forces for daily operations. It also includes crisis action planning in the event of hostilities directed against the United States and its allies. CDRUSSTRATCOM ensures the most efficient and effective use of space assets by integrating and synchronizing DOD space capabilities. JP 3-14 states that "USSTRATCOM operates assigned space forces through Joint Functional Component Command for Space—JFCC Space, in coordination with Service component commands, USSTRATCOM functional component commands, and other agencies and organizations."[9]

Joint Functional Component Command for Space. The goal of JFCC Space, as defined in JP 3-14, "is to provide unity of command and unity of effort in unimpeded delivery of joint space capabilities to supported commanders and, when directed, to deny the benefits of space to adversaries."[10] CDR JFCC Space is the primary point of contact for military space operations and is the primary interface between USSTRATCOM and the supported commanders. As the focal point for military space operations, JFCC Space has been charged with numerous responsibilities:

- Plan and conduct space operations.
- Conduct operational-level command and control (C2) of assigned forces.
- Maintain and make available to all authorized users and mission partners a common space picture, to include satellite constellation maintenance and state-of-health operations.
- Coordinate space operations between USSTRATCOM and the National Reconnaissance Office (NRO).
- If designated SCA, coordinate joint space operations with each combatant command's SCA.
- Support CDRUSSTRATCOM as the DOD manager for human spaceflight support.
- Perform radio frequency deconfliction and laser clearinghouse operations.
- Provide indications, warnings, and assessments of attacks on space systems.
- Provide missile warnings.

- Integrate navigation warfare (NAVWAR) operations.
- Identify and assess current and future space requirements.
- Exploit joint space operations in support of CDRUSSTRATCOM requirements.

The Joint Space Operations Center (JSpOC) directly supports the CDR JFCC Space mission by providing continuous C2 capabilities to conduct space operations. The JSpOC also develops and provides an integrated space picture to enhance the CCDR's space situational awareness and supports both CDRUSSTRATCOM and CDR JFCC Space on all aspects of the space mission.

Other US Strategic Command Functional Components. In addition to JFCC Space, USSTRATCOM has five other functional components.

1. Joint Task Force-Global Network Operations (JTF-GNO): Directs the operation and defense of the Global Information Grid.

2. Joint Functional Component Command for Intelligence, Surveillance, and Reconnaissance (JFCC ISR): Formulates the plan to integrate global ISR capabilities associated with mission requirements into combatant command planning and operations.

3. Joint Functional Component Command for Network Warfare (JFCC NW): Responsible for the cyber warfare mission in support of the joint force.

4. Joint Functional Component Command for Integrated Missile Defense (JFCC IMD): Responsible for integrated missile defense planning and operational support.

5. Joint Functional Component Command for Global Strike (JFCC GS): "Provides planning and force management in order to deter attacks against the United States, its territories, possessions, and bases, and when directed, defeat adversaries through decisive joint global strike."[11]

Service Component Operations. Service component commands play an important role in supporting USSTRATCOM's space operations mission by training, equipping, and providing the necessary forces. USSTRATCOM works through JFCC Space to coordinate with the service components and their operations centers. The service component commands include the US Army Space and Missile Defense Command/Army Forces Strategic Command (USASMDC/ARSTRAT); Naval Network Warfare Command (NETWARCOM); Marine Corps Forces, US Strategic Command (MARFORSTRAT); and Air Force Space Command (AFSPC). Although each service component performs its own unique mission, common responsibilities do exist. Each service component is responsible for

advocating for space requirements within their respective Services, providing a single point of contact for access to Service resources and capabilities, making recommendations to USSTRATCOM on appropriate employment of Service forces, providing assigned space forces to CDRUSSTRATCOM and CCDRs as directed, assisting in planning in support of space operations and assigned tasking, and supporting CDRUSSTRATCOM and other CCDRs with space mission area expertise and advocacy of desired capabilities as requested.[12]

Theater Support. JFCs and their components are responsible for requesting space services and capabilities early in the planning process. Individuals, either assigned or resident on staffs, assist the SCA with theater space operations by creating, gathering, and prioritizing space capability requirements. Space service support can also be provided by other DOD and national agencies.

Combat Support Agencies. Space forces are a limited resource and are constantly in high demand. Often CCDR space requirements cannot be entirely satisfied by DOD systems alone and must be augmented by national, civil, commercial, and/or foreign systems. USSTRATCOM is the primary organization responsible for coordinating non-DOD space support to fulfill CCDR requirements. Three major agencies provide support in this area:

1. National Geospatial-Intelligence Agency (NGA): Provides geospatial intelligence in the form of imagery analysis to "describe, assess, and visually depict physical features and geographically referenced activities on the Earth."[13]

2. National Security Agency/Central Security Service (NSA/CSS): A unified organization that helps protect the United States by providing signals intelligence products to national-level decision makers.

3. Defense Intelligence Agency (DIA): Provides intelligence support to include "all-source military analysis, measures and MASINT [measurement and signature intelligence], HUMINT [human intelligence], counterintelligence, IO [information operations], personnel recovery, peacekeeping and coalition support, indications and warning, targeting, BDA [battle damage assessment], collection management, and intelligence support to operations planning."[14] Other important elements of the DIA are the Defense Intelligence Operations Coordination Center (DIOCC), the Missile and Space Intelligence Center (MSIC), and the Defense Special Missile and Aerospace Center (DEFSMAC).

Other Agencies and Organizations. Other agencies with a role in joint space operations include:

1. National Reconnaissance Office (NRO): A joint organization that researches, develops, acquires, launches, and operates overhead reconnaissance systems to obtain information in support of intelligence community and DOD requirements.

2. National Air and Space Intelligence Center (NASIC): The primary agency for foreign air and space threat assessments.

3. National Oceanic and Atmospheric Administration (NOAA): Operates numerous programs that provide information in support of military, commercial, civil, and interagency operations, including Operational Significant Event Imagery (OSEI), National Geophysical Data Center, Space Weather Prediction Center (SWPC), Earth weather satellites, and search and rescue satellite-aided tracking (SARSAT).

Commercial Space Operations. The benefits of space operations can go far beyond their military application. Space operations are infused in the day-to-day activities of society on a global scale. According to JP 3-14, "due to the demand for space-based products and services, the [US government] has established policy to foster the use of US commercial space capabilities around the globe."[15] Such capabilities include remote sensing; position, navigation, and timing; and commercial satellite imagery.

Multinational Space Operations. Unlike the United States, most other nations' space operations are dominated by their civilian and commercial segments, but space operations often provide support to military operations. For example, the United States relies heavily on foreign environmental space capabilities to augment its own systems. It is essential to understand US disclosure policy regarding the release of space-derived products when working with allied or coalition forces. NATO has established offices to coordinate specific programs and integrate space capabilities. For NATO, the

Consultation, Command, and Control Agency is responsible for commercial space imagery and satellite communications (SATCOM) programs.

Planning

Planning is an essential component of space operations, as prescribed in JP 3-14: "Commanders address space operations in all types of plans and orders, at all levels of war. Additionally, plans must address how to effectively integrate capabilities, counter an adversary's use of space, maximize use of limited space assets, and to consolidate operational requirements for space capabilities."[16]

Operational Art and Design. JP 5-0, *Joint Operation Planning*, defines operational art and design:

> Operational art is the application of creative imagination by commanders and staffs—supported by their skill, knowledge, and experience—to design strategies, campaigns, and major operations and organize and employ military forces. Operational art integrates ends, ways, and means across all levels of war. . . .
>
> Operational design is the conception and construction of the framework that underpins a joint operation plan and its subsequent execution. While operational art is the manifestation of informed vision, operational design is the practical extension of the creative process.[17]

Successfully synchronized, operational art and design combine to help commanders and staffs visualize the flow of a campaign. There are 17 elements of operational design that must be considered during the planning process: termination, end state and objectives, effects, centers of gravity, decisive points, direct versus indirect, lines of operation, operational reach, simultaneity and depth, timing and tempo, forces and functions, leverage, balance, anticipation, synergy, culmination, and arranging operations.

Key Planning Considerations. Space planners must understand the capabilities and limitations of space systems and how they can support mission requirements. Space operations have their own unique challenges that must be understood and considered during planning. These include the predictability of satellite orbits, the vulnerabilities of space systems, the limited nature of space resources and the long lead times to replenish or supplement on-orbit assets, timing considerations, legal aspects associated with laws and treaties, and the impacts of multinational space operations.

Control and Coordinating Measures. The joint space tasking cycle is used to coordinate and deconflict space assets and missions. The joint space tasking order is used to task units with specific missions but does not incorporate non-DOD space assets.

Air Force Doctrine for Space Operations

Air Force doctrine for space operations is articulated in AFDD 2-2, *Space Operations*. Air Force doctrine establishes guidance for the integration of space power across the range of military operations and recommends command and control constructs. This doctrine provides the foundation upon which Air Force commanders plan, execute, and assess space operations, as well as integrate space capabilities throughout joint operations.[18] Eleven foundational doctrinal statements about space operations drive the development of Air Force space doctrine. AFDD 2-2 follows the general construct of the previous version of JP 3-14 by describing a foundation for military space operations, command and control of space forces, support for space planning, and military space operations. Although similar to the previous version, the January 2009 version of JP 3-14 has changed slightly and now describes the fundamentals of military space operations, space mission areas, command and control of space forces, roles and responsibilities, and support for space planning.

An important assumption made in Air Force doctrine is that the commander, Air Force forces (COMAFFOR) will be assigned simultaneously as a joint force air (and space) component commander (JFACC). Additionally, Air Force doctrine assumes that through the JFACC it will execute tactical control of both joint air and space forces through the air (and space) operations center (AOC).[19] The relatively new change in terminology to include "and space" in both the JFACC and AOC titles is significant and reflects the Air Force's view of its role as the executive agent for space.

Foundational Doctrine Statements

Air Force doctrine explicitly states the basic principles and beliefs upon which the doctrine is built. These foundational doctrine statements drive Air Force space doctrine:[20]

- Space power should be integrated throughout joint operations as both an enabler and a force multiplier.

- Space capabilities contribute to situational awareness; highly accurate, all-weather weapon system employment; rapid operational tempo; information superiority; increased survivability; and more efficient military operations.

- Space power operates differently from other forms of military power due to its global perspective, responsiveness, and persistence.

- Global and theater space capabilities may be best employed when placed under the command of a single Airman through appropriate command relationships, focused expeditionary organization and equipment, "reachback," and specialized talent.

- Space is a domain—like the air, land, sea, and cyberspace—within which military operations take place.

- Space coordinating authority is an authority within a joint force aiding in the coordination of joint space operations and integration of space capabilities and effects. SCA is an authority, not a person.

- The combined force air and space component commander (CFACC) should be designated as the supported commander for counterspace operations.

- To plan, execute, and assess space operations, the COMAFFOR typically designates a director of space forces, an Air Force senior space advisor who facilitates coordination, integration, and staffing activities.

- Space operations should be integrated into the joint force commander's contingency and crisis action planning to magnify joint force effectiveness.

- Integration of theater space requirements must consider both a global and a theater perspective.

- An established relationship between the CFACC and the commander, Joint Functional Component Command for Space is essential to ensure flexibility and responsiveness when integrating space operations.

Space Operations Fundamentals

The space operations fundamentals chapter in AFDD 2-2 includes a discussion of the Airman's perspective on space power, the effects-based approach to operations, and key space operations principles.

Air Force doctrine views space power as a key ingredient for achieving battlespace superiority. Space is considered the ultimate high ground, and control of space is critical for space superiority to ensure availability of the force-multiplying capabilities of space power. Space power should be integrated throughout joint operations as both an enabler and a force multiplier. Space power adds another dimension to the joint force's ability to posture quickly and achieve battlespace superiority. Additionally, space power bolsters the US global presence because it is not limited by terrestrial antiaccess concerns.[21]

The ability to create accurate effects is crucial in military operations, and space power contributes significantly to this requirement. Space capabilities contribute to situational awareness; highly accurate, all-weather weapon system employment; rapid operational tempo; information superiority; increased survivability; and more efficient military operations. Precision, based on space capabilities, benefits weapons delivery and has many other applications, such as mapping terrain and environmental conditions, collecting detailed imagery, and detecting and characterizing inbound missiles. Space capabilities significantly increase the flexibility of military operations. Space-based communications allow much greater freedom of movement for terrestrial forces and enhance their command and control. Intelligence derived from space capabilities fills critical gaps in situational awareness, further augmenting joint force command and control capability.[22]

An Airman's Perspective on Space Power. Space power operates differently from other forms of military power due to its global perspective, responsiveness, and persistence. Because space-related effects and targeting can be global in nature, space power can be used to accomplish an effects-based approach based on functional capabilities rather than geographic limitations. The Air Force leverages the strengths of space platforms to produce effects based on this global perspective and responsiveness and the unique degree of persistence provided by assets in the space domain.[23]

The Air Force is focused on "operationalizing" space at the operational and tactical levels of war. This requires significant integration with other assets and capabilities. The synergistic effect of combining space capabilities with traditional surface, subsurface, and airborne systems delivers persistence over the joint operations area.[24]

Space operations and the space domain are unique. Space power defies a single model for organization and operations because it requires both a theater and a global perspective. Global and theater space capabilities may be best employed when placed under the command of a single Airman through appropriate command relationships, focused expeditionary organization and equipment, reachback, and specialized talent.[25]

Space is viewed as a physical domain where space-centric activities are conducted to achieve objectives. Space is a domain—like the air, land, sea, and cyberspace—within which military operations take place.[26]

Key Space Operations Principles. To share a common perspective on space operations, Airmen should understand key principles and concepts—the four space mission areas and the categories of space capabilities—and know the relevant space-related terminology.

70

There are four space mission areas: space control, space support, space force enhancement, and space force application. The discussion of these four areas in Air Force doctrine is consistent with that of joint doctrine with one notable exception. The Air Force uses the term *counterspace* as equivalent to the space control mission, as this term aligns more appropriately with other Air Force functions, provides less ambiguity, and provides a common Air Force language.[27]

Three terms are used to describe different categories of space capabilities: space systems, space assets, and space forces. The term *space systems* refers to the equipment required for space operations, which is comprised of nodes and links. This includes all the devices and organizations forming the space network, which consists of spacecraft; ground and airborne stations; and data links among spacecraft, mission, and user terminals.[28] *Space assets* include military and civil space systems, commercial and foreign entities, ground control elements, operators, and space-lift vehicles.[29] *Space forces* are military space assets and personnel used by the joint force, which are normally organized as units. There are both global space forces and theater space forces. Global space forces support multiple theater and/or national objectives and are controlled by the commander, USSTRATCOM. Theater space forces support individual theater requirements and generally fall under control of the geographic combatant commander.[30]

Executing Space Operations

The employment of space forces at the operational level of war is accomplished through tasking orders that deconflict, synchronize, and integrate space operations with theater operations. Although no authority exists for control over nonmilitary space assets, the joint force must integrate with enabling space operations conducted by nonmilitary space assets.[31]

Space AOC/Joint Space Operations Center

The Air Force provides a Space AOC that forms the core of the Joint Space Operations Center (JSpOC) at Vandenberg AFB, California. It includes the personnel, facilities, and equipment necessary to plan, execute, and assess space operations and to integrate space power. The JSpOC tracks assigned and attached space forces and space assets and also provides reachback support to organic theater space personnel. The JSpOC also creates the space tasking order (STO), based on CDRUSSTRATCOM operation orders (OPORD) and CDR JFCC Space guidance. The STO tasks and directs assigned and attached space forces to fulfill theater and global mission requirements in support of national objectives.[32]

Integrating Global with Theater Space Operations. Control of military space forces is normally retained by USSTRATCOM due to the inherently global nature of most space assets. Thus, support is the normal command relationship used to integrate USSTRATCOM space operations with theater operations. The JSpOC normally synchronizes its supporting operations with the theaters because they (as the supported commander) drive tasking requirements. An established relationship between the JFACC and the CDR JFCC Space is essential to ensure flexibility and responsiveness when integrating space operations.[33]

Execution of Space Forces in-Theater. There are multiservice space forces that can deploy to support operations in-theater. Some of these forces are designed to integrate into various levels of command within the joint force, while others possess capabilities that must be integrated into the overall military campaign. The secretary of defense may attach these forces to geographic combatant commanders conducting combat operations.[34]

When deployed, Air Force space forces are normally attached to an air and space expeditionary task force (AETF) under the operational control of the COMAFFOR. When the COMAFFOR is also assigned as the JFACC, the JFACC is normally given tactical control (TACON) of other service space forces that exceed their organic requirements (similar to how the JFACC would receive TACON of any Navy aviation sorties that exceed the Navy's organic requirements).[35]

Integrating Civil, Commercial, and Foreign Space Assets. Many civil, commercial, and foreign organizations contribute space capabilities to military operations. These nonmilitary space assets provide invaluable alternatives to meet the military's operational needs. Thus, the integration of nonmilitary space assets may become vital to mission accomplishment. In most cases, the geographic combatant commander's staff will determine the appropriate avenue for using these assets.[36]

Civil, commercial, and foreign space assets often must be requested on an unplanned basis; therefore, preestablished agreements can significantly enhance effectiveness and responsiveness. Additionally, space planners must understand that civil, commercial, and foreign space assets may be specialized and not have sufficient flexibility for dynamic retasking, may require unique procedures and equipment, and may not meet critical requirements for military operations.[37]

Army Doctrine for Space Operations

US Army doctrine for space operations is articulated in FM 3-14, *Space Support to Army Operations*. Central to this document is the understanding that the objective of Army use of space is to support Army land dominance. Space capabilities are well integrated into Army operations and are critical to Army and joint war fighting.[38]

Space Operations Overview

The Army leverages space capabilities to accomplish a wide variety of missions. Space-based and space-enabled communications; position, velocity, and timing; environmental monitoring; ISR; and missile-warning support are all necessary for success on the battlefield.[39] Robust space capabilities enhance both information superiority and situational awareness. Space operations are conducted by space forces and other personnel who routinely facilitate the use of space assets to support the war fighter.

Army space operations fall into two categories: controlling space and exploiting space. Controlling space means to affect space to benefit US efforts or detract from adversary efforts and falls within the space-control joint space mission area. Exploiting space is making space-based capabilities available to benefit operations and falls within the space force-enhancement joint space mission area.[40] The ability of the Army to capitalize on space systems, along with the ability to protect them and attack the adversary's capability to use them, yields military power.[41]

Key Terms and Organizations

The US Army Space and Missile Defense Command (USASMDC), a major Army command, is the Army proponent for space. USASMDC is also the Army service component command (ASCC) for USSTRATCOM, and in this capacity it is called Army Strategic Command (ARSTRAT).[42]

ARSTRAT executes command and control of ARSTRAT space forces worldwide and is the focal point for the employment and integration of ARSTRAT space forces into global, national, and military operations. ARSTRAT commands a space brigade consisting of three battalions that provide theater missile warning, space control, and other space-based capabilities and expertise to the war fighter. The satellite control battalion provides communication satellite network and payload control.[43]

Controlling and Exploiting Space to Enhance Land War-fighting Power

Army space operations consist of those activities concerned with controlling and exploiting space to enhance land war fighting; Army space power is a terrestrial entity and is land-warfare-centric.[44] The prerequisite to exploiting space is to control the domain of operations. The armed forces require maximum control of particular space assets at particular times; this requires the ability to exercise control of any space asset at any time (which differs from controlling all space assets all the time). The essence of space control for land force purposes is to exercise the Army's will at decisive points for space operations in support of land campaigns. Having space superiority maximizes the contribution space can make to land war-fighting dominance.[45]

Having established space control, the United States can then exploit space to gain military advantage. Land forces should see first, understand first, act first, and finish decisively as the means to achieve tactical success. Space systems provide critical support to each of these capabilities.

Army space operations are guided by five mission-essential tasks included in the Army space policy:

1. Enable situational understanding and joint battle command.
2. Support precision maneuver, fires, and sustainment.
3. Contribute to continuous information and decision superiority.
4. Support increased deployability by reducing the in-theater footprint.
5. Protect the force during all phases of operations.

To accomplish these tasks, space-based capabilities and services provide assured, responsive, and timely support.[46]

Army Joint Space Operations Relationships

Space operations, by their nature, are joint operations. Each service component contributes to an integrated whole that is synchronized by the joint force headquarters. Army space operations support joint force missions and receive support from service and other joint force, government, civil, and commercial space assets. The joint operations concepts document, provided by the secretary of defense, sets the goal of being full-spectrum dominant, which is a driver for the Army's development of space operations capabilities.[47]

JP 3-14 lays the foundation of joint space doctrine by establishing principles for the integrated employment of space capabilities. JP 3-14 recognizes that the services have unique roles to play in providing space capabilities, including specific Army roles:

The Army is to provide space control operations and space support to the joint force and Army component, coordinate and integrate Army resources in the execution of [USSTRAT-COM] plans and operations, provide theater missile warning through employment of joint tactical ground stations (JTAGS), provide space support through the use of Army space support teams, and perform Defense Satellite Communications System payload and network control. Additionally, [USASMDC/ARSTRAT] functions as the SATCOM system expert for Wideband Gapfiller System super-high frequency (SHF) communications satellites and is the parent command for regional satellite communications support centers servicing all combatant commands, their components, and the Defense agencies and other users. U.S. Army Space and Missile Defense Command is the U.S. Army major command that organizes, trains, equips, and provides forces to [USASMDC/ARSTRAT] and plans for national missile defense.[48]

The G3 Section and Space Operations

The corps and division G3 (Operations) has overall coordinating staff responsibility for space operations at its level. The G3 section normally has an assigned space element that provides space operations planning and coordinates space mission execution. Additionally, the G3 coordinates the space-related activities of other staff sections, primarily the G2 (Intelligence) and G6 (Communications).

The G3 space element serves as the staff focal point for coordination of most space activities. The primary function of the space element is to synchronize space mission-area (space control and space force enhancement) activities throughout the operations process. Additionally, space element members coordinate space operations objectives and tasks with their counterparts at higher and lower echelons.[49]

The Functional Area 40 space operations officer is familiar with corps and division operations and plans and is thoroughly educated in space capabilities available for theater operations. Space operations officers identify opportunities for space capabilities to provide effective solutions for war-fighting problems. The space operations officer advises the G3 to request an Army space support team for contingencies or exercises when space operations activities would otherwise overwhelm the space element. The space element and space operations officer also recommend to the G3 and commander other space capabilities that should be used to support the mission.[50]

Army Space Command and Control

At the direction of the secretary of defense, the CDRUSSTRATCOM transfers designated space capabilities to the supported combatant commander or subordinate joint force commander. These capabilities are forces that, for the Army, are normally provided via USASMDC/ARSTRAT.[51]

The Space and Missile Defense Command Operations Center (SMDCOC) provides the USASMDC/ARSTRAT commander the means to communicate and execute command and control of USASMDC space and missile defense assets. The SMDCOC provides command situational awareness and maintains command asset operational status. Additionally, the SMDCOC provides around-the-clock reach for space operations officers and deployed space assets (in a function very similar to that of the JSpOC/Air Force Special Operations Command [AFSOC]).[52]

74

To ensure overall synchronization of space efforts, the joint force commander designates a space authority to coordinate theater space operations and integrate space capabilities. Similarly, the USASMDC/ARSTRAT commander may designate an Army space coordination authority in support of the ASCC for the regional combatant commander, Army forces (ARFOR) commander or joint force land component commander (JFLCC), and theater space authority.[53]

Differences in Service Doctrine

Much, if not most, of the current Army and Air Force space-related doctrine is similar. Apparently, both services agree on the most significant issues. For the most part, the doctrine differs only in the format of its presentation. The Army doctrine is unique in that it incorporates the relevant guidance from the National Space Policy and demonstrates how the Army policy and doctrine align with this guidance.[54] The Air Force doctrine does not address national or DOD policy, but it does include foundational doctrine statements at the beginning of the document, which are the Air Force's space-related fundamental principles that guided the development of the manual.[55] As an additional helpful formatting technique, these foundational doctrine statements are presented in bold font wherever they appear later in the text.

In addition to these relatively minor formatting discrepancies, there are at least three noteworthy differences to be found in the two sets of doctrine. The areas that differ include the focus for space capabilities, the emphasis on the four space mission areas, and the role of each service with regard to space coordinating authority.

The first notable difference between the Army and Air Force doctrine is the focus. The Army doctrine is quite clear that the purpose of space forces, assets, and capabilities is for achieving land dominance;[56] the Army is committed to "using space to its best advantage."[57] Throughout the Army doctrine it is apparent that the Army vision for space is rather land-centric, whereas the Air Force doctrine regarding space is somewhat more "joint-minded," focusing on complete battlespace dominance, rather than dominance in any single domain.[58]

The second significant difference between service doctrines concerns the space mission areas. The Air Force is responsible for executing tasks in all four of the joint space mission areas and has space forces and assets related to each. The Army, however, is currently concerned with only two functions: controlling space and exploiting space.[59] Army forces exploit space by making space-based capabilities available to enhance Army operations. Space control means to affect space to benefit US efforts or to detract from adversary efforts. Army forces play an important part in executing the space-control mission area by affecting adversary land-based space forces and assets; terrestrial-based space control is an Army responsibility.[60] Space support and space force application, however, are two joint space mission areas that the Army is currently not concerned with, as the service does not have the forces, assets, or capabilities to execute operations within these mission areas.

The final significant difference between Army and Air Force space doctrine concerns the delegation of SCA. The SCA coordinates space operations, integrates space capabilities, and has primary responsibility for in-theater joint space operations planning. The Army doctrine mentions that the ARFOR commander/JFLCC may be designated as the space authority at the discretion of the JFC. This is likely to happen if the Army has the preponderance of space capabilities in-theater and has adequate command and control to fully coordinate space issues.[61] The nature and duration of the overall mission are also factors when assigning space authority.

The Air Force assumes that the JFC should delegate space authority to the COMAFFOR/JFACC.[62] Air Force doctrine does mention that space authority might be delegated to the functional component commander with the preponderance of space assets and the ability to best command and control them, but this point is not emphasized, and several paragraphs follow which justify a JFC appointing SCA to the COMAFFOR/JFACC. The point here is not to say that this perspective is unjustified, but rather simply to highlight that the "tone" of the two documents differs significantly with regard to this issue.

The Air Force plans and trains "to employ forces through a COMAFFOR who is also dual-hatted as a JFACC."[63] This statement is particularly noteworthy, as the service has adopted new naming conventions to emphasize its role which assume that the COMAFFOR will be delegated space coordinating authority. According to JP 1-02, the acronym JFACC stands for joint forces air component commander; however, the Air Force has notably inserted "and space" (joint forces air *and space* component commander) into the acronym.[64] Similarly, the Air Force has renamed the joint air operations center (JAOC)[65] as the joint air *and space* operations center,[66] while the joint air operations plan (JAOP)[67] has been renamed the joint air *and space* operations plan.[68]

Together, these three issues—focus for space capabilities, emphasis on the four space mission areas, and the role of each service with regard to space coordinating authority—comprise the most significant differences between Army and Air Force space operations doctrine.

Notes

1. JP 3-14, *Space Operations*, 6 January 2009, i.
2. Ibid., I-1.
3. Ibid., II-1.
4. Ibid., x.
5. Ibid., xi.
6. Ibid.
7. Ibid.
8. Ibid., IV-1.
9. Ibid., xii.
10. Ibid., IV-3.
11. Ibid., IV-7.
12. Ibid., IV-8.
13. Ibid., IV-12.
14. Ibid., IV-13.
15. Ibid., IV-17.
16. Ibid., V-1.
17. JP 5-0, *Joint Operation Planning*, 26 December 2006, IV-2.
18. AFDD 2-2, *Space Operations*, 27 November 2006, v.
19. Ibid., vi.
20. Ibid., vii.
21. Ibid., 1.
22. Ibid., 2.
23. Ibid.
24. Ibid., 3.
25. Ibid.

26. Ibid.
27. Ibid., 5.
28. Ibid.
29. Ibid.
30. Ibid., 6.
31. Ibid., 29.
32. Ibid., 29-30.
33. Ibid., 32-33.
34. Ibid., 34.
35. Ibid.
36. Ibid., 35.
37. Ibid.
38. FM 3-14, *Space Support to Army Operations*, 18 May 2005, 1-1.
39. Ibid.
40. Refer to chapter 8 of this *Space Primer* for details on the joint space mission areas.
41. FM 3-14, *Space Support*, 1-2.
42. Refer to chapter 10 of this *Space Primer* for additional discussion of US Army space organizations.
43. FM 3-14, *Space Support*, 1-6.
44. Ibid., 1-9.
45. Ibid., 1-10.
46. Ibid.
47. Ibid., 1-15.
48. JP 3-14, *Space Operations*, II-3.
49. FM 3-14, *Space Support*, 1-16.
50. Ibid.
51. Ibid., 3-8.
52. Ibid., 3-9.
53. Ibid.
54. FM 3-14, *Space Support*, 1-6.
55. AFDD 2-2, *Space Operations*, vii.
56. FM 3-14, *Space Support*, 1-9.
57. Ibid., 1-1.
58. AFDD 2-2, *Space Operations*, 1.
59. FM 3-14, *Space Support*, 1-2.
60. Ibid., 2-12.
61. Ibid., 3-8.
62. AFDD 2-2, *Space Operations*, 13.
63. AFDD 1, *Air Force Basic Doctrine*, 17 November 2003, 65.
64. JP 1-02, *Department of Defense Dictionary of Military and Associated Terms*, 12 April 2001 (as amended through 17 October 2008), 287.
65. Ibid., A-73.
66. AFDD 2-2, *Space Operations*, vii.
67. JP 1-02, *Dictionary*, 284.
68. AFDD 2-2, *Space Operations*, 20.

Chapter 5

US Military Space Planning

Maj Bryan Eberhardt, USAF; and MAJ Wes Young, USA

If you find yourself in a fair fight, you didn't plan your mission properly.

—Col David Hackworth

Successful planning will lead to successful integration of space capabilities into the joint fight. Space planning takes time and must begin early in order to bring effective capabilities into the joint campaign. Once a crisis occurs, it can be too late to integrate space effects. Air Force Doctrine Document (AFDD) 2-2, *Space Operations*, stresses this by mentioning integration five times on the first page of the space operations planning chapter.[1] This integration is key to building the operation plan (OPLAN), the geographic and functional combatant commander's (CCDR) key planning product for a theater of operations.[2]

The Operation Plan

The OPLAN defines the tasks and responsibilities of the supported CCDR and supporting CCDRs, administration and logistics requirements, and command and control of forces. OPLANs are used both for long-term planning and for responding to crises. According to Joint Publication (JP) 5-0, *Joint Operation Planning*, "A joint OPLAN is the most detailed of the planning products, and provides a complete concept of operations (CONOPS), all annexes applicable to the plan, and the time-phased force and deployment data (TPFDD) for the specific operation."[3] A CCDR's OPLAN is the result of the seven steps of the joint operation planning process (JOPP).[4] OPLANs contain plans for responding to potential crises within a theater of operations.

Execution of an OPLAN is conducted in six phases:

1. Phase 0: Shape
2. Phase I: Deter
3. Phase II: Seize the initiative
4. Phase III: Dominate
5. Phase IV: Stabilize
6. Phase V: Enable civil authority[5]

For space to be effective in phase 0, "agreements with space-faring nations and commercial and international organizations are essential in order to shape the international space community and ensure that potential adversaries are denied needed space capabilities."[6] Satellite communications and space situational awareness (SSA) also provide capabilities to "shape the operational environment."[7]

SSA in conjunction with defensive space control (DSC) also helps in phase I by monitoring satellite assets and deterring others "from initiating attacks against space and terrestrial capabilities."[8] The US Strategic Command's (USSTRATCOM) Joint

Functional Component Command for Integrated Missile Defense (JFCC-IMD) and the JFCC for Global Strike and Integration also continuously utilize strategic space assets for deterrence.[9]

In order to seize the initiative in phase II, the United States combines SSA with global coverage. This global surveillance creates the ability to "seize the initiative with in-place communication, navigation, environmental, intelligence, surveillance and reconnaissance (ISR), and warning systems to exploit an adversary's weaknesses."[10]

Phase III dominance in the space arena has always been inherent in the military's ability to always hold the high ground, which is critical in military operations.[11] This dominance leads to space superiority and the ability to conduct military operations "at a given time and place without prohibitive interference by the opposing force."[12]

As space capabilities are routinely used by the commercial and civilian sectors, the defense of these assets will be required to complete the stabilization phase and to eventually enable civil authority. Conducting SSA of "civil space capabilities and operations"[13] and providing imagery, satellite communications, remote sensing, and search and rescue support all help civil authorities in the execution of their various duties.[14]

The space operations annex (Annex N) provides details of the above capabilities, phase-by-phase and as integrated across time, space, and purpose with the CCDR's OPLAN. As part of the OPLAN, the space operations annex covers the contributions space assets will bring to the fight. The space operations annex should cover the space operations contributions to the CCDR mission (friendly space systems), as well as enemy space capabilities that may threaten mission accomplishment.[15]

Annex N is tied into the Joint Operation Planning and Execution System (JOPES), which is the principal system within the Department of Defense for responding "to requirements from the President, the [Secretary of Defense], or the CJCS [chairman of the Joint Chiefs of Staff]. It specifies policies, procedures, and reporting structures—supported by modern communications and computer systems—for planning the mobilization, deployment, employment, sustainment, redeployment, and demobilization of joint forces."[16]

Additional information on space planning can be obtained from JP 3-14, *Space Operations*; AFDD 2-2, *Space Operations*; and Army Field Manual (FM) 3-14, *Space Support to Army Operations*.

Joint Operation Planning and Execution System

JOPES is a system that includes a set of publications and documents to guide the development and operational planning process that develops OPLANs and operations orders (OPORD); JOPES also includes a computer support system for processing support.[17] According to AFDD 2-2, "Annexes B (Intel), C (Operations), K (Communications), N (Space), and S (Special Technical Operations) of supported commander OPLANs and campaign plans contain space contributions to the overall effort. Development of these annexes is the supported commander's responsibility but requires coordinated effort between the JFC and component staffs and USSTRATCOM staffs at joint and Service component levels."[18]

JP 3-14 directs that "once the supported commander develops a joint OPLAN with annexes, the supporting combatant commanders will write CONPLANs [concept plans] in support of the OPLAN."[19] The Joint Forces Component Command for Space (JFCC

Space) now has day-to-day responsibility within USSTRATCOM for planning space operations with "other USSTRATCOM joint functional components, other combatant commanders through their space coordinating authority (SCA), and other Department of Defense (DoD), and when directed, non-DoD partners to ensure unity of effort in support of military, national security operations, and support to civil authorities."[20]

The CONPLAN is a capabilities-based vice a requirements-based plan. This means the plan discusses capabilities within Strategic Command's means to control and operate assets in space. According to AFDD 2-2.1, *Counterspace Operations*, "An effects-based methodology of planning places the highest priority on achieving a given desired outcome, in order to attain or directly contribute to the attainment of military and political objectives."[21]

The plan provides tasks and responsibilities for both the supported commander and supporting commanders, including USSTRATCOM: "Because much of theater space integration involves forces controlled by USSTRATCOM, they need to be consulted when building plans."[22] Responsibilities for USSTRATCOM and JFCC Space include:

Taking lead for Space control, Space situational awareness, Space offensive and defensive operations, Space force enhancements such as Intelligence, Surveillance and Reconnaissance; ITW/AA [integrated tactical warning and attack assessment]; environmental monitoring; Satellite Communication; Positioning, Navigation and Timing; and also in Space support (lift and satellite operations) and Space force applications. JFCC-Space is also the day to day manager of missile warning capability and serves as the supporting commander to JFCC-Integrated Missile Defense and JFCC-Intelligence Surveillance and Reconnaissance for management of the missile warning centers and data.[23]

Integrating Space into Operation Plans

According to AFDD 2-2, "The challenge for campaign planners is to ensure space operations are integrated throughout the joint force commander's (JFC's) scheme of maneuver across all levels of war—strategic, operational, and tactical."[24] Annex N is only one part of the overall effort, but it is a critical part. In order to be fully effective, space support and thinking must be integrated throughout as many of the JOPES annexes as possible. Of prime importance are the intelligence, operations, and communications annexes. The execution checklists must also contain information showing what space support to expect at various times.

Most planners consider space a separate entity, much like maintenance or communications. This thinking must be revised, and space should be incorporated as an integral part of all planning and war fighting. Though it can be challenging, integrating space into joint operations is a necessity.

As CCDR staffs are populated with increasing numbers of Space Weapons School graduates, or space weapons officers (SWO), they will assume greater responsibility for authoring the theater or functional space operations annexes of their respective OPLANs. These SWOs will also play an increasingly important role in the development of the joint space operations plan (JSOP) in much the same way as the joint force air component commander's (JFACC) staff develops the joint air operations plan (JAOP). "The JSOP details how joint space operations will support both global missions and theater requirements. The JSOP prioritizes space operations across all AORs [areas of responsibility] and functions based on geographic and functional combatant commander's requests and CDRUSSTRATCOM [commander, USSTRATCOM] priorities. Theater strategists should include theater space requirements in the JAOP."25

Previously, Air Force space support teams (SST) would "supplement the supported commander's staff to assist in integrating space into the joint campaign plan and provide tailored space support through space support team personnel to train and/or assist Service forces."26 Today, highly trained space professionals from across the Air Force have replaced these SSTs in order to provide the best integrated space-planning efforts across the globe.27

Annex N: Space Operations

Annex N resulted from a review of Desert Storm operations, which revealed that space systems were not integrated into OPLANs because operators were not aware of space-system capabilities or how to access or request space-system support. This led to the generation of SSTs and USSTRATCOM support plans, which were a result of direction from the CJCS to incorporate space system education into all professional and technical military education curriculums,28 with a focus "on how satellite systems enhance warfighting."29

OPLAN 1002-90, begun in March 1990, was to serve as a blueprint for a war with Iraq:

Annex N to OPLAN 1002-90 was supposed to describe the concept of operations and explain theater-wide space forces support required by US Central Command's employment plan. However, the level of detail reflected the relative immaturity of the space mission. Some space force functional areas, such as communications, weather, and intelligence, contained enough detail to be of use. On the other hand, navigation, early warning, and geodesy lacked even basic information. Any good planning found in Annex N can be largely attributed to the fact that there were separate, detailed annexes in some functional areas, such as communications, intelligence, and weather. Nevertheless, even in these areas preplanning was not totally acceptable. For example, SATCOM communications links had to be altered at least 75 times, and the intelligence dissemination network worked backwards. The lack of planning for interoperability between service dissemination systems forced intelligence data collected by one service to be routed from the theater back to the Pentagon, then transmitted back to the theater. Consequently, throughout the Gulf War operations space support took on an ad hoc character because of inadequate planning for the use of space forces.30

Annex N, the space operations annex included in a CCDR's OPLAN, provides planning guidance concerning space-related support and capabilities for the supported CCDR for use during the campaign. The annex describes how capabilities will be utilized by phase and "should include a prioritized list of those space forces and capabilities critical to the success of the plan."31 Specifically, space forces provide the following four capabilities: space force enhancement, space control (or counterspace), space force application, and space support:

Space force enhancement (SFE) capabilities contribute to maximizing the effectiveness of military air, land, sea, and space operations (e.g., ISR, warning, communication, PNT [position, navigation, and timing], blue force tracking, space environment monitoring, and weather services). *Space control* (SC) capabilities attain and maintain a desired degree of space superiority by allowing friendly forces to exploit space capabilities while denying an adversary's ability to do the same (e.g., surveillance, protection, prevention, and negation). The Air Force uses *counterspace* as an equivalent definition of the space control mission. Counterspace aligns more appropriately to other Air Force air and space power functions (i.e., counterair, counterland, and countersea), provides less ambiguity, and provides common Air Force language. *Space force application* (SFA) capabilities execute missions with weapons systems operating in, through or from space which hold terrestrial-based targets at risk (e.g., intercontinental ballistic missiles [ICBM], ballistic missile defense, and force projection). *Space support* (SS) capabilities provide critical launch and satellite control infrastructure, capabilities and technologies that enable the other mission areas to effectively perform their missions.[32]

Annex N also addresses how the above capabilities are utilized or exploited by potential enemies, friendly forces, and allies in-theater. Planning assumptions should include identifying shortfalls, limiting factors, an understanding of the world situation, and the ability to replace on-orbit assets "in the event of the loss of space forces or services."[33] Additional Annex N information will be discussed further in the Annex N template provided at the end of this chapter.

Developing a Theater Annex N

Before developing an Annex N, planners need situational awareness of red, blue, and even grey space assets. Space planners must also be aware of the supported commander's objectives and tasks, by phase, for the operation. One example is that counterspace requirements may be "emphasized early in an operation and be de-emphasized once space superiority is firmly established."[34] USSTRATCOM is responsible for planning on the global level and the geographic CCDR is responsible for theater integration.[35]

To develop the Annex N, one first needs to ask some basic questions. For example, what kinds of space support are required by the supported CCDR? The answer to this question might include satellite communications (SATCOM), PNT support, intelligence, surveillance, imagery, attack warning, weather, and multispectral imagery (MSI). PNT support should include combat search and rescue.[36] Environmental monitoring information should include weather and MSI for terrain/water-depth analysis, map updates, and ground cover classification.[37]

As the campaign evolves and deployment to a theater nears, more specific questions need to be discussed and resolved, such as the following:

- What are the supported/supporting relationships for required space capabilities?
- What are the decision points between the phases of the campaign?[38]
- What are in-theater system capabilities? Can theater units receive information from satellites properly and in a timely manner? Is additional equipment needed?
- What are area and target coverage requirements? Can target imagery or wide area coverage be pinpointed?
- What is the response time of various satellite systems? How do we get data in real time or near real time to the theater?
- What are the resolution and accuracy of satellite information?
- What are the availability and survivability of space systems?

Next, we will need to know specific, unique theater requirements.

- Do users have the proper terminal or receiver equipment to obtain the needed support data and information (e.g., weather terminals and tactical data processors)?

- Have connectivity and interoperability among the service components (and allies) been determined and resolved (e.g., super-high frequency [SHF] versus ultra-high frequency [UHF] communications; imagery dissemination)?[39]
- Has maintenance support, especially of dissimilar equipment, been addressed and resolved?
- Has training and exercise space support to the theater been practiced so that deployments do not present personnel with new situations or unknown systems?

Allies also need to be knowledgeable about what US systems there are and how they can be used to maximum advantage.[40]

Here are some additional hints on preparation of the Annex N and supporting appendices:

- Focus on unique space capabilities and their application to the operation.
- Refer to the Annex N of the next higher command's OPLAN.
- Cross-reference with and avoid repeating information in other annexes.

* * * * * *

Excerpt of a Sample Annex N

The following excerpt of a sample Annex N is from CJCS Manual 3122.03, *Joint Operation Planning and Execution System*, vol. 2, *Planning Formats and Guidance*.[41] Amplifying information not in CJCS Manual 3122.03 is italicized within the sample Annex N below. Italicized information is not required in accordance with the JOPES format and is for information only.

ANNEX N—SPACE OPERATIONS

HEADQUARTERS, US EUROPEAN COMMAND
APO AE 09128
25 May 200X

ANNEX N TO USEUCOM OPLAN 4999-05
SPACE OPERATIONS

References: List documents essential to this annex. *List Annex N of the next higher command's OPLAN or OPORD and other documents, maps, overlays and standard operating procedures (SOP) that provide guidance and information for use with this annex. Applicable annexes include A, B, C, J, K, N, and S, "at a minimum."*[42]

1. Situation

a. General. Identify political decisions needed to use space operations to support the mission. *Describe planned and available space support to the OPLAN. Explain how to obtain and coordinate space support and list operational constraints and shortfalls, especially potential legal considerations.*[43] *Describe relationships between supporting and supported organizations. Refer to other annexes or provide enough information about the* overall situation to give subordinate and supporting units a clear understanding of the operations contemplated which require space operations support.

b. Enemy. Identify enemy capabilities to interfere with the space operations. Refer to Annex B, Intelligence, for amplifying information. Describe enemy space capabilities, how they will be used, and their value to the enemy.[44]

1. Estimate the impact of enemy space capabilities on friendly operations. Describe notification or warning reports to friendly units of enemy space activities to include enemy reconnaissance, surveillance, and target acquisition of friendly forces by manned and unmanned space systems. Discuss the enemy's ability to use friendly space systems to support operations. Refer to Annex B, Intelligence, for amplifying information.

2. Identify enemy space weaknesses and vulnerabilities such as inadequate coverage, poor resolution, inability to launch new or replacement systems, and inability to counter the capabilities of friendly space systems.

3. Describe what the enemy is capable of doing and probably will do with space, air, surface, or subsurface assets to interfere with friendly space systems and space operations that support the missions and tasks envisioned in this plan. Note the hostile space activities that deny unrestricted friendly access to space, deny the full capabilities of friendly space assets, or restrict friendly surface resources required by these space assets. Refer to Annex B, Intelligence, for amplifying information.

c. Friendly. Identify all friendly space forces and assets in theater and to be deployed to theater. Identify systems available for communications, environmental, navigation, surveillance, tactical warning, space control, nuclear detonation detection, or other application categories. Identify friendly space weaknesses and vulnerabilities.[45] Describe changes or modifications to established procedures, memorandums of agreement, or memorandums of understanding that may be in effect. Use an appendix for detailed information. Refer to the Annex N of the next higher command and adjacent commands.

d. Assumptions. State any assumptions not included in the basic plan relating to friendly, enemy, or third-party capabilities that may affect, negate, or compromise space capabilities. If any assumptions are critical to the success of the plan, indicate alternative courses of action.

2. Mission

State in concise terms the space tasks to be accomplished in support of the operations in the basic plan and describe desired results in support of this OPLAN.[46]

3. Execution

Space activities may range from satellite communication and intelligence support to space control operations. The functions required may vary greatly within the area of operations or between phases of the operation. This paragraph, therefore, may require considerable detail and possibly alternative courses of action to accomplish the mission. Appendixes should be used as necessary to provide detailed guidance.

a. Concept of Operations. Describe how space operations support the operation. Emphasize the aspects of the basic plan that will require space support and that may affect space capabilities.

1. *General: State the general concept of space operations required to support the forces in the task organization of the OPLAN and briefly describe how space operations fit into the entire operation or refer to the basic plan. Emphasize the aspects of the basic plan that will require space support and that may affect space capabilities. State OPSEC planning guidance for tasks assigned in this annex, and cross-reference other OPSEC planning guidance for functional areas addressed in other annexes.*

2. *Employment: If the operation is phased, discuss the employment of space assets during each phase. Include discussion of priorities of access, usage, and capabilities in each phase. Discuss ability to launch new or replacement space systems.*

b. Space Support. *Identify space support and procedures that will support the OPLAN. Use appendixes for detailed discussion and information.*

1. *Communications: Describe space systems that will support communications plans as described in Annex K. List military and commercial satellites and ground systems that will provide support. If any satellites are not in geostationary orbit, provide orbital data sufficient to determine the time and duration of their availability. Include procedures for obtaining additional SATCOM space and ground assets and allocations. Refer to Annex K, Command, Control, and Communications Systems, for amplifying information.*

2. *Environmental: Describe meteorological, oceanographic, geodetic, and other environmental support information provided by space assets. List receivers and processors available to receive Defense Meteorological Satellite Program (DMSP) and civil weather satellite data. Describe availability of data from the various weather satellites based on transmission schedules, orbital parameters, and so forth. Describe capabilities, products, and availability of multispectral satellite data. Describe provisions to acquire, receive, or gain access to data from weather, multispectral, and other satellites that cannot be received by systems in the theater of operations. Describe provisions to deny the enemy access to data from civil weather satellites. Refer to Annex H, Meteorological and Oceanographic Operations, or Annex L, Environmental Considerations, for amplifying information.*

3. *Precision, Navigation, and Timing: Describe the capabilities of space-based navigation systems that will aid the position location and navigation of ships, vehicles, personnel, or spacecraft. Describe types of GPS receivers available to subordinate units. Identify which receivers are not able to compensate for selective availability. If continuous 3-D coverage is not available, describe outage periods or times of reduced coverage. Describe requirements to jam or spoof GPS receivers that may be in use by the enemy. Describe requirements for differential GPS.*

4. *Reconnaissance, Intelligence, Surveillance, and Target Acquisition (RISTA): Describe capabilities available to friendly forces to include imagery intelligence (IMINT), signals intelligence (SIGINT), measurement and signature intelligence (MASINT), nuclear detonation (NUDET), multispectral, and others. Describe intertheater and intratheater dissemination architecture and procedures. Describe which systems can be used and the type of information they provide. Describe availability of multispectral data, its processing, and products. Refer to Annex B, Intelligence, for amplifying information.*

5. *Tactical Warning: Describe the capabilities of space systems to detect an enemy ballistic missile, attack by space-based weapons, or other enemy activities. Describe coordination and channels needed to disseminate warnings quickly. Identify additional resources needed. Describe linkage and coordination with ground- and air-based radar systems. Identify whether tactical warning data will be passed to allied military forces and civil agencies and the channels to do so. Refer to Annex B, Intelligence, for amplifying information.*

6. *Space Control: Describe actions performed by space, air, or surface assets to ensure friendly forces access to space or deny enemy forces unrestricted use of space and space assets. Include planned or anticipated actions in response to the enemy's use of space or denial of friendly access to space and space systems.*

c. Tasks. Identify tasks for each applicable subordinate unit, supporting command, or agency that provides support to the plan. Provide a concise statement of the task with sufficient detail to ensure that all elements essential to the operational concept are described properly.

d. Coordinating Instructions. Provide necessary guidance common to two or more components, subdivisions, or agencies. Describe liaison requirements, if any.

4. Administration and Logistics. Identify administrative and logistics support for space operations. Address support of mobile or fixed space assets within the theater here, or refer to the annex where this information is available. Reference to Annex D, Logistics, or pertinent command directives may suffice. Identify augmentation requirements for headquarters requiring space operations personnel. Identify operations security (OPSEC) planning guidance and cross-reference other OPSEC planning guidance for functional areas addressed in other annexes. Describe support needed and who will provide it for any space-related ground stations supporting the command. Describe resupply procedures for cryptological supplies.

5. Command and Control (C2)

a. Command Relationships. Identify unique command and control channels and command relationships for space activities. Refer to the appropriate sections of Annex J, Annex K, or the basic plan for general C2 support of space activities. If applicable, state requirements for augmentation of appropriate headquarters with space operations personnel.

b. Command, Control, Communication, and Computer (C4) Systems. Summarize requirements for general C4 support of space activities. Refer to appropriate sections of Annex K.

t /
General
Commander
OFFICIAL
s /
t /
Major General
Director, J-3

* * * * *

Notes

1. AFDD 2-2, *Space Operations*, 27 November 2006, 18.

2. Ibid.

3. JP 5-0, *Joint Operation Planning*, 26 December 2006, I-12.

4. Ibid., III-20.

5. Ibid., IV-34.

6. JP 3-14, *Space Operations*, 6 January 2009, I-4.

7. Ibid., II-7.

8. Ibid.

9. Ibid., IV-10–IV-11.

10. Ibid., I-3.

11. AFDD 2-2, *Space Operations*, 1.

12. JP 1-02, *Department of Defense Dictionary of Military and Associated Terms*, 12 April 2001 (as amended through 17 October 2008), 500.

13. JP 3-14, *Space Operations*, IV-3.

14. Ibid., IV-24–IV-25.

15. CJCS Manual 3122.03, *Joint Operation Planning and Execution System*, vol. 2, *Planning Formats and Guidance*, 17 August 2007, E-N-1.

16. JP 5-0, *Joint Operation Planning*, xi.

17. Ibid.

18. AFDD 2-2, *Space Operations*, 18.

19. JP 3-14, *Space Operations*, V-2.

20. USSTRATCOM, "Joint Functional Component Command for Space Fact Sheet," http://www.stratcom.mil/fact_sheets/fact_space.html (accessed 17 March 2008).

21. AFDD 2-2.1, *Counterspace Operations*, 2 August 2004, 38.

22. AFDD 2-2, *Space Operations*, 19.

23. Maj J. Dave Price, USA, "Life in the Joint Side of Space," *Army Space Journal* 6, no. 1 (Winter 2007): 22.

24. AFDD 2-2, *Space Operations*, 3.

25. Ibid., 20.

26. JP 3-14, *Space Operations*, viii.

27. The Army still utilizes the SST concept.

28. General Accounting Office (GAO), *Improvements Needed in Military Space Systems' Planning and Education* (Washington, DC: GAO, May 2000), 33–34.

29. Ibid., 5.

30. "OPLAN 1002 Defense of the Arabian Peninsula," GlobalSecurity.org, http://www.globalsecurity.org/military/ops/oplan-1002.htm (accessed 24 February 2008).

31. JP 3-14, *Space Operations*, V-2.

32. AFDD 2-2, *Space Operations*, 4–5.

33. JP 3-14, *Space Operations*, V-2.

34. AFDD 2-2, *Space Operations*, 21.

35. Ibid.

36. Lt Col Kendall K. Brown, USAFR, ed., *Space Power Integration: Perspectives from Space Weapons Officers* (Maxwell AFB, AL: Air University Press, 2006), 5.

37. JP 3-14, *Space Operations*, IV-8.

38. AFDD 2-2, *Space Operations*, 21.

39. Ibid., 14.

40. Ibid., 39.

41. CJCS Manual 3122.03, *Joint Operation Planning and Execution System*, vol. 2, E-N-1–E-N-2.

42. JP 3-14, *Space Operations*, V-1.

43. AFDD 2-2, *Space Operations*, 26.

44. Ibid., 32.

45. Ibid., 23.

46. Ibid., 18–19.

Chapter 6

Orbital Mechanics

Maj Edward P. Chatters IV, USAF;

Maj Bryan Eberhardt, USAF; and Maj Michael S. Warner, USAF

Knowledge of orbital motion is essential for a full understanding of space operations. Motion through space can be visualized using the laws described by Johannes Kepler and understood using the laws described by Sir Isaac Newton. Thus, the objectives of this chapter are to provide a conceptual understanding of orbital motion and discuss common terms describing that motion. The chapter is divided into three sections. The first part focuses on the important information regarding satellite orbit types to provide an understanding of the capabilities and limitations of the spaceborne assets supporting the war fighter. The second part covers a brief history of orbital mechanics, providing a detailed description of the Keplerian and Newtonian laws. The third section discusses the application of those laws to determining orbit motion, orbit geometry, and orbital elements. This section has many facts, figures, and equations that may seem overwhelming at times. However, this information is essential to understanding the fundamental concepts of orbital mechanics and provides the necessary foundation to enable war fighters to better appreciate the challenges of operating in the space domain.

Orbit Types

An orbit for a satellite is chosen based on the mission of that particular satellite. For instance, the lower the altitude of a satellite, the better the resolution an onboard camera can have and the shorter the time it takes to travel around the earth (period). On the other hand, the farther out a satellite is, the more of the earth's surface it can observe at one time. Also, the farther the orbit is tilted away from the equator, the more of the earth's surface a satellite will observe over the course of an orbit. These parameters (which will be described in more detail later in the chapter) drive the four basic orbit types: low Earth orbit (LEO), medium Earth orbit (MEO), geosynchronous Earth orbit (GEO), and highly elliptical orbit (HEO). Table 6-1 lists the various orbit types and the missions associated with each one.

Low Earth Orbit Satellites

LEO satellites orbit the earth at an altitude between approximately 100 and 1,000 statute miles (160 to 1,600 km) by the laws of orbits corresponding to periods of about 100 minutes to go around the earth. At these altitudes, onboard sensors have the best resolution, communication systems require the least power to talk to the earth, and rockets require the least energy to get them to orbit. LEO satellites can be divided into three general categories: polar sun-synchronous, polar non-sun-synchronous, and inclined nonpolar.

Table 6-1. Orbit types

Orbit Type	Mission	Altitude	Period	Tilt[a]	Shape
LEO					
• Polar sun-synchronous	Remote sensing/ weather	~150–900 km	~98–104 min	~98°	circular
• Inclined nonpolar	International Space Station	~340 km	~91 min	~51.6°	circular
• Polar non-sun-synchronous	Earth observing, scientific	~450–600 km	~90–101 min	~80–94°	circular
MEO					
• Semisynchronous	Navigation, communications, space environment	~20,100 km	~12 hours	~55°	circular
GEO					
• Geosynchronous	Communication, early warning, nuclear detection, weather	~35,786 km	~24 hours (23h 56m 04s)	~0°	circular
• Geostationary					
HEO					
• Molniya	Communications	Varies from ~495 km to ~39,587 km	~12 hours (11h 58m)	63.4°	long ellipse

[a]Orbits roughly stay in the same plane. This indicates the tilt or inclination of this plane relative to the equator. Near zero is along the equator, and near 90° is over the poles. Greater than 90° indicates against the rotation of the earth.

The term *inclined nonpolar orbit* refers to all LEO satellites that are not in near-polar orbits.[1] The inclination of the orbit is equal to the maximum latitude the satellite will pass over. Thus, this type of orbit is used when global coverage of the earth is not needed. The chosen inclination is ordinarily the latitude of the launch site to maximize the amount of energy gained from the rotation of the earth. The International Space Station and space shuttle fall into this orbit category. Figure 6-1 shows an example of an inclined nonpolar orbiting satellite ground track.

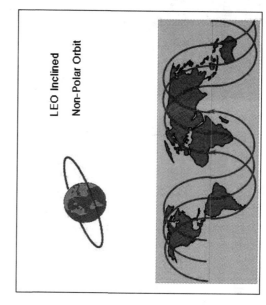

LEO Inclined Non-Polar Orbit

Figure 6-1. Inclined nonpolar orbit. (*Created by* Air Command and Staff College [ACSC])

90

A polar non–sun-synchronous orbit is like the previous orbit except that the inclination is nearly polar. This type of orbit is used to maximize the coverage of the earth—every latitude will ultimately be passed over, and because of the fast period, a large part of the earth's surface will be seen each day. All the earth's surface will ultimately be overflown. This type of orbit is commonly used for constellations of communication satellites.

One phenomenon affecting a polar, non–sun-synchronous orbit is that, because the earth is not a perfect sphere, the orbit will drift (or precess) over time. If the designers want the orbit to pass over a specific point on the earth at a specific time each day, a polar sun-synchronous orbit is needed. In this type of orbit, a specific altitude and inclination are picked such that the natural orbit precession exactly matches the rate that the earth orbits the sun [(360° per year)/(365.25 days per year) = .986° per day].[2] An example of a polar sun-synchronous satellite orbit and corresponding ground track is shown in figure 6-2.

Medium Earth Orbit Satellites

MEO satellites orbit the earth at an altitude between approximately 1,000 and 12,000 statute miles (1,600 to 19,300 km), corresponding to periods between 100 minutes and 12 hours. Medium Earth orbits are used to provide longer dwell times over a given region and a larger coverage area of the earth as compared to LEO satellites. In addition, the higher altitude above the earth reduces the effects of atmospheric drag to effectively zero. MEO satellite missions include navigation systems such as GPS.[3]

An example of an MEO satellite, a semisynchronous satellite ground track, can be seen in figure 6-3. This orbit, with an orbital period of approximately 12 hours, repeats twice a day. Since the earth turns halfway on its axis during each complete orbit, the points where the sinusoidal ground tracks cross the equator coincide pass after pass, and the ground tracks repeat each day as shown. This predictability is very helpful for ground stations monitoring the satellite.

Geosynchronous Earth Orbit Satellites

GEO satellites orbit the earth at an altitude of 22,236 statute miles (35,786 km). At this altitude, a satellite in a circular orbit and zero inclination will have an orbital period equal to the earth's rotational period (approximately 24 hours). This allows a satellite to remain relatively fixed over a particular point on the earth's surface. At an altitude of 22,236 miles, one geosynchronous satellite has a commanding field of view of almost one-third of the earth's surface from approximately 75° south latitude to

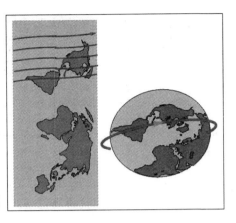

Figure 6-2. Sun-synchronous orbit. (*Adapted from* Air University, *Space Primer,* unpublished book, 2003, 8-18.)

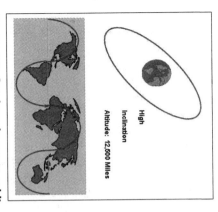

High
Inclination
Altitude: 12,500 Miles

Figure 6-3. Semisynchronous orbit. (*Adapted from* Air University, *Space Primer,* unpublished book, 2003, 8-18.)

approximately 75° north latitude.[4] Therefore, geosynchronous orbits are desirable for communications and early warning systems. However, this altitude and inclination are the most difficult to achieve, especially for nations without an equatorial launch site.

The terms *geosynchronous* and *geostationary* have been used interchangeably, but there is a distinct difference between the two. *Geosynchronous* refers to a satellite with a 24-hour period, regardless of inclination. *Geostationary* refers to a satellite with a 24-hour period, in a near-circular orbit, with an inclination of approximately zero. It appears to hover over a spot on the equator as shown in figure 6-4. All geostationary orbits must be geosynchronous, but not all geosynchronous orbits are necessarily geostationary.[5] An example of a nongeostationary satellite would be the *Syncom 2*, launched in 1963 into a geosynchronous orbit with a 33° inclination.[6]

Now take the same orbit and give it an inclination of 30°. The period and orbit shape remain the same. The ground trace will retrace itself with every orbit, in this case in a figure-eight pattern. The ground trace will also vary between 30° north and 30° south latitude due to its 30° inclination. In another example, if the geostationary satellite has an eccentricity near zero and an inclination of 60°, the ground trace would follow a similar, larger figure-eight path between 60° north and 60° south latitude as shown in figure 6-5.

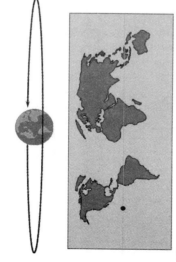

Figure 6-4. Geostationary orbit/ground track. (*Adapted from* Air University, *Space Primer*, unpublished book, 2003, 8-17.)

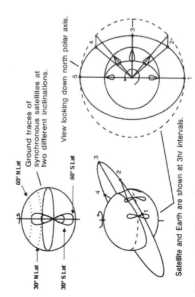

Figure 6-5. Ground traces of inclined, circular, synchronous satellites. (*Adapted from* Air University, *Space Primer*, unpublished book, 2003, 8-17.)

Highly Elliptical Orbit Satellites

All the orbits discussed thus far have been circular. However, orbits can also take on an elliptical shape. HEO satellites are the most common noncircular orbits, and they orbit the earth at altitudes which vary between approximately 660 and 24,000 statute miles (1,060 and 38,624 km) in a single period.[7] Satellites travel faster the closer they are to the earth, so HEO orbits enable long dwell times as well as large fields of view when at their farthest points from the earth (apogee). They are primarily used for communications, scientific research, and intelligence, surveillance, and reconnaissance (ISR) missions when GEO orbits are inaccessible.

The most popular highly elliptical orbit is the "Molniya" orbit, named after the Russian word for lightning to describe the speed at which a satellite in this particular orbit travels through its closest point of approach (perigee).[8] Figure 6-6 shows a typical Molniya orbit that might be used for northern hemispheric communications.

With an orbital period of 12 hours, the ground track retraces itself every day, just like the medium Earth, semisynchronous orbit of GPS.

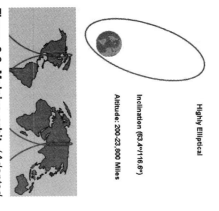

Figure 6-6. Molniya orbit. (*Adapted from Air University,* Space Primer, *unpublished book, 2003, 8-18.*)

Highly Elliptical

Inclination (63.4°/116.6°)

Altitude: 200-23,800 Miles

A History of the Laws of Motion

The modern orbit types have been developed based on theories dating back centuries. The early Greeks initiated the orbital theories, postulating that the earth was fixed, with the planets and other celestial bodies moving around it—a geocentric universe.[9] About 300 BC, Aristarchus of Samos suggested that the sun was fixed and the planets, including Earth, were in circular orbits around the sun—a heliocentric universe.[10] Although Aristarchus was more correct (at least about a heliocentric solar system), his ideas were too revolutionary for the time. Other prominent astronomers/philosophers were held in higher esteem, and since they favored the geocentric theory, Aristarchus's heliocentric theory was rejected, and the geocentric theory continued to be predominately accepted for many centuries.

In the year 1543, some 1,800 years after Aristarchus proposed a heliocentric system, a Polish monk named Nicolas Koppernias (better known by his Latin name, Copernicus) revived the heliocentric theory when he published *De Revolutionibus Orbium Coelestium* (*On the Revolutions of the Celestial Spheres*). This work represented an advance, but there were still some inaccuracies. For example, Copernicus thought that the orbital paths of all planets were circles around the center of the sun.[11]

Tycho Brahe established an astronomical observatory on the island of Hven in 1576. For 20 years, he and his assistants carried out the most complete and accurate astronomical observations of the period. However, Brahe did not accept Copernicus's heliocentric theory and instead believed in a geo-heliocentric model that had the moon and sun revolving around the earth while the rest of the celestial bodies revolved around the sun.[12]

German astronomer Johannes Kepler, born in 1571, wondered why there were only six planets and what determined their separation. His theories required data from observations of the planets, and he realized that the best way to acquire such data was to become Brahe's assistant.

In 1600, Brahe set Kepler to work on the motion of Mars. This task was particularly difficult because Mars's orbit was the second most eccentric (of the then-known planets) and defied the circular explanation. After Brahe's death in 1601, Kepler finally discovered that Mars's orbit (and that of all planets) was represented by an ellipse with the sun at one of its foci.[13]

Kepler's Laws of Planetary Motion

Kepler's discovery of Mars's elliptical orbit led to another discovery—the first of his three laws of planetary motion, which describe the orbit of the planets around the sun.

Kepler's First Law (Law of Ellipses). *The orbits of the planets are ellipses with the sun at one focus.*[14] Figure 6-7 shows an ellipse where O^1 is one focus and O is the other. This depiction illustrates that, by definition, an ellipse is a closed curve such that the sum of the distances ($R1$ and $R2$) from any point (P) on the curve to the two foci (O^1 and O) remains constant.[15]

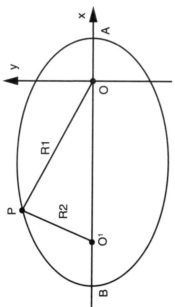

Figure 6-7. Kepler's first law. *(Created by ACSC)*

The maximum diameter of an ellipse is called its major axis; the minimum diameter is the minor axis. The size of an ellipse depends in part upon the length of its major axis. The shape of an ellipse is denoted by eccentricity (*e*), which is the ratio of the distance between the foci to the length of the major axis (see the orbit geometry section in this chapter).

The paths of ballistic missiles (not including the powered and reentry portion) are also ellipses; however, they happen to intersect the earth's surface (as shown in fig. 6-8).

Kepler's Second Law (Law of Equal Areas). *The line joining the planet to the sun sweeps out equal areas in equal times.*[16] Based on his observation, Kepler reasoned that a planet's speed depended on its distance from the sun.

Kepler's second law is easy to visualize in figure 6-9, where t_0, t_1, and so forth indicate time. If the object in figure 6-9 were in a circular orbit (versus the elliptical orbit shown), its speed and radius would both remain constant, and, therefore, over a given interval of time the "shape" of area 1 and area 2 would be identical. It is also apparent from figure 6-9 that the closer a planet is to the sun along the elliptical orbit, the faster it travels. The same principle applies to satellites orbiting the earth, as especially noted in the Molniya orbit discussed earlier.

Kepler's Third Law (Law of Harmonics). *The square of the orbital period of a planet is proportional to the cube of the mean distance from the sun.*[17] Kepler's third law directly relates the square of the period to the cube of the mean distance for orbiting

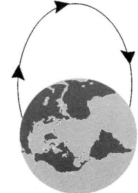

Figure 6-8. Ballistic missile path. *(Adapted from Air University, Space Primer, unpublished book, 2003, 8-5.)*

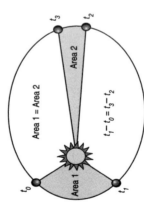

Figure 6-9. Kepler's second law. *(Adapted from Air University, Space Primer, unpublished book, 2003, 8-6.)*

objects. By this law, the altitude of a circular orbit uniquely determines how long it will take to travel around the earth and vice versa.[18] Thus, geostationary orbits, which must have a period of 24 hours, must be at an altitude of 24,000 miles. LEO satellites likewise cannot hover over a spot on the earth.

Newton's Laws of Motion

The laws Kepler developed describe very well the observed motions of the planets, but they made no attempt to describe the forces behind those laws. The laws regarding those forces would be key to ultimately developing artificial satellites. This work was formulated by Sir Isaac Newton.

In 1665, an outbreak of the plague forced the University of Cambridge to close for two years. During those two years, the 23-year-old genius Isaac Newton conceived the law of gravitation, the laws of motion, and the fundamental concepts of differential calculus. Twenty years later the result appeared in *The Mathematical Principles of Natural Philosophy*, or simply the *Principia*,[19] which formulated a grand view that was consistent and capable of describing and unifying the mundane motion of a falling apple and the motion of the planets.

Newton's First Law (Inertia). *Every body continues in a state of rest, or of uniform motion in a straight line, unless it is compelled to change that state by a force imposed upon it.*[20] Newton's first law describes undisturbed motion. Inertia is the resistance of mass to changes in its motion.

Newton's Second Law (Changing Momentum). *When a force is applied to a body, the time rate of change of momentum is proportional to, and in the direction of, the applied force.* Newton's second law describes how motion changes. It is important to define momentum before describing the second law. Momentum is a measure of an object's motion. Momentum (**p**) is a vector quantity (denoted by boldface type) defined as the product of an object's mass (*m*) and its relative velocity (**v**).

$$p = mv$$

If there is a change in momentum (Δp), assuming the mass of the object remains the same, then there must be a change in velocity (Δv) of the object as well. As a result, we have the following equation:

$$\Delta p = m\,\Delta v$$

Force (**F**) is defined as the time rate of change of an object's momentum.

$$F = \frac{\Delta p}{\Delta t} = \frac{m\,\Delta v}{\Delta t}$$

95

Acceleration (a) is defined as the change in velocity over time ($\Delta v / \Delta t$). As a result, this second law becomes Newton's famous equation:

$$F = ma$$

Newton's Third Law (Action-Reaction). *For every action there is a reaction that is equal in magnitude but opposite in direction to the action.*[21] This law hints at conservation of momentum. If forces are always balanced, then the objects experiencing the opposed forces will change their momentum in opposite directions and equal amounts.

Newton's Law of Universal Gravitation. *Every particle in the universe attracts every other particle with a force that is proportional to the product of the masses and inversely proportional to the square of the distance between the particles.*[22]

$$F_g = G \left(\frac{M_1 m_2}{R^2} \right)$$

In the above equation, F_g is the force due to gravity, G is the universal gravitational constant with a set value of 6.67259×10^{-11} m³kg⁻¹s⁻², M_1 and m_2 are the masses of the central body (the earth, for example) and orbiting bodies, and R is the distance between the centers of the two bodies.[23] This law, in association with the second law, allows scientists and engineers to connect the forces applied (such as gravity) to the acceleration. When the position and velocity are known, the gravity force can be calculated. Knowing the gravity acceleration will change the position and velocity. Plotting the altitude over time for a satellite yields an orbit.

In this way, engineers can also calculate the necessary orbit velocities and the subsequent amounts of force necessary to launch a satellite into space.[24] The force (F) required will determine the type of booster (Delta IV, Delta II, space shuttle, etc.) that is selected to launch the satellite.

Once the satellite is at the right spot (position) going a certain speed (velocity), the orbit will be established and predictable using the laws above. The solutions to the equations above also match Kepler's observations of the planets, thus establishing that satellites would move the same way. However, with additional velocity, satellites do not have to travel only in ellipses; they can also travel on parabolas or hyperbolas. This knowledge is key to understanding interplanetary travel.

Orbital Motion

So what is the velocity and position a body needs to get into orbit? According to Newton's second law, for a body to change its motion a force must be imposed upon it. An example is playing catch—when a ball is thrown or caught, its motion is altered. Thus, gravity is compensated for by throwing the ball upward by some angle allowing gravity to pull it down, resulting in an arc. When the ball leaves the hand, it starts accelerating toward the ground according to Newton's laws (at sea level on the earth the acceleration is approximately 9.8 meters per second [m/s] or 32 feet [ft.] per second straight down).[25] If the ball is initially motionless, it will fall straight down. However, if the ball has some horizontal motion, it will continue in that motion while accelerating toward the ground. Figure 6-10 shows a ball released with varying lateral (or horizontal) velocities.

In figure 6-10, if the initial height of the ball is approximately 4.9 meters (16.1 ft.) above the ground, then at sea level, it would take one second for the ball to hit the ground. How far the ball travels along the ground in that one second depends on its horizontal velocity (table 6-2).

Eventually one would come to the point where the earth's surface drops away as fast as the ball drops toward it. As figure 6-11 depicts, the earth's surface curves down about five meters for every eight kilometers.[26]

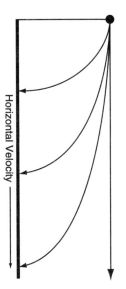

Figure 6-10. Newton's second law. (*Adapted from Air University, Space Primer, unpublished book, 2003, 8-9.*)

Horizontal Velocity →

Table 6-2. Gravitational effects.

Horizontal velocity (m/s)[a]	Distance travelled in one second (m)	
	Vertical	Horizontal
1	4.9	1
2	4.9	2
4	4.9	4
8	4.9	8
16	4.9	16

[a] All values are in meters and meters per second.

hit the ground, the earth will have curved away from the body.

At the earth's surface (without accounting for the atmosphere, mountains, or other structures), a satellite would have to travel at approximately 8 km/second (km/sec) (or about 17,900 mph) to fall around the earth without hitting the surface. In other words, the satellite would have to travel 17,900 mph to remain in orbit at the earth's surface (at a height of approximately zero). This is fundamentally what it means to be in orbit—travelling fast enough forward that by the time the orbiting body would ordinarily

However, the earth does have an atmosphere, and to stay in a relatively stable orbit, a satellite has to be positioned at an orbital height above the denser parts of the earth's atmosphere. The minimum height is approximately 150 km (about 93 miles) above the earth's surface. To remain in orbit at this height, a satellite must travel at 7.8 km/sec (or 17,500 mph).[27] At this speed, the orbital period of

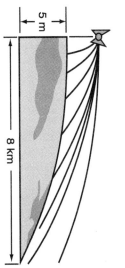

Figure 6-11. Earth's curvature. (*Adapted from Air University, Space Primer, unpublished book, 2003, 8-10.*)

5 m

8 km

the satellite would be 87.5 minutes. A period of less than 87.5 minutes indicates that the object is "decaying" due to the effects of atmospheric drag and will eventually reenter the earth's atmosphere and fall back to Earth. This would ordinarily cause the object to burn up. Thus, the job of a rocket is to carry a satellite above the main part of the atmosphere and then get it travelling at the right speed. Once the satellite is released, it is in orbit.

At higher altitudes, the speed needed to maintain an orbit is less, much like the speed needed to keep a ball on the end of a string horizontal. Figure 6-12 shows how differing velocities affect a satellite's trajectory or orbital path. The figure depicts a satellite at an altitude of one Earth radius (6,378 km above the earth's surface). At this distance, a satellite would have to travel at 5.59 km/sec (12,500 mph) to maintain a circular orbit, and this speed is known as the satellite's circular velocity for this altitude. As the satellite's speed increases, it moves away from the earth, and its trajectory becomes an elongating ellipse until the speed reaches 7.91 km/sec (17,700 mph). At this speed and altitude the satellite has enough energy to leave the earth's gravity and never return. Its trajectory has now become a parabola, and this velocity is known as its escape velocity for this altitude.[28] The equations for circular velocity (v_c) and escape velocity (v_e) are as follows:

$$v_c = \sqrt{\frac{GM_E}{r}} \qquad v_e = \sqrt{\frac{2GM_E}{r}}$$

In these equations, G is the gravitational constant (6.67259 x 10^{-11} m³kg⁻¹s⁻²), M_E is the mass of the earth (approximately 5.977 x 10^{24} kilograms [kg]), and r is the distance of the satellite from the center of the earth (i.e., the altitude plus 6,378 km).

As an example, from a low Earth orbit of 161 km (100 miles), the escape velocity becomes 11.2 km/sec (25,050 mph). In figure 6-12, the two specific velocities (5.59 km/sec and 7.91 km/sec) correspond to the circular and escape velocities for the specific altitude of one Earth radius (6,378 km).

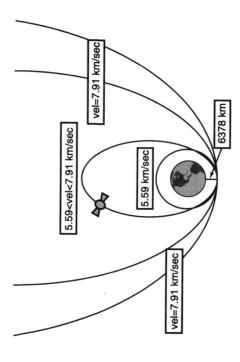

Figure 6-12. Velocity versus trajectory. (*Adapted from Air University, Space Primer, unpublished book, 2003, 8-10.*)

Constants of Orbital Motion: Momentum and Energy

For a satellite, if you know the position and velocity when the satellite is released from the rocket, you can use Newton's laws to plot out the long-term trajectory. However, to compare orbits, it is helpful to have some common parameters to describe them (like altitude and eccentricity, as described above). This section explores how to find some of those constants to help visualize an orbit.

For a system such as a satellite affected only by gravity (i.e., no drag or thrust), some basic properties remain constant or fixed; that is, they are conserved. Energy and momentum are two such properties which are conservative in such a closed system.

Momentum. Linear momentum is the product of mass times velocity, as discussed previously in Newton's second law. For rotating or spinning bodies, such as a satellite orbiting the earth, a second form of this law is formulated to describe motion in angular terms. Angular momentum ($\bar{H}$) is the product of the linear momentum of an object (i.e., satellite) times the object's position from the center of rotation (the center of the earth): $\bar{H} = m(\bar{r} \times \bar{v})$.[29] This property remains constant for orbiting objects which are not torqued.

In an elliptical orbit, the radius (R) is constantly varying. Thus, for angular momentum to be conserved, the orbital speed must change. Hence, there is greater velocity at perigee than at apogee. Also, since the direction of the angular momentum is also conserved, the plane formed by the rotating object is fixed. Thus, unless an orbit is torque, the orbit plane will not drift through space.

Energy. A system's mechanical energy can also be conserved. Total mechanical energy (E) is derived from an object's position and motion and is usually depicted as the sum of kinetic energy (KE) and gravitational potential energy (PE):[30]

$$E = KE + PE$$

Kinetic energy is the energy associated with an object's motion, and gravitational potential energy is the energy associated with an object's position. Potential energy is measured relative to the center of the earth (hence, it is not the "mgh" you may have learned in high school). Potential energy is the mass of an object (m_1) times the earth's gravitational acceleration (M_2G) over the height above the earth's center. Kinetic energy (KE) is expressed as one-half an object's mass times the square of the object's velocity.[31] These equations are expressed as follows:

$$KE = \frac{1}{2}mv^2 \qquad PE = m_1M_2G/R$$

The Law of Conservation of Energy in its simplest form states that, under the premise that energy cannot be created or destroyed, the sum of all energies (in this case total mechanical energy [E]) in a particular system remains constant unless energy is added (such as by thrust) or taken away (such as by drag).[32] Therefore, any increase in kinetic energy will result in a proportional decrease in gravitational potential energy (KE) is expressed as one-half an object's mass times the square of the object's velocity since the value of total mechanical energy (E) will not change.

Hence, in a circular orbit where the radius remains constant, so will the velocity, as both gravitational potential and kinetic energy remain constant. In all other orbits (elliptical, parabolic, and hyperbolic), the "radius" and speed both change, and therefore, so do both the gravitational potential and kinetic energies in such a way that the total mechanical energy of the system remains constant. Again, for an elliptical orbit, this results in greater velocity at perigee than apogee.

Orbit Geometry

When Newton's second law is combined with his gravitational law, the solutions are all conic sections, which are shapes that can be made by slicing off sections of a cone at various angles. The conic section an object will follow depends on its kinetic and potential energy as described above. Conic sections consist of four types: circular, elliptical, parabolic, and hyperbolic. If an object lacks the velocity (insufficient kinetic energy, $KE < PE$) to overcome the earth's gravitational attraction, then it will follow a closed-path orbit in the form of a circle or ellipse. However, if the object has enough velocity (kinetic energy equal in magnitude to the gravitational potential energy in the absence of friction resistance, $KE = PE$) to overcome the earth's gravitational attraction, then the object will follow an open path in the shape of a parabolic orbit. Finally, if the object has excess velocity (more than sufficient kinetic energy, $KE > PE$) to overcome the earth's gravitational attraction, then the object will follow an open path in the shape of a hyperbolic orbit.[33] Figure 6-13 shows a three-dimensional representation of the various possible conic sections (orbit geometries).

Figure 6-14 shows a two-dimensional representation of the conic section geometry. The parameters that describe the size and shape of the conic are its semimajor axis (a) and eccentricity (e). The semimajor axis, a measure of the orbit's size, is half the distance between perigee and apogee; it is also the average distance from the attracting body's center. Eccentricity, which describes the orbit's shape, is the ratio of the linear eccentricity (c) to the semimajor axis. The linear eccentricity (c) is half the distance between the two foci.

These parameters apply to all trajectories. A circular orbit is a special case of the elliptical orbit where the foci coincide ($c = 0$). Figure 6-15 depicts a satellite orbit with additional parameters whose conic section is an ellipse.

Coordinate Reference Systems and Orbital Elements

All positions and velocities have to be measured with respect to a fixed frame of reference. Many such frames exist—which is used depends on the situation and the nature of the knowledge to be retrieved. Table 6-3 lists several common coordinate reference systems that are used for space applications.[34] For describing the orbit itself, the Earth-centered inertial (ECI) system is used, while the other two describe how the satellite is oriented within that frame.

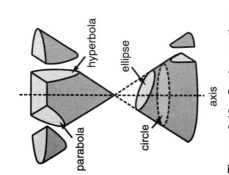

Figure 6-13. Conic sections. (*Reprinted from* David P. Stern, "Kepler's Three Laws of Planetary Motion: An Overview for Science Teachers," http://www.phy6.org/stargaze/Kep3laws.htm [accessed 18 April 2008].)

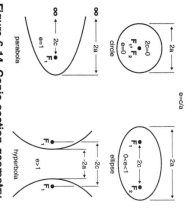

Figure 6-14. Conic section geometry. *(Adapted from* Air University, *Space Primer,* unpublished book, 2003, 8-11.)

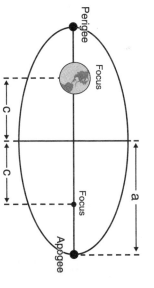

Figure 6-15. Elliptical geometry. *(Adapted from* Air University, *Space Primer,* unpublished book, 2003, 8-11.)

Table 6-3. Coordinate reference systems.

Coordinate Name	Fixed with Respect to	Center	Z-axis or Pole	X-axis or Reference Direction	Applications
Earth-centered inertial (ECI)	Inertial space	Earth	Celestial pole	Vernal equinox (J2000.0 reference frame)	Orbit analysis, astronomy, inertial motion
Spacecraft-fixed	Spacecraft	Defined by engineering drawings	Spacecraft axis toward nadir	Spacecraft axis in direction of velocity vector	Position and orientation of spacecraft instruments
Roll, pitch, yaw	Orbit	Spacecraft	Nadir	Perpendicular to nadir toward velocity vector	Earth observation attitude maneuvers

Adapted from Wiley J. Larson and James R. Wertz, ed., *Spacecraft Mission Analysis and Design,* 3rd ed. (El Segundo, CA: Microcosm Press, 1999), 96.

In three-dimensional space, the position and velocity each have three components in each dimension. Therefore, any element set defining a satellite's orbital motion contains at least six parameters to fully describe that motion. The Keplerian, or classical, element set is useful for space operations and tells us four attributes of orbits: orbit size, orbit shape, orientation (to include orbital plane in space and orbit within plane), and location of the satellite at any point in time during its orbit. The most popular Keplerian element set format is the two-line element (TLE) set, which will be discussed later in this chapter.

Orbit Size. The orbit size is described by the semimajor axis (a)—half the distance between apogee and perigee on the ellipse.

Orbit Shape. Eccentricity (e) measures the shape of an orbit. Recall from the discussion of orbit geometry above that eccentricity is a ratio of the foci separation (linear eccentricity [c]) to the size (semimajor axis [a]) of the orbit.

$$e = c/a$$

Size and shape relate to orbit geometry and tell what the orbit looks like. The other orbital elements deal with orientation of the orbit relative to a fixed point in space. With energy being conserved, both e and a are constant.

Orientation. The first angle used to orient the orbital plane is inclination (i)—a measurement of the orbital plane's tilt relative to the equatorial plane. It is measured counterclockwise at the point at which an object crosses the equatorial plane traveling north in its orbit (the ascending node) while looking toward Earth as shown in figure 6-16.[35]

Inclination is utilized to define several general classes of orbits as shown in figure 6-17. Orbits with inclinations equal to 0° or 180° are equatorial orbits, because the orbital plane is contained within the equatorial plane. If an orbit has an inclination of 90°, it is a polar orbit, because it travels over the poles. If 0°≤i<90°, the satellite orbits in the same direction as the earth's rotation (orbiting eastward around the earth) and is called a prograde orbit. If 90°<i≤180°, the satellite orbits in the opposite direction of the earth's rotation (orbiting westward about the earth) and is in a retrograde orbit.

The second measure used to orient the orbital plane is the right ascension of the ascending node (Ω—uppercase Greek letter omega). It measures where the ascending node is relative to a reference line within the ECI coordinate system eastward to the ascending node (0°≤Ω≤360°) as shown in figure 6-18.[36] It is mostly used to space out constellations of similar satellites.

The reference line is established by drawing a line from the center of the sun through the center of the earth and extending out into space as the earth crosses the sun's equatorial (ecliptic) plane.[37] These crossings occur twice a

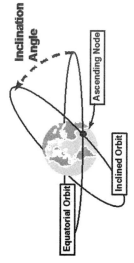

Figure 6-16. Inclination tilt. (*Adapted from Air University, Space Primer, unpublished book, 2003, 8-13.*)

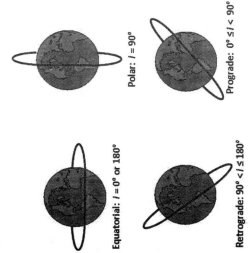

Figure 6-17. Orbital inclination types. (*Created by ACSC*)

year and are called the vernal or autumnal equinox (the first day of spring or fall). For astronomical purposes we use the spring or vernal equinox to establish our reference point. When first established as the reference point, this line pointed to the constellation Aries, hence the name "first point of Aries" (fig. 6-19).[38]

Argument of Perigee. Inclination and right ascension fix the orbital plane in space. The orbit must also be fixed within the orbital plane. For elliptical orbits, the perigee is the reference point in the orbit. The argument of perigee (ω—lowercase Greek letter omega) is used, and it is the angle within the orbital plane from the ascending node to perigee in the direction of satellite motion (0°≤ω≤360°) (fig. 6-20).[39]

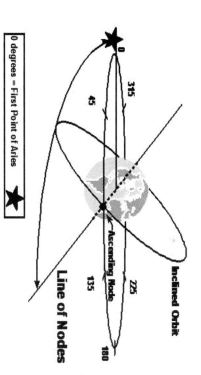

Figure 6-18. Right ascension of the ascending node. (*Adapted from* Air University, *Space Primer*, unpublished book, 2003, 8-11.)

True Anomaly. At this point all the orbital parameters needed to visualize the orbit in space have been specified. In fact, due to conservation of momentum and energy, the parameters are all constant unless the orbit is perturbed. The final step is to locate the satellite within its orbit. Trueanomaly(v—lowercase Greek letter nu) is an angular measurement that describes where the satellite is in its orbit at a specified time. It is measured within the orbital plane from perigee to the satellite's position in the direction of motion (0°≤v≤360°).[40]

True anomaly locates the satellite with respect to time and is the only orbital element that changes with time.[41] The true anomaly cannot be defined in cases where the eccentricity is exactly zero (perfectly circular orbit) since there would be no perigee from which to measure. Likewise, the argument of perigee is undefined for a circular orbit (which has no perigee), and the right ascension of the ascending node is undefined for an equatorial orbit (which never crosses the equator).

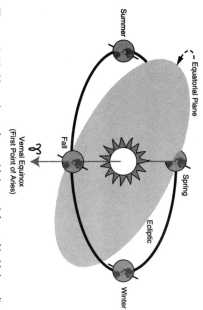

Figure 6-19. Vernal equinox. (*Adapted from* Air University, *Space Primer*, unpublished book, 2003, 8-14.)

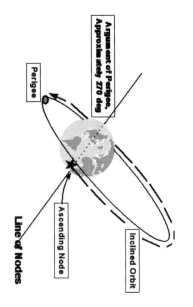

Figure 6-20. Argument of perigee. (*Adapted from* Air University, *Space Primer*, unpublished book, 2003, 8-13.)

103

Table 6-4 summarizes the Keplerian orbital element set and orbit geometry and its relationship to the earth.[42]

Table 6-4. Classical orbital elements.

Element	Name	Description	Definition	Remarks
a	semimajor axis	orbit size	half the long axis of the ellipse	orbital period and energy depend on orbit size
e	eccentricity	orbit *shape*	ratio of half the foci separation (c) to the semimajor axis (a)	closed orbits: $0 \le e < 1$ open orbits: $e \ge 1$
i	inclination	orbital plane's *tilt*	angle between the orbital plane and equatorial plane, measured counterclockwise at the ascending node	equatorial: $i = 0°$ or $180°$ prograde: $0° \le i < 90°$ polar: $i = 90°$ retrograde: $90° < i \le 180°$
Ω	right ascension of the ascending node	orbital plane's *rotation* about the earth	angle, measured eastward, from the vernal equinox to the ascending node	$0° \le \Omega < 360°$ undefined when $i = 0°$ or $180°$ (equatorial orbit)
ω	argument of perigee	orbit's *orientation* in the orbital plane	angle, measured in the direction of satellite motion, from the ascending node to perigee	$0° \le \omega < 360°$ undefined when $i = 0°$ or $180°$, or $e = 0$ (circular orbit)
ν	true anomaly	satellite's *location* in its orbit	angle, measured in the direction of satellite motion, from perigee to the satellite's location	$0° \le \nu < 360°$ undefined when $e = 0$ (circular orbit)

Two-Line Element Sets

The way the orbital elements are usually presented to space personnel is through the TLE set. It is used by agencies such as NASA and USSTRATCOM to describe the location of satellites orbiting the earth. The two-line element set actually has three lines. The first line is reserved for the satellite's name.[43] The next two lines in essence describe the "address" of the satellite (fig. 6-21). The components of the two-line element set are defined by NASA as follows:[44]

Name of Satellite (*NOAA 6*). This is simply the name associated with the satellite. *NOAA 6* is a weather satellite operated by the National Oceanic and Atmospheric Administration.

International Designator (*84 123A*). The *84* indicates that the launch year was 1984. The *123* indicates that this launch was the 123rd of the year and *A* shows it was the first object resulting from this launch.

Figure 6-21. TLE set format. (*Reprinted from NASA, "Definition of Two-Line Element Set Coordinate System," Human Space Flight Web site, http://spaceflight.nasa.gov/realdata/sightings/SSapplications/Post/JavaSSOP/SSOP_Help/tle_def.html [accessed 18 April 2008]).*

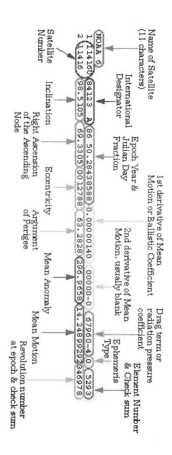

Epoch Date and Julian Date Fraction (86 50.28438588). The Julian date fraction is just the number of days passed in the particular year. For example, the date above shows 86 as the epoch year (1986), and the Julian date fraction of 50.28438588 means a little over 50 days after 1 January 1986. The resulting time of the vector would be 1986/050:06:49:30.94, computed as follows:

Start with 50.28438588 days (days = 50)

50.28438588 days - 50 = 0.28438588 days

0.28438588 days x 24 hours/day = 6.8253 hours (hours = 6)

6.8253 hours - 6 = 0.8253 hours

0.8253 hours x 60 minutes/hour = 49.5157 minutes (minutes = 49)

49.5157 - 49 = 0.5157 minutes

0.5157 minutes x 60 seconds/minute = 30.94 seconds (seconds = 30.94)

Ballistic Coefficient (0.00000140). Also called the first derivative of mean motion, the ballistic coefficient is the daily rate of change in the number of revolutions (revs) the object completes each day, divided by two. Units are revs/day. This is a "catch all" term used in the Simplified General Perturbations (SGP4) USSTRATCOM predictor to represent the atmospheric drag slowing down a satellite. Mean motion is the average angular rate of a satellite, reflecting that any satellite with a distinct apogee and perigee would change speeds over the course of an orbit. For a circular orbit, the ballistic coefficient would be a constant.

Second Derivative of Mean Motion (00000-0 = 0.00000). The second derivative of mean motion is a second-order drag term in the SGP4 predictor used to model terminal orbit decay. It measures the second time derivative in daily mean motion, divided by six. Units are revs/day^3. A leading decimal must be applied to this value. The last two characters define an applicable power of 10 (12345-5 = 0.0000012345).

Drag Term (67960-4 = 0.000067960). Also called the radiation pressure coefficient (or BSTAR), the parameter is another drag term in the SGP4 predictor. Units are Earth radii^-1. The last two characters define an applicable power of 10. Do not confuse this parameter with "B-Term," the USSTRATCOM special perturbations factor of drag coefficient, multiplied by reference area, divided by weight.

Element Set Number and Check Sum (5293). The element set number is a running count of all TLE sets generated by USSTRATCOM for this object (in this example, 529). Since multiple agencies perform this function, numbers are skipped on occasion to avoid ambiguities. The counter should always increase with time until it exceeds 999, when it reverts to one. The last number of the line is the check sum of line one. A check sum (or checksum) is simply a value used in computer programming to verify the validity of the information contained within that particular line of information or line of computer code. It is used to check whether errors occurred during the transmission or storage of data.[45]

Satellite Number (11416U). This is the catalog number that USSTRATCOM has designated for this object. A *U* indicates an unclassified object.

Inclination (98.5105). The angle, in degrees, is the mean inclination.

Right Ascension of the Ascending Node (69.3305). The angle, in degrees, is the mean right ascension of the ascending node.

Eccentricity (0012788). The value is the mean eccentricity over the orbit. A leading decimal must be applied to this value.

Argument of Perigee (63.2828). This value is the mean argument of perigee over the orbit.

Mean Anomaly (296.9658). The mean anomaly is the angle, in degrees, measured from perigee of the satellite location in the orbit referenced to a circular orbit with the radius equal to the semimajor axis.

Mean Motion (14.24899292). The value is the mean number of orbits per day the object completes. There are eight digits after the decimal, leaving no trailing space(s) when the following element exceeds 9999. The period of the satellite's orbit can be determined by taking the total number of minutes in a sidereal day (1,436 minutes) and dividing it by the mean motion. For this particular satellite, the period would be 1,436 ÷ 14.24899292 = 101.06 minutes.

Revolution Number and Check Sum (346978). This is the orbit number at epoch time. This time is chosen very near the time of true ascending node passage as a matter of routine. At the time of this element set, the *NOAA 6* had completed 34,697 revolutions around the earth. The last digit is the check sum for line two.

Ground Tracks

The orbit parameters determine which points on the earth a satellite flies over and when. The fly-over points will be key for controlling or communicating with satellites from fixed ground stations and also knowing where on the earth a satellite sensor can see. To determine the fly-over points, a line is drawn between the earth's center and the satellite. The point on the line at the surface of the earth is called the satellite subpoint, or nadir.[46] The path the satellite subpoint traces on the earth's surface over time is referred to as the satellite ground track, or ground trace, as shown in figure 6-22.

Since the earth is rotating under the satellite, the intersection of the orbital plane and the earth's surface is continually changing. Because of this relative

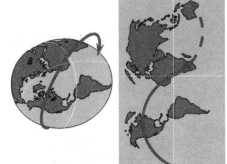

Figure 6-22. Ground track. (*Adapted from* Air University, *Space Primer*, unpublished book, 2003, 8-16.)

106

motion, ground tracks come in various forms and shapes based on the orbit parameters discussed above.

Inclination. Inclination defines the tilt of the orbital plane and therefore defines the maximum latitude, both north and south of the ground track. A satellite with a 50° inclination will have a ground track that moved between 50° north and 50° south latitude. In fact, due to symmetry, if a satellite passes over 50° north, it *must* pass as far south as 50°. Any orbit passes over the pole if, and only if, it has an inclination of 90°.

Period. With a nonrotating Earth, the ground track would be a circle passing over the same terrestrial points every orbit. Because the earth does rotate 15° per hour, by the time the satellite returns to the same place in its orbit after one revolution, the earth has rotated eastward by some amount. The ground track therefore looks like it has moved westward on the earth's surface (westward regression). The amount of regression is proportional to the time it takes for one orbit (i.e., the period). The orientation of the satellite's orbital plane does not change in space; the earth has just rotated beneath it.

The example in figure 6-23 shows a satellite in a circular orbit with a period of 90 minutes and an inclination of approximately 50°. With a 90-minute period, the satellite's ground trace regresses 22.5° westward per revolution (15°/hour × 1.5 hours = 22.5°) around the earth. This figure shows three successive orbits around the earth.

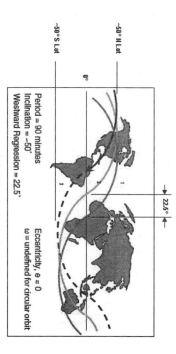

~50° N Lat

0°

~50° S Lat

22.5°

3   1   2

Period = 90 minutes
Inclination = ~50°
Westward Regression = 22.5°

Eccentricity, e ≈ 0
ω = undefined for circular orbit

Figure 6-23. Earth's rotation effects. (*Adapted from Air University, Space Primer, unpublished book, 2003, 8-16.*)

Eccentricity. The above example shows a circular orbit ($e \approx 0$), which produces sinusoidal ground tracks. Eccentricity affects the ground track because the satellite spends different amounts of time in different parts of its orbit (it is moving faster or slower). This means it will spend more time over certain parts of the earth than others. This has the effect of creating an unsymmetrical ground track.

Argument of Perigee. The argument of perigee skews the ground track. For a prograde orbit, at perigee the satellite will be moving faster eastward than at apogee, in effect tilting the ground track. A great example of this type of effect on a ground track can be seen in figure 6-6, which shows the track of a Molniya orbit.

Launch Considerations

When a satellite is launched, it is targeted for a specific orbit. Several factors must be taken into consideration such as launch window, launch azimuth, desired orbital inclination, desired orbital altitude, and launch booster type. These factors are addressed in two general categories: launch location and launch velocity. The final and probably most important consideration is the launch cost.

Launch Location. The location of the launch site is extremely important because it usually determines the range of possible orbital inclinations in which to insert a satellite. Most satellites launched into orbit are considered direct launch satellites. Note that a direct launch from a latitude of 28° will by definition have an inclination of at least 28° since the orbital plane must pass through the launch site and the center of the earth. Lower inclinations will require an on-orbit plane change or maneuver, which has significant fuel penalties.

A launch window is defined as the period of time during which a satellite can be launched directly into a specific orbital plane from a specific launch site.[47] If the orbital plane inclination is greater than the launch site latitude, the launch site will pass through the orbital plane twice a day, producing two launch windows per day. The direction to point is known as the launch azimuth, measured from the north clockwise.

If the inclination of the orbital plane is equal to the launch site latitude, the launch site will be coincident with the orbital plane once a day, producing one launch window per day at a launch azimuth of 90º (due east). If the inclination is less than the launch site latitude, the launch site will not pass through, or be coincident with, the orbital plane at any time, so there will not be any launch windows for a direct launch.[48]

A simplified model for determining inclination (i) from launch site latitude (L) and launch azimuth (Az) is:

$$\cos(i) = \cos(L) \bullet \sin(Az)$$

The launch azimuths allowed (in most countries) are limited due to the safety considerations that prohibit launching over populated areas or foreign airspace. This restriction further limits the possible inclinations from any launch site.[49]

Launch Velocity. When a satellite is launched, a tremendous amount of energy is imparted to it. Such forces are necessary to overcome the gravitational force of the earth as discussed previously. To maintain a minimum circular orbit at an altitude of 90–100 miles, the satellite has to travel at about 17,500 mph. Due to the earth's rotation, more or less kinetic energy may need to be supplied, depending on launch azimuth. The starting velocity at the launch site varies with latitude and can be determined by multiplying the cosine of the latitude by 1,037 mph. For example, at an altitude of 45° north latitude, the starting velocity would be determined in the following manner:

$$\cos(45) \times 1,037 \text{ mph} = 0.7071068 \times 1,037 \text{ mph} = 733.3 \text{ mph}$$

A satellite launched from the equator in the same direction as the earth's rotation (due east) has an initial speed of 1,037 mph. Therefore, 16,463 mph must be supplied (17,500 mph – 1,037 mph = 16,463 mph) to launch a satellite into that particular orbit

108

(90–100 mile altitude). If launched from the equator in a retrograde orbit (against the rotation of the earth), 18,537 mph must be supplied. Launching with the earth's rotation saves energy and allows for larger payloads for any given booster. In addition, the above equations show substantial energy savings when locating launch sites close to the equator.

Launch Costs. Launching a satellite into space is an extremely expensive venture. A very common standard used to estimate the cost of putting a satellite in orbit has been $10,000 per pound. In reality, the cost per pound varies greatly. Factors such as the type of launch payload, the launch booster, and orbit type (LEO, GEO, etc.) affect the costs. In one study of the current commercial launch costs, it was determined that the average cost per pound was between $3,632 and $4,587 for LEO launches and between $9,243 and $11,243 for GEO launches.[50] The actual launch costs used to determine these averages ranged from $5 million for a Russian Strategic Arms Reduction Treaty (START) launch vehicle (LEO) on the lower end to $180 million for a European Space Agency *Ariane 5* launch vehicle (GEO) on the higher end.[51]

Orbital Maneuvers

An orbital maneuver is a deliberate change in the size, shape, and/or orientation of a satellite's orbit. The reasons for conducting an orbital maneuver include (but are not limited to) the following: increasing the satellite's field of view, countering the effects of atmospheric drag or other perturbations, increasing imaging resolution, rendezvousing with another satellite, or deorbiting a satellite.[52] Perturbations and deorbits will be discussed further in later sections.

Delta-v. As previously mentioned, a satellite's velocity and position determine its orbit. To change one of these requires the application of force, which then accelerates the vehicle by Newton's second law. This acceleration produces an impulsive change in velocity, known as delta-v (Δv), which changes the size of the orbit by either adding or subtracting energy.[53] For any single Δv orbital change, the desired orbit must intersect the current orbit, and the point of intersection is where the change is applied. Otherwise it will take at least two Δv's to achieve the final orbit, one to leave the current orbit and another to join the final desired orbit. The amount of Δv required can be determined by subtracting the present vector from the desired vector.

Mission Considerations. Mission planners must ensure that a satellite is provided with sufficient fuel to perform the above maneuvers once in orbit. Additional fuel on board a satellite results in a heavier payload and may require a more powerful booster to place the satellite in orbit, so these maneuvers must be planned carefully. There are two types of orbital maneuvers: in plane and out of plane.

In-plane maneuvers are the most common type of orbital maneuvers performed since they require much less fuel and energy to perform. These maneuvers are conducted to change a satellite's period (size), argument of perigee, or true anomaly.[54] The majority of in-plane maneuvers are performed to counter the external forces, or perturbations, that are constantly acting upon the satellite and changing its orbit.

Out-of-plane maneuvers result in a change in inclination or right ascension of the ascending node.[55] This type of maneuver requires a much larger amount of fuel to generate the sufficient velocity vectors (Δv) to change the satellite's orbital plane. For example, a $28°$ plane change, such as would be necessary for a Kennedy Space Center–launched satellite to become equatorial, requires a Δv of about 3.5 km/s. This same Δv

applied in-plane would be enough for the two burns needed to raise an LEO satellite to geostationary.

Perturbations

Some orbit maneuvers are done simply to maintain the given orbit in the light of perturbations, which were ignored earlier in our discussion to simplify the orbital elements. However, in the real world, all satellites are subject to external forces acting upon a satellite that affect its otherwise constant orbital parameters. These forces have a variety of causes, origins, and effects. For instance, because of drag, the eccentricity of a satellite orbiting the earth can never truly equal zero. These forces are named and categorized in an attempt to model their effects. The major perturbations are:

- Earth's oblateness
- Atmospheric drag
- Third-body effects
- Solar wind/radiation pressure
- Electromagnetic drag

Earth's Oblateness. The earth is not a perfect sphere. It is somewhat asymmetrical at the poles and bulges at the equator. This squashed shape is referred to as oblateness, or the J2 effect. The north polar region is more pointed than the flatter south polar region, producing a slight "pear" shape. Also, the equator is not a perfect circle; it is slightly elliptical when looking down on it from the top. The effects of the earth's oblateness are gravitational variations or perturbations, which have a greater influence the closer a satellite is to the earth. For low to medium orbits, these influences are significant.[56]

One effect of the earth's oblateness is nodal regression. Westward regression due to the earth's rotation under the satellite was discussed above in the section on ground tracks. Nodal regression is an actual rotation of the orbital plane about the earth (the right ascension changes) relative to the fixed reference line—the first point of Aries. If the orbit is prograde, the orbital plane rotates westward around the earth (right ascension decreases); if the orbit is retrograde, the orbital plane rotates eastward around the earth (right ascension increases).

In most cases, perturbations must be counteracted. However, in the case of sun-synchronous orbits, perturbations can be advantageous. Picking a specific slightly retrograde orbit, the angle between the orbital plane and a line between the earth and the sun remains constant and thus "sun-synchronous." This works because as the earth orbits eastward around the sun, the orbital plane drifts due to the J2 effect around the earth at the same rate.

A sun-synchronous orbit is beneficial because it allows a satellite to view the same place on Earth with the same sun angle (or shadow pattern) every day. This is very valuable for remote sensing missions because they use shadows to measure object height. With a constant sun angle, the shadow lengths give away any changes in height, or any shadow changes give clues to exterior configuration changes.[57]

Another significant effect of Earth's asymmetry is apsidal line rotation. This effect appears as a rotation of the orbit within the orbital plane, that is, the argument of perigee changes. This is true for all orbits except at an inclination of 63.4° (and its retrograde complement, 116.6°), where this rotation happens to be zero. The Molniya orbit was specifically designed with an inclination of 63.4° to take advantage of this perturbation. With the zero effect at a 63.4° inclination, the stability of the Molniya orbit improves, limiting the need for considerable onboard fuel to counteract this rotation. Without this effect, the apogee point would rotate away from the desired communications zone (i.e., from the Northern to Southern Hemisphere), and the satellite would be useless.[58]

The ellipticity of the equator has an effect that shows up most notably in geostationary satellites (also in inclined geosynchronous satellites). Because the equator is elliptical, most satellites are closer to one of the lobes and experience a slight gravitational misalignment. This misalignment affects geostationary satellites more because they view the same part of the earth's surface all the time, resulting in a cumulative effect. The elliptical force causes the subpoint of the geostationary satellite to move east or west with the direction depending on its location. There are two stable points at 75° east and 105° west and two unstable stable points 90° out (165° east and 5° west). This movement would be bad not only because the satellite would no longer "hover" over the point of interest, but also because it would cause collisions if all the GEO satellites drifted to these two nodes.

Atmospheric Drag. The earth's atmosphere does not suddenly cease; rather it trails off into space. The current atmospheric model is not perfect because of the many factors affecting the upper atmosphere, such as the earth's day-night cycle, seasonal tilt, variable solar distance, fluctuation in the earth's magnetic field, the sun's 27-day rotation, and the 11-year sun spot cycle. Even a very thin atmosphere causes a drag force due to the high orbital speeds of the satellites. The drag force also depends on the satellite's coefficient of drag and frontal area, which varies widely between satellites.[59] Up to 1,000 km (620 miles), the slowing effect it has on satellites must be taken into account.

The uncertainty in these variables causes predictions of satellite decay to be accurate only for the short term. An example of changing atmospheric conditions causing premature satellite decay occurred in 1978-79, when the atmosphere received an increased amount of energy during a period of extreme solar activity. The extra solar energy expanded the atmosphere, causing several satellites to decay prematurely, most notably the US space station Skylab.[60]

The highest drag occurs when the satellite is closest to the earth (at perigee) and has an effect similar to performing a retro-rocket delta-v at perigee; it decreases the apogee height, circularizing the orbit. On every perigee pass, the satellite loses more kinetic energy (negative delta-v), circularizing the orbit more and more until the whole orbit is experiencing significant drag and the satellite spirals in, enters the earth's atmosphere, and falls back to the earth.[61] For example, the International Space Station currently drops in altitude 30 km per month and thus requires a reboost at every shuttle rendezvous.

Third-Body Effects. According to Newton's Law of Universal Gravitation, every object in the universe attracts every other object in the universe. The greatest third-body effects come from those bodies that are very massive and/or close, such as the sun, Jupiter, and the moon. These forces affect satellites in orbit as well. The farther a satellite is from the earth, the greater the third-body forces are in proportion to Earth's gravitational force, and therefore, the greater the effect on the high-altitude orbits.[62]

Radiation Pressure. The sun is constantly expelling atomic matter (electrons, protons, and Helium nuclei). This ionized gas moves with high velocity through interplanetary space and is known as the solar wind. Satellites are like sails in this solar wind, alternately being speeded up and slowed down, producing orbital perturbations.[63]

Electromagnetic Drag. Satellites are continually traveling through the earth's magnetic field. With all their electronics, satellites produce their own localized magnetic fields which interact with the earth's, causing torque on the satellite. This torque mainly turns the satellite within its orbit rather than affecting the orbit itself as the other perturbations do.

Deorbit and Decay

So far the concern has been with placing and maintaining satellites in orbit. Low Earth orbit satellites have an expected mission duration (life expectancy). Once a payload has completed its mission, it is essentially "taking up space" in space. In addition, when a payload is launched into orbit, other pieces from that launch such as the rocket body, platform, or debris may also remain in orbit. Due to the effects of perturbations, most of these objects will eventually reenter the earth's atmosphere. The only questions are when and how. The answers can be determined by mission planners, who are responsible for deciding whether to deorbit an object or allow it to naturally decay.

A deorbit is the deliberate, controlled reentry of an object into the earth's atmosphere to a specific location.[64] This is usually done to recover something of value, such as people in the case of the space shuttle returning from the International Space Station. It is also done to protect civilians by controlling the reentry of large objects that may survive reentry through the earth's atmosphere as was the case with the deorbit of the Russian Mir space station in March 2001.[65] Most LEO objects are not payloads but rather space junk and therefore cannot be controlled by satellite operators for a possible deorbit. These objects are left to decay naturally back to the earth.

A decay is the uncontrolled reentry of an object into the earth's atmosphere. The effects of perturbations, most notably atmospheric drag, will eventually reduce a satellite's orbital altitude to the point where it can no longer remain in orbit. As discussed in a previous section, this altitude is approximately 150 km (93 miles). It is possible for these decaying objects to be detected through the Space Surveillance Network, discussed in chapter 19. In addition, predictions for reentry dates and locations for decaying objects can be determined by USSTRATCOM's Joint Space Operations Center, as discussed in chapter 12.

In some situations, the satellites are in such stable orbits that natural perturbations will not do the disposal job. In these instances, the satellite must be removed from its operational orbit to another location. To return a satellite to Earth without destroying it takes a considerable amount of energy. Obviously, it is impractical to return old satellites to Earth from a high Earth orbit. The satellite is usually boosted into a slightly higher orbit to get it out of the way, and there it will remain for thousands of years. This practice is common for geosynchronous satellites. By boosting the orbit even higher (> 22,236 miles) above the earth, the satellite is placed in what is called a supersynchronous orbit.[66]

Notes

1. NASA Global Change Master Directory, "Ancillary Description Writer's Guide, 2008," http://gcmd.nasa.gov/User/suppguide/platforms/orbit.html (accessed 18 April 2008).

2. US Centennial of Flight Commission, "Sun Synchronous Orbit," http://www.centennialofflight.gov/essay/Dictionary/SUN_SYNCH_ORBIT/DI155.htm (accessed 18 April 2008).

3. Joint Publication 3-14, *Space Operations*, 6 January 2009, F-5.

4. Michel Broussely, *Industrial Applications of Batteries: From Cars to Aerospace and Energy*, ed. Gianfranco Pistoia (Cambridge, MA: Elsevier Science, 2007), 274.

5. NASA Global Change Master Directory, "Ancillary Description."

6. NASA National Space Science Data Center, "Syncom 2," http://nssdc.gsfc.nasa.gov/nmc/masterCatalog.do?sc=1963-031A (accessed 18 April 2008).

7. JP 3-14, *Space Operations*, F-3–F-6.

8. Ibid., F-5.

9. Eric Chaisson and Steve McMillan, *Astronomy Today* (Englewood Cliffs, NJ: Prentice Hall, 1993), 32.

10. George Kish, *A Source Book in Geography* (Cambridge, MA: Harvard University Press, 1978), 51–53.

11. Jerry Jon Sellers, *Understanding Space: An Introduction to Astronautics*, 3rd ed. (New York, NY: McGraw Hill, 2005), 35.

12. Ibid., 36.

13. Ibid., 37–38.

14. Chaisson and McMillan, *Astronomy Today*, 47.

15. Douglas C. Giancoli, *Physics for Scientists and Engineers with Modern Physics* (Englewood Cliffs, NJ: Prentice Hall, 1989), 129–30.

16. Chaisson and McMillan, *Astronomy Today*, 47.

17. Giancoli, *Physics for Scientists*, 130.

18. Sellers, *Understanding Space*, 39.

19. Chaisson and McMillan, *Astronomy Today*, 51.

20. Ibid., 52.

21. Ibid.

22. Ibid.

23. John E. Prussing and Bruce A. Conway, *Orbital Mechanics* (New York: Oxford University Press, 1993), 21.

24. Ibid., 6.

25. Giancoli, *Physics for Scientists*, 25.

26. Sellers, *Understanding Space*, 106.

27. "Space Environment and Orbital Mechanics," Federation of American Scientists, http://www.fas.org/spp/military/docops/army/ref_text/chap5im.htm (accessed 18 April 2008).

28. Prussing and Conway, *Orbital Mechanics*, 21.

29. Sellers, *Understanding Space*, 113.

30. Ibid., 124.

31. Ibid.

32. Giancoli, *Physics for Scientists*, 161.

33. Victor G. Szebehely, *Adventures in Celestial Mechanics: A First Course in the Theory of Orbits* (Austin, TX: University of Texas Press, 1989), 36–37.

34. Wiley J. Larson and James R. Wertz, eds., *Space Mission Analysis and Design*, 3rd ed. (El Segundo, CA: Microcosm Press, 1999), 96.

35. Vladimir A. Chobotov, ed., *Orbital Mechanics*, 3rd ed. (Reston, VA: American Institute of Aeronautics and Astronautics, Inc., 2002), 28–29.

36. Ibid., 29.

37. Prussing and Conway, *Orbital Mechanics*, 46–48.

38. Note that this is a simplification, as the star reference does drift over time.

39. Chobotov, ed., *Orbital Mechanics*, 29.

40. Sellers, *Understanding Space*, 136.

41. Ibid., 160.

42. Sellers, *Understanding Space*, 161.

43. Amateur Radio Satellite Corporation. "Keplerian Elements Formats," http://www.amsat.org/amsat/keps/formats.html (accessed 18 April 2008).

44. NASA. "Definition of Two-line Element Set Coordinate System." Human Space Flight Web site. http://spaceflight.nasa.gov/realdata/sightings/SSapplications/Post/JavaSSOP/SSOP_Help/tle_def.html (accessed 18 April 2008).

45. William J. Beyda, *Data Communications: From Basics to Broadband*, 3rd ed. (Boston, MA: Pearson Custom Publishing, 2002), 69.

46. Navy, "Aerographer's Mate Non-Resident Training Course, April 1999," http://www.combatindex.com/store/NRTC/Sample/AEROGRAPHERS_MATE/Aerographers_Mate_Module_3.pdf (accessed 18 April 2008).

47. Civil Air Patrol (CAP) Advanced Technology Group, "Satellite Tool Kit Lesson Plans: Orbital Mechanics PP Slides Day 2," http://atg.cap.gov/ (accessed 23 March 2008).

48. Sellers, *Understanding Space*, 299–300.

49. Ibid.

50. Barry D. Watts, "The Military Use of Space: A Diagnostic Assessment," Center for Strategic Budget Assessment, http://www.csbaonline.org/4Publications/PubLibrary/R.20010201.The_Military_Use_o/R.20010201.The_Military_Use_o.pdf (accessed 18 April 2008).

51. Ibid.

52. CAP Advanced Technology Group, "Satellite Tool Kit Lesson Plans."

53. Sellers, *Understanding Space*, 194.

54. Ibid.

55. CAP Advanced Technology Group, "Satellite Tool Kit Lesson Plans."

56. Sellers, *Understanding Space*, 273–74.

57. Ibid., 275.

58. Ibid.

59. Ibid., 273.

60. NASA Kennedy Space Center, "Project Skylab," http://science.ksc.nasa.gov/history/skylab/skylab-operations.txt (accessed 18 April 2008).

61. Larson and Wertz, eds., *Spacecraft Mission Analysis and Design*, 144–45.

62. Sellers, *Understanding Space*, 277.

63. Ibid., 415–16.

64. CAP Advanced Technology Group, "Satellite Tool Kit Lesson Plans."

65. NASA, "Shuttle-Mir: The U.S. And Russia Share History's Highest Stage," http://history.nasa.gov/SP-4225/multimedia/deorbit.htm (accessed 18 April 2008).

66. Zoe Parsons, "Lunar Perturbations of a Supersynchronous Geo Transfer Orbit in the Early Orbit Phase," https://dspace.lib.cranfield.ac.uk/bitstream/1826/1767/1/ZParsons_Thesis%20MSc.pdf (accessed 18 April 2008).

Chapter 7

Space Environment

Maj Jeffrey D. Lanphear, USAF;
and Maj Gabriel A. Medina, Dominican Republic Air Force

Special consideration must be given to the design and fabrication of systems that must operate in the harsh environment of space. Our increased dependence on space-based systems to meet war-fighter objectives and needs, coupled with the increasing use of microelectronics and a move to nonmilitary specifications for satellites, increases our vulnerability to the loss of critical satellite functions or entire systems. Therefore, it is essential to further our understanding of the space environment.

An Introduction to the Space Environment

The study and analysis of the space environment is a relatively new science. Each day we gather and process new information that increases our understanding of this environment and its effects on systems that operate within it. One conclusive fact is that space is a hostile environment for both man and machine. The more we learn and understand about the space environment, the more effectively we can lessen the negative impacts on both our space and ground systems. Events such as solar flares can have a direct impact not only on our terrestrial communications, but also on the functioning and survivability of our satellites.[1]

Our command, control, and communications systems have advanced rapidly, and at the same time we have developed a vulnerable dependence on space-based systems for passing information. From commercial communications to highly secure and survivable military systems, space-based assets provide a link to the information age. The war fighter's reliance and dependence upon space-based assets will continue to grow in the future. The expanding use of microelectronics and nonmilitary, commercial off-the-shelf products increases the risk to the war fighter that operational systems may fail or be degraded because of solar activity. This is why expanding our knowledge of the sun and the space environment is so important.

First, it is important to understand the nature of the space environment.[2] It is neither empty nor benign and is impacted by extreme forces of nature. The primary force in our corner of the universe is our sun. The sun is constantly radiating enormous amounts of energy across the entire electromagnetic spectrum containing x-rays, ultraviolet, visible light, infrared, and radio waves. The sun also radiates a steady stream of charged particles—primarily protons, electrons, and neutrons—known as the solar wind. Threats from electromagnetic and charged particle radiations are enhanced greatly when there is an increase in solar activity.[3]

The magnetosphere is the earth's geomagnetic field. The magnetopause is the outer boundary of the magnetosphere. The magnetosphere is partially flattened on the sunlit side of the earth. This flattening is a direct result of pressure applied to the magnetosphere by the solar wind.[4] As the solar wind passes by the earth and over the magnetosphere, it causes the earth's geomagnetic field lines to be stretched out on the side opposite that facing the sun. These geomagnetic field lines extend past the earth for millions of miles. This is referred to as the magnetotail.[5] Next, we will look at some aspects of solar radiation and energy.

Radiation

Radiation is "the emission or propagation of waves or particles."[6] Particle radiation is the result of atomic or subatomic particle collision, fusion—which is the primary atomic reaction that keeps the sun burning—or the natural decomposition of a radioactive material such as plutonium. In such events, subatomic particles, generally in the form of protons, neutrons, and electrons, are physically projected from one place to another.[7]

Electromagnetic radiation is sometimes referred to as light or radiant energy. Traditionally, we have viewed it as an electrical-type waveform that can travel through a vacuum as easily as it can travel through air and moves at the speed of light. The sun continuously emits electromagnetic radiation across the entire spectrum. To understand the space environment we need to understand more about electromagnetic radiation.

The orderly arrangement of accepted categories of electromagnetic energy is called the electromagnetic spectrum (fig. 7-1). It ranges from the highest energy and shortest wavelength (cosmic rays) to the lowest energy and longest wavelength (TV and radio).

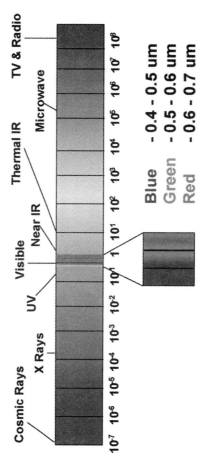

Figure 7-1. Electromagnetic spectrum. (*Reprinted from Air University, Space Primer, unpublished book, 2004, 8-4.*)

It is interesting to note that visible light, which is by far the most obvious to human senses, occupies a mere 2 percent of the electromagnetic spectrum. Distribution of energy is such that the most intense portion falls in the visible part of the spectrum. Substantial amounts also lie in the near-ultraviolet and infrared portions. Less than 1 percent of the sun's total emitted electromagnetic radiation lies in the extreme ultraviolet (EUV)/x-ray and radio-wave portions of the spectrum.[8] However, despite the bulk of the sun's electromagnetic radiation being in the visible bands, we still have a problem in the other areas. DOD radar, communications, and space systems work in the EUV/x-ray and radio-wave energy bands. The sun's radiation in these bands is of no direct use to us in these DOD applications, and, in fact, their constant presence has to be overcome as naturally occurring "background noise." During periods of increased solar activity, the amount of emitted EUV and x-ray energy can be multiplied by a factor of 100, and radio-wave energy by a factor of tens of thousands over the normal solar output. This can cause numerous extensive DOD system problems.[9]

Coronal Mass Ejection and Solar Flares

Adding to the normal energy output from the sun, there are periodic and random solar activities that result in massive increases in ambient energy. The prime events in solar activity are the coronal mass ejection (CME) and the solar flare. To understand these phenomena, we need to address the forces at work.

The outer solar atmosphere is called the corona. It is structured by strong magnetic fields. Where these fields are closed, often above sunspot groups, the confined solar atmosphere can build up enormous pressure and violently erupt, releasing bubbles or tongues of gas and magnetic fields called CMEs. A large CME can contain 10 billion tons of matter that can be accelerated to several million miles per hour in a spectacular eruption. Solar material streaks out through space, impacting anything in its path, such as planets or spacecraft. CMEs are sometimes associated with flares but usually occur independently.[10]

A solar flare is an explosive release of energy, consisting of both electromagnetic and charged particles, within a relatively small but greater-than-Earth-sized region of the lower solar atmosphere. The energy released is substantial, equivalent to the simultaneous detonation of a trillion five-megaton nuclear weapons, but it represents only one hundred-thousandth of the normal total solar output. However, the enhanced x-ray, EUV, radio wave, and particle emissions from a flare are sufficient to affect DOD space and ground systems significantly.[11]

We now know that sunspots, their magnetic fields, flares, and CMEs are very closely related and can have significant impacts on DOD space systems. Solar flares and CMEs tend to occur in regions of sunspot activity, and the level of sunspot activity generally follows an 11-year cycle. The peaks are known as the solar maximums (sometimes called solar max) and the valleys as the solar minimums. In short, as the number of observed sunspots increases, so does solar activity.

The most recent solar minimum occurred in early 2006, while the most recent solar maximum occurred in late 2000.[12] Although an increase in flares and CMEs generally coincides with the 11-year solar cycle's period of solar max, they can occur at any time. What are the effects on Earth from increased solar activity? One of them is called a geomagnetic storm. A geomagnetic storm is the mechanism by which the solar wind disrupts our magnetosphere and adversely affects radar, communications, and space operations.[13]

Generally, the stronger a solar flare or CME, the more severe the event's impacts on the near-Earth environment and on DOD systems operating in that environment. Unfortunately, the impacts discussed in this section would not likely occur singly or sequentially, but would most likely occur simultaneously in combinations of more than one thing. The stronger the solar activity, the more simultaneous effects a system or systems may experience.

The earth's magnetic field deflects solar particles, preventing direct access to the near-Earth environment, except for the funnel-like cusps above the polar caps. However, when an enhanced solar wind, caused by a solar flare or a CME, sweeps past the earth, its impact sends shockwaves rippling through the magnetosphere. Out in the magnetosphere's tail, drawn-out magnetic field lines reconnect and, like a snapping rubber band, shoot trapped particles back toward the earth's night side, that is, the side of the earth that is in darkness. Some of these particles stay near the equatorial plane and feed into the Van Allen radiation belts; others follow geomagnetic field lines and fall into the high northern and southern latitudes, or auroral zones. The result is a disturbance called a geomagnetic and ionospheric storm.

DOD system impact occurrences make sense when one looks at the night-side particle injection mechanism just described. The vast majority of radar, communications, and spacecraft problems occur in the night sector and not in the daylight sector.

Van Allen Radiation Belts

The outer and inner Van Allen radiation belts are two concentric, toroid (or donut-shaped) regions of stable, trapped charged particles that exist because the geomagnetic field near the earth is strong and field lines are closed. The inner belt has a maximum proton density approximately 5,000 km above the earth's surface and contains mostly high-energy protons produced by cosmic ray collisions with the earth's upper atmosphere. The outer belt has a maximum proton density at an altitude ranging from 16,000 to 20,000 km and contains low- to medium-energy electrons and protons whose source is the influx of particles from the magnetotail during geomagnetic storms.[14]

The Ionosphere

The ionosphere is a part of the earth's atmosphere that has a significant impact on communications. Solar radiation ionizes this layer. When we attempt communication by either ground or satellite, the ionosphere plays a major role in its success or failure.

The ionosphere begins in the mesosphere, around 45 miles above the earth's surface, and continues upward until it merges with the ionized interplanetary medium at the exosphere, normally around 250 miles above the earth. The variation of electron density as altitude increases has led to the subdivision of the ionosphere into what are termed the D-, E-, and F-layers. The F-layer is further divided into two regularly occurring layers, F1 and F2.

The D-layer is the lowest portion of the ionosphere and is characterized by relatively weak ionization. It is mainly responsible for absorption of high-frequency radio waves.

The E-layer is above the D-layer and is useful for returning radio signals to the earth. These layers, however, are only capable of refracting radio signals during sunlight hours and practically disappear after sundown.

The F-layer, the uppermost layer of the ionosphere, is the region mainly responsible for long-distance communications. It ionizes very rapidly at sunrise and decays very slowly after sunset, reaching minimum ionization just before sunrise. During the day, the F-region is split into two layers, F1 and F2. F1 does not impact propagation, and like the D- and E-layers, it decays after sunset but is replaced by a broadened F2-layer. The F2-region is the primary medium supporting high-frequency (HF) communications.[15]

We have now looked at the sun's impact on the space environment and the earth's atmosphere. However, there are other naturally occurring threats that can literally impact satellites.

Comets and Meteor Showers

Comets are space objects believed to be mainly composed of ammonia, methane, carbon dioxide, and water (ice) traveling in large, highly elliptical orbits around the sun. Comets are often referred to as dirty snowballs. When seen from Earth, they are characterized by their long, vaporous tail. As the comet approaches the sun, it heats, and some of the core material begins to slough off, forming the tail. If the comet's orbit crosses Earth's orbit, our planet will cross through it on all subsequent yearly orbits of the sun. This gives rise to rather spectacular meteor showers.[16]

The Leonids meteor shower results from the earth passing through the orbit of the comet 55P/Tempel-Tuttle. The name *Leonids* is derived from the resulting meteor shower, which appears to emanate from the constellation Leo. The Leonids is only one of several passages of the earth through comet trails each year. Some others include the Perseids in August, Geminids in December, and the Lyrids in April.[17]

The most obvious danger from comet debris is high-speed collision. There can be physical damage to solar panels, reflective surfaces, and even internal components as a result of particle bombardment. However, there is another potential problem. Today's population of satellites uses circuitry that runs in milli-volt ranges using microcircuits and sensitive chips. Plasma generation can damage and degrade these expensive and possibly defenseless systems.

The Space Environment and System Impacts

It is important to emphasize again the reason that this information on the space environment is of paramount interest to the war fighter. We cannot change the sun's activity level or type. However, we can understand what is happening to us because of solar activity. We can then provide alternate means to ensure that the mission of the war fighter is continued and brought to a successful conclusion.

As we have learned, there are several types of enhanced solar emissions, each with its own characteristics and impacts. We will discuss the impacts that result from the three main categories of emissions:

- Electromagnetic radiation
- High-energy particles
- Low- to medium-energy particles

In the case of solar electromagnetic radiation effects, the enhanced x-rays, EUV, and radio waves reach the earth at the speed of light, in about eight minutes, and can cause environmental and DOD system impacts anywhere over the earth's sunlit hemisphere. Fortunately, these effects tend to last only a bit longer than the flare that produced them, normally a few minutes to an hour or two.

Operational Impacts

Each solar-geophysical phenomenon or event has the potential to affect radar, communications, and space systems.[18] The next sections explore the many operational impacts on DOD and non-DOD systems that a war fighter may experience. Those impacts are presented first in general, then individually.

DOD System Impacts. Generally, the stronger a solar flare, the denser/faster/more energetic a particle stream, or the sharper a solar wind discontinuity or enhancement, the more severe the event's impacts will be on the near-Earth environment and on DOD systems operating in that environment. Unfortunately, the DOD system impacts discussed in this section do not occur one at a time, but will most likely occur in combinations of more than one thing. The stronger the causative solar-geophysical activity, the greater number of simultaneous effects a system may experience. Each of the three general categories of solar radiation has its own characteristics and types of immediate or delayed DOD system impacts (fig. 7-2).

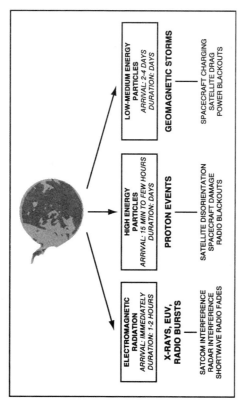

Figure 7-2. Solar radiation particle types and effects. (*Adapted from Air University, Space Primer*, unpublished book, 2003, 6-2.)

Non-DOD System Impacts. DOD systems are not the only ones affected by solar-geophysical activity. Some of these "non-DOD" impacts can indirectly affect military operations. For example, system impacts from a geomagnetic storm can include (1) induced electrical currents in power lines that can cause transformer failures and power outages and (2) magnetic field variations, which can lead to compass errors and interfere with geological surveys.

Electromagnetic (Immediate) versus Particle (Delayed) Effects

Every solar event is unique in its exact nature and the enhanced emissions it produces. Some solar events cause little or no impact on the near-Earth environment because their enhanced particle and/or electromagnetic (x-ray, EUV, and/or radio wave) emissions are too feeble or their particle streams may simply miss hitting the earth. For those events that do affect the near-Earth environment, effects can be both immediate and delayed, depending on the exact type of enhanced radiation emitted. The following paragraphs summarize the three general categories of solar radiation and the immediate or delayed DOD system impacts they produce.

Electromagnetic Radiation. We detect flares by the enhanced x-ray, ultraviolet, optical, and/or radio waves they emit. All of these wavelengths travel to the earth at the speed of light (in about eight minutes), so by the time we first observe a flare, it is al-

120

ready causing immediate environmental effects and DOD system impacts. These impacts are almost entirely limited to the earth's sunlit hemisphere, as the radiation does not penetrate or bend around the earth. Since enhanced electromagnetic emissions cease when the flare ends, the effects tend to subside as well. As a result, these effects tend to last from only a few tens of minutes to an hour or two. Sample system effects include satellite communications (SATCOM) and radar interference (specifically, enhanced background noise), long-range aid to navigation (LORAN) errors, and absorption of HF (6–30 megahertz [MHz]) radio communications.

High-Energy Particles. These particles (primarily protons, but occasionally cosmic rays) can reach the earth within 15 minutes to a few hours after the occurrence of a strong solar flare. Not all flares produce these high-energy particles (and the earth is a rather small target 93 million miles from the sun), so predicting solar proton and cosmic ray events is a difficult challenge. The major impact of these protons is felt over the polar caps, where, as explained earlier, the protons have ready access to low altitudes through funnel-like cusps (Earth's magnetic field lines that terminate into the North and South Poles) in Earth's magnetosphere. The impact of a proton event can last for a few hours to several days after the flare ends. Sample impacts include satellite disorientation, physical damage to satellites and spacecraft, false sensor readings, LORAN navigation errors, and absorption of HF radio signals. Proton events are probably the most hazardous of space weather events (fig. 7-3). Proton events occur when solar flares eject high-energy particles (mainly protons) that arrive at the earth in 30 minutes.

Low- to Medium-Energy Particles. Particle streams (composed of both protons and electrons) may arrive at the earth about two to three days after a flare. Such particle streams can also occur at any time due to other nonflare solar activity. These particles cause geomagnetic and ionospheric storms, which can last from hours to several days. Typical problems include spacecraft electrical charging, drag on low-orbiting satellites, radar interference, space tracking errors, and radio wave propagation anomalies. Again, we frequently experience these impacts in the night sector of the earth.

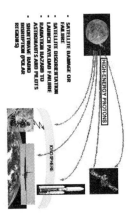

HIGH-ENERGY PROTONS

IONOSPHERE

- SATELLITE DAMAGE OR FAILURE
- SATELLITE DISORIENTATION
- LAUNCH PAYLOAD FAILURE
- RADIATION HAZARD TO ASTRONAUTS AND PILOTS
- SHORTWAVE RADIO DISRUPTION (POLAR REGION)

Figure 7-3. High-energy particle impacts. (Adapted from Air University, *Space Primer*, unpublished book, 2003, 6-3.)

Electromagnetic (Immediate) Effects

The first of the specific DOD system impacts to be discussed will be the shortwave fade (SWF), which is caused by solar flare x-rays. The second impact covered will be SATCOM and radar interference caused by solar flare radio bursts. These electromagnetic impacts are almost entirely limited to the earth's sunlit hemisphere and occur simultaneously (immediately or within eight minutes) with the solar flare that caused them.

Shortwave Fade Events

The high-frequency (6–30 MHz) radio band is also known as the shortwave band. Thus, an SWF refers to an abnormally high fading (or absorption) of an HF radio signal.

HF Radio Communications. The normal mode of radio wave propagation in the HF range is by refraction using the ionosphere's strongest (or F-) layer for single hops and by a combination of reflection and refraction between the ground and the F-layer for multiple hops (fig. 7-4). It should be noted that the ionosphere is defined as that portion of the earth's atmosphere above 45 miles where ions and electrons are present in quantities sufficient to affect the propagation of radio waves. HF radio waves are refracted by

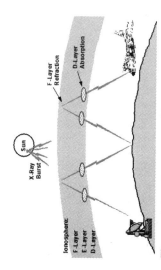

Figure 7-4. HF communications. (*Adapted from* Air University, *Space Primer,* unpublished book, 2003, 6-4.)

the ionosphere's F-layer. However, each passage through the ionosphere's D-layer causes signal absorption, which is additive.

Maximum Usable Frequency. The portion of the ionosphere with the greatest degree of ionization is the F-layer (normally between about 155 and 250 miles altitude). The presence of free electrons in the F-layer causes radio waves to be refracted (or bent), but the higher the frequency, the less the degree of bending. As a result, surface-to-surface radio operators use medium or high frequencies (300 kilohertz [kHz] to 30 MHz), while SATCOM operators use very high frequencies (VHF) to extremely high frequencies (EHF) (30 MHz–300 gigahertz [GHz]). The maximum usable frequency (MUF) is that frequency above which radio signals encounter too little ionospheric refraction (for a given take-off angle) to be bent back toward the earth's surface (i.e., they become transionospheric). Normally, the MUF lies in the upper portion of the HF band.

Lowest Usable Frequency. The lowest layer of the ionosphere is the D-layer (normally between altitudes of 45 to 55 miles). At these altitudes, there are still a large number of neutral air atoms and molecules coexisting with the ionized particles. As a passing radio wave causes the ions and free electrons to oscillate, they will collide with the neutral air particles, and the oscillatory motion will be damped out and converted to heat. Thus, the D-layer acts to absorb passing radio wave signals. The lower the frequency, the greater the degree of signal absorption. The lowest usable frequency (LUF) is that frequency below which radio signals encounter too much ionospheric absorption to permit them to pass through the D-layer. Normally, the LUF lies in the lower portion of the HF band.

HF Propagation Window. The HF radio propagation window is the range of frequencies between an LUF (complete D-layer signal absorption) and an MUF (insufficient F-layer refraction to bend back the signal). This window varies by location, time of day, season, and level of solar and/or geomagnetic activity. HF operators choose propagation frequencies within this window so their signals will pass through the ionosphere's D-layer and subsequently refract from the F-layer. Typical LUF/MUF curves show a normal daily variation. During early afternoon, incoming photo-ionizing solar radiation (some x-rays, but mostly ultraviolet) is at a maximum, so the D- and F-layers are strong and the LUF and MUF are elevated. During the night, the removal of ionizing sunlight causes all ionospheric layers to weaken (the D- and E-layers disappear altogether), and the LUF and MUF become depressed.

HF radio waves above the MUF encounter insufficient refraction and pass through the ionosphere into space. Those below the LUF suffer total absorption in the ionosphere's lowest layer. The result is a usable frequency window.

The SWF Event. X-ray radiation emitted during a solar flare can significantly enhance D-layer ionization and absorption (thereby elevating the LUF) over the entire sunlit hemisphere of the earth. This enhanced absorption is known as an SWF and may, at times, be strong enough to close the HF propagation window (called a shortwave blackout) completely (fig. 7-5). The amount of signal loss depends on a flare's x-ray intensity, the location of the HF path relative to the sun, and design character-

istics of the system. An SWF is an immediate effect, experienced simultaneously with observation of the causative solar flare. As a result, it is not possible to forecast a specific SWF event. Rather, forecasters can only predict the likelihood of an SWF event based on the probability of flare occurrence determined by an overall analysis of solar features and past activity. However, once a flare is observed, forecasters can quickly (within seven minutes of event onset) issue an SWF warning, which contains a prediction of the frequencies to be affected and the duration of signal absorption. Normally SWFs persist only for a few minutes past the end of the causative flare, that is, for a few tens of minutes up to an hour or two.

Other Sudden Ionospheric Disturbances. An SWF is the most common and troublesome of a whole family of sudden ionospheric disturbances (SID) caused by the influence of solar flare x-rays on the ionosphere. Other SIDs describe additional impacts. For example, flare x-rays can also cause the altitude of the D-layer's base to lower slightly. This phenomenon (called a sudden phase anomaly) will affect very low-frequency (VLF) (6–30 kHz) and low-frequency (LF) (30–300 kHz) transmissions and can cause LORAN navigation errors.

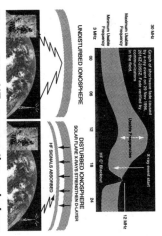

Figure 7-5. HF propagation windows. (*Adapted from* Air University, *Space Primer,* unpublished book, 2003, 6-5.)

SATCOM and Radar Interference

Several kinds of disturbances can interfere with SATCOM and radar systems. Knowing about these disturbances can help the operator diagnose the cause of interference.

Solar Radio Bursts. Radio bursts from solar flares can cause the amount of radio wave energy emitted by the sun—the background level of solar noise—to increase by a factor of tens of thousands over certain frequency bands in the VHF to super-high-frequency (SHF) range (30 MHz–30 GHz). If the sun is in the field of view of the receiver and if the burst is at the right frequency and is intense enough, it can produce direct radio frequency interference (RFI) on a SATCOM link or missile-detection/space-tracking radar. Knowledge of a solar radio burst can allow a SATCOM or radar operator to isolate the RFI cause and avoid time-consuming investigation of possible equipment malfunction or jamming.

Radio bursts are another immediate effect, experienced simultaneously with observation of the causative solar flare. Consequently, it is not possible to forecast the occurrence of radio bursts, let alone what frequencies they will occur on and at what intensities. Rather, forecasters can only issue rapid warnings (within seven minutes of event onset) that identify the observed burst frequencies and intensities. Radio burst impacts are limited to the sunlit hemisphere of the earth. They will persist only for a few minutes up to tens of minutes, but usually not for the full duration of the causative flare.

Solar Conjunction. There is a similar geometry-induced effect called solar conjunction, which occurs when the ground antenna, satellite, and sun are in line. This accounts for interference or blackouts (e.g., static or "snow" on TV signals) in geosynchronous communication satellites during brief periods on either side of the spring and autumn equinoxes. This problem does not require a solar flare to be in progress, but its effects are definitely greatest during solar max when the sun is a strong background radio emitter.

Solar Radio Noise Storms. Sometimes a large sunspot group will produce slightly elevated radio noise levels, primarily on frequencies below 400 MHz. This noise may persist for days, occasionally interfering with communications or radar systems using an affected frequency.

Particle (Delayed) Effects

The discussion of specific DOD system impacts continues with the major delayed (or charged particle–induced) system impacts. These impacts tend to occur hours or up to several days after the solar activity that caused them. They persist for up to several days and are mostly felt in the nighttime sector (as the particles that cause them usually come from the magnetosphere's tail) although they are not strictly limited to that time/geographic sector.

Particle Events. The sources of the charged particles (mostly protons and electrons) include solar flares, CMEs, disappearing filaments, eruptive prominences, and solar sector boundaries (SSB) or high-speed streams (HSS) in the solar wind. Except for the most energetic particle events, the charged particles tend to be guided by the interplanetary magnetic field (IMF), which lies between the sun and the earth's magnetosphere. The intensity of a particle-induced event generally depends on the size of the solar flare, filament or prominence, its position on the sun, and the structure of the intervening IMF. Alternately, the sharpness of an SSB or the density/speed of an HSS will determine the intensity of a particle-induced event caused by these phenomena.

Recurrence. One important factor in forecasting particle events is that some of the causative phenomena (like SSBs and coronal holes, the source region for HSSs) persist for months. Since the sun rotates once every 27 days, there is a tendency for these long-lasting phenomena to show a 27-day recurrence in producing geomagnetic and ionospheric disturbances.

High-Frequency Absorption Events

High-frequency SWFs over the sunlit hemisphere (caused by solar flare x-rays enhancing D-layer absorption) were discussed above. There are similar HF absorption events at high geomagnetic latitudes (above 55º). However, at high latitudes, the enhanced ionization of D-layer atoms and molecules (which produce signal absorption) is caused by particle bombardment from space. Another difference is that these high-latitude absorption events can last for hours up to several days and usually occur simultaneously with other radio transmission problems.

Polar Cap Absorption Events. For a polar cap absorption (PCA) event, the enhanced ionization is caused by solar flare or CME protons that gain direct access to low altitudes (as low as 35 km) by entering through the funnel-like cusps in the magnetosphere above the earth's polar caps.

Auroral Zone Absorption Events. For an auroral zone absorption (AZA) event, the enhanced ionization is caused by particles (primarily electrons) from the magnetosphere's tails, which are accelerated toward the earth during a geomagnetic storm and guided by magnetic field lines into the auroral zone latitudes. These same ionizing particles cause the aurora or northern and southern lights.

Ionospheric Scintillation

The intense ionospheric irregularities found in the auroral zones and at plus or minus 20° of the geomagnetic equator are the primary causes of ionospheric scintillation. Scintillation of radio wave signals is the rapid, random variation in signal amplitude, phase, and/or polarization caused by small-scale irregularities in the electron density along a signal's path (fig. 7-6). Ionospheric radio-wave scintillation is very similar to the visual twinkling of starlight or heat shimmer over a hot road caused by atmospheric turbulence. The result is signal fading and data dropouts on satellite command uplinks, data downlinks, or communications signals.

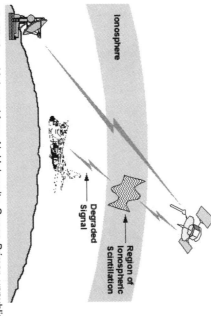

Ionosphere

Degraded Signal

Region of Ionospheric Scintillation

Figure 7-6. Ionospheric scintillation. (*Adapted from Air University, Space Primer, unpublished book, 2003, 6-8.*)

Scintillation tends to be a highly localized effect. An impact will be felt only if the signal path penetrates an ionospheric region where these small-scale electron density irregularities are occurring. Low-latitude, nighttime links with geosynchronous communications satellites are particularly vulnerable to intermittent signal loss due to scintillation. In fact, during the Persian Gulf War, allied forces relied heavily on SATCOM links, and scintillation posed an unanticipated, but very real, operational problem.

GPS and Scintillation

GPS satellites, which are located at semisynchronous altitude, are also vulnerable to ionospheric scintillation. Signal strength enhancements and fades, as well as phase changes due to scintillation, can cause a GPS receiver to lose signal lock with a particular satellite.

The reduction in the number of simultaneously usable GPS satellites may result in a potentially less accurate position fix. Since scintillation occurrence is positively correlated with solar activity and the GPS network has received widespread use only recently during a quiet portion of the 11-year solar cycle, the true environmental vulnerability of the GPS constellation is yet to be observed. Nevertheless, even during low solar activity levels, it has been shown under strong scintillation that the GPS signals cannot be seen through the background noise due to the rapid changes in the ionosphere, even with the use of dual-frequency receivers. Figure 7-7 is a plot of the actual signal-to-noise ratio graph measured during a moderate scintillation event. A war fighter may lose total GPS signal lock during such events. This includes dual-frequency systems.

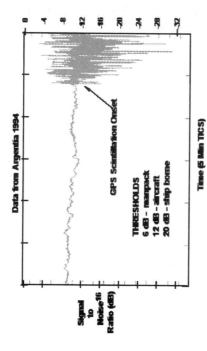

Figure 7-7. Scintillation effect on GPS signal. (*Reprinted from* Air University, *Space Primer*, unpublished book, 2003, 6-9.)

Scintillation Occurrence

There is no fielded network of ionospheric sensors capable of detecting real-time scintillation occurrence or distribution (fig. 7-8). Scintillation is frequency dependent—the higher the radio frequency (all other factors held constant), the lesser the impact of scintillation. Since we do not presently have a dedicated network of sensors that can detect real-time scintillation, we are heavily dependent on its known association with other environmental phenomena (such as aurora) and scintillation climatology.

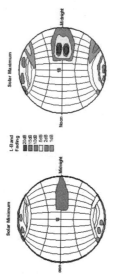

Figure 7-8. Scintillation occurrence. (*Reprinted from* Air University, *Space Primer*, unpublished book, 2003, 6-9.)

From a war fighter's perspective, it is important to know that scintillation is strongest from local sunset until just after midnight and during periods of high solar activity. At high geomagnetic latitudes (the auroral and polar regions), scintillation is strong, especially at night, and its influence increases with higher levels of geomagnetic activity.

The effects of particle bombardment mostly cause scintillation in the high latitudes by protons. Knowledge of solar activity periods and the portions of the ionosphere where conditions are conducive to scintillation permits operators to reschedule mission-critical activities and/or to switch to less susceptible radio frequencies or satellite links.

GPS and Total Electron Content

The total electron content (TEC) along the path of a GPS signal can introduce positioning errors. Just as the presence of free electrons in the ionosphere causes HF radio waves to be bent (or refracted), the higher frequencies used by GPS satellites will suffer some bending (although to a much lesser extent than with HF radio waves). This signal bending increases the signal path length. In addition, passage through an ionized medium causes radio waves to be slowed (or retarded) somewhat from the speed of light. Both the longer path length and slower speed can introduce up to 300 nanoseconds (equivalent to about 100 meters) of error into a GPS location fix—unless some compensation is made for the effect.

The solution is relatively simple for two-frequency GPS receivers, since signals of different frequency travel at different speeds through the same medium. Measuring the difference in signal phases for the two frequencies allows computation of the local phase delay for a particular receiver and elimination of 99 percent of the error introduced in a location fix. Unfortunately, this approach will not work for single-frequency receivers. For them, a software algorithm is used to model ionospheric effects based on the day of the year and the average solar ultraviolet flux for the previous few days. This method produces a gross correction for the entire ionosphere. However, as already stated, the ionosphere varies rapidly and significantly over geographical area and time. Consequently, the algorithm can eliminate, at best, about 50 percent of the error and a far smaller percentage of the error in regions where an enhanced degree of ionization is found (such as in the auroral latitudes and near the geomagnetic equator during evening hours).

Radar Aurora Clutter and Interference

A geomagnetic and ionospheric storm will cause both enhanced ionization and rapid variations (over time and space) in the degree of ionization throughout the auroral oval. Visually, this phenomenon is observed as the aurora or northern and southern lights. This enhanced, irregular ionization can also produce abnormal radar signal backscatter on poleward looking radars, a phenomenon known as radar aurora (fig. 7-9). The strength of radar aurora signal returns and the amount of Doppler frequency shifting are aspect dependent. Impacts can include increased clutter and target masking, inaccurate target locations, and even false target or missile launch detection. While improved software screening programs have greatly reduced the frequency of false aircraft or missile launch detection, such occurrences have not been eliminated. (Radar aurora is a separate phenomenon from the weak radio wave emission produced by the recombination/de-excitation of atmospheric atoms and molecules in the auroral oval, a process that also produces the much stronger infrared, visible, and ultraviolet auroral emissions.)

Surveillance Radar Errors

The presence of free electrons in the ionosphere causes radio waves to be bent (or refracted) as well as slowed (or retarded) somewhat from the speed of light. Missile detection

127

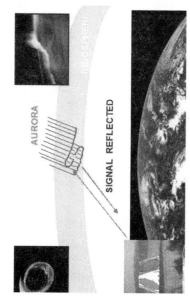

Figure 7-9. Radar aurora. (*Reprinted from* Air University, *Space Primer,* unpublished book, 2003, 6-10.)

and spacetrack radars operate at ultra-high frequencies (UHF) (300–3,000 MHz) and SHFs (3,000–30,000 MHz) to escape most of the effects of ionospheric refraction so useful to HF surface-to-surface radio operators. However, even radars operating at these much higher frequencies are still susceptible to enough signal refraction and retardation to produce unacceptable errors in target bearing and range.

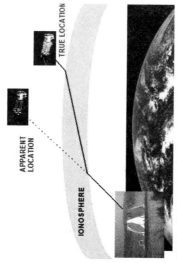

Figure 7-10. Surveillance radar errors. (*Reprinted from* Air University, *Space Primer,* unpublished book, 2003, 6-11.)

Bearing and Range Errors. A bearing (or direction) error is caused by signal bending, while a range (or distance) error is caused by both the longer path length for the refracted signal and the slower signal speed (fig. 7-10). For range errors, the effect of longer path length dominates in UHF signals, while slower signal speed dominates for SHF signals.

Correction Factors. Radar operators routinely attempt to compensate for these bearing and range errors by applying correction factors that are based on the expected ionospheric TEC along a radar beam's path. These predicted TEC values/correction values are based on time of day, season, and the overall level of solar activity. Unfortunately, individual solar and geophysical events will cause unanticipated, short-term variations from the predicted TEC values and correction factors. These variations (which can be either higher or lower than the anticipated values) will lead to inaccurate position determinations or difficulty in acquiring targets. Real-time warnings when significant TEC variations are occurring help radar operators minimize the impacts of their radar's degraded accuracy.

Space-Based Surveillance. The bearing and range errors introduced by ionospheric refraction and signal retardation also apply to space-based surveillance systems. For example, a space-based sensor attempting to lock on to a ground radio emitter may experience a geolocation error.

Over-the-Horizon Backscatter Surveillance Radars. Over-the-horizon backscatter (OTH-B) radars use HF refraction through the ionosphere to detect targets beyond the horizon. OTH-B operators need to be aware of existing and expected ionospheric conditions (in detail) over a wide geographical area. Otherwise, improper frequency selection will reduce target detection performance, or incorrect estimation of ionospheric layer heights will give unacceptable range errors.

Atmospheric Drag

Another source for space-object positioning errors is the presence of either more or less atmospheric drag than expected on low orbiting objects (generally at less than about 1,000 km altitude). Energy deposited in the earth's upper atmosphere by EUV, x-ray, and charged particle bombardment heats the atmosphere, causing it to expand outward. Low Earth orbiting satellites and other space objects then experience denser air and more frictional drag than expected. This drag decreases an object's altitude and increases its orbital speed. The result is that the object will be some distance below and ahead of its expected position when a ground radar or optical telescope attempts to locate it (fig. 7-11). Conversely, exceptionally calm solar and/or geomagnetic conditions will cause less atmospheric drag than predicted, and an object could be higher and behind where it was expected to be found.

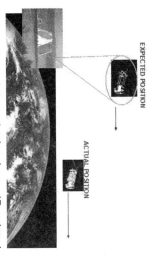

Figure 7-11. Atmospheric drag. (*Reprinted from Air University, Space Primer, unpublished book, 2003, 6-12.*)

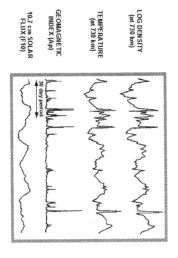

LOG DENSITY
(at 730 km)

TEMPERATURE
(at 730 km)

GEOMAGNETIC
INDEX (Ap)

10.7 cm SOLAR
FLUX (F10)

30 day period

Figure 7-12. Factors contributing to atmospheric drag. (*Reprinted from Air University, Space Primer, unpublished book, 2003, 6-13.*)

Impacts of Atmospheric Drag. The consequences of atmospheric drag include: (1) satellite locations may be inaccurate, which can hinder rapid acquisition of SATCOM links for commanding or data transmission; (2) costly orbit maintenance maneuvers may become necessary; and (3) deorbit predictions may become unreliable. A classic case of the latter was *Skylab*. Geomagnetic activity was so severe, for such an extended period, that the expanded atmosphere caused *Skylab* to deorbit and burn in before a planned space shuttle rescue mission was ready to launch.

Contributions to Drag. There are two space environmental parameters used by current models to predict the orbits of space objects. The first is the solar F10 index. Although the F10 index is a measure of solar radio output at 10.7 centimeters (or 2,800 MHz), it is a very good indicator of the amount of EUV and x-ray energy emitted by the sun and deposited in the earth's upper atmosphere. In figure 7-12 the solar flux (F10) graph shows a clear, 27-day periodicity caused by the sun's 27-day period of rotation and the fact that hot, active regions are not uniformly distributed on the sun's surface. The second parameter is the geomagnetic Ap index, which is a measure of the energy deposited in the earth's upper atmosphere by charged particle bombardment. This index shows strong spikes corresponding to individual geomagnetic storms. The upper two graphs, which show upper atmospheric temperature and density (observed by a satellite at 730 km altitude), clearly reflect the influence of these two indices. Since it takes time for the atmosphere to react to a change in the amount of energy being deposited in it, drag impacts first tend to be noticeable about six hours after a geomagnetic storm starts and may persist for about 12 hours after the storm ends.

Impact of Geomagnetic Storms on Orbit Changes.

We have discussed two impacts of geomagnetic storms on space tracking radar. The first is bearing and range errors induced by inadequate compensation for TEC changes, which cause *apparent* location errors. The second is atmospheric drag, which causes *real* position errors. These effects can occur simultaneously. During a severe geomagnetic storm in March 1989, over 1,300 space objects were temporarily misplaced (fig. 7-13). It took almost a week to reacquire all

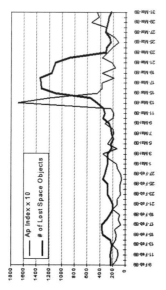

Figure 7-13. Geomagnetic storms and orbit changes. (*Reprinted from Air University, Space Primer, unpublished book, 2003, 6-14.*)

the objects and update their orbital elements. This incident led to a revision in operating procedures. Normally drag models do not include detailed forecasts of the F10 and Ap indices. However, when severe conditions are forecast, more comprehensive model runs are made, even though they are also more time-consuming. Figure 7-13 demonstrates how a geomagnetic storm can change the orbits of space objects unexpectedly, causing difficulty for those who maintain orbital data.

Space Launch and Payload Deployment Issues

When objects are being launched into space, the potential effects of atmospheric drag and particle bombardment must be considered.

Atmospheric Drag. Excessively high or low geomagnetic conditions can produce atmospheric density variations along a proposed launch trajectory. The ability of a launch vehicle to compensate for these variations may be exceeded. In addition, the atmospheric density profile based on changes in altitude will determine how early the protective shielding around a payload can be jettisoned. If the protective shielding is jettisoned too early, the payload is exposed to excessive frictional heating.

Particle Bombardment. Charged particle bombardment during a geomagnetic storm or proton event can produce direct physical damage on a launch vehicle or its payload, or it can deposit an electrical charge on or inside the spacecraft. The electrostatic charge deposited may be discharged (lead to arcing) by onboard electrical activity such as vehicle commanding. In the past, payloads have been damaged by attempted deployment during geomagnetic storms or proton events.

Radiation Hazards

Despite all engineering efforts, satellites are still quite susceptible to the charged particle environment. In fact, with newer microelectronics and their lower operating voltages, it will actually be easier to cause electrical upsets than on older, simpler vehicles. Furthermore, with the perceived lessening of the nuclear threat, there has been a trend to build new satellites with less nuclear radiation hardening. However, the previous hardening also protected the satellites from space environmental radiation hazards. Both low and high Earth orbiting spacecraft and satellites are subject to a number of environmental radiation hazards, such as direct physical damage and/or electrical upsets caused by charged particles. These charged particles may be: (1) trapped in the Van Allen radiation belts, (2) in directed motion during a geomagnetic storm, or (3) protons/cosmic rays of direct solar or galactic origin.

Geosynchronous Orbit. Geosynchronous orbit (35,782 km or 22,235 statute miles altitude) is commonly used for communication satellites. Unfortunately, it lies near the outer boundary of the outer Van Allen belt and suffers whenever that boundary moves inward or outward. Semisynchronous orbit (used for GPS satellites) lies near the middle of the outer belt (in a region called the ring current) and suffers from a variable, high-density particle environment. Both orbits are particularly vulnerable to the directed motion of charged particles that occurs during geomagnetic storms. Particle densities observed by satellite sensors can increase by a factor of 10 up to 1,000 over a period as short as a few tens of minutes.

Geomagnetic Storms. Charged particles emitted by the sun cause problems primarily on the night side of the earth. Their arrival causes a shock wave to ripple through the magnetosphere, causing magnetic field lines out in the magnetosphere's tail to recombine, and previously stored particles are then shot toward the earth's night-side hemisphere. Some of these particles stay near the plane of the equator and feed the ring current in the outer Van Allen radiation belt, while other particles follow magnetic field lines up (and down) toward auroral latitudes.

Radiation Belt Particle Injections. The particles from the night-side magnetosphere (or magnetotail) which stayed near the plane of the equator will feed the ring currently in the outer Van Allen belt. The electrons and protons, since they are oppositely charged, tend to move in opposite directions when they reach the ring current (fig. 7-14). Furthermore, the protons and electrons have about the same amount of energy, but the electrons (since they are 1,800 times lighter) move 40 times faster. Finally, the electrons are about 10 to 100 times more numerous than the protons. Figure 7-14 shows a cross-section of the magnetosphere taken in the plane of the earth's geomagnetic equator.

The result of all these factors is that electrons are much more effective at causing physical damage due to collision and electrical charging than the protons. This fact explains why the preponderance of satellite problems occur in the midnight to dawn (0001 to 0600 local) sector, while the evening (1800 to 2359 local) sector is the second most common location for problems. This explanation is well supported by the rather large number of satellite anomalies which actually can be observed in the midnight to dawn sector.

Auroral Particle Injections. Some of the particles from the night-side magnetosphere follow geomagnetic field lines up (and down) toward the Northern and Southern Hemisphere auroral latitudes. These particles will penetrate to very low altitudes (as low as 35 km) and can cause physical damage and electrical charging on high-inclination, low-altitude satellites or space shuttle missions.

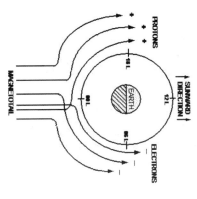

Figure 7-14. Geomagnetic storms—radiation belt particle injections. (*Reprinted from Air University, Space Primer, unpublished book, 2003, 6-15.*)

Electrical Charging

Spacecraft charging is a problem for satellites and can be produced by an object's motion through a medium containing charged particles. This phenomenon is referred to as wake charging, which is a significant problem for large objects like the space shuttle. Spacecraft charging is also caused by particle bombardment, as occurs during geomagnetic storms and proton events, and even from solar illumination. The impact of each phenomenon is strongly influenced by variations in an object's shape and the materials used in its construction (fig. 7-15).

An electrical charge can be deposited either on the surface or deep within a satellite. Solar illumination and wake charging are surface

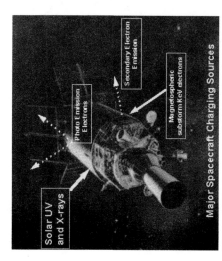

Figure 7-15. Spacecraft charging. (*Adapted from* Air University, *Space Primer,* unpublished book, 2003, 6-16.)

charging phenomena. During direct particle bombardment, the higher the energy of the particles, the deeper the charge can be placed. Normally electrical charging will not in itself cause an electrical upset or damage. It will deposit an electrostatic charge, which will stay on the vehicle for perhaps many hours until some triggering mechanism causes a discharge or arcing, similar to a small thunderbolt inside the vehicle. Such triggering mechanisms include a change in particle environment, a change in solar illumination such as moving from eclipse to sunlight, or onboard vehicle activity or commanding.

In extreme cases, the satellite's life span can be significantly reduced, necessitating an unplanned launch of a replacement satellite. Warnings of environmental conditions conducive to spacecraft charging allow operators to reschedule vehicle commanding, reduce onboard activity, delay satellite launches and deployments, or reorient a spacecraft to protect it from particle bombardment. Should an anomaly occur, an environmental post-analysis could help operators or engineers determine whether the environment contributed to it and determine if satellite functions need to be reactivated or reset.

Single-Event Upsets

High-energy protons and cosmic rays can penetrate through a satellite and ionize material deep inside the spacecraft. A single particle can cause physical damage and/or deposit enough charge to cause an electrical upset such as causing a circuit to switch, inducing a false command, or causing the computer memory to be changed or lost. High-energy protons can also physically damage satellite components. Hence, these occurrences are called single-event upsets (SEU).

SEUs are random, unpredictable events. They can occur at any time during the 11-year solar cycle. In fact, SEUs are actually most common near solar minimum, when the interplanetary magnetic field emanating from the sun is weak and unable to provide the earth much shielding from cosmic rays originating outside the solar system. During severe geomagnetic storms, particles low in the atmosphere move toward the equator and can therefore similarly affect satellites in lower-inclination orbits.

132

Satellite Disorientation

Many satellites rely on electro-optical sensors to maintain their orientation in space. These sensors lock onto certain patterns in the background stars and use them to achieve precise pointing accuracy. These star sensors are vulnerable to cosmic rays and high-energy protons, which can produce flashes of light as they influence a sensor. The bright spot produced on the sensor may be falsely interpreted as a star. When computer software fails to find this false star in its star catalogue or incorrectly identifies it, the satellite can lose attitude lock with respect to the earth. When com- tions antennas, sensors, and solar cell panels will then correspondingly fail to acquire their intended targets. The result may be loss of communications with the satellite, loss of satellite power, and in extreme cases, loss of the satellite due to drained batter- ies (gradual star sensor degradation can also occur under constant radiation expo- sure). Disorientation occurs primarily when solar activity is high and on geosynchronous or polar-orbiting satellites.

Geomagnetic Storm Surface Impacts

Geomagnetic storms cause rapid fluctuations in the earth's magnetic field and in- crease the amount of precipitating energetic particles impinging on the earth's iono- sphere. The rapid fluctuations can lead to induced currents in power grids, causing the power grid to fail (fig. 7-16). This can—and has—happened, predominately in the higher latitudes. (In March 1989, the Canadian province of Quebec suffered a power grid fail- ure of this type.) Such fluctuations can also cause orientation errors for those relying on magnetic compasses for navigation. In addition to the ionospheric disturbances discussed earlier, localized, rapidly changing ionospheric activity can occur. This activ- ity may not be picked up by space environment sensors but can cause HF communica- tion users to suffer sporadic interference or total localized blackouts.

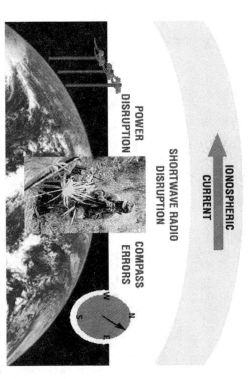

Figure 7-16. Geomagnetic storm surface impacts. (*Reprinted from Air University, Space Primer, unpublished book, 2003, 6-18.*)

Space Environmental Support

The United States leads the world in the study of the space environment. The space environment is becoming a critical factor in the nation's economy and security. We need to accurately provide reliable space weather predictions, forecasts, and warnings to users whose systems can be affected by solar disturbances. The Space Environmental Center and the 55th Space Weather Squadron lead US efforts to predict space weather for global civil and DOD users.

Space Environmental Center

Non-DOD federal and civilian customers receive support from the Department of Commerce, specifically the NOAA Space Environment Center (SEC), located in Boulder, Colorado. The SEC is one of the nation's official sources of space weather alerts and warnings. The center continually monitors and forecasts Earth's space environment; provides accurate, reliable, and useful solar-terrestrial information; and leads programs to improve services.

The SEC conducts research into phenomena affecting the sun-Earth environment, including the emission of electromagnetic radiation and particles from the sun, the transmission of solar energy to Earth via solar wind, and the interactions between the solar wind and Earth's magnetic field, ionosphere, and our atmosphere.

Together with personnel from the US Air Force, the SEC operates the Space Weather Operations (SWO) Center that monitors solar and geomagnetic activity 24 hours a day. They issue products such as the SEC Space Weather Outlook along with other warnings and predictions. The SWO Center also provides real-time data, or "nowcasts," that include forecasts and summaries of solar activity to customers interested in the solar-terrestrial environment.

In addition to current data slides, the SWO Center provides users with a synopsis of the current space weather. Data from both ground- and space-based observatories and sensors are monitored and analyzed to provide users with the best information currently available. Significant solar events are seen in the forecast centers within two minutes of detection, which allows the forecast centers in turn to issue alerts of potential system impacts to customers within an additional five minutes.

The SEC and the 55th Space Weather Squadron also watch the sun for indications as to when major solar flares might occur. Predictions of solar activity are made in the solar flare watch forecast, in which groups of sunspots are numbered and tracked based upon their type and level of expected activity.

The NOAA space weather scales were introduced in November 1999 as a way to communicate to the public the current and future space weather conditions and their possible effects on people and systems. Many of the SEC products describe the space environment, but few have attempted to define or describe in lay terms the effects that can be experienced as the result of these space environment disturbances. The space weather scales then should be a useful reference to those who are interested in space weather effects. Printable copies of the space weather scales are available on CD as well as from the SEC Web site.[19]

The geomagnetic storm scale index was developed to convey the potential severity of solar storms using numbered levels, analogous to the numerical scales that describe hurricanes, tornadoes, and earthquakes. The index lists the possible effects at each

134

level of geomagnetic storm. It also shows how often such events occur and gives a measure of the intensity of the physical causes.

Air Force Weather Agency Space Weather Flight

Forecasters in the Space Weather Flight, 2nd Weather Squadron, 2nd Weather Group at the Air Force Weather Agency (AFWA) look at the sun's emissions and provide mission-tailored analyses, forecasts, and warnings. Their products are used for mission planning and environmental situational awareness by national agencies, DOD operators, war fighters, and decision makers.

Although solar emissions can occur at any time, the sun undergoes an 11-year activity cycle. The last solar peak, or period of maximum activity, occurred in 2000, producing a large number of solar flares and sun spots. This heightened activity creates an increase in solar emissions traveling to and interacting with the earth's atmosphere. Solar emissions also cause the aurora borealis or northern lights. However, most interactions are not visible to the human eye.

AFWA space weather technicians located at Offutt AFB, Nebraska, and at solar observatories around the globe never let the sun slip from view. Each month, they provide updated space weather information on the Internet for military and DOD personnel issuing approximately 100 textual and graphical products warning of significant solar activity. Under these conditions, the environmental situational awareness of space weather can be as important as thunderstorms or other terrestrial weather phenomena to our nation's military. AFWA is committed to providing a complete terrestrial and space weather program, looking at the environment from "the mud to the sun."[20]

Notes

1. Jerry Jon Sellers, *Understanding Space: An Introduction to Astronautics*, 2nd ed. (Boston: McGraw Hill, 2004), 79.

2. Much of the following discussion of the space environment and its impact is based on Air Force Space Command Pamphlet (AFSPCPAM)15-2, *Space Environmental Impacts on DOD Operations*, 1 October 2003, certified current 7 December 2007.

3. NASA, "The Solar Wind," Solar Physics Web site at Marshall Space Flight Center, http://solarscience.msfc.nasa.gov/SolarWind.shtml (accessed 16 April 2009).

4. NASA, "What Is the Magnetosphere?" Marshall Space Flight Center Space Plasma Physics Web site, http://science.nasa.gov/ssl/pad/sppb/edu/magnetosphere/ (accessed 16 April 2009).

5. European Space Agency Science and Technology, "Plasma Regions: The Magnetotail," http://sci.esa.int/science-e/www/object/index.cfm?fobjectid=33272&fbodylongid=1171 (accessed 16 April 2009).

6. *American Heritage Dictionary*, 4th ed., s.v. "radiation."

7. Sellers, *Understanding Space*, 93.

8. NASA, "Electromagnetic Spectrum," Imagine the Universe Web site at Goddard Space Flight Center, http://imagine.gsfc.nasa.gov/docs/science/know_11/emspectrum.html (accessed 16 April 2009).

9. Maj Michael J. Muolo, ed., *Space Handbook: A War Fighter's Guide to Space*, vol. 2, *An Analyst's Guide* (Maxwell AFB, AL: Air University Press, 1993), 16.

10. NASA, "Coronal Mass Ejections," Solar Physics Web site at Marshall Space Flight Center, http://solarscience.msfc.nasa.gov/CMEs.shtml (accessed 16 April 2009).

11. NASA, "Solar Flares," Solar Physics Web site at Marshall Space Flight Center, http://solarscience.msfc.nasa.gov/flares.shtml (accessed 16 April 2009).

12. NASA, "Solar Minimum Has Arrived," NASA Web site, http://www.nasa.gov/vision/universe/solarsystem/06mar_solarminimum.html (accessed 16 April 2009).

13. Muolo, ed., *Space Handbook*, vol. 2, 14.

14. Ibid., 13.

15. National Geophysical Data Center, "Definition of the Ionospheric Regions (Structures)," http://www.ngdc.noaa.gov/stp/IONO/ionostru.html (accessed 16 April 2009).

16. Lunar and Planetary Institute, "About Comets," http://www.lpi.usra.edu/education/explore/comets/ (accessed 16 April 2009).

17. International Meteor Organization (IMO), "IMO Meteor Shower Calendar 2007," http://www.imo.net/calendar/2007 (accessed 16 April 2009).

18. The discussion of the impacts of the space environment is based on AFSPCPAM 15-2, 13–29.

19. AFSPCPAM 15-2, 30–31. See the SEC Web site at http://www.swpc.noaa.gov/.

20. AFWA, "AFWA Space Weather Flight," http://www.afweather.af.mil/library/factsheets/factsheet.asp?id=5090 (accessed 16 April 2009).

Chapter 8

Joint Space Mission Areas

Maj Christopher J. King, USAF; and MAJ Kenneth G. Kemmerly, USA

Adm Alfred Thayer Mahan saw the earth's oceans as a medium for force projection and commerce which begged the development of strategy, policies, and doctrine to ensure their effective use. Similarly, the use of and dependence on space by the US military necessitates the development of effective policies and doctrine to ensure its proper employment.[1] This chapter provides the reader with a general understanding of the underpinning doctrinal concepts of US military space operations captured in Joint Publication (JP) 3-14, *Space Operations;* AFDD 2-2.1, *Space Operations;* AFDD 2-2, *Space Operations;* AFDD 2-2.1, *Counterspace Operations;* Air Force Doctrine Document (AFDD) 2-2, *Space Operations;* and Army Field Manual (FM) 3-14, *Space Support to Army Operations.*

JP 3-14 states that "this publication establishes a framework for the use of space capabilities and the integration of space operations into joint military operations."[2] Therefore, this chapter also intends to provide an understanding of these concepts in order to facilitate the successful integration of space into joint operations so space becomes a significant force multiplier to the war fighter.[3] To achieve true joint integration, it is necessary to view space operations within the construct of joint space mission areas, which are divided into four categories: space control, space force enhancement, space support, and space force application.

Space Control

As noted, Mahan sought to develop strategies and doctrine for the use of a medium that, when used effectively, theoretically provides a nation an advantage in economic and military terms. If a nation wants to enjoy the use of a medium, it must control it because, as Jim Oberg points out, "the history of mankind has proven time and again that anything that enhances the power of an individual or group—be it political, economic, or military strength—will be coveted by others."[4] Thus, Mahan advocated the principle of "sea control" for the unfettered use of the oceans for a nation's purposes. An application of this principle to space attempts to achieve the same result.

Space control operations provide freedom of action in space for friendly forces and, when directed, deny it to an adversary. Space control also includes the protection of the space systems belonging to the United States and its allies and the negation of adversary space systems. Oberg stresses the need for protection by emphasizing that "a basic tenet of space control is a requirement that all elements of space power, whether orbital or terrestrial be protected."[5] Space control operations encompass all elements of the space defense mission. Space control may include some or all activities conducted by land, sea, air, space, and/or special operations forces. FM 3-14 states it succinctly: "Space control is used to deny communications and propaganda tools, such as TV and radio, to adversary leadership. Space surveillance systems monitor the status of enemy and commercial satellite operations to determine potential threat to friendly forces."[6]

To gain space superiority, space forces must have surveillance of space and terrestrial areas of interest (AOI) that may impact space activities; protect the ability to use space; prevent adversaries from exploiting US, allied, or neutral space services; and negate the ability of adversaries to exploit space capabilities. These forces are applied against space systems or facilities identified through the targeting process. Space control operations provide freedom of action in space for friendly forces and, when directed, deny the same freedom to the adversary. They include offensive and defensive operations by friendly forces to gain and maintain space superiority and situational awareness of events that impact space operations. In particular, space control operations are comprised of several types of missions, including surveillance of space, protection, prevention, and negation functions. These operations change in nature and intensity as the type of military operation changes. Prevention efforts can range from deterrence or diplomacy to military action. If prevention efforts fail, protection and negation functions may be performed to achieve space superiority. Negation focuses on denying an adversary's effective use of space. Prevention, protection, and negation efforts all rely on the ongoing surveillance of space and Earth to make informed decisions and to evaluate the effectiveness of their efforts.

Surveillance of Space

Situational awareness is fundamental to the ability to conduct the space control mission. It requires robust space surveillance for continual awareness of orbiting objects; real-time search and targeting-quality information; threat detection, identification, and location; predictive intelligence analysis of foreign space capability and intent in a geopolitical context; and a global reporting capability for friendly space systems. Space surveillance is conducted to detect, identify, assess, and track space objects and events to support space operations. Space surveillance is also critical to space support operations, such as placing satellites in orbit. Further, space situational awareness data can be used to support terrestrially based operations, such as reconnaissance avoidance and missile defense.

Protection

Active and passive defensive measures ensure that US and friendly space systems perform as designed by overcoming an adversary's attempts to negate friendly (US and allies) exploitation of space or to minimize adverse effects if the US or its allies attempt negation of the adversary's ability to use space. Such measures also provide some protection from space environmental factors. Protection measures must be consistent with the criticality of the mission's contribution to the war fighter and are applied to each component of the space system, including launch, to ensure that no weak links exist. Means of protection include, but are not limited to, ground facility protection (security; covert facilities; camouflage, concealment, and deception; and mobility), alternate nodes, spare satellites, link encryption, increased signal strength, adaptable waveforms, satellite radiation hardening, and space debris protection measures. The system of protection measures should provide unambiguous indications of whether a satellite is under attack or in a severe space weather environment when any satellite anomaly or failure occurs. Some attack indications could be so subtle or dispersed that, when indications are considered individually, an attack is not detectable. At a

138

minimum, a common fusion point for possible indications from all US government satellites should be provided to allow centralized analysis.

Prevention

Prevention measures are designed to preclude an adversary's hostile use of US or third-party space systems and services. Prevention can include military, diplomatic, political, and economic measures as appropriate.

Negation

Negation measures aim to deceive, disrupt, deny, degrade, or destroy an adversary's space capabilities. Negation can include action against the ground, link, or space segments of an adversary's space system.

Deception. Deception measures are designed to mislead the adversary by manipulation, distortion, or falsification of evidence to induce the adversary to react in a manner prejudicial to its interests.

Disruption. Disruption results in the temporary impairment (diminished value or strength) of the utility of space systems, usually without physical damage to the space system. These operations include the delaying of critical, perishable operational data to an adversary.

Denial. Denial seeks the temporary elimination (total removal) of the utility of an adversary's space systems, usually without physical damage. This objective can be accomplished by such measures as interrupting electrical power to the space ground nodes or computer centers where data and information are processed and stored. For example, denying US adversaries position navigation information could significantly inhibit their operations.

Degradation. Permanent partial or total impairment of the utility of space systems, usually with physical damage, is the goal of degradation. This option includes attacking the ground, control, or space segment of any targeted space system. All military options, including special operations, conventional warfare, and information warfare, are available for use against space targets.

Destruction. Destruction seeks the permanent elimination of the utility of space systems. This option includes attack of critical ground nodes; destruction of uplink and downlink facilities, electrical power stations, and telecommunications facilities; and attacks against mobile space elements and on-orbit space assets.

Space Force Enhancement

Force enhancement operations multiply joint force effectiveness by enhancing battlespace awareness and providing needed war-fighter support. There are five force enhancement functions: (1) intelligence, surveillance, reconnaissance (ISR); (2) integrated tactical warning and attack assessment (ITW/AA); (3) environmental monitoring; (4) communications; and (5) position, velocity, time, and navigation. They provide significant advantages by reducing the confusion inherent in combat situations. They also improve the lethality of air, land, sea, space, and special operations forces. Force enhancement functions are also often provided by agencies such as the National

Reconnaissance Office (NRO), National Security Agency (NSA), National Geospatial-Intelligence Agency (NGA), National Aeronautics and Space Administration (NASA), National Oceanic and Atmospheric Administration (NOAA), commercial organizations, and consortiums. Missions are discussed below.

Intelligence, Surveillance, and Reconnaissance

Monitoring terrestrial (air, land, and sea) AOIs from space helps reveal location, disposition, and intention at the tactical, operational, and strategic levels of war. Such information provides warning of attack, operational combat assessment, tactical battle damage assessment (BDA), and feedback on how well US forces are affecting the adversary's understanding of the battlespace. ISR support is requested through established collection-management channels within the intelligence community. Dissemination down to the user/war-fighter level must be timely and assured.

Integrated Tactical Warning and Attack Assessment

Satellite- and ground-based systems are crucial for providing timely detection and communicating warning of an adversary's use of ballistic missiles or nuclear detonations to US strategic forces, tactically deployed forces, and allies. ITW/AA is a composite term in satellite and missile surveillance. Tactical warning is a notification to operational command centers that a specific threat event is occurring. The component elements that describe threat events are: (1) country of origin—country or countries initiating hostilities; (2) event type and size—identification of the type of event and determination of the size or number of weapons; (3) country under attack—determined by observing trajectory of an object and predicting its impact point; and (4) event time—time the hostile event occurred. Attack assessment is an evaluation of information to determine the potential or actual nature and objectives of an attack for the purpose of providing information for timely decisions.

Environmental Monitoring

Space forces provide data on meteorological, oceanographic, and space environmental factors that might affect operations in other battlespace dimensions. Additionally, space forces provide forecasts, alerts, and warnings of conditions in space. Imagery capabilities such as multispectral imagery can provide joint force planners with current information on surface conditions such as surface trafficability, beach conditions, vegetation, and land use. Knowledge of these factors allows forces to avoid adverse environmental conditions (such as poor surface conditions or severe weather), while taking advantage of other conditions to enhance operations. Such monitoring also supports intelligence preparation of the battlespace by providing the commander with information needed to identify and assess potential adversary courses of action.

Communications

Space-based communications offers many unique advantages that allow the joint force commander (JFC) and subordinate commanders to shape the battlespace. Using military satellite communications and, in some cases, civil, commercial, and international systems, the JFC and subordinate commanders can execute reachback operations, draw from planning support databases in the continental United States, sustain the two-way flow of data, and disseminate plans, orders, and force status over long distances, thereby increasing command and control (C2) effectiveness, especially in areas with limited or no communications infrastructure. Satellite communications provide critical connectivity for maneuver forces whose rapid movement and nonlinear deployments take them beyond inherent line-of-sight (LOS) communication networks.

Position, Velocity, Time, and Navigation

Space forces provide precise, reliable position and timing information that permits joint forces to more effectively plan, train, coordinate, and execute operations. Space-based force tracking will improve C2 of assets and provide enhanced situational awareness while decreasing the chances of fratricide.

The Navstar GPS provides the primary space-based source for US and allied position, velocity, and timing requirements.[7] Certain ground-based systems, primarily allied equipment, also utilize similar information from the Russian GLONASS satellite constellation. This information enables precise location, velocity, and timing for such uses as navigation of terrestrial forces, combat identification, and target weaponeering for some precision munitions. However, GPS information does have limitations. Like communications satellite uplinks and downlinks, a GPS signal is also susceptible to hostile jamming and spoofing. Additionally, satellite information is only as accurate as the information uploaded to satellites. As such, errors in position, timing, and velocity can be induced into the downlinked information by uploading erroneous information to the satellite. Current satellite systems require continual monitoring and routine uploading of information in order to ensure accurate terrestrial position, velocity, and timing.

Space Support

Space support operations consist of operations that launch, deploy, augment, maintain, sustain, replenish, deorbit, and recover space forces, including the C2 network configuration for space operations. Specific functions consist of spacelift, satellite operations, rendezvous and proximity operations, and reconstitution of space forces.

Spacelift

Spacelift is the ability to deliver satellites, payloads, and material into space. Spacelift operations are conducted to deploy, sustain, or augment satellite constellations supporting US military operations. During periods of increased tension or conflict, a spacelift objective is to launch and deploy new or replacement space assets and capabilities necessary to maintain, augment, or add to the operational capability of space systems to achieve national security objectives. This requires responsive, affordable launch capabilities.

Satellite Operations

Satellite operations are conducted to maneuver, configure, and sustain on-orbit forces and to activate on-orbit spares. Military satellite operations are executed through a host of dedicated and common-user networks. The Air Force operates the Air Force Satellite Control Network (AFSCN) for common-use satellite operations. The Naval Satellite Control Network provides satellite operations of communications, oceanographic, and research satellites and packages in support of all joint war fighters. Several systems utilize dedicated antennas for both mission data retrieval and routine satellite telemetry, tracking, and commanding (TT&C). The various networks combined ensure total C2 of space resources.

Rendezvous and Proximity Operations

Rendezvous refers to those operations that intentionally bring two resident space objects operationally close together. *Proximity* refers to on-orbit operations that deliberately and necessarily place and maintain a space object within a close distance of another space object for some specific purpose.

Rendezvous and proximity operations (RPO) can be used for on-orbit activities such as assembly and servicing and include the capability to support a wider range of future US space capabilities. All RPO activities must be coordinated to reduce on-orbit collision risks and to ensure flight safety procedures are in place.

Reconstitution of Space Forces

Reconstitution refers to plans and operations for replenishing space forces in the event of loss of space assets. This could include repositioning and reconfiguring surviving assets, augmentation by civil and commercial capabilities, and replacement of lost assets.

Space Force Application

The application of space force would consist of attacks against terrestrial-based targets carried out by military weapons systems operating in or through space. The force application mission area includes ballistic missile defense and force projection. In accordance with current US space policy, there are no force application assets operating in space. However, there are many strategists arguing for a reversal of this policy. See Dr. Everett C. Dolman's book *Astropolitik* for an in-depth discussion and argument on the subject of placing force application assets in space.

Space operations will continue to grow in importance due to the enabling capabilities they provide to the JFC and will continue to become more integrated into the overall military mission. A thorough understanding of the four mission areas of space operations will greatly contribute to mission success for all joint operations.

Notes

1. Everett C. Dolman, *Astropolitik: Classical Geopolitics in the Space Age* (New York: Frank Cass Publishers, 2002), 32.
2. JP 3-14, *Space Operations*, 6 January 2009, xiv.
3. Ibid, I-1.
4. James E. Oberg, *Space Power Theory* (Washington, DC: Government Printing Office, 1999), 137.
5. Ibid., 13.
6. FM 3-14, *Space Support to Army Operations*, 18 May 2005, 3-7.
7. Air Force Space Command, "Global Positioning System Constellation Status," http://gps.afspc.af.mil/gps/ (accessed 17 April 2009).

Chapter 9

US Government Space Organizations and Missions

Maj Burton Catledge, USAF; and MAJ Dillard Young, USA

Since 11 September 2001, there has been a growing dependence on other government agencies (OGA) to provide defense and security capabilities, and space has been no exception. The principle space OGAs are the National Reconnaissance Office (NRO), National Geospatial-Intelligence Agency (NGA), National Aeronautics and Space Administration (NASA), and National Oceanic and Atmospheric Administration (NOAA).

National Reconnaissance Office

The National Reconnaissance Office "designs, builds and operates" US reconnaissance satellites:

NRO products, provided to an expanding list of customers like the Central Intelligence Agency (CIA) and the Department of Defense (DoD), can warn of potential trouble spots around the world, help plan military operations, and monitor the environment. As part of the 16-member Intelligence Community, the NRO plays a primary role in achieving information superiority for the US Government and Armed Forces. A DoD agency, the NRO is staffed by DoD and CIA personnel. It is funded through the National Reconnaissance Program, part of the National Foreign Intelligence Program.[1]

According to the NRO mission statement, "The NRO is a joint organization engaged in the research and development, acquisition, launch, and operation of overhead reconnaissance systems necessary to meet the needs of the Intelligence Community and of the Department of Defense. The NRO conducts other activities as directed by the Secretary of Defense and/or the Director of National Intelligence."[2]

In recent years, the NRO has declassified some of its operations: "The organization was declassified in September 1992, followed by the location of its headquarters in Chantilly, Virginia, in 1994. In February 1995, CORONA, a photoreconnaissance program in operation from 1960 to 1972, was declassified, and 800,000 CORONA images were transferred to the National Archives and Records Administration." In December 1996, the NRO made its first advance announcement of the launch of a reconnaissance satellite.[3]

National Geospatial-Intelligence Agency

The National Geospatial-Intelligence Agency supports national security objectives by providing "timely, relevant, and accurate geospatial intelligence," which the agency defines as "the exploitation and analysis of imagery and geospatial information to describe, assess and visually depict physical features and geographically referenced activities on the Earth. Geospatial intelligence consists of imagery, imagery intelligence, and geospatial (e.g., mapping, charting and geodesy) information." NGA information is tailored for the customer's requirements:

By giving customers ready access to geospatial intelligence, NGA provides support to civilian and military leaders and contributes to the state of readiness of U.S. military forces. NGA also contributes to humanitarian efforts, such as tracking floods and disaster support, and to peacekeeping. NGA is a member of the U.S. Intelligence Community and a Department of Defense (DoD) Combat Support Agency. Headquartered in Bethesda, MD, NGA operates major facilities in the St. Louis and Washington, D.C. areas. The Agency also fields support teams worldwide.[4]

National Aeronautics and Space Administration

NASA conducts its work in four principle organizations, called mission directorates:

1. *Aeronautics*: Pioneers and proves new flight technologies that improve our ability to explore and which have practical applications on Earth.
2. *Exploration Systems*: Creates new capabilities and spacecraft for affordable, sustainable human and robotic exploration.

144

3. *Science:* Explores Earth, the moon, Mars and beyond; charts the best route of discovery; and reaps the benefits of Earth and space exploration for society.

4. *Space Operations:* Provides critical enabling technologies for much of the rest of NASA through the space shuttle, the International Space Station, and flight support.[5]

NASA's mission is to advance and communicate scientific knowledge and understanding of the earth, the solar system, and the universe; advance human exploration, use, and development of space; and research, develop, verify, and transfer advanced aeronautics and space technologies.[6]

National Oceanic and Atmospheric Administration

NOAA's mission is to understand and predict changes in the earth's environment and conserve and manage coastal and marine resources to meet our nation's economic, social, and environmental needs.[7] NOAA's National Environmental Satellite, Data, and Information Service (NESDIS) is dedicated to providing timely access to global environmental data from satellites and other sources to promote, protect, and enhance the nation's economy, security, environment, and quality of life. To fulfill its responsibilities, NESDIS acquires and manages the nation's operational environmental satellites, provides data and information services, and conducts related research.[8]

National Security Space Office

The National Security Space Office (NSSO) was established in May 2004 and was formed by combining the National Security Space Architect, the National Security Space Integration Office, and the Transformational Communications Office. The NSSO facilitates the integration and coordination of defense, intelligence, civil, and commercial space activities. The NSSO is the only office specifically focused on cross-space enterprise issues, providing direct support to the Air Force, NRO, Joint Staff, Office of the Secretary of Defense, Office of the Director of National Intelligence, White House, Congress, as well as other services, agencies, and national-security space stakeholders.[9]

Notes

1. NRO, "Welcome to the NRO," http://www.nro.gov/index.html (accessed 1 March 2008).

2. Ibid.

3. Ibid.

4. NGA, "NGA Fact Sheet," http://www.nga.mil/NGASiteContent/StaticFiles/OCR/nga_fact.pdf (accessed 1 March 2008).

5. NASA, "About NASA," http://www.nasa.gov/about/highlights/what_does_nasa_do.html (accessed 1 March 2008).

6. NASA Ames Conference Center, "NASA Mission Statement," http://naccenter.arc.nasa.gov/NASAMission.html (accessed 1 March 2008).

7. NOAA, "About NOAA," http://www.noaa.gov/about-noaa.html (accessed 1 March 2008).

8. NOAA Satellite and Information Service, "About NESDIS," http://www.nesdis.noaa.gov/About/about.html (accessed 1 March 2008).

9. NSSO, Web site, http://www.acq.osd.mil/nsso/index.htm (accessed 2 April 2008).

Chapter 10

US Military Space Organizations

Maj Burton Catledge, USAF; and MAJ Dillard Young, USA

The military's space functions are spread among the Air Force, Navy, and Army, each with its own space-related organizations. This chapter provides an overview of the relevant organizations and their functions.

Air Force Space Command

Most Air Force space organizations fall under the Air Force Space Command (AFSPC) at Peterson AFB, Colorado. As of this writing, AFSPC has two numbered air forces and two centers (fig. 10-1). AFSPC's mission is to deliver space and missile capabilities to America and its war-fighting commands.[1]

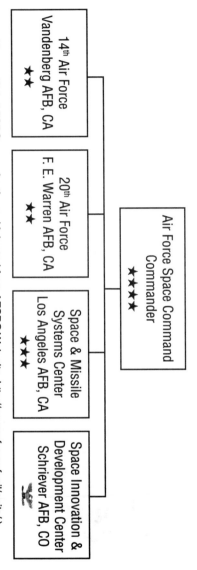

Figure 10-1. AFSPC organizations. *(Adapted from AFSPC Web site, http://www.afspc.af.mil/units/.)*

147

Fourteenth Air Force

Fourteenth Air Force at Vandenberg AFB, California, manages the generation and employment of space forces to support US Strategic Command (USSTRATCOM) and North American Aerospace Defense Command operational plans and missions. Fourteenth Air Force is the Air Force space task force to USSTRATCOM. The mission of the Fourteenth Air Force is to control and exploit space for global and theater operations. The organization is comprised of a headquarters, a space operations command and control center, and five subordinate wings that conduct a full range of space operations. As the day-to-day operators of AFSPC's space forces, the Fourteenth Air Force provides space capabilities that ensure global presence, vigilance, and reach for the nation. Fourteenth Air Force has five key missions:

1. *Command and control (C2) of space forces*—Plan, task, direct, and synchronize space operations to support global and theater missions.

2. *Space superiority*—Provide surveillance, tracking, and intelligence of more than 9,000 man-made objects, ranging from active and inactive satellites to vehicle fragments, using a variety of sensors such as phased-array radars and optical surveillance systems. Conduct defensive and offensive counterspace operations and space environment assessments.

3. *Surveillance, warning, and battlefield characterization*—Provide global and theater ballistic-missile warning (strategic and tactical) and tracking capabilities to the United States and allied nations through the employment of satellite sensors and phased-array radars.

4. *Satellite and network operations*—C2 of over 100 satellites that provide weather, communications, navigation, and surveillance-warning capabilities and operate a global network of satellite control centers and stations supporting a variety of defense and civil users.

5. *Space launch and range*—Provide assured access to space and conduct launch operations from western and eastern US launch sites to support military, civil, and commercial users. Operate ranges to include testing and evaluating space, air, and missile systems.[2]

Twentieth Air Force

Twentieth Air Force at F. E. Warren AFB, Wyoming, operates and maintains the nation's nuclear intercontinental ballistic missile (ICBM) weapon systems in support of USSTRATCOM war plans. Designated as USSTRATCOM's Task Force 214, Twentieth Air Force provides on-alert, combat-ready ICBMs to the president. Combined with bombers and submarines, USSTRATCOM forces protect the United States with a formidable nuclear deterrent umbrella.[3] As of this writing, Twentieth Air Force has been designated one of the two numbered air forces of Air Force Global Strike Command (AFGSC), the new command entrusted with the US nuclear ICBM and bomber missions. The exact date of Twentieth Air Force's transition from AFSPC to AFGSC is unknown at this time.

Space Innovation and Development Center

The third numbered-air-force–equivalent unit under AFSPC is the Space Innovation and Development Center (SIDC) at Schriever AFB, Colorado. The SIDC is chartered with "unlocking the potential" as premier innovators, integrators, and operational testers of air, space, and cyberspace power for the war fighter. The center's mission is to advance full-spectrum warfare through rapid innovation, integration, training, testing, and experimentation.[4]

Space and Missile Systems Center

The mission of the Space and Missile Systems Center (SMC) at Los Angeles AFB, California, is to develop, acquire, field, and sustain the world's best space and missile systems for the joint war fighter and the nation.[5] SMC designs and acquires all Air Force and most Department of Defense space systems. It oversees launches and completes on-orbit checkouts prior to turning systems over to user agencies. It supports the Program Executive Office for Space on the global positioning, Defense Satellite Communications, and military strategic and tactical relay (Milstar) systems. SMC also supports the evolved expendable launch vehicle, Defense Meteorological Satellite, the Defense Support Program, Air Force Satellite Control Network/launch range modernization programs, and the space-based infrared system. In addition, it supports development and acquisition of land-based ICBMs for the Air Force Program Executive Office for Strategic Systems.[6]

Twenty-fourth Air Force

The Air Force recently established a new numbered air force, Twenty-fourth Air Force, under AFSPC. Twenty-fourth Air Force has command of the Air Force's cyberspace mission. Its permanent headquarters and subordinate units have yet to be finalized at the time of this writing.

Air Force Global Strike Command

As previously mentioned, the USAF established AFGSC to execute its nuclear ICBM and bomber missions. The command will consist of Twentieth Air Force at F. E. Warren AFB, Wyoming, and Eighth Air Force at Barksdale AFB, Louisiana. Barksdale AFB has been chosen as the permanent headquarters for AFGSC.

Naval Network Warfare Command

The Naval Network Warfare Command (NETWARCOM) in Norfolk, Virginia, is the Navy space type commander and a functional component for space to USSTRATCOM (fig. 10-2). In close coordination with Fleet Forces Command (FLTFORCOM), Second Fleet, and carrier and expeditionary strike commanders, NETWARCOM works to improve fleet combat effectiveness with smarter, more aggressive use of space effects and a better understanding of how space effects support maritime operations. FLTFORCOM designated NETWARCOM as the Naval Space Campaign lead as directed in Chief of Naval Operations Guidance 2005. NETWARCOM is also the functional authority for the Navy Space Cadre, ensuring operational space expertise is increased throughout the Fleet Readiness Training Program and deployments. The Naval Satellite Operations Center (NAVSOC) is a subordinate command that operates satellite constellations to provide military ultra-high frequency (UHF) narrow-band communications (fleet satellite), military UHF narrow-band, extremely high frequency (EHF), and Global Broadcast System communications (UHF follow-on) and support ionospheric research. NAVSOC also operates the Geodetic/Geophysical Satellite (GEOSAT) Follow-on radar altimeter that provides ocean surface height information to naval meteorological centers, and polar-orbiting host satellites that provide additional EHF communications to military users.[7]

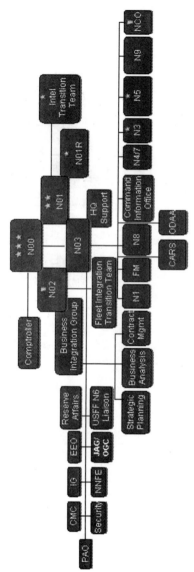

Figure 10-2. Naval NETWARCOM. (*Reprinted from* Naval NETWARCOM, http://www.netwarcom .navy.mil/about-us/org-chart.htm [accessed 20 May 2009].)

US Army Space and Missile Defense Command/Army Strategic Command

The Space and Missile Defense Command (SMDC)/Army Strategic Command (AR-STRAT) at Redstone Arsenal, Alabama, conducts space and missile defense operations and provides planning, integration, control, and coordination of Army forces and capabilities in support of USSTRATCOM missions; serves as proponent for space- and ground-based midcourse defense; is the Army operational integrator for global missile defense; conducts mission-related research, development, and acquisition in support of Army Title 10 responsibilities; and serves as the focal point for desired characteristics and capabilities in support of USSTRATCOM missions (fig. 10-3).[8]

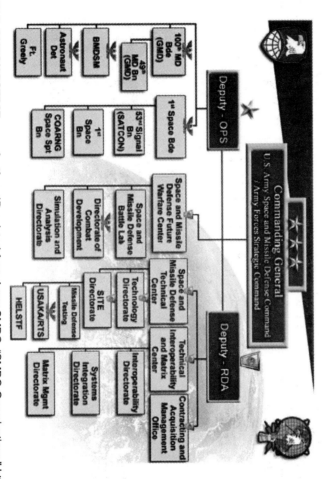

Figure 10-3. SMDC/ARSTRAT organization. (*Reprinted from* Army SMDC, "SMDC Organizations," http://www.smdc.army.mil/SMDC/org_poc.html [accessed 1 March 2008].)

Notes

1. AFSPC, "AFSPC Fact Sheet," http://www.af.mil/factsheets/factsheets/factsheet.asp?id=155 (accessed 1 March 2008).

2. Ibid.

3. Air Force, "20th Air Force," Fact Sheet, http://www.warren.af.mil/library/factsheets/factsheet.asp?id=4697 (accessed 1 March 2008).

4. AFSPC, "Space Innovation and Development Center," Fact Sheet, http://www.afspc.af.mil/library/factsheets/factsheet.asp?id=3651 (accessed 1 March 2008).

5. SMC, *The SMC Story*, 2, http://www.losangeles.af.mil/shared/media/document/AFD-080606-04pdf, 2 (accessed 20 May 2009).

6. SMC, Web site, http://www.losangelesafb.com/smc/smc.html (accessed 20 May 2009).

7. Naval NETWARCOM, "Space," http://www.netwarcom.navy.mil/space.htm (accessed 1 March 2008).

8. Army SMDC, "About USASMDC," http://www.smdc.army.mil/SMDC/About.html (accessed 1 March 2008).

Chapter 11

Command and Control of Space Forces

MAJ Kenneth G. Kemmerly, USA; and Maj Jeffrey D. Lanphear, USAF

Nothing is more important in war than unity of command.

—Napoleon Bonaparte

> The majority of the following information is excerpted directly from Air Force Doctrine Document (AFDD) 2-2, *Space Operations*, chapter 2, "Command and Control of Space Operations," 27 November 2006.

Unity of command and unity of effort are immutable principles of war which are just as applicable to the medium of space as to the domains of ground, air, and sea. However, the characteristics of space and allocation of space capabilities throughout several federal agencies with no one central controlling authority present unique challenges to the command and control (C2) of space forces. Interagency responsibilities with authority are often split between organizations. Further exacerbating the situation is the interdependence between global and theater space forces. Theater missile defense during Operation Desert Storm illustrates the challenges of C2 of space forces. Army Patriot missile defense batteries received missile launch notifications from the Air Force's Defense Support Program (DSP) and the Army-Navy joint tactical ground station (JTAGS) system. This integrated missile-defense warning data was crucial to the combined force air component commander (CFACC) in his responsibility as the area air defense commander (AADC).

Other challenges occur when one organization owns an asset while another has responsibility for the actual operation, or when one organization operates the platform while another has responsibility over the onboard payload. For example, Defense Meteorological Satellite Program (DMSP) weather satellites, which provide weather data for Department of Defense (DOD) and national operations, currently fall under the combatant command of US Strategic Command (USSTRATCOM), but are operated on a daily basis by the National Oceanic and Atmospheric Administration (NOAA) under the Department of Commerce, and requirements for onboard sensor tasking are provided by the Air Force Weather Agency, an Air Force field operating agency.

Given the inherent challenges to C2 space forces and the ever-increasing role of space operations to achieve the objectives of a joint force commander (JFC), this chapter provides a doctrinal construct for C2 of space operations. However, it does not discuss the "ongoing debate over deployable space forces, such as CCS [Counter Communications System], which will undoubtedly be part of a growing OCS [offensive counterspace] component of theater campaign plans."[1] A compelling argument for the need of a doctrinal approach to C2 of "deployable space forces," if the reader chooses to explore this subject further, is made by Maj Mark Schuler, USAF, in his treatise "It Isn't Space, It's Warfare!"[2] Schuler notes that DOD space doctrine at the time of his publication is "unclear what the official belief is regarding the C2 of deployable space forces."[3] Therefore, this chapter discusses the C2 of space assets of global and theater spaces forces to include C2 considerations. The chapter concludes with the CFACC's authority and role in theater space operations. This construct has proven to be effective in recent operations and exercises and will remain the typical arrangement for the foreseeable future.

Global and Theater Considerations

Many space assets support joint operations in more than one geographic area. Space assets may be used to fulfill single-theater, multiple-theater, or global objectives. Thus, the C2 structure established for integrating space assets and forces must be robust enough to account for these various operating areas.

When the employment of space assets meets global or multiple-theater requirements, a structure that bridges more than one theater and is capable of dealing with non-DOD agencies is normally necessary. In this case, USSTRATCOM usually provides such a structure. A geographic combatant commander (GCC) may control those space forces which produce strategic, operational, or tactical effects within his or her theater. Furthermore, the combatant commander will usually delegate operational control (OPCON) of theater space forces to the appropriate service component commander and tactical control (TACON) to the appropriate functional component commander if needed by a joint force. The CFACC is usually best suited to integrate space operations within a combined/joint force. Within that force, the commander, Air Force forces (COMAFFOR) is best suited to integrate Air Force space operations because of his or her ability to exercise C2 of space capabilities and the COMAFFOR's theater-wide war-fighting perspective.

When the situation arises that there are no Air Force forces attached to a joint task force (JTF), the COMAFFOR to the joint force commander may be tasked in a supporting relationship to the JTF to integrate and provide space capabilities and effects. For example, multiple JTFs in US Central Command's area of responsibility (AOR) require space effects for the ongoing global war on terrorism. The CFACC provides/coordinates these effects for JTFs in Afghanistan, Iraq, and the Horn of Africa.

Although not operated or controlled by USSTRATCOM, nonmilitary US space assets also provide critical space capabilities for war fighters. Some assets belong to national agencies such as NASA, the National Reconnaissance Office, and NOAA. International consortia such as the International Telecommunications Satellite (INTELSAT) Organization and the International Maritime Satellite (INMARSAT) Organization own other space assets. USSTRATCOM has established coordination channels with some US nonmilitary organizations.

If such channels are not already established, a JFC may request USSTRATCOM assistance in coordinating with these nonmilitary organizations for integration of their capabilities. The secretary of defense and combatant commanders develop processes to streamline discussions, policies, procedures, and rules of engagement for space forces. These assets are important in establishing space superiority for global and theater operations.

154

USSTRATCOM Joint Functional Component Commands

USSTRATCOM executes assigned missions through a number of subordinate elements called joint functional component commands (JFCC) in lieu of JTFs. These commands are responsible for the day-to-day planning and execution of primary USSTRATCOM mission areas: space; global strike and integration; intelligence, surveillance, and reconnaissance; network warfare; integrated missile defense; and combating weapons of mass destruction. The commander, JFCC Space (CDR JFCC Space) serves as USSTRATCOM's single point of contact for military space operational matters to plan, task, direct, and execute space operations. The CDR JFCC Space will conduct space operational-level planning, integration, and coordination with other JFCCs, combatant commanders, and other DOD and non-DOD partners to ensure unity of effort in support of military and national security operations. The CDR JFCC Space will be the primary USSTRATCOM interface for operational space effects. The mission of the CDR JFCC Space includes employing joint space forces for missile warning; position, navigation, and timing; communications; space lift; and counterspace operations.

Command and Control of Global Space Forces

The Unified Command Plan establishes USSTRATCOM as the functional unified command with overall responsibility for military space operations. The commander, USSTRATCOM (CDRUSSTRATCOM) has combatant command (COCOM), or command authority, of all space forces as assigned by the secretary of defense in the "Forces for Unified Commands" memorandum. CDRUSSTRATCOM employs these forces to support worldwide operations.

Command and Control of Theater Space Forces

Theater commanders integrate space effects throughout joint military operations. Space effects are created by a mix of global and theater space forces. Global space forces normally support national objectives and multiple theaters and produce effects for theater operations. Theater space forces move forward to conduct operations in a specific theater or consist of organic space forces assigned in theater. Global space forces and theater space forces require different command relationships and levels of coordination to achieve effects within the theater.

Space experts on theater staffs facilitate space integration. The Air Force embeds space expertise within its component and air and space operations center (AOC) staff. Also, the Air Force augments theater staffs with additional space expertise, when requested, to assist with integration of global space effects and control of theater space forces.

Integrating Global Space Forces

When a theater requests global space forces to produce effects, the secretary of defense specifies a command relationship between CDRUSSTRATCOM and the combatant commander—normally a supporting/supported relationship. This will be employed at appropriate levels within both the supporting and supported commands. These support relationships fall into four categories: general, mutual, direct, and close support. General support is used when the support is given to the supported force as a whole. Mutual support is that support which units render each other against an enemy because of their assigned tasks, their position relative to each other and to the enemy, and their inherent capabilities. Direct support is used when a mission requires a force to directly support another specific force. Close support is used to describe actions by a supporting force in close proximity against objectives near the supported force which require detailed integration of the supporting actions of the supporting force.

For space forces providing effects via a support relationship, it is important for both supported and supporting commanders to document their requirements in an establishing directive. The establishing directive should specify the purpose of the support relationship, the effect desired, and the scope of the action to be taken. Additional information includes:

- The space forces and resources allocated to the supporting commander's effort.
- The time, place, level, and duration of the supporting commander's effort.
- The relative priority of the supported commander's effort.
- The degree of authority exercised by the supported and supporting commanders over the effort, to include processes for reconciling competing requirements and emergency events expeditiously, as required.

To facilitate a support relationship, an appropriate level of coordination should occur between the involved commanders. This facilitates planning the detailed integration of space capabilities and effects with theater operations and enables theater war fighters to coordinate directly at either the same or differing organizational levels.

Typically, CDRUSSTRATCOM will retain control of global space forces. However, a theater commander may require a greater degree of command authority than specified by a support relationship. This assumes the requisite expertise, ability, and means to perform C2 of space forces exist in theater. In those instances, the secretary of defense may transfer control over specified global space forces conducting operations affecting an individual theater.

Examples of Space Support

The four categories of space support relationships—general, mutual, direct, and close—have all been employed in recent conflicts to provide space support crucial to accomplishing the mission.

General Support. During the major combat operations phase of Operation Iraqi Freedom (OIF), USSTRATCOM provided general support from space operations to the Iraqi theater of operations. This support relationship helped the joint force integrate space capabilities, such as positioning, navigation, and timing from GPS, and counterspace effects.

Mutual Support. During the counterinsurgency phase of OIF, the combatant commander assigned the CFACC the task of space superiority. For this objective, the JFC designated the CFACC as the supported commander with other component commanders in a mutual support relationship for space operations.

Direct Support. During Operation Allied Force (OAF), a direct support relationship was established between the CFACC and the 11th Space Warning Squadron (SWS). This relationship allowed the AOC to directly task 11th SWS personnel and exchange real-time information from the DSP satellite for time-critical actions like personnel recovery after aircraft shoot-downs.

Close Support. Future space capabilities will be responsive to the war fighter. These space forces may operate in close proximity with theater forces and will require detailed integration to provide close support to theater operations. These types of forces could emerge as technologies based on the Air Force's operationally responsive space and joint war-fighting space operating concepts.

Theater Space Forces

If space forces are tasked to impact only a single theater, the secretary of defense may direct CDRUSSTRATCOM to attach the forces with specification of OPCON or TACON to the GCC with the mission requirement. It is the responsibility of the secretary of defense to specify the command relationship the gaining commander will exercise. The typical relationship for attached forces is OPCON, but a TACON or support relationship may be appropriate depending on the ability of the theater commander to C2 space operations, as well as other factors, including the nature and duration of the operation. Usually, the GCC delegates OPCON of attached forces to the service component commander who requires those forces and has the capability to C2 them. In the case of attached Air Force space forces, this is the COMAFFOR, who also is usually dual-hatted as the CFACC, and designated supported commander for counterspace operations in the joint operations area (JOA).

Theater-Organic Space Forces

GCCs exercise COCOM of assigned theater space forces. Service component commanders are normally then delegated OPCON of those forces. During contingencies, those forces may be incorporated into a joint force. Within the joint force, the appropriate functional component commander normally exercises TACON of forces made available by service component commanders. For space forces, this component commander should be the CFACC if one is designated.

Presentation of Forces

If a contingency operation requires a joint force, Air Force forces will be presented as an air and space expeditionary task force (AETF). The commander, Air Force Space Command (AFSPC/CC) is responsible for providing Air Force space forces to an AETF when required. Within the AETF, space forces may be attached to an air expeditionary wing, group, or squadron. Attached space forces are commanded by the COMAFFOR who commands the AETF through an A-staff and controls forces through an AOC. The AOC coordinates integration of space effects with the Space AOC/Joint Space Operations Center (JSpOC), and execution of assigned, attached, and supporting space forces (direct liaison authority) should be authorized for coordinated planning between the AOC and Space AOC/JSpOC.

CFACC's Authority and Role in Theater Space Operations

The CFACC is normally delegated space coordinating authority (SCA) and designated the supported commander for counterspace operations by the JFC. In cases where the CFACC is other than an Air Force officer, the COMAFFOR will fill designated billets within the CFACC staff to ensure proper employment of space assets. If a CFACC is not appointed, the JFC may delegate SCA to the COMAFFOR, designate another component/service commander SCA, or opt to retain SCA.

Space Coordinating Authority

Space coordinating authority is an authority within a joint force aiding in the coordination of joint space operations and integration of space capabilities and effects. SCA is an authority, not a person. As such, the commander with SCA serves as the focal point for gathering space requirements from the JFC's staff and each component commander. This provides unity of effort for space operations in support of the JFC's campaign. These requirements include requests for space forces (e.g., deployed space forces), requests for space capabilities (e.g., support to personnel recovery operations), and requests for implementation of specific command relationships (e.g., a support relationship between the CFACC and CDR JFCC Space). The commander with SCA develops a recommended prioritized list of space requirements for the joint force based on JFC objectives. The sphere of influence and focus of SCA in theater is the JOA. While a commander with SCA can facilitate nontraditional uses of space assets, planning staffs should use the established processes for fulfilling intelligence and communications requirements.

Because component commanders normally execute forces, the JFC may delegate SCA to the component-commander level. Coordination should be done at the operational level because that is where requirements are prioritized to support the operations of the component commanders, which in turn support the overall campaign. Moreover, the commander-delegated SCA should have a theater-wide perspective and a thorough understanding of integrating space operations with all other military activities.

SCA is a specific type of coordinating authority where authority is delegated to a commander or individual for coordinating specific space functions and activities involving forces of two or more military departments, functional components, or two or more forces of the same service. The commander with SCA has the authority to require consultation among the agencies involved but does not have the authority to compel agreement. The common task to be coordinated will be specified in the establishing directive without disturbing the organizational relationships in other matters. Coordinating authority is a consultation relationship between commanders, not an authority by which command may be exercised.

Space coordinating authority carries with it several responsibilities:

- Recommend appropriate command relationships for space forces to the JFC or JFACC.

- Establish, deconflict, prioritize, and recommend military space requirements.

- Recommend guidelines for employing space capabilities, such as rules of engagement, for the joint force.

- Guide strategy development, operational planning, and space integration.

158

- Provide status of space assets that affect the JOA to key theater staffs.
- Maintain space situational awareness.
- Ensure optimum interoperability of space assets with coalition forces.

Delegation of SCA is tied to force assignment, and it is normally delegated to the functional component commander with the preponderance of space forces, expertise in space operations, and the ability to C2 space assets, including reachback. The preponderance of space forces is based on a component's space capabilities affecting the theater, through the C2 of space forces assigned, attached, and in support. Users of space capabilities are not a factor in the determination of preponderance; it is based solely on the ability to operate space capabilities and produce effects with space forces.

During times of conflict or large-scale contingencies, it is important to have a coordinating authority for space within the joint force structure to appropriately represent the space requirements of the joint force. With each component and many allies having their own organic space capability, there is a requirement to integrate, synchronize, and deconflict among the space operations, redundant efforts, and conflicting support requests. By designating SCA for the joint force to a single commander, the JFC can optimize space operations in the JOA. To facilitate unity of effort within theater space operations and with global space assets, the JFC normally delegates SCA to the CFACC.

There are several reasons why the JFC normally delegates SCA to the CFACC. First, the CFACC has space expertise embedded in his or her staff. Second, the CFACC has the ability to command and control space forces via the AOC, including reachback to the Space AOC/JSpOC. Lastly, unlike the land or maritime component commanders, who are assigned specific areas of operations (AO) within a theater, the CFACC maintains a JOA and theater-wide perspective. This perspective is essential for coordinating space operations that also support the JFC throughout the theater.

Supported Commander for Counterspace Operations and Strategic Attack

To ensure unity of command, the JFC should designate the CFACC as the supported commander for counterspace operations. These operations are designed to maintain space superiority. With US dependence on space capabilities for our asymmetric advantages in the operational environment and the proliferation of various threats to space systems, it is critical to have a single component commander focused on maintaining space superiority using all available capabilities as part of the overall joint campaign.

The CFACC is well suited to execute counterspace operations for the JFC as part of the overall campaign for several reasons. First, the Air Force has the overwhelming majority of satellite operations, maintenance, and C2 experience, making it especially qualified to plan, execute, and assess offensive and defensive space activities. This expertise is integrated into the CFACC's staff. Second, the CFACC has a complete AOR perspective due to range, speed, and flexibility and is able to employ various methods to attack the user/user equipment through kinetic and nonkinetic means, both directly and indirectly. Also, the CFACC, as the COMAFFOR, can recommend theater defensive measures to ensure that tactics, techniques, and procedures as well as infrastructure reduce or mitigate potential threats. For example, the CFACC could provide guidance in the special instructions that units should be prepared to employ weapons in a GPS-hostile environment. Third, the CFACC, through its organic C2 centers (to include reachback), has the ability to integrate assets to deliver effects when and where needed. Fourth, the Air

Force understands the treaty, legal, and policy considerations associated with space operations. For these reasons, the CFACC should be designated as the supported commander for counterspace operations. In this role, the CFACC has the authority to designate target priority, effects, and timing of these operations and attack targets across the entire JOA (to include targets within the land and maritime AOs, although operations within a surface AO must be coordinated with the AO commander).

To coordinate with the JFC and other component commands, the CFACC may collocate an air component coordination element (ACCE) within their respective staffs. The purpose of the ACCE is to act as the CFACC's liaison to other commanders. The CFACC will normally integrate space expertise (and counterspace expertise, if designated the supported commander for counterspace) in the ACCE (or other liaison elements) to coordinate space-related issues with the JFC and component commanders, on his or her behalf.

In future operations and consistent with treaty obligations, assigning theater activities for force application from or through space to the CFACC would enhance unity of command. The CFACC, as the supported commander for strategic attack, would integrate these capabilities into the overall joint campaign. The CFACC has the ability within the AOC to integrate and deconflict all strategic attack capabilities to meet the JFC's objectives. All Air Force strategic attack capabilities should be integrated throughout joint operations to achieve the commander's desired effects.

Director of Space Forces

To plan, execute, and assess space operations, the COMAFFOR typically designates a director of space forces (DIRSPACEFOR), an Air Force senior space advisor who facilitates coordination, integration, and staffing activities. In the preferred construct of a dual-hatted COMAFFOR/CFACC, the DIRSPACEFOR serves as the senior space advisor to the CFACC in an appropriate capacity, such as special staff, to tailor space operations as part of the JFC's campaign plan. Also, this position normally requires a small support staff to work requirements specific to the JOA and ongoing military operations. Because the intended scope includes coordination with both Air Force and other service space forces, the DIRSPACEFOR accomplishes joint responsibilities, especially given the normal situation where the CFACC is delegated SCA and designated supported commander for counterspace operations. The DIRSPACEFOR is a senior Air Force officer with broad space expertise and theater familiarity, nominated by AFSPC/CC and approved by the theater CFACC. AFSPC ensures DIRSPACEFORs are trained and certified to perform their responsibilities, and the CFACC provides theater-specific information and orientation.

When the situation arises that there are no Air Force forces attached to a JTF, the COMAFFOR to the joint force commander may be tasked in a supporting relationship to the JTF to integrate and provide space capabilities and effects. In the situation of multiple JTFs, the DIRSPACEFOR should work for the theater COMAFFOR/CFACC, who normally is delegated SCA, to provide space effects to the JTF based on JFC priorities.

The DIRSPACEFOR has the following tasks:

- Recommend appropriate command relationships for space forces.
- Establish, deconflict, prioritize, and recommend operational military space requirements.

160

- Recommend policies for employing space capabilities, such as rules of engagement.
- Provide senior space perspective for strategy and daily guidance development, effects and target selection, and space integration throughout joint force operations.
- Monitor status of space forces that affect the JOA, and provide status to JFC staff and components.
- Maintain space situational awareness.
- Request space inputs from JFC staff during planning and operations.
- Ensure optimum interoperability of space assets with coalition forces.
- Execute day-to-day SCA responsibilities on behalf of the CFACC, or act as the CFACC's representative to the SCA if the authority is retained by the Combined Forces Command or delegated to another component; assist the COMAFFOR with command and control of Air Force space forces if another component is designated CFACC.

The Air Force organizes, trains, and equips space forces for employment during military operations based on the construct of a COMAFFOR/CFACC. However, there may be exceptional circumstances which fall outside the bounds of this construct. First, for the rare instances when the CFACC is not delegated SCA (e.g., a JFC retains SCA or delegates SCA to another component commander), the DIRSPACEFOR will continue to work space-related issues on behalf of the COMAFFOR/CFACC. Second, for the special case when the JFC chooses to organize and employ military forces through service components and does not designate a CFACC, the DIRSPACEFOR works for the COMAFFOR, who is expected to be delegated SCA. In all these special circumstances, theaterwide coordination will be the responsibility of the component commander delegated SCA, who will normally be aided by a senior space advisor. The Air Force recommends a senior space advisor handle day-to-day SCA responsibilities on behalf of the component commander delegated SCA.[4]

The space assets available to the DIRSPACEFOR are available under the auspices of USSTRATCOM, who in turn leverages the operational capabilities of its respective service component commands: Army Space Command (ARSPACE), Naval Network Warfare Command (NETWARCOM), and Space Air Forces (SPACEAF).

These components have distinct space missions. The mission of ARSPACE is to provide space control operations and space support to the joint force and Army component, coordinate and integrate Army resources in the execution of USSTRATCOM plans and operations, provide theater missile warning through employment of joint tactical ground stations, provide space support through the use of Army space support teams, and perform Defense Satellite Communications System payload and network control. Additionally, ARSPACE functions as the satellite communications (SATCOM) system expert (SSE) for Wideband Global SATCOM super-high frequency (SHF) communications satellites and is the parent command for the regional satellite communications support centers servicing all combatant commands, their components, the defense agencies, and other users. US Army Space and Missile Defense Command is the Army major command that organizes, trains, equips, and provides forces to ARSPACE and plans for national missile defense.

NETWARCOM's mission is to ensure space-based support to naval war fighters. This mission is accomplished via four means: providing operations and operational support;

161

providing space expertise and training; performing requirements advocacy; and fostering the advancement of space technologies.

Additionally, NETWARCOM operates the Naval Space Operations Center (NAVSPOC) to provide integrated support to naval and joint war fighters as well as other members of the space community. The primary goal of the NAVSPOC is to provide situational awareness by monitoring not only space activity, but also fleet deployments to ensure that space-based support is optimized. The NAVSPOC is capable of pushing space-related intelligence and other data products to fleet and fleet Marine forces on a continuous basis. Additional support and products may be provided as requested. The NAVSPOC also serves as operational manager of ultra-high frequency (UHF) communications systems, provides satellite sustainment, and coordinates commercial satellite communications support. NETWARCOM also operates other space-based communications, meteorological and oceanographic (METOC), and research and development systems in support of naval needs. NETWARCOM also provides manpower and training support for the Army's JTAGS units.

Important to the continuity and survivability of C2 operations, the NAVSPOC serves as the alternate space control center, providing C2 of the space surveillance network in support of USSTRATCOM operations. NAVSPOC formerly operated the Naval Space Surveillance Radar Fence, which detects and tracks objects in space.[5] However, operations were transferred to Air Force control on 1 October 2004, and the fence was renamed the Air Force Space Surveillance System (AFSSS).

The aforementioned C2 construct for joint space operations has served as a fundamental and workable construct, in which the CDRUSSTRATCOM currently has COCOM of all space forces. Moreover, the CDRUSSTRATCOM employs these forces to support worldwide operations. In conclusion, lessons learned concerning C2 of space operations from Operations Iraqi Freedom and Enduring Freedom will require inclusion into future doctrine. Moreover, space capabilities are certain to increase and with them the demand for those capabilities to support the JFC in a responsive manner. Space capabilities will be a subject of discussion and exploration which the secretary of defense, CDRUSSTRATCOM, and COCOM commander will no doubt address for future doctrine to ensure the necessary responsiveness.

Notes

1. Maj Mark A. Schuler, "It Isn't Space, It's Warfare!" in *Space Power Integration: Perspectives from Space Weapons Officers*, ed. Lt Col Kendall K. Brown, (Maxwell AFB, AL: Air University Press, 2006), 6.

2. Ibid., 65–88.

3. Ibid., 73.

4. AFDD 2-2, *Space Operations*, 27 November 2006, 8–17.

5. Joint Publication 3-14, *Space Operations*, 6 January 2009, II-4.

Chapter 12

Space Event Processing

Maj Edward P. Chatters IV, USAF

Space systems have become a critical component of US military operations. Military commanders rely on navigation, communications, environmental surveillance, and warning information received from or provided via space systems. Any degradation to these systems could have a significant impact on the success of a military operation. In addition, the United States must protect its ground assets from intelligence collection by other countries.

The US Space Command (USSPACECOM) was established in 1985 to normalize the use of space in support of US deterrence capabilities and to centralize all military activity related to US space systems. USSPACECOM advocated the space requirements of the other unified commanders. In 2002 USSPACECOM functions were transferred to the US Strategic Command (USSTRATCOM), and USSPACECOM was inactivated.[1]

USSTRATCOM conducts space operations through its joint functional component command, JFCC Space, which is headquartered at Vandenberg AFB, California, and commanded by the Fourteenth Air Force commander.[2]

Space Events

A space event is an activity impacting on a US space asset or an activity involving another nation's space assets. Possible space events include the following:

- New foreign launch (NFL)
- Antisatellite (ASAT) launch
- Preplanned launch (PPL)
- Maneuvers
- Separations
- Reentries
- Breakups

A new foreign launch is defined as the launch of a satellite by a foreign country or agency without prior coordination with USSTRATCOM. An ASAT launch is a specific type of NFL that is designed to destroy or degrade the capabilities of a satellite belonging to the United States or another nation. An ASAT launch is typically considered to be a hostile act by the launching nation. The space surveillance network (SSN) is used to detect, track, identify, and catalog the objects from these space launches. The SSN will be discussed in further detail in chapter 19.

A preplanned launch is a space launch in which USSTRATCOM has received advance notification and launch information from the launching agency and/or payload(s) owner about the payload mission, launch profile, and parameters. There are two types of PPLs: cooperative and domestic. A domestic launch refers to a PPL that is launched from within the United States or from a US platform. A cooperative launch refers to a PPL that is launched by a nation other than the United States but with prior coordination with USSTRATCOM.

A maneuver is simply a change in orbit of a satellite. This change can occur with the satellite orbit's size (shape), its inclination (orbital plane), or both.[3] Most satellite maneuvers are considered station keeping, which means the satellite is being moved slightly in order to keep it in a particular orbit around the earth. However, there are cases where a satellite may maneuver for repositioning, end-of-life preparations, or other reasons. In these cases the Joint Space Operations Center (JSpOC) will coordinate with various intelligence sources to determine the purpose of these maneuvers and send warnings to forward users if necessary.[4]

A separation is the intentional disconnection of one or more parts of a satellite from its main body. There are certain satellites that have been specifically designed to perform separation missions. Satellite separations are usually confirmed by intelligence sources.

A reentry refers to a near-Earth space object that, due to the drag force of the atmosphere and gravitational effects, can no longer remain in orbit and falls back to Earth. Objects that survive reentry may generate false indications of a missile threat to the US or Russian missile-warning systems. As a result, the JSpOC manages a reentry assessment program that predicts atmospheric reentry times for these reentering space objects and provides notification to the National Military Command Center (NMCC).

A satellite breakup is defined as the unintentional separation of several objects from the main body of a payload, rocket body, or other orbiting object. Most breakups are believed to have been caused by propulsion-related events or accidental detonations; however, the causes of some satellite breakups are simply unknown. The number of new objects detected as a result of a breakup will vary greatly. Such variation is due to the satellite's orbital parameters, collision variants, and the availability of space surveillance sites that have coverage of the event.

Responding to Space Events

When a space event occurs, the JSpOC at Vandenberg AFB, California, is responsible for determining if the event is accidental, incidental, or the result of a hostile action directed against the United States and forwarding its assessment to USSTRATCOM. The JSpOC gathers information from a variety of sources, especially its Combat Operations Division's Space Situational Awareness Operations (SSA OPS) Cell (fig. 12-1) to make this determination.

Once the USSTRATCOM commander has been provided with the JSpOC's report, the commander may request a space event conference from the NMCC. During the space event conference, USSTRATCOM describes the activity and provides one of the following assessments:

- NO—An attack against a space system has not occurred nor is one in progress.
- CONCERN—Events are occurring that have raised the level of concern. Further assessment is necessary to determine the nature of the activity involved. Pending

164

completion of the ongoing assessment, precautionary measures to enhance responsiveness or survivability are suggested.

- YES—A verified attack against a space system has occurred. This means that all source data confirms the hostile event has occurred or is occurring.

The assessment provided by USSTRATCOM will determine what courses of action to take in response to the space event.

Figure 12-1. JSpOC SSA OPS Cell operator. (USAF photo)

Conclusion

The nature of space operations is such that its theater of operations is not normally host to the personnel affected. Also, all space ground facilities are located in another combatant commander's area of responsibility. As a result, when a verified attack occurs or is in progress, USSTRATCOM relies on the other unified commanders to protect US assets and, when necessary, respond to space events with force. The Joint Space Operations Center, along with other agencies within the space and intelligence community, provides the unified commanders with the information necessary to avert or mitigate threats to space systems and their associated ground-support systems. For additional information regarding space event processing, contact the JSpOC Combat Operations Division at Vandenberg AFB.

Notes

1. USSTRATCOM, "U.S. Strategic Command History," http://www.stratcom.mil/about-ch.html (accessed 16 January 2008).

2. USSTRATCOM, "Functional Components," http://www.stratcom.mil/organization-fnc_comp.html (accessed 16 January 2008).

3. David Wright, Laura Grego, and Lisbeth Gronlund, *The Physics of Space Security: A Reference Manual*, 183, http://www.amacad.org/publications/Physics_of_Space_Security.pdf (accessed 23 January 2008).

4. Briefing, 1st Space Control Squadron, 614th Space Operations Group, subject: Welcome to the 1st Space Control Squadron, 4 June 2007.

Chapter 13

US Space-Based Intelligence, Surveillance, and Reconnaissance

Maj Brian Crothers, USAF; Maj Jeff Lanphear, USAF; Maj Brian Garino, USAF; Maj Paul P. Konyha III, USAF; and Maj Edward P. Byrne, USAF

I wouldn't want to be quoted on this, but we've spent 35 or 40 billion dollars on the space program. And if nothing else had come out of it except the knowledge we've gained from space photography, it would be worth 10 times what the whole program cost. Because tonight we know how many missiles the enemy has and, it turned out, our guesses were way off. We were doing things we didn't need to do. We were building things we didn't need to build. We were harboring fears we didn't need to harbor. Because of satellites, I know how many missiles the enemy has.

—Pres. Lyndon B. Johnson
Remarks to educators in Nashville, TN
16 March 1967

Intelligence, surveillance, and reconnaissance (ISR) is the collection of data and information on an object or in an area of interest (AOI) on a continuing, event-driven, or scheduled basis. Collection over relatively continuous periods of time is called surveillance. Collection that is event-driven, is scheduled over shorter periods, is repeated, or occurs on a relatively brief one-time basis is generally referred to as reconnaissance. Orbital characteristics and numbers of systems applied to a target over time can determine whether reconnaissance or surveillance is conducted. The joint force commander (JFC) and the components have access to space systems that can collect diverse military, political, or economic information that can be valuable for planning and executing throughout the range of military operations (including peacekeeping) and humanitarian or disaster-relief missions. More specifically, information can be collected, processed, exploited, and disseminated on such diverse subjects as indications and warning (to include ballistic missile attack), targeting analysis, friendly course-of-action (COA) development, adversary capability assessment, battle damage assessment (BDA), or battlespace characterization. Types of data and information collected from space can include signals intelligence (SIGINT), imagery intelligence (IMINT), and measurement and signature intelligence (MASINT).

ISR and Space Systems

ISR capabilities allow commanders and decision makers to collect information to aid them in planning and decision making. Space systems are vital to the military's ISR functions.

Intelligence

Intelligence is the product resulting from the collection, processing, integration, analysis, evaluation, and interpretation of available information concerning foreign countries or areas. Space systems contribute to the development of intelligence through surveillance and reconnaissance activities.[1]

Surveillance

Space systems offer commanders continuous observation of space, air, surface areas, places, persons, or things by visual, electronic, photographic, or other means that provide situational awareness within a given area. Surveillance from space does not infer that a single satellite or "system" must be continuously collecting. Satellites that are able to provide a snapshot in time can be augmented by additional systems collecting in the same or even different areas of the electromagnetic spectrum. There will be short gaps in collection (minutes or a few hours), but systems will be concentrating on a target, which over time constitutes surveillance. These "following" systems can continue collecting on a target as the previous satellite moves out of the area of access in its orbit. Several satellites in low and medium Earth orbits can provide coverage of targets on the order of minutes. Geosynchronous satellites can provide true surveillance, as their orbits allow them to have continuous access to large portions of the earth. Collection from geosynchronous systems may, by necessity, be prioritized based on area of the world and where within the electromagnetic spectrum they can be tasked to collect. In many instances, the number of requirements levied against a system may also necessitate a prioritization of collection. Satellites may also be a contributor to an overall surveillance effort consisting of space, terrestrial, and airborne systems that together provide continuity in surveillance when space systems alone do not have continuous access or are unavailable.[2]

Reconnaissance

Single low and medium Earth orbiting systems or architectures that provide limited numbers of low or medium orbital systems are well-suited to the reconnaissance mission. Generally their access to specific targets are limited in time based on their orbits, such that data collected will be a "snapshot" of events in the portion of the electromagnetic spectrum where the systems can collect. Geosynchronous or geostationary satellites are capable of performing reconnaissance from space as well, focusing their collection efforts on a target or region for relatively short amounts of time before focusing on another area.[3]

Imagery Intelligence

Imagery intelligence is defined by the Department of Defense (DOD) as intelligence derived from the exploitation of collection by visual photography, infrared sensors, lasers, electro-optics, and radar sensors such as synthetic aperture radar, wherein images of objects are reproduced optically or electronically on film, electronic display devices, or other media.[4]

Background

Military reconnaissance was one of the first applications of space technology in the United States. The first attempted launch of an imagery collection satellite occurred in February 1959, but that launch failed. However, in August 1960 the first successful imagery launch took place under the CORONA program. In September 1961, the National Reconnaissance Office (NRO) was formed to execute the national reconnaissance program.[5] The CORONA program operated in secret from August 1960 to May 1972, collecting over 800,000 images from space. The existence of the NRO was declassified in 1992, and the CORONA program was declassified under executive order on 24 February 1995.[6] Although the CORONA program was the earliest pioneer in space-based IMINT, there have been many other programs since.

The NRO manages all data collection from national satellite systems. The NRO and National Geospatial-Intelligence Agency (NGA) work jointly to process this data. Data collected at the theater and tactical levels by airborne collection systems and through other methods are managed by the military services. The services are responsible for providing this data to national-level databases. The NGA is responsible overall for managing, disseminating, and archiving data.

Commercial and civil entities also contribute significantly to these databases.[7] Today, at least seven other countries and multinational organizations operate space-based imaging platforms.[8] In addition to state-owned and operated programs, there are numerous commercial space-based imaging programs in operation. The NGA is the executive agent for the purchase of commercial satellite imagery within DOD and has the capability to buy rights in two distinct forms. It can purchase imagery for immediate use, or it can purchase the rights to selected imagery for future distribution, depending on specific requirements. The Commercial Satellite Imagery Library (CSIL) contains an archive of all DOD-purchased commercial satellite imagery and is maintained by the Defense Intelligence Agency (DIA) for the NGA.[9]

Resolution

The detail discernible in an image is dependent on the spatial resolution of the sensor and refers to the size of the smallest possible feature that can be detected. Spatial resolution of passive sensors depends primarily on their instantaneous field of view (IFOV). The IFOV is the angular cone of visibility of the sensor and determines the area on the earth's surface that is "seen" from a given altitude at one particular moment in time. The size of the area viewed is determined by multiplying the IFOV by the distance from the ground to the sensor. This area on the ground is called the resolution cell and determines a sensor's maximum spatial resolution. To detect a homogeneous feature, its size generally has to be equal to or larger than the resolution cell. If the feature is smaller than this, it may not be detectable, as the average brightness of all features in that resolution cell will be recorded. However, smaller features may sometimes be detectable if their reflectance dominates within a particular resolution cell allowing subpixel or resolution-cell detection.

With current systems, resolution is usually referred to in meters, and each pixel will sample a square area on the ground in terms of meters. Most remote sensing images are composed of a matrix of picture elements, or pixels, which are the smallest elements of an image that can be detected. Image pixels are normally square and represent a certain area on an image. Reflected energy is received by a sensor array in the form of individual brightness values or picture elements (pixels). In a digital system, a pixel represents an area on the earth's surface. For example, the Satellite Pour L'Observation de la Terre (SPOT) panchromatic sensor has pixels that are the average of the light reflected from a 10-meter by 10-meter (10 m x 10 m) area on the ground.[10] Therefore, SPOT panchromatic imagery can be said to have 10 m pixels.

It is important to distinguish between pixel size and spatial resolution—they are not interchangeable. Spatial resolution is a measure of the smallest angular or linear separation between two objects that can be resolved by the sensor. More simply put, it is the smallest separation between two objects where the objects can still be detected as separate. This type of resolution is related to the ground sampling distance (GSD) of a system. GSD is defined as the distance between centers of pixels or, in other words, the centers of areas sampled on the ground. An image from the LANDSAT Thematic Mapper (TM) sensor, for example, which has a GSD of 28.5 m, will not normally allow for detection of an object that is 5 m.[11]

If a sensor has a spatial resolution of 20 m and an image from that sensor is displayed at full resolution, each pixel represents an area of 20 m x 20 m on the ground. In this case, the pixel size and resolution are the same. However, it is possible to display an image with a pixel size different from the resolution. Many posters of Earth satellite images have their pixels averaged to represent larger areas, although the original spatial resolution of the sensor that collected the imagery remains the same.

Images where only large features are visible are said to have coarse or low resolution. In fine- or high-resolution images, small objects can be detected. Military sensors, for example, are designed to view much greater detail and therefore have very fine resolution. Commercial satellites typically provide imagery with resolutions varying from a few meters to several kilometers. Generally speaking, the finer the resolution, the less total ground area can be seen. See figures 13-1 through 13-4 for examples of GSD.

Figure 13-1. 48-inch GSD. (*Reprinted from* Jeffrey J. Hemphill, "ITEK Optical Reconnaissance Camera System: Comparing Resolution and Area Coverage," http://www.geog.ucsb.edu/~jeff/115a/militaryintelligence/itek.html [accessed 5 April 2008].)

Figure 13-2. 24-inch GSD. (*Reprinted from* Jeffrey J. Hemphill, "ITEK Optical Reconnaissance Camera System: Comparing Resolution and Area Coverage," http://www.geog.ucsb.edu/~jeff/115a/militaryintelligence/itek.html [accessed 5 April 2008].)

Figure 13-3. 12-inch GSD. *(Reprinted from Jeffrey J. Hemphill, "TEK Optical Reconnaissance Camera System: Comparing Resolution and Area Coverage," http://www.geog.ucsb.edu/~jeff/115a/militaryintelligence/itek.html [accessed 5 April 2008].)*

Figure 13-4. 6-inch GSD. *(Reprinted from Jeffrey J. Hemphill, "TEK Optical Reconnaissance Camera System: Comparing Resolution and Area Coverage," http://www.geog.ucsb.edu/~jeff/115a/militaryintelligence/itek.html [accessed 5 April 2008].)*

Types of Space-Based Imagery Systems

There are several types of spaced-based imagery systems that collect IMINT.

Film Return Capsule. The CORONA program operated as a film-return capsule system (fig. 13-5). Photographs were taken on a film roll system stored within the satellite. Film canisters were then ejected from the satellite and returned to Earth. Once the capsule had penetrated Earth's atmosphere, a small parachute would open, and the capsule would fall slowly over the ocean until it was recovered in mid-air by a US Air Force C-119 aircraft.[12]

This method of collecting film capsules from space is quite challenging and not very timely. Several IMINT programs from around the world still use film-return capsule systems to access and process imagery data. Another good example of a film-return

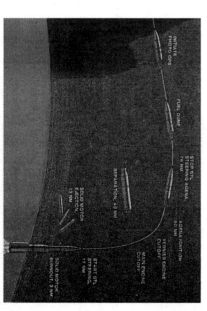

Figure 13-5. CORONA film capsule recovery sequence. *(Reprinted from NRO, "Corona System Information,"* http://www.nro.gov/corona/sysinfo2.html [accessed 5 March 2008].)

171

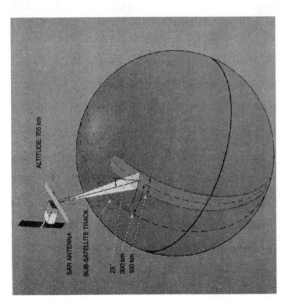

Figure 13-6. SAR satellite. (*Reprinted from* NASA, "What Is SAR, Anyway?" http://southport.jpl.nasa.gov/polar/sar.html [accessed 5 March 2008].)

capsule system is the Russian Resurs-F system. Russia flew 42 space missions with the Resurs-F system from May 1986 to September 1999 conducting remote sensing work. Each mission lasted less than 30 days and carried a film camera system, which returned to Earth in a 2.2 m spherical descent capsule. The capsules were reused an average of three times, and some camera systems were also refurbished and reflown.[13]

Electrical-Optical Imagery. Today most space-based imagery is collected by space-based camera systems and transmitted electronically to Earth. Electro-optical imagery is imagery collected from the portion of the electromagnetic spectrum visible to the human eye. The Indian Remote Sensing (IRS) P-5, or CARTOSAT-1 satellite system, is an example of an electro-optical imagery satellite. CARTOSAT-1 carries two panchromatic (PAN) cameras that take black and white stereoscopic pictures of the earth in the visible region of the electromagnetic spectrum. It also carries a solid state recorder to store the images taken by its cameras. The stored images can be downlinked when the satellite comes within the visibility zone of Shadnager Ground Station and processed and distributed by India's National Remote Sensing Agency.[14]

With an electro-optical imagery system, images can be transmitted to Earth electronically whenever in view of a receiving station. Those images can then be processed and distributed almost instantly. This provides imagery in a much more timely fashion than film-return capsule systems, with which it took weeks or months to view an image taken from space. With electro-optical systems that timeline can be reduced to minutes.

Space-Based Radar Imagery. Space-based radar systems rely on synthetic aperture radar (SAR) systems (fig. 13-6). Using SAR, a space-based radar sends out a pulse of radio waves which bounces off the object to be depicted. The scattered pulses then return to the radar, where they are captured by the receiving antenna. The antenna is the radar's aperture—its opening on the world. SAR antennas are a type of radar antenna designed to take advantage of their satellite's movement, thus creating a "synthetic" aperture or opening.[15]

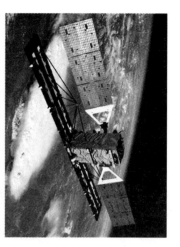

Figure 13-7. RADARSAT-2. *(Reprinted from Canadian Space Agency, Web site, http:// www.asc-csa.gc.ca/images/recherche/.)*

SAR images, which resemble photographs, are actually maps in which the brightness shown is a measure of the radar energy reflected back to the antenna. Water droplets in fog and clouds are transparent to radio waves of the proper frequency just as window glass is to light waves of the visible frequency. Hence, a SAR instrument can gather data in conditions where optical sensors would be useless, that is, it can provide excellent images of what the radar detected even in fog, clouds, or darkness.[15]

The Canadian Space Agency designed, constructed, launched, and now operates the RADARSAT. RADARSAT-2, launched on 14 December 2007, is the world's most powerful commercial radar remote-sensing satellite totally dedicated to operational applications (fig. 13-7).[17]

Infrared Imagery. Some imaging satellites contain sensors that collect images in the infrared (IR) portion of the electromagnetic spectrum. Infrared light lies between the visible and microwave portions of the electromagnetic spectrum. Infrared light has a range of wavelengths, just like visible light has wavelengths that range from red light to violet.[18] IR sensors on satellites are used to determine temperature variations of the object being imaged. This capability is useful in a number of situations. Due to temperature variations in an image, it is possible to determine if oil is running through a pipeline, if a nuclear reactor is active, or if a vehicle is operating or not. These are just a few obvious applications, but a more common use for IR sensors on a satellite is weather monitoring.

Many weather satellites have IR sensors to monitor temperature differences on Earth. Some of these sensors can be extremely sensitive to temperature variations. The French-owned and operated SPOT-4 Earth observation satellite has an additional sensor which can image objects in the shortwave infrared (SWIR) band. This information is used to discriminate between different types of crops and plant cover.[19]

Multispectral Imagery. Multispectral imagery (MSI) is steadily growing in popularity within DOD as a digital means for a variety of important taskings to include mission planning, thermal signature detection, and terrain analysis. Presently, it is frequently used as a map substitute when standard mapping, charting, and geodesy (MC&G) products are outdated or inadequate. The ability to record spectral reflectances in different portions of the electromagnetic spectrum is the main attribute of MSI, which can be useful in a number of applications. MSI typically provides such things as terrain information over broad areas in an unclassified format. This attribute make MSI convenient to share with personnel and organizations that are not usually privileged with controlled information from "national" assets. Multinational forces, news media, and civil authorities can all share the benefits of MSI.

The IKONOS satellite (fig. 13-8) is the world's first commercial satellite to collect black-and-white images with 1 m resolution and multispectral imagery with 4 m resolution. Imagery from the panchromatic and multispectral sensors can be merged to create 1 m color imagery (pan-sharpened). Commercial and governmental organizations rely on high-resolution IKONOS imagery to view, map, measure, monitor, and manage global activities. Applications range from national security and disaster assessment to urban planning and agricultural monitoring.[20]

Figure 13-8. IKONOS satellite. *(Reprinted from* Colorado State University, Environmental Observing Satellites, http://www.cira.colostate. edu/cira/RAMM/hillger/Ikonos_image.jpg.)

Signals Intelligence

Signals intelligence is the collection of broadcast transmissions from communication systems, as well as radars and other electronic systems. The SIGINT arena is comprised of three sub-areas—electronic intelligence (ELINT), communications intelligence (COMINT), and foreign instrumentation signals intelligence (FISINT)—which are differentiated based on the type of analysis to be performed and the nature of the emitter.

Background

The Soviet Union's launch of *Sputnik*, the world's first orbiting artificial satellite, impelled the United States to explore the concept of a space-based reconnaissance program. Along with the CORONA imagery system, President Eisenhower approved the development of a SIGINT satellite system in August 1959 called the Galactic Radiation and Background (GRAB) satellite, referring to its unclassified cover mission (fig. 13-9).[21] After the shootdown of Francis Gary Powers' high-altitude U-2 spy plane in May 1960, President Eisenhower cancelled all further U-2 overflights of the Soviet Union, cementing America's need for satellite reconnaissance. Along with its imagery cousin CORONA, GRAB and its successor, Poppy, became the original cornerstone of satellite reconnaissance in the 1960s and 1970s.[22]

GRAB and Poppy were ELINT satellites developed by the Naval Research Laboratory (NRL) and were designed to intercept Soviet radar emissions. The GRAB satellite was a 20-inch diameter metal ball packed with electronic equipment and antennas that provided reception of signals. It also featured a larger and separate turnstile antenna that received commands and transmitted telemetry and ELINT data.[23] The GRAB system included two successful satellite launches, failing twice at a third.[24] Following the conclusion of *GRAB 2*'s mission, the United States launched the first of six GRAB successor satellites, *Poppy 1*, in 1962. The early Poppy spacecraft had a stretched spherical shape, while later satellites featured a 12-sided

Figure 13-9. GRAB satellite. (Photo provided courtesy of the Naval Research Laboratory)

multiface design (fig. 13-10).[25] As Soviet terrestrial radars emitted their signals above the horizon, GRAB and Poppy satellites collected each radar pulse in a specified bandwidth and sent a corresponding signal to NRL ground stations. Personnel at the ground stations then transmitted the data to NRL, Air Force Strategic Air Command, and the National Security Agency (NSA) to exploit the data and generate technical intelligence about the Soviet radars.[26]

Intelligence derived from the GRAB and Poppy systems supported a wide range of applications during the Cold War. It provided cues to locations and capabilities of

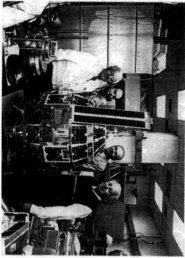

Figure 13-10. Poppy satellite with multiface design. (Photo taken by the NRL and provided courtesy of the NRO)

Soviet radar sites, characteristics and locations of Soviet air defense equipment, ocean surveillance information for Navy commanders, and a more complete picture of the actual Soviet military threat.[27] The GRAB and Poppy satellite systems were declassified in 1998 and 2004, respectively. They created the critical operations and exploitation paradigm for signals collection that established the foundation of the current overhead SIGINT reconnaissance architecture.

The SIGINT satellites of today are developed and launched jointly by the USAF and the National Reconnaissance Office, with support from the National Security Agency. The NRO's relationship with the NSA for the SIGINT mission mirrors the relationship it has with the National Geospatial-Intelligence Agency for the IMINT mission. The NRO collects signals from overhead satellite systems and delivers the data to the NSA for processing, analysis, dissemination, and exploitation.[28]

Signals Intelligence Types

Unlike imagery satellites, the United States deploys SIGINT spacecraft in all orbits—geosynchronous orbits to pick up ultra-high frequency (UHF) and very high frequency (VHF) communications, and low to medium Earth orbits to collect signals from air defense and early warning radars.[29] Highly elliptical orbits give satellites both long dwell times at high altitudes and short dwell times at low altitudes, maximizing signals collection over multiple regions for specific and repeating durations or frequencies.[30] The type of SIGINT collected often dictates which orbit will be used for a particular satellite.

Electronic Intelligence. ELINT involves the collection and analysis of intercepted signals by other than the intended recipient. It involves the exploitation of signal "externals," referring to the characteristics of the actual transmitted signal (including frequency of carriers and subcarriers, modulation, bandwidth, power level, etc.), beam footprint parameters, and emitter location and motion. A collection signal parameter can be used to obtain a radio frequency (RF) fingerprint for each emitter/emitter platform, which can then be used to locate and rapidly identify the specific emitter or emitter type in subsequent intercepts. Generally, ELINT requires the least amount of analysis of the three SIGINT sub-areas. Typically, systems that are designed to perform ELINT collection may also be capable of performing COMINT and/or FISINT activities.

Traffic analysis is an ELINT technique applicable to COMINT targets wherein the level and timing of activity associated with a specific communication or data-transmission system is assessed by determining whether or not data is present in the link. This determination is based on an examination of the actual RF signal; it is not necessary to actually demodulate the signal and recover the raw data (although this would be more reliable). Because of this, the technique is useful against encrypted links in which it is not possible to recover the raw data. Traffic analysis can be used for indications and warning purposes. Combined with emitter location data, traffic analysis can be used to specify users and user locations (by examining, over time, signal up and down times and assessing visibility between the targeted emitter and the list of potential users).

Communications Intelligence. COMINT involves the collection and analysis of intercepted signals used in communication systems by other than the intended recipient. Generally, the intercepted signal is demodulated, and the original data streams are extracted (voice, electronic messages, computer data, facsimile, etc.), which can then be processed by computer or analyzed by human analysts. For encrypted communication systems, it may not be possible to extract the original data streams, but traffic analysis techniques can still be used to extract some useful intelligence data. COMINT thus involves the exploitation of signal "internals," where *internal* is a reference to the actual data contained in the signal. COMINT analysis is more apt to provide information about the users of the communication link and their activities and is less apt to provide information about the communication system itself. COMINT is routinely used to meet other intelligence requirements and generally requires more analytical effort than ELINT but less than FISINT. Typically, systems that are designed to perform COMINT collection may also be capable of performing ELINT and/or FISINT activities.

Foreign Instrumentation Signals Intelligence. FISINT involves the collection and analysis of intercepted signals used in noncommunication data-transmission systems (telemetry systems, tracking/fusing/arming/command systems, beacons, certain video transmission systems, etc.). Generally, the intercepted signal is demodulated, and the original data streams are extracted. For encrypted communication systems, it may not be possible to extract the original data stream(s), but traffic analysis techniques can still be used to extract some useful intelligence data. Like COMINT, FISINT thus involves signal internals. However, unlike COMINT, FISINT can be used to determine the configuration, characteristics, and capabilities of the emitter and, more importantly, the overall system of which the emitter is a part. Generally, FISINT requires the most analytical effort of the three SIGINT sub-areas. Typically, systems that are designed to perform FISINT collection may also be capable of performing COMINT and/or ELINT activities.

Requirements

Although exact requirements vary with the emitter being targeted and its capabilities, a basic SIGINT system is comprised of a receiving antenna, a preamplifier, a receiver, and demodulation equipment. The quality of the SIGINT components will be dictated by the nature of the intercepted link (effective radiated power, bandwidth, beamwidth, etc.). Normally, the SIGINT antenna should be in the footprint of the emitter; that is, the SIGINT receiver must be physically located at a site which has access to the main beam of the emitter transmit antenna. With the trend of using increasingly smaller antenna beamwidths, this could mean being physically close to the intended receiver site. However, if sufficient receiver gain is available, then it may be possible to collect from a location which is in a sidelobe of the emitter transmit antenna, greatly increasing the allowable distance between the SIGINT systems and the intended receiver. Also, it is usually necessary to be within the physical line of sight of the emitter. However, for some lower frequency (high frequency [HF]) links, the beam will alternatively bounce off the atmosphere and the ground, allowing over-the-horizon (not within line of sight) collection.

Targets for SIGINT collection include space system components which emit electromagnetic waves—either uplink, downlink, or crosslink transmitters. Such emitters may be located at ground facilities and/or on satellites. In some situations, it may also be possible to collect signals of interest as they are reflected off of another object. For example, it may be possible to collect an uplink signal as it is reflected off of the satellite containing the uplink receiver. This is called a bistatic collect. Bistatic collection is very difficult because the power of the received signal is typically very low. Another potential target would be COMINT emitters not directly related to an operational space system, but which convey information related to a space system. One example would be the communications at a launch range that occur before, during, and after a new satellite launch.

Timeliness is an important quality of any intelligence operation. ELINT and COMINT (for relatively simple unencrypted systems) can be conducted in real time by trained personnel. FISINT, however, requires significant amounts of time. For example, a limited understanding of what is in a telemetry signal might be gained in a period of days or weeks. However, a thorough assessment of what each telemetry channel represents (there may be hundreds) may require years and would likely involve fusion of data from the other kinds of intelligence. In all cases, the amount of time required to answer a specific intelligence question is a function of the skill and experience of the analysts involved.

Locating an Emitter

A major goal of any SIGINT operation is to precisely locate the source of a signal. This is the direction finding (DF) process. Such data can be used to target weapons against the emitter and the platform to which it is attached (either a ground facility or a satellite). Generally, SIGINT systems can only provide bearing information (based on the direction of arrival of the intercepted signal), not the range to the emitter (bearing and range together would uniquely locate the emitter). However, by combining a single bearing fix with bearing fixes from SIGINT systems located elsewhere, it is possible to locate the emitter. It may also be possible to obtain range data from a single SIGINT collector using interferometric (superimposing or comparing multiple signals to detect differences) techniques. Finally, single bearing data, coupled with data from other intelligences, could be used to pinpoint an emitter, assuming the other intelligences can provide a list of potential emitters.

The most widely used DF technique is to vary the SIGINT antenna pointing angles and look for the point of maximum received signal. A very narrow-beam antenna must be used for an accurate measurement. With a broad-beam antenna, the signal variation is slight as the antenna is rotated off boresight or DF. Therefore, it is sometimes necessary to estimate the point of maximum signal. The directional antenna technique has the advantage of relatively high gain because the DF is taken on the peak of the antenna beam.

A somewhat more accurate method of DF is to use an antenna with one or two nulls in its radiation pattern. The antenna is rotated until the received signal strength is minimal. This technique is more accurate than the previous because the signal variation around the null is more rapid than the signal variation around the beam maximum (for most antennas). The disadvantage of this technique is that DF is done at a point of very low gain in the antenna pattern. If the signal is weak, it may be lost around the null, eliminating any DF capability.

Probably the best DF technique is lobe comparison. Two antennas are placed near one another so that their patterns overlap. When the two antennas receive equal strength signals, the antennas are both pointed at the target emitter. Another way to use this system is to take the difference between the two antenna outputs. When the antenna is on boresight, the difference should be zero so that the combined antenna pattern has a deep null. The two techniques are generally used together and called sum and difference direction finding. The high-gain sum pattern is used to pick out the approximate DF. Then the difference pattern is used for exact DF.

In the phase method, the phase difference between two separated antennas is measured to determine direction of arrival of the incoming signal. The antenna type consists of at least two antenna elements physically separated in space by some portion of a wavelength of the received signal. In general, the more antennas used to accomplish DF, the more accurate the resulting bearing measurement.

Identifying the Emitter

Identification of the emitter (name and mission) and the platform on which it is located is another major goal of a SIGINT program. The amount of effort required to identify the emitter will depend on the fidelity of the result. It may be possible to characterize the type of emitter from a few basic ELINT parameters (radar, communication systems, telemetry system, etc.). On the other hand, identifying the specific emitter and developing a detailed assessment of its mission may require COMINT/FISINT analysis of the data contained in the signal (for data transmission systems). It is also possible (even likely) that a single platform will have multiple emitters, providing additional data for the construction of an RF signature.

Determining Characteristics of Emitter and Emitter Platform

SIGINT can significantly contribute to an overall understanding of the configuration, capabilities, and characteristics of the emitter and the emitter platform. All sub-areas can contribute to this analysis. ELINT can provide overall emitter characteristics and power requirements. COMINT can provide more detailed emitter characteristics. (COMINT might also provide, indirectly, a number of other system details.) FISINT is probably the most useful technique, especially the analysis of unencrypted telemetry signals. Telemetry systems are intended by the system owner/operator to provide the ability to monitor many aspects of system operation. Telemetry can be used by the SIGINT analyst to identify system components and their characteristics; identify sensors, their characteristics, and sensor event timing; identify the status or health of individual components; identify the interconnections between various components;

and determine the criticality of individual components. Data signals are also useful; the exploitation of data signals can provide very detailed sensor parameters.

Analysis of SIGINT (ELINT, COMINT, and/or FISINT where applicable) can also determine the status or health (active, inactive, reduced capabilities, etc.) of emitters and their platforms and, in some cases, system users. This capability would be useful just prior to a counterspace operation (ground segment attack, space segment attack, or electronic attack), so as to avoid needlessly conducting an operation against a non-functioning or improperly identified/misidentified target. The ability to determine systems/user status would also be useful just after a counterspace operation, to assist in performing kill assessment.

SIGINT is also crucial to the successful conduct of any electronic attack (EA). SIGINT will provide RF characteristics of the target link so that the EA systems can be selected or developed. SIGINT would also likely be used to monitor the effects of an attack while it is occurring (as in a counterspace operation).

Identifying the Users

COMINT exploitation of communication signals transponded through a communication satellite can be used to identify the users of the communication system (by the association of can signs, etc.). Also, it is possible to assess, based on the identity of the users or by looking at the data itself, how critical the communication system is to a country's overall military activities.

Measurement and Signature Intelligence

Measurement and signature intelligence is defined as "intelligence obtained by quantitative and qualitative analysis of data (metric, angle, spatial, wavelength, time dependence, modulation, plasma, and hydromagnetic) derived from specific technical sensors for the purpose of identifying any distinctive features associated with the emitter or sender, and to facilitate subsequent identification and/or measurement of the same. The detected feature may be either reflected or emitted."[31] MASINT basically covers technical intelligence derived from the rest of the electromagnetic spectrum plus other measurable "signatures" that can reveal information about an adversary. Together, MASINT, IMINT, and SIGINT provide full-spectrum technical intelligence of an adversary system or action.

While IMINT targets externals and SIGINT targets internals, MASINT targets distinctive features not previously exploited by the former two disciplines.[32] These distinctive features include other information that can be derived from collected raw data of IMINT and SIGINT sensors as well as signatures (changes in characteristics) from acoustic, magnetic, nuclear, radar, multi- and hyper-spectral, electro-optic, and other measurable phenomena.[33]

MASINT is described in terms of its six subdisciplines: radar, radio frequency, geophysical, nuclear radiation, materials, and electro-optical. However, the difficulty in defining MASINT in this manner is that the sensor platforms of each of these subdisciplines can be owned and controlled by different entities with different objectives. Thus, a single integrated intelligence picture is difficult to draw.[34]

Another way of describing MASINT is as a family of systems. Under this construct, a loose collection of signature sensors is employed with a single purpose of discerning adversary capability or intent.[35] By processing and comparing various measurements and signature data, additional complementary information beyond the capability of IMINT and SIGINT sensors can be gleaned. For example, a simple visual-spectrum image can reveal the external characteristics of an adversary weapon system. MASINT sensors could use the raw visible-light data along with other sensor data to reveal the material composition of the weapon (e.g., metal or composite material).

Space-based MASINT capabilities (technically) are thus any space-based remote sensing capability other than IMINT and SIGINT that can be employed individually or collectively to derive technical intelligence on an adversary capability or intent.

Block IIR GPS systems have onboard optical, x-ray, dosimeter, and electromagnetic pulse (EMP) sensors referred to as the Nuclear Detection System (GPS/NDS). This sensor array measures light, infrared, gamma, atomic, and electromagnetic signatures. The data is fused and analyzed to determine the location and yield of a nuclear detonation.[36] Note that the system is a collection of different sensors analyzing different phenomenology or signatures for a common purpose of providing the location and yield of a nuclear detonation. This is categorically a MASINT operation.

Similarly, the Defense Satellite Program (DSP) system and its follow-on systems (e.g., SBIRS) also perform MASINT-like functions. DSP satellites are equipped with two different infrared sensors and nuclear signature sensors. The infrared sensors measure changes and characteristics in infrared signatures and can determine if a ballistic missile has been launched and its probable impact point. The nuclear sensors, like the GPS/NDS system, are designed to provide the location and yield of a nuclear detonation.[37] These platforms look for distinguishing features, not necessarily externals or signal internals, in order to determine action or intent, making them inherently MASINT.

In short, MASINT is an ISR discipline, though not necessarily an ISR platform. Space-based remote sensing systems can derive MASINT by measuring and analyzing various phenomenologies or signatures to extract distinguishing characteristics. These sensors can reside on single or multiple space platforms. They need only be employed for a common purpose of deriving additional technical intelligence beyond traditional SIGINT and IMINT capabilities.

Notes

1. Joint Publication (JP) 3-14, *Space Operations*, 6 January 2009, A-1.

2. Ibid.

3. Ibid., A-2.

4. Interagency Operations Security (OPSEC) Support Staff, "OPSEC Glossary of Terms," http://www .ioss.gov/docs/definitions.html (accessed 27 April 2009).

5. Bill Sweetman and Kimberley Ebner, eds., *Jane's Space Systems and Industry; 2007–2008* (Alexandria, VA: Jane's Information Group, 2007), 267.

6. NRO, "Corona Facts," http://www.nro.gov/corona/facts.html (accessed 1 March 2008).

7. National System for Geospatial Intelligence Publication 1-0, *Geospatial Intelligence (GEOINT) Basic Doctrine*, September 2006, http://www.nga.mil/NGASiteContent/StaticFiles/OCR/geopub1.pdf (accessed 5 March 2008).

8. Sweetman and Ebner, eds., *Jane's Space Systems and Industry*, 247–86.

9. Jim Olsen and Bill Small, "NGA Transforms Dissemination While Improving CENTCOM Support," *Pathfinder: The Geospatial Intelligence Magazine* 6, no. 1 (January/February 2008): 9, http://www.nga.mil/NGASiteContent/StaticFiles/OCR/pf_janfeb08.pdf (accessed 5 March 2008).

10. Sweetman and Ebner, eds., *Jane's Space Systems and Industry*, 250.

11. NASA, "Data Properties," in *Landsat 7 Science Data Users Handbook*, http://landsathandbook.gsfc.nasa.gov/handbook/handbook_htmls/chapter6/chapter6.html (accessed 5 April 2008).

12. NRO, "Corona System Information," http://www.nro.gov/corona/sysinfo2.html (accessed 5 March 2008).

13. Sweetman and Ebner, eds., *Jane's Space Systems and Industry*, 262.

14. Ibid., 252.

15. NASA, "What Is SAR, Anyway?" http://southport.jpl.nasa.gov/polar/sar.html (accessed 5 March 2008).

16. Ibid.

17. Sweetman and Ebner, eds., *Jane's Space Systems and Industry*, 247.

18. NASA, "The Electromagnetic Spectrum," http://science.hq.nasa.gov/kids/imagers/ems/infrared.html (accessed 9 March 2008).

19. Sweetman and Ebner, eds., *Jane's Space Systems and Industry*, 249.

20. GeoEye Satellite Constellation, "IKONOS," http://www.geoeye.com/corporate/constellation.htm#IKONOS.

21. Robert A. McDonald and Sharon K. Moreno, *Raising the Periscope: Grab and Poppy: America's Early ELINT Satellites* (Chantilly, VA: NRO, 2005), 4.

22. Ibid., 2.

23. Ibid., 7.

24. Ibid., 8.

25. Ibid., 11.

26. Ibid., 7.

27. Ibid., 15.

28. Peter L. Hays, James M. Smith, Alan R. Van Tassel, and Guy M. Walsh, eds., *Spacepower for a New Millennium: Space and U.S. National Security* (New York: McGraw-Hill, 2000), 119.

29. Steven Lambakis, *On the Edge of the Earth: The Future of American Space Power* (Lexington, KY: University Press of Kentucky, 2001), 33.

30. Ibid., 60.

31. JP 2-0, *Joint Intelligence*, 22 June 2007, GL-13.

32. Interagency OPSEC Support Staff, *Operations Security Intelligence Threat Handbook*, April 1996, revised May 1996, 6, http://www.fas.org/irp/nsa/ioss/threat96/part02.htm (accessed 18 March 2008).

33. William K. Moore, "MASINT: New Eyes in the Battlespace," *Military Intelligence Professional Bulletin*, January–March 2003, 1, http://findarticles.com/p/articles/mi_mOIBS/is_1_29/ai_97822088 (accessed 18 March 2008).

34. Air Force Institute of Technology Center for MASINT Studies and Research, "Intelligence: Toward a Better Definition," http://www.afit.edu/cmsr/Intelligence2.cfm (accessed 18 March 2008).

35. Ibid.

36. National Security Space Architect (NSSA), "National Security Space Roadmap," http://www.fas.org/spp/military/program/nssrm/initiatives/usnds.htm (accessed 18 March 2008).

37. Sweetman and Ebner, eds., *Jane's Space Systems and Industry*, 244–45.

Chapter 14

Satellite Communications

Maj Bryan Eberhardt, USAF;
MAJ Kenneth Kemmerly, USA; and Maj Paul Konyha III, USAF

This is the President of the United States speaking. Through the marvels of scientific advance, my voice is coming to you from a satellite traveling in outer space. My message is a simple one: Through this unique means I convey to you and all mankind, America's wish for peace on Earth and goodwill toward men everywhere.

—Pres. Dwight D. Eisenhower
19 December 1958

On 19 December 1958, a recorded Christmas message from Pres. Dwight D. Eisenhower was broadcast worldwide via shortwave radio frequency from the Army's Signal Communications by Orbiting Relay Equipment (SCORE), which lasted for only 13 days until the battery failed. This led to the realization of British scientist Arthur C. Clarke's vision, in 1945, for global communications via artificial satellites in 24-hour orbits stationed above the earth.[1] Through countless developments since the SCORE broadcast, the US military has become increasingly dependent on satellite communications (SATCOM) for military operations.

This chapter purposely minimizes technical jargon as much as possible and provides the war fighter and his or her staff with a basic understanding of the capabilities of primarily military, but also some commercial, SATCOM systems. Military dependency on SATCOM for bandwidth grew 30 times within the 13 years from Operation Desert Storm to Operation Iraqi Freedom (OIF).[2] Furthermore, over 80 percent of SATCOM bandwidth used by the military to conduct OIF and Operation Enduring Freedom (OEF) has been commercial SATCOM. United States Strategic Command (USSTRATCOM), who forwards bandwidth requirements to the Defense Information Systems Agency (DISA), determines commercial SATCOM requirements. As the Department of Defense (DOD) designated contracting authority, DISA obtains commercial services via an existing contract vehicle or generates a new contract as necessary.[3]

Military SATCOM (MILSATCOM) provides minimum essential war-fighting connectivity, including systems designed to provide antijam and survivable nuclear command and control. It is unlikely (and unaffordable) that future MILSATCOM systems will fully meet rapidly expanding capacity requirements. Therefore, commercial SATCOM (COMSATCOM) will be needed to fill the gap.

The dependency on radio repeaters in space (i.e., satellites) will only increase in the future because satellites are a key method of connecting the isolated war fighter to the US military's Global Information Grid (GIG) and ultimately enabling network-centric warfare. The GIG is defined as the globally interconnected end-to-end set of information capabilities, associated processes, and personnel for collecting, processing, storing, disseminating, and managing information on demand to war fighters, policy makers, and support personnel.[4] All encompassing, the GIG includes all owned and leased communications, computing systems and services, software applications, system data, security, and other associated services necessary to achieve information superiority. Eventually, the GIG will connect all soldiers, weapons platforms, sensors, and command and control nodes. At its basic level, the GIG is "networks which provide voice, data, video, and facilitate more than just the passing of targeting information through sensor-to-shooter loops; such a grid also provides, for example, real-time collaboration and dynamic planning."5

Satellite Communications Basics

Simplistically, SATCOM is a large radio repeater or relay situated on high ground. In this case, the high ground is space. Meanwhile, on Earth, satellite terminals are required for picking up (receiving) and sending (transmitting) the signals (frequencies) from and to the satellite. The frequency used by a SATCOM terminal to the satellite is the uplink frequency, and the frequency from the satellite to the SATCOM terminal is the downlink frequency. A SATCOM terminal is defined as any terminal used to connect a user to a satellite through the electromagnetic spectrum. The terminal may be an airborne, naval, or ground facility and can be fixed, mobile, or stand-alone.

The purpose of the space-based radio relay is to overcome the challenges of distance or obstructions inherent in terrestrial-based architectures for radios like microwave transmitters. However, the disadvantage posed by the great distances involved is the signal attenuation, or loss of some signal over the distance, requiring much greater transmit power and receiver sensitivity. In today's current satellite systems, this delay time primarily affects voice communications and can take "nearly 240 milliseconds [due to the] required propagation time."6 Additionally, the great distances produce signal attenuation, or loss of some signal over the distance.

These satellite systems also contain segments that have space, satellite, and ground components. The space segment is the area of the electromagnetic spectrum between the ground terminal and the physical satellite, through which the satellite signals pass, and includes the orbits and coverage areas of the satellite (see chapter 6). The physical satellite itself is typically a member of a constellation of other satellites that can provide continuous coverage to an area of responsibility. The ground terminal can be the user terminal (either mobile or fixed) or the ground control station that provides the user with connectivity back to the GIG or has personnel who operate and maintain the satellite.7 Note that joint, Army, and Air Force doctrine describes these segments a little differently; however, the inherent meanings are still similar (table 14-1).

Table 14-1. Names for segments in joint, Army, and Air Force doctrine.

Document	Segment		
	Space	Satellite	Ground
Joint Publication (JP) 3-14[a]	Link	Space	Ground/control
Field Manual (FM) 3-14[b]	Communication links	Satellite	Ground station/user segment
Air Force Doctrine Document (AFDD) 2-2[c]	Data links (control and mission)	Spacecraft	Ground and airborne stations

a JP 3-14, *Space Operations*, 6 January 2009, IV-7.
b FM 3-14, *Space Support to Army Operations*, May 2005, D-3.
c AFDD 2-2, *Space Operations*, 27 November 2006, 5.

Communications Satellite Modules

In general, a communications satellite is comprised of two modules: the spacecraft bus or service module and the communications payload. Generally, the spacecraft bus or service module consists of five subsystems:

1. The *structural subsystem* provides the mechanical base structure and shields the satellite from extreme temperature changes and micrometeorite damage.

2. The *telemetry subsystem* monitors the onboard equipment operations, transmits equipment operation data to the earth control station, and receives the earth control station's commands to perform equipment operation adjustments.

3. The *power subsystem* is comprised of solar panels and batteries. The solar panels charge the batteries, and the batteries supply power to the satellite subsystems, including when the satellite passes into Earth's shadow.

4. The *thermal control subsystem* helps protect electronic equipment from extreme temperatures due to intense sunlight or the lack of sun exposure on different sides of the satellite's body.

5. The *attitude and orbit control subsystem* is typically comprised of reaction wheels, electromagnets, and small rocket thrusters, which work together to keep the satellite in the correct orbital position and keep antennas pointing in the right directions.

The second major module, the communications payload, contains the transponders, antennas, and, for some communications satellites, crosslinks. A transponder provides the capability to amplify received radio signals from the uplink antennas. It also sorts the input signals and directs the output signals through input/output signal multiplexers to the proper downlink antennas. The antennas receive radio signals from SATCOM terminals and transmit to SATCOM terminals. Crosslinks provide connectivity between satellites without going through a SATCOM terminal.

Radio Spectrum

According to AFDD 2-2, "Where communication lines cannot be laid, or when terrain and other line-of-sight radio frequency limitations hamper terrestrial based communications, space communications keep forward and rear echelons in contact."[8] SATCOM systems contain a number of components that provide the ability to communicate effectively worldwide. These include the frequencies available for utilization within the electromagnetic spectrum through which SATCOM systems operate.

The SATCOM systems used today typically operate in the ultra-high frequency (UHF), super-high frequency (SHF), or extremely high frequency (EHF) ranges. Some of the systems that operate in these frequency ranges are described below in table 14-2, which also provides information on the radio spectrum, or the bands used by respective satellites, and the corresponding utilization of those bands.

Table 14-2. Bands and their utilization.

Band	Frequencies	Utilization
UHF	300 MHz to 3 GHz	TV broadcast, mobile satellite, land mobile, radio astronomy, air traffic control radar, global positioning systems, Mobile User Objective System (MUOS), UHF follow-on (UFO)
L band	1 to 2 GHz	Aeronautical radio navigation, radio astronomy, Earth exploration satellites
S band	2 to 4 GHz	Space research, fixed satellite communication
SHF	3 to 30 GHz	Satellite TV, Defense Satellite Communications System (DSCS), Wideband Global SATCOM (WGS)
C band	4 to 8 GHz	Fixed satellite communication, meteorological satellite communication
X band	8 to 12 GHz	Fixed satellite broadcast, space research
Kurtz-under (Ku) band	12 to 18 GHz	Mobile and fixed satellite communication, satellite broadcast
K band	18 to 27 GHz	Mobile and fixed satellite communication
Kurtz-above (Ka) band	27 to 40 GHz	Intersatellite communication, mobile satellite communication
EHF	30 to 300 GHz	Remote sensing, military strategic and tactical relay (Milstar), Advanced Extremely High Frequency (AEHF) System, Transformational Satellite (TSAT) Communications System
Millimeter	40 to 300 GHz	Space research, intersatellite communications

Adapted from K. V. Prasad, Principles of Digital Communication Systems and Computer Networks (Boston, MA: Charles River Books, 2004), 154; and Sky Scan, "The Electromagnetic Spectrum," http://www.skyscan.ca/the_electromagnetic_spectrum.htm (accessed 21 January 2008).

Current Military Satellite Communications Enterprise

The current MILSATCOM enterprise consists of four areas: protected, wideband, wideband broadcast, and narrowband. See figure 14-1 for the capabilities inherent in each of these areas. A fifth area, commercial SATCOM systems, also integrates with MILSATCOM services to give war fighters additional capacity and greater flexibility through redundancy.

Each system within these five areas offers unique advantages, making it particularly suitable to fulfill specific war-fighting needs. Together, they provide a robust, cost-effective integrated MILSATCOM architecture that satisfies critical Department of Defense requirements.

Today, the DOD SATCOM enterprise architecture comprises four primary systems (all in geosynchronous orbits), operating in UHF, SHF, and EHF ranges:

1. UHF follow-on (UFO) satellites.
2. SHF Defense Satellite Communications System (DSCS).
3. Wideband Global SATCOM (WGS) satellites.
4. EHF Milstar satellites.

Ultra-High Frequency Communications

After replacing the Navy's fleet SATCOM system, the UFO constellation became the primary DOD system for tactical mobile communications. Now providing UHF, EHF,

186

and Global Broadcast Service (GBS) capabilities on a worldwide basis, the UFO satellite system plays a vital role in meeting DOD's voice, data, and video transmission needs. The most prevalent users are ground forces (both Army and Marine Corps) which "account for 85 percent of the users of ultra-high frequency satellite communications."[9] As mentioned earlier, the Air Force oversees most of DOD's space systems; the Navy is responsible for narrowband satellite communications. The UFO constellation consists of "eight active spacecraft plus an in-orbit spare,"[10] which are in geosynchronous orbits. In addition to supporting ground forces, UFO "supports the Navy's global communications network, serving ships at sea"[11] and other government entities, including the White House, State Department, and Department of Homeland Security.

Besides the basic capabilities of the UFO satellites, specific satellites have additional capabilities depending upon when the satellites were fielded. For example, starting with UFO satellite Flight 4 (F4):

The EHF subsystem . . . provides enhanced anti-jam telemetry, command, broadcast, and fleet interconnectivity communications, using advanced signal processing techniques. Beginning with UFO F7, the EHF package was enhanced to provide 20 channels through the use of advanced digital integrated circuit technology. The GBS payload carried on F8 through F10 includes four 130-watt, 24 megabits-per-second (Mbps) military Ka-band transponders with three steerable downlink spot beam antennas as well as one steerable and one fixed uplink antenna. This modification resulted in a 96 Mbps capability per satellite.[12]

Also, satellites F8 and F10 (F9 is no longer active) "include protected fleet broadcast to all Navy ships plus command and control networks to selected aircraft, ships, submarines and ground forces. UFO F11 is equipped with a UHF and EHF payload and an advanced tunable digital receiver that will enable this spacecraft to offer 41 channels. The F11 spacecraft [will] sustain the constellation until the advent of DoD's next-generation Mobile User Objective System."[13] The most recent UFO, F11, was successfully launched 17 December 2003.[14]

Figure 14-1. DOD SATCOM enterprise overview. (*Adapted from* Keith Hollinger, USA SMDC, "Narrowband SATCOM Support—Current/Future," presentation, 2006 LandWarNet Conference, 23 August 2006).

PROTECTED	WIDEBAND	WIDEBAND BROADCAST	NARROWBAND	COMMERCIAL
EHF Q/Ka-Band MILSTAR I/II	SHF S/Ka-Band DSCS	Ka-Band UFO	UHF P/L-Band UFO	L, C, Ku, Ka-Band
Military and Commercial Satellite Systems Are Essential to Provide Critical Communications for the Deployed War Fighter				
• High protection (AJ, LPI, LPD, EMP) • Comm crosslinks • Survivable comm	• High data rates for tactical and enterprise users • Reachback for DISN • Some AJ	• GBS Ka payload on UFO satellites • High throughput COTM • Small antennas • Smart push/pull	• Lightweight, mobile, terminals; • Low data rate • Push-to-talk combat C2	• Growing capability • High throughput —CSS —Telemedicine —Split-based ops —Video
AEHF • Some AJ • Improved throughputs • Improved coverage	WGS • Increased throughputs • Platform COTM • Adds Ka-band	WGS • WGS—X & Ka bands • Return channel; 2-way Ka-band	MUOS • 6–10X legacy capacity • Handheld terminals • Full GIG integration	• No protection • Pay for services • Mobile Satellite System for COTM
TSAT • Wideband/protected • Platform COTM • IP-based, network-centric				

UHF satellite end-user terminals, or antennas, are typically "small and portable enough to be carried deep into military theaters of operation. The UHF frequency offers the capability of penetrating jungle foliage and inclement weather, as well as urban canyons."[15] There are around 20,000 terminals in use across the DOD today.[16]

Super-High Frequency Communications

Two military satellite systems operate in the SHF range: the Defense Satellite Communications System and the Wideband Global SATCOM satellites.

Defense Satellite Communications System. The Defense Satellite Communications System is a worldwide military satellite network managed under USSTRATCOM by DISA. DSCS consists of space and satellite segments along with ground terminals that operate in the SHF band to provide long-haul multichannel communications connectivity.[17] The system is an important part of the comprehensive plan to support globally distributed military users on the ground, at sea, or in the air.

DSCS evolved in three phases, starting with the Initial Defense Communications Satellite Program (IDCSP) satellites in Phase I (sometimes called DSCS I). Phase II began in 1971 with the launch of two DSCS II satellites. The third phase began in 1982 with the launch of the first DSCS III satellite.[18] Currently, there are 14 operational DSCS satellites with five Phase III DSCS satellites in geosynchronous orbit circling the earth at an altitude of 22,300 miles.[19] The five primary DSCS III satellites provide overlapping footprints for worldwide communications between 65° north latitude and 65° south latitude.[20] This highlights one of the disadvantages of geostationary satellites in "that they cannot be seen from the polar regions. . . . Fortunately, there is not a heavy telecommunications demand in these part[s] of the earth."[21] The five-satellite constellation of DSCS allows some Earth terminals to access two satellites (fig. 14-2).

The satellite system includes single- and multiple-beam antennas. Each DSCS III satellite also carries a special-purpose single-channel transponder used for disseminating emergency action and force-direction messages to nuclear-capable forces.[22] Each DSCS satellite has six SHF transponder channels (one of which provides limited antijam capability) capable of providing worldwide secure-voice and high-data-rate communications.[23] A single steerable dish antenna provides an increased power spot beam that is flexible to suit the needs of different sizes of user terminals.[24]

Figure 14-2. DSCS satellite. (USAF photo)

The DSCS III spacecraft is a three-axis, momentum-stabilized vehicle with an on-orbit weight of about 2,550 pounds with propellant. The spacecraft's rectangular body is 6.5 feet on each side, with a 38-foot span (with solar arrays deployed). The solar arrays generate 1,100 watts, decreasing to 837 watts after five years.[25]

The DSCS frequency plan falls within the SHF spectrum (X band) with uplink frequencies of 7,900 MHz to 8,400 MHz, which the transponders down-translate to the downlink frequencies of 7,250 MHz to 7,750 MHz.[26] The DSCS service life extension program (SLEP) upgraded the last four DSCS III satellites with improved solar panels and transponders providing more power, more sensitive receivers, and additional antenna connectivity options.[27]

The DSCS system is flexible enough to meet many different needs: "The DSCS Earth Terminals come in many shapes and sizes, conforming to the needs of the users it [sic] supports. There are two general types of terminal categories in the ground segment that are directly related to the type of user: strategic [enterprise] and tactical."[28] Key sites, known as teleports, are located around the world and are primarily used to connect to the GIG or to interface between systems.

DSCS launch, on-orbit operations (station-keeping), telemetry analysis, tracking data for orbit determination, and commanding of onboard subsystems are the responsibility of the 3rd Space Operations Squadron (3 SOPS). 3 SOPS is a component of the 50th Operations Group, 50th Space Wing at Schriever AFB, Colorado.[29]

Under the Army Space and Missile Defense Command (SMDC), 1st Space Brigade, the 53rd Signal Battalion's (Satellite Control) mission at Ft. Detrick, Maryland, is to provide communications network control for the DSCS.[30] The battalion operates the wideband operations centers (WOC) at five SATCOM locations around the world to oversee all use of the DSCS, ensuring that users receive the optimal SATCOM support authorized. They control the satellite links for tactical and strategic war-fighter communications networks. The battalion also provides payload control to the satellite as well as the technical and troubleshooting assistance required to ensure maximum support to the user. The WOCs provide real-time monitoring and control for the DSCS and perform payload control, which involves making changes to transponder and antenna configuration.[31]

Wideband Global SATCOM.

The Wideband Global SATCOM (fig. 14-3), previously known as the Wideband Gapfiller Satellite System, provides additional capability to the current DSCS constellation and will eventually take over for DSCS and reduce the amount of commercial satellite communications capability that is required by the Department of Defense today. The WGS Block I satellites provide DOD with the "highest capacity communication satellite, offering a quantum leap in communications bandwidth for airmen, soldiers, sailors and Marines."[32]

Although planning for the WGS constellation began during the 1990s, the first WGS was successfully launched on 10 October 2007 and was transferred to the Air Force on 18 January 2008. DOD has contracted for a total of six WGS satellites. Two more were launched during 2008, one will be launched in 2011, and the last two in 2012 and 2013. The first satellite, WGS-1, is currently located over the Pacific and met initial operational capability in January 2009. The next two satellites will be placed over the European Command and Central Command areas of responsibility. These new satellites are expected to provide service to DOD for 14 years.[33]

The system includes eight X-band phased-array antennas, 10 Ka-band gimbaled-dish antennas, and one X-band coverage antenna. The eight X-band antennas are considered steerable due to the advances inherent in phased-array technology.[34]

The WGS spacecraft is based on a commercial Boeing design and has an on-orbit weight of about 7,600 pounds.[35] The commercial satellite platform provides enhanced technologies such as "xenon-ion propulsion system (XIPS), highly efficient triple-junction gallium arsenide solar cells, and deployable radiators with flexible heat pipes."[36] The XIPS is nearly 10 times as efficient as conventional fuel and requires less fuel for station keeping.[37] The solar arrays generate 11 kilowatts, nearly 10 times the current DSCS satellite power.[38] The radiators and heat pipes provide a "more stable thermal environment" for the satellite, thus increasing "reliability over service life."[39]

The WGS frequency plan falls within the SHF spectrum using X band and Ka band in the 7–8 GHz and 20–21 GHz frequency range, respectively, with the ability to cross-band between the X and Ka bands.[40] The Block II satellites, first launching in 2011, will provide a radio-frequency bypass for airborne intelligence, surveillance, and reconnaissance (ISR) assets to provide high bandwidth to unmanned aerial vehicles (UAV).[41] The WGS will provide enough bandwidth to allow UAVs to utilize military SATCOM resources in order to reduce today's complete reliance on commercial SATCOM.[42]

Figure 14-3. WGS satellite. (USAF photo)

Transmission rates for end-user terminals depend on user requirements, antenna size, and modulation utilized. Typical throughput for each WGS satellite will be between 2.1 gigabits per second (Gbps) and 3.6 Gbps. In comparison, "a DSCS III satellite will support up to 0.25 Gbps."[43]

After the WGS satellites complete their initial systems checks by Boeing, they are turned over to the 3 SOPS to take over monitoring and control of the satellites.[44] The Army will control the payloads from four wideband satellite operations centers (WSOC) that allow them to control up to three satellites at one time with Boeing-designed software and hardware.[45]

Extremely High Frequency Communications

Although the term Milstar was originally based on the Military Strategic and Tactical Relay acronym, government sources no longer refer to it as an acronym, but a system (i.e., Milstar vice MILSTAR). The Milstar satellite system is a joint asset developed by the Air Force and has a satellite cross-linking capability that enables control from anywhere on Earth. Milstar provides highly robust, secure, and survivable communications among fixed-site and mobile terminals. Milstar's unique capabilities enable US forces to maintain information superiority throughout all levels of conflict, enhancing full-dimensional protection and ensuring that war fighters retain freedom of action through continuous, secure, jam-resistant communication.[46]

Milstar has a couple of features that distinguish it from earlier satellite communication systems. First, the Milstar satellite serves as a smart switchboard in space, allowing users to establish critical communication networks on the fly. Secondly, the Milstar system uses a satellite-to-satellite cross-link to provide worldwide connectivity without the use of vulnerable and expensive ground relay stations.[47] Milstar's flexible capabilities also allow users to utilize crossbanding and processed UHF-to-UHF communications. Crossbanding is the ability for EHF/SHF terminals to communicate with UHF terminals.[48] Milstar provides replacement of the Air Force SATCOM UHF networks by crossbanding EHF/SHF command systems to modified UHF Air Force SATCOM terminals on bombers and other force elements. Milstar will provide this until the legacy UHF terminals can be replaced with EHF terminals around 2014. AEHF will not continue the crossbanding capability.

The first Milstar satellite launched on 7 February 1994, and the final satellite successfully reached orbit on 8 April 2003. The Milstar constellation consists of five satellites positioned around the earth in low-inclined geosynchronous orbits at an altitude of approximately 22,300 miles. They provide coverage from 65° north to 65° south latitude in their assigned orbital position.[49]

The first two satellites possess the original strategic communications low-data-rate (LDR) payload (75–2,400 bps) capability. The third and subsequent satellites add the medium-data-rate (MDR) payload (to 1.544 Mbps) in addition to the LDR. Lockheed produced four Block II vehicles; however, the first Milstar II failed to reach orbit in April 1999 due to a Centaur stage software error.[50] The higher data rates provided by the Block II satellites "provide the user the ability to transmit large amounts of data in a short period of time."[51] See figure 14-4 for additional details.

Protected SATCOM	Milstar I LDR	Milstar II MDR	AEHF XDR
Throughput	0.002 Mbps	1.5 Mbps	8 Mbps
Air Tasking Order 1.1 MB	1.02 hr	5.7 sec	1.07 sec
Tomahawk Tasking Order 0.03 MB	100 sec	0.16 sec	0.03 sec
Imagery 8x10 Annotated 24 MB	22.2 hr	2.07 min	23.6 sec
# Networks # Terminals Reconfig Time	30–100 1,000 Months	~1,500 1,000 Days–months	4,000 6,000 Minutes

Figure 14-4. Data throughput. (*Adapted from Lt Col Luke Schaub, "Advanced EHF Overview," presentation, 20 May 2005.*)

The Milstar satellite extends 51 feet across its payload axis, and the massive solar arrays generate nearly 5,000 watts of power (fig. 14-5).[52] Its payloads have onboard computers that perform resource monitoring and control functions supporting worldwide voice, data, video, teletype, and facsimile communications.[53] The Milstar II also has "a nulling antenna that nullifies enemy jamming attempts."[54]

Milstar provides interoperable communications capabilities to terminals located on submarines, ships, land-based systems, and mobile systems.[55] Today over 1,000 fielded terminals meet service-specific platform requirements while also supporting joint communications to all US military users with antenna diameters "from 14 centimeters for submarine terminals to 3 meters for fixed command-post terminals."[56] The terminal segment of Milstar "consists of a family of multi-Service ground, shipborne, submarine,

Figure 14-5. Milstar satellite. (USAF photo)

and airborne terminals functionally interoperable. . . . These terminals consist of the Air Force air and ground command post terminals, the Navy Extremely High Frequency Satellite Program (NESP) ship, shore, and submarine terminals, and the Army's Single-Channel Anti-jam Man-Portable (SCAMP) terminal and Secure, Mobile, Anti-jam, Reliable, Tactical Terminal (SMART-T)."[57]

The 4th Space Operations Squadron (4 SOPS), a component of the 50th Operations Group, 50th Space Wing, Schriever AFB, Colorado, is responsible for overall command and control and payload management of the Milstar constellation.[58] The control segment is controlled through the Milstar Satellite Operations Center (MSOC), which performs "satellite command and control, communications resource management, systems engineering support, mission planning, user support and anomaly resolution."[59] The MSOC utilizes two distinct command and control resources to operate the Milstar system, depending on mission requirements. The majority of satellite contacts are completed using three fixed constellation control stations (CCS)—two located at Schriever AFB, and one located at Vandenberg AFB, California, and operated by the 148 SOPS, California Air National Guard. Additionally, mobile CCSs execute satellite command and control and enhance mission survivability in support of the US Northern Command and contingency operations with operators from 4 SOPS.[60]

Commercial SATCOM Systems

As mentioned earlier, most operational SATCOM is provided by commercial SATCOM, which is consistent with US national space policy:

It is in the interest of the United States to foster the use of U.S. commercial space capabilities around the globe and to enable a dynamic, domestic commercial space sector. To this end, departments and agencies shall: Use U.S. commercial space capabilities and services to the maximum practical extent; purchase commercial capabilities and services when they are available in the commercial marketplace and meet United States Government requirements; and modify commercially available capabilities and services to meet those United States Government requirements when the modification is cost effective.[61]

SATCOM requirements are determined by USSTRATCOM in its role as SATCOM operational manager of both MILSATCOM and commercial SATCOM for DOD. Meanwhile, DISA serves as the contracting authority for commercial SATCOM services. DISA describes the Enhanced Mobile Satellite Services (EMSS) as follows:

EMSS is a satellite-based telephone and data communication service, utilizing a commercial satellite infrastructure to provide voice and low data rate services from a mobile, lightweight terminal through a DoD dedicated gateway which accesses the Defense Information System Network (DISN). It is capable of providing . . . secure voice service and non-secure access to commercial and DSN [Defense Switch Network] telephone services. . . . EMSS also provides the following special features: Broadcast Service, Protected Paging, Unclassified but Sensitive Internet Protocol Router Network (NIPRNet) Connectivity, Short Burst Messaging, Conference Calling and Secret Internet Protocol Router Network (SIPRNet) Connectivity (2008).[62]

The typical end terminal utilized with EMSS is the Iridium commercial satellite phone, which can be secured with "a removable National Security Agency (NSA) approved . . . Communications Security (COMSEC) sleeve. EMSS is available through DISA to DOD, other federal departments and agencies, state and local governments, and Joint Staff (J-6) approved foreign and allied government users."[63]

Future Military SATCOM Systems

New military SATCOM systems are under development. These future systems will give DOD a greater capacity for transmitting data, higher transmission speed, and increased user access to data.

Mobile User Objective System

The Mobile User Objective System (MUOS) is the next generation of US military tactical UHF SATCOM developed by the US Navy for DOD. The MUOS constellation will replace the UFO satellite constellation currently in operation and will significantly increase both the capability of users and the number of potential users. When fully fielded, MUOS will provide an aggregate of 40.216 Mbps for the war fighter, compared to the legacy UFO system's aggregate of 2.666 Mbps. The increase means future war fighters will have more than 16,332 simultaneous accesses (voice, video, data) at 2.4 kilobits per second (kbps), compared to 1,111 accesses provided by the present UFO satellite system at the same data rate.[64] Consequently, more terminals will be used for mobile connectivity at the lowest tactical level.

The war fighter's MUOS terminals will be available in a couple of different types. The Army is currently scheduled to employ the Joint Tactical Radio System (JTRS) as its satellite terminal. Meanwhile, other users will use portable receivers that are approximately the "same size as today's Iridium satellite handheld phones."[65] Currently, the US Army is projected to be the largest user of MUOS. Additionally, MUOS will operate in several network configurations for internet routing.

With four satellites and one spare planned for geostationary orbits, MUOS will be fully compatible with the legacy UFO system and its associated terminals. Additionally, MUOS will employ four Earth stations as its main hubs: Italy, Australia, Hawaii, and Virginia. This next-generation UHF satellite system provides the war fighter 10 times more capacity with higher data rates than today's UHF military system. It supports hand-held terminals, which will enable the war fighter, whether mobile or static, to access the GIG.[66]

Advanced Extremely High Frequency

The joint-service Advanced Extremely High Frequency (AEHF) system "is the follow-on to the Milstar system, augmenting and improving on the capabilities of Milstar, and expanding the MILSATCOM architecture. AEHF will provide connectivity across the spectrum of mission areas, including land, air, and naval warfare; special operations; strategic nuclear operations; strategic defense; theater missile defense; and space operations and intelligence."[67] As of this publication, the first AEHF system is scheduled to be launched in September 2010.[68]

According to the Air Force Space Command, "On-board signal processing will provide protection and ensure optimum resource utilization and system flexibility among the Armed Forces and other users who operate terminals on land, sea, and air."[69] The AEHF system will be backward compatible with the LDR and MDR capabilities of legacy Milstar satellites and terminals, while providing extended data rate (XDR) and other improved functionality at less cost than the previous system.[70] XDR replaces both LDR and MDR. XDR improves LDR missions for national/nuclear command and control with a 75 bps to 19.2 kbps highly survivable waveform. XDR improves MDR missions by extending the data rate to 8.192 Mbps. Additionally, AEHF significantly improves on Milstar's MDR by providing full Earth coverage. Milstar's MDR coverage was provided with eight small-footprint steerable antennas—Earth coverage was not available on MDR (Earth coverage was LDR only).

Each satellite in the constellation will weigh approximately 9,000 lb. when in geo-synchronous orbit. The satellite utilizes a commercial infrastructure "based on Lockheed Martin's flight-proven A2100 geosynchronous spacecraft series"[71] (fig. 14-6). It will use cross-banded EHF communications and communicate via SHF downlinks and EHF uplinks."[72] Three satellites were originally ordered. Recently, a fourth satellite was requested by the Pentagon "to ensure continuity of service to commanders around the globe until TSAT becomes operational."[73]

The system will serve a terminal segment comprised of terminals used by all the services and international partners. The AEHF satellites "will respond directly to service requests from operational commanders and user terminals, providing real-time point-to-point connectivity and network services on a priority basis."[74] The XDR capability has also been successfully tested with the international variant of the Secure

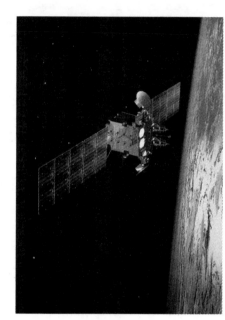

Figure 14-6. AEHF satellite. (USAF photo)

194

Mobile Antijam Reliable Tactical Terminal (SMART-T), and Lincoln Laboratory's Advanced Universal System Test Terminal (AUST-T).[75]

The AEHF program is currently on contract with Lockheed Martin Space Systems to develop and field the three satellites and the mission control segment (MCS). The new MCS will be used for both Milstar and the AEHF systems. The MILSATCOM Program Office is the contract manager of the AEHF program.[76]

Transformational Satellite

Transformational Satellite (TSAT) will provide further enhancement of AEHF satellites to include integrated Internet-like networking functionality. TSAT extends the ground-based GIG to deployed and mobile users. The system will also employ IP networks and onboard network routing to significantly increase and automate connectivity for the war fighter. TSAT increases bandwidth capacity up to 2 Gbps per satellite compared with 450 Mbps for AEHF. User RF data rates up to 45 Mbps are planned, while future laser communication links are capable of 1–10 Gbps. Higher throughput translates to faster download speeds, which means the war fighter can make decisions faster and act faster. As an example, an 8 x 10 image with a size of 24 megabytes (MB) can be transmitted in less than a second by TSAT, compared to a Milstar II communications satellite, which can transfer that same image in about two minutes. See figure 14-4 above for additional details.

The TSAT program is comprised of three segments: space, terminal, and TSAT Mission Operations System (TMOS). TMOS encompasses overall TSAT mission planning capability, network management, network services, and GIG border functions and interoperability. It will provide circuit and packet mission planning and policy management, external network coordination, network operations, key management, and a common operational picture.[77]

Currently, the space segment baseline consists of five satellites connected via crosslinks. The TSAT terminals will use at least one of the TSAT waveforms, and they may be backwards compatible with AEHF terminals.[78]

Five TSAT satellites are scheduled for launch beginning in 2019 to provide a wideband survivable network-centric capability to service the GIG in support of strategic and tactical war fighters. TSAT will employ packet switching with bulk and packet encryption/decryption to support secure information dissemination. TSAT's IP routing capability will connect thousands of users through interconnected networks rather than limited point-to-point connections. Initially TSAT satellites will use traditional RF cross-links to AEHF satellites to achieve integration and support transition from circuit-switched to packet-switched service delivery. Eventually TSAT satellites are intended to be interconnected by highly secure wideband laser cross-links.[79] (Note: As of April 2009, it is very likely that TSAT will suffer from major funding cuts, causing either an extremely long delay in fielding or possibly cancelation of the program.)

As a summary, figure 14-7 provides a timeline of key developments in military SATCOM systems.

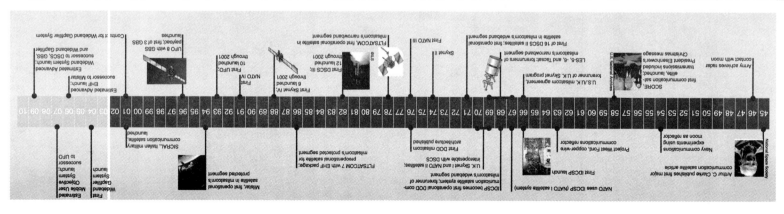

Figure 14-7. SATCOM timeline. (*Reprinted from* Donald H. Martin, "A History of U.S. Military Satellite Communication Systems," Crosslink 3, no. 1 [Winter 2001/2002], 56. Used by permission of The Aerospace Corporation, http://www.aero.org/.)

Notes

1. August E. Grant and Jennifer H. Meadows, eds., *Community Technology Update*, 8th ed. (St. Louis, MO: Focal Press, 2002), 274.

2. Joe Leland and Isaac Porche, *Future Army Bandwidth Needs and Capabilities* (Santa Monica, CA: RAND Corporation, 2004), 21.

3. Lt Col Roy Snodgrass, "Commercial SATCOM Support—Current/Future," presentation, LandWarNet 2007, Annual Armed Forces Communications and Electronics Association Conference, Ft. Lauderdale, FL, 21 August 2007.

4. "U.S. Stealth Bombers to Use EHF SatCom from Northrop Grumman," *MilsatMagazine* 1, no. 1 (First Quarter 2007): 7–8.

5. Leland and Porche, *Future Army Bandwidth Needs and Capabilities*, 11.

6. K. V. Prasad, *Principles of Digital Communication Systems and Computer Networks* (Boston, MA: Charles River Books, 2004), 41.

7. Chairman of the Joint Chiefs of Staff (CJCS) Instruction 6250.01, *Satellite Communications*, 30 April 2007, A-3.

8. AFDD 2-2, *Space Operations*, 2.

9. Sandra I. Erwin, "High Frequency: Navy Upbeat about Communications Spacecraft, Despite Radio Troubles," *National Defense*, July 2007.

10. Navy, "UHF Follow-On Program," Navy Fact Sheet, http://www.spaceflightnow.com/atlas/ac203/03121 1uhfprogram.html (accessed 2 April 2008).

11. Ibid.

12. Navy, "UHF Follow-On Program."

13. Ibid.

14. Boeing, "Successful Launch Orbits the 11th Boeing-Built UHF Follow-On Naval Satellite," http://www.boeing.com/news/releases/2003/q4/nr_031217o.html (accessed 7 April 2008).

15. Navy, "UHF Follow-On Program."

16. Ibid.

17. Air Force, "Defense Satellite Communications System," Air Force Fact Sheet, http://www.losangeles.af.mil/library/factsheets/factsheet.asp?id=5322 (accessed 21 January 2007).

18. Donald H. Martin, "A History of U.S. Military Satellite Communication Systems," *Crosslink* 3, no. 1 (Winter 2001/2002): 8–13.

19. Air Force, "Defense Satellite Communications System."

20. "DSCS-3," GlobalSecurity.org, http://www.globalsecurity.org/space/systems/dscs_3.htm (accessed 11 February 2008).

21. Mark R. Chartrand, *Satellite Communications for the Nonspecialist* (Bellingham, WA: SPIE: The International Society for Optical Engineering, 2004), 160.

22. "DSCS-3."

23. Air Force, "Defense Satellite Communications System."

24. Kostas Liopiros and Edward Lam, "Extremely High Frequency Satellites Offer Flexibility," *Signal* 44, no. 11 (July 1990): 77.

25. "DSCS-3."

26. Ibid.

27. Air Force, "Defense Satellite Communications System."

28. CW2 Garth R. Hahn, CW2 Anthony Kellar, and CW2 Steven Stubblefield, "Satellite Communications: Operating Together for National Defense," *Army Space Journal* 3, no. 1 (Winter/Spring 2004): 25.

29. Air Force, "3rd Space Operations Squadron," Fact Sheet, http://www.schriever.af.mil/library/factsheets/factsheet.asp?id=3914 (accessed 13 February 2008).

30. "Ft. Detrick Base Guide: 53rd Signal Battalion," dcmilitary.com, http://www.dcmilitary.com/special_sections/sw/082807_Detrick/ss_140741_31958.shtml (accessed 13 February 2008).

31. Hahn, Kellar, and Stubblefield, "Satellite Communications," 26.

32. "Boeing Completes On-Orbit Handover of Wideband Global SATCOM Satellite to USAF," Space War, http://www.spacewar.com/reports/Boeing_Completes_On_Orbit_Handover_Of_Wideband_Global_SATCOM_Satellite_To_USAF_999.html (accessed 14 February 2008).

33. Turner Brinton, "Longer Life Expected for First WGS Satellite," *Space News*, https://halfway.peterson.af.mil/NSSI/NSSISpaceNewsArchives/20080201_NSSISpaceNews.doc (accessed 14 February 2008).

34. Peter A. Buxbaum, "Wideband Comms: Change Is in the Air," *Defense Systems*, December 2007.

35. Air Force Space Command (AFSPC), "Wideband Global SATCOM Satellite," http://www.afspc.af.mil/library/factsheets/factsheet.asp?id=5582 (accessed 14 February 2008).

36. Boeing, "Wideband Global SATCOM Backgrounder," http://www.boeing.com/defense-space/space/bss/factsheets/702/wgs/docs/WGS overview.pdf (accessed 14 February 2008).

37. Boeing, "Integrated Defense Systems: Boeing 702 Fleet," http://www.boeing.com/defense-space/space/bss/factsheets/702/702fleet.html (accessed 20 March 2008).

38. "Wideband Gapfiller System: Satellite Design," GlobalSecurity.org, http://www.globalsecurity.org/space/systems/wgs-satdesign.htm (accessed 14 February 2008).

39. Boeing, "Integrated Defense Systems," http://www.boeing.com/defense-space/space/bss/factsheets/702/702fleet.html.

40. Buxbaum, "Wideband Comms."

41. Boeing, "Transformational Wideband Communication Capabilities for the Warfighter," http://www.boeing.com/defense-space/space/bss/factsheets/702/wgs/wgs_factsheet.html (accessed 14 February 2008).

42. DOD, Unmanned Aerial Vehicles Roadmap 2002–2027 (Washington, DC: Office of the Secretary of Defense, December 2002), 107.

43. Boeing, "Transformational Wideband Communication."

44. "Boeing Completes On-Orbit Handover."

45. Boeing, "Transformational Wideband Communication."

46. AFSPC, "MILSTAR Satellite Communications," Fact Sheet, http://www.af.mil/factsheets/factsheet.asp?fsID=118 (accessed 12 February 2008).

47. Ibid.

48. Boeing, "Boeing Satellites: Milstar II," http://www.boeing.com/defense-space/space/bss/factsheets/government/milstar_ii/milstar_ii.html (accessed 19 February 2008).

49. Air Force, "MILSTAR," Fact Sheet, http://www.losangeles.af.mil/library/factsheets/factsheet.asp?id=5328 (accessed 25 November 2007).

50. "Milstar," Astronautix.com, http://www.astronautix.com/craft/milstar.htm (accessed 19 February 2008).

51. Air Force, "MILSTAR."

52. Lockheed Martin, "MILSTAR," http://www.lockheedmartin.com/products/Milstar/index.html (accessed 19 February 2008).

53. AFSPC, "MILSTAR Satellite Communications."

54. Muhammed El-Hasan, "Northrop Hopes for Satellite Bid," Daily Breeze.com, 26 October 2007.

55. Air Force, "MILSTAR."

56. Martin, "A History of U.S. Military Satellite Communication Systems," 12.

57. Director, Operational Test & Evaluation, DOD, "Military Strategic and Tactical Relay (MILSTAR) Satellite System," FY99 Annual Report, http://www.globalsecurity.org/military/library/budget/fy1999/dot-e/airforce/99milstar.html (accessed 29 February 2008).

58. AFSPC, "MILSTAR Satellite Communications."

59. Air Force, "4th Space Operations Squadron," Fact Sheet, http://www.schriever.af.mil/library/factsheets/factsheet.asp?id=3915 (accessed 29 February 2008).

60. Ibid.

61. White House Office of Science and Technology Policy, U.S. National Space Policy, 31 August 2006.

62. DISA, "Enhanced Mobile Satellite Services (EMSS)," http://www.disa.mil/services/emss.html (accessed 2 April 2008).

63. Ibid.

64. Keith Hollinger, "Narrowband SATCOM Support—Current/Future," presentation, 2006 LandWarNet Conference, 23 August 2006.

65. Ron Sherman, "MUOS: Milsatcom's Cutting Edge," Avionics Magazine, 1 June 2005, http://www.avtoday.com/av/categories/military/936.html (accessed 4 April 2008).

66. Virgil Labrador, "Military Satellite Market: Opportunities and Challenges," MilsatMagazine 1, no. 1 (First Quarter 2007): 16.

67. Air Force, "Advanced Extremely High Frequency (AEHF) System," Fact Sheet, http://www.losangeles.af.mil/library/factsheets/factsheet.asp?id=5319 (accessed 25 November 2007).

68. Amy Butler, "Fourth Satellite Busts Budget," Aviation Week, 4 March 2008, http://www.aviationweek.com/aw/generic/story_channel.jsp?channel=space&id=news/AEHF03048.xml (accessed 15 March 2008).

69. AFSPC, "Advanced Extremely High Frequency System," Fact Sheet, http://www.afspc.af.mil/library/factsheets/factsheet.asp?id=7758 (accessed 1 May 2009).

70. Ibid.

71. Steve Tatum, "Lockheed Martin Delivers Key Hardware for Third Advanced EHF Military Communication Satellite," Lockheed Martin press release, 22 December 2006.

72. Air Force, "Advanced Extremely High Frequency System."

73. Butler, "Fourth Satellite Busts Budget."

74. AFSPC, "Advanced Extremely High Frequency System."

75. "Northrop Grumman Demonstrates Compatibility of AEHF Satellite Interface with Terminals Using Extended-Data-Rate Waveform," SpaceDaily, 4 February 2008, http://www.spacedaily.com/reports/Northrop_Grumman_Demonstrates_Compatibility_Of_AEHF_Satellite_Interface_With_Terminals_Using_Extended_Data_Rate_Waveform_999.html (accessed 2 March 2008).

76. Air Force, "Advanced Extremely High Frequency."

77. Ibid.

78. Ibid.

79. Ibid.

Chapter 15

Weather/Environmental Satellites

Maj Edward P. Chatters IV, USAF;
and Maj Gabriel Medina, Dominican Republic Air Force

Timely knowledge of weather conditions is of extreme importance in the planning and execution of military operations. Real-time night and day observations of current weather conditions provide the operational commander with greater flexibility in the use of resources for imminent or ongoing military operations. The military has firmly established the importance of meteorological data from satellites in the effective and efficient conduct of military operations. Satellite-based remote sensors provide situational awareness of environmental conditions to areas that otherwise would not be accessible via aircraft or other terrestrial means. The purpose of this chapter is to describe in detail the current fleet of Defense Meteorological Satellite Program (DMSP) satellites and their capabilities. This chapter will also describe other civil and foreign weather satellites and look ahead to the future of the weather satellite program, the National Polar-Orbiting Operational Environmental Satellite System.

Why Do We Need Weather/Environmental Satellites?

Weather and environmental satellites are capable of providing joint force commanders with essential data required for accurate, dependable weather forecasting in support of air, land, and maritime operations. Cloud cover data are needed to determine weather conditions in data-denied and data-sparse regions and to forecast target-area weather, theater weather, en-route weather (including refueling areas), and recovery weather. Surface and upper-level wind data are used to support all aspects of military operations, such as assessing radioactive fallout conditions; nuclear, biological, and chemical weapon effects; movement of weather systems; and predicting winds for weapons delivery.

Precipitation information (type and rate) is required to forecast soil moisture, soil trafficability, river stages, and flooding conditions that could impact land-based force deployment/employment. Ocean tides information is vital to naval operations for the safe passage in and out of ports and river entrances and for the landing of amphibious craft. Sea ice conditions can have a significant impact on surface/subsurface ship operations. The location of open water areas or areas of thin ice is crucial to submarine surfacing operations, submarine missile launch, and penetration by air-dropped sonobuoys, which are used for detecting submarines. Knowledge of the location and size of icebergs is also imperative for the safe navigation of surface ships and submarines. This information could provide an important advantage over adversaries in submarine and antisubmarine warfare. Most of this information is currently acquired through the use of the Defense Meteorological Satellite Program.

Defense Meteorological Satellite Program

The DMSP mission is to provide an enduring and survivable capability to collect and disseminate global visible and infrared cloud data and other specialized meteorological, oceanographic, and solar-geophysical data in support of worldwide DOD operations. It was designed to provide the military with a dedicated weather observing system. Under peacetime conditions, weather data is also available from civil weather satellites, such as geostationary operational environmental satellites (GOES) and polar operational environmental satellites (POES). The National Oceanic and Atmospheric Administration (NOAA) operates these systems. While such systems provide useful information, the DMSP has specialized meteorological capabilities to meet specific military requirements. Through DMSP satellites, military weather forecasters can detect developing patterns of weather and track existing weather systems over remote areas. The DMSP accomplishes its mission through a system of space- and ground-based assets categorized into three segments: the space segment; the command, control, and communications segment; and the user segment.

Space Segment

The space segment consists of the expendable launch vehicle, the spacecraft (vehicle), and the individual sensor payloads. Previously, the DMSP satellite was launched on the Titan II launch vehicle from Vandenberg AFB, California. The last DMSP satellite, *DMSP Flight 17 (DMSP F17)*, was launched on a Delta IV-M. The next DMSP launch will be aboard an Atlas V launch vehicle. This satellite has been designated as *DMSP F18*. Details about the capabilities of these launch vehicles can be found in chapter 20 of this handbook. In addition to *DMSP F18*, there are two satellites remaining in the DMSP series: Flights 19 and 20. The launch dates of the remaining DMSP satellites will be determined by the status of the current satellites in orbit.[1] As these satellites begin to reach the end of their operational lifetime, new satellites will be launched to replace them.

The launch weight of the satellite is 2,720 pounds, with a final on-orbit weight of 2,552 pounds (including the 772-pound sensor payload).[2] The satellite is injected into a near-circular, sun-synchronous, 450 nautical mile (nm), near-polar orbit with a period of 101.6 minutes and an inclination of 98.75 degrees. As discussed in chapter 6, a sun-synchronous orbit is one in which the orbital plane rotates eastward around the earth at the same rate at which the earth orbits the sun. This enables the satellite to orbit a location on the earth's surface at roughly the same local time each day. For example, if a satellite flies over New York City at 9:30 a.m. eastern time, then roughly three hours later it will fly over San Francisco at 9:30 a.m. Pacific time. Later that day it will fly over Beijing at 9:30 a.m. Beijing time.[3]

The space-based portion of DMSP nominally consists of two satellites, both of which orbit the earth a little over 14 times a day. Each satellite is capable of crossing any point on the earth twice a day.[4] The on-orbit satellites operational at the end of December 2000 were designated as the Block 5D-2 as shown in figure 15-1.

The DMSP spacecraft are three-axis stabilized, Earth-oriented vehicles. Using a hands-off, precision attitude-control system, the spacecraft are capable of maintaining a 0.01 degree pointing accuracy in all three axes.[5] This pointing accuracy is required to avoid optical distortion in the primary sensor, the operational linescan system, which will be explained in detail in a later section. The vehicles carry redundant onboard computers in both the spacecraft body and primary sensor. This redundancy has reduced the possibility of a single-point failure and increased the mean on-orbit lifetime of the spacecraft to three to four years. However, in some cases, for example *DMSP F13*, which was launched in 1995, the operational lifetime exceeded expectations by almost 10 years.[6]

The latest version of DMSP satellites is the Block 5D-3. Block 5D-3 satellites consist of the same major component subsystems as the Block 5D-2 satellites. However, 5D-3 satellites have increased payload capacity, increased power capability, improved on-orbit autonomy (60 days), and a design-life duration of five years. The first launch of a 5D-3 satellite (*DMSP F16*) occurred on 18 October 2003.[7] Although *DMSP F15*, launched in December 1999, featured the new 5D-3 satellite bus, it carried the legacy 5D-2 sensors. The 5D-3 designation has been reserved for DMSP Flights 16–20. The latest 5D-3 satellite is *DMSP F17*, launched on 4 November 2006.

Each satellite carries an operational linescan system (OLS) as the primary sensor. Up to 12 additional mission sensors can be carried on board the satellites. The combination of the OLS and the other mission sensors results in an existing capability for the DMSP to satisfy many of DOD's meteorological requirements. While each of the sensors provides valuable mission data, only the OLS and the special sensor microwave imager (SSMI) will be addressed in detail. A brief description of the other sensors will follow.

Operational Linescan System. The OLS is the primary sensor on board the satellite for providing visual and infrared imagery. The OLS, built by Westinghouse Corporation, is a sophisticated cloud imager consisting of an oscillating-scan radiometer, data processor, and storage system.[8] It is designed to gather, process, and output data in real time to tactical sites and store (on four recorders) both day and night visual data and infrared spectrum imagery. An example of an OLS image is shown in figure 15-2. The recorders on 5D-3 satellites have been upgraded from digital tape recorders to a reliable solid-state design. The OLS scanning radiometer (in reality, a Cassegrainian telescope) oscillates at six cycles per second and scans a 1,600 nm–wide swath with little or no distortion at the edges.[9]

Figure 15-1. DMSP deployed. (USAF image)

Figure 15-2. Operational linescan system image. (NOAA photo)

Imagery collected by an OLS is formatted into three data types:

1. The thermal detector collects thermal fine-resolution data continuously day and night.

2. Light (visual) fine data is gathered during daylight only. Fine-resolution data has a nominal linear resolution of 0.3 nm. However, satellite contact duration (typically 10 minutes) limits the vast quantity of fine-resolution data which can be stored for subsequent transmission to the ground. As a solution, the capability exists on board the spacecraft to digitally average or "smooth" the fine data into a 1.5 nm-resolution format.[10]

3. Data smoothing permits global coverage in both the thermal smooth (TS) and visual light smooth (LS) modes. Nighttime collection of visual imagery can be accomplished in the LS mode by using a low-resolution photo multiplier tube (PMT). The PMT is effective under one-quarter or better moonlight conditions.[11] The OLS also has the capability to combine fine-resolution data, interleaved with "smooth," for real-time downlink to remote ground terminals.

The capacity for on-orbit storage of fine-resolution data for subsequent transmission to the ground is limited to 40 minutes. This is less than half of the satellite's 101-minute single-orbit period. The stored data is transmitted down to a ground station at a 4:1 ratio during a single satellite contact. Smoothing the fine-resolution data inputs permits global coverage in an LS or TS mode. Up to 400 minutes of smoothed recorded data can be played back at a 40:1 ratio during typical ground station contact.

The OLS data-management unit has a capability for acquiring, processing, recording, and outputting data from up to 12 other mission sensors. One of the most significant of these sensors is the SSMI.

Special Sensor Microwave Imager. The SSMI is a seven-channel, passive microwave radiometer sensing radiation at 19, 22, 37, and 85 GHz. It detects the horizontal and vertical polarizations at 19, 37, and 85 GHz. The microwave brightness temperatures are converted to environmental parameters such as sea surface wind speeds, rain rates, cloud water, liquid water, solid moisture, ice edge, and ice age. The SSMI data are processed at centralized weather facilities and some tactical sites. The data are collected in a swath width of almost 760 nm. The resolution is 13.6 nm at the lower three frequencies and 7.8 nm at 85 GHz.[12]

Other Sensors. Other DMSP sensors include:

- Microwave temperature sounder (SSM/T-1): A passive microwave sensor used to obtain radiometric measurements at seven frequencies. The data provides atmospheric temperature profiles for pressure levels between the earth's surface to 30 km.[13]

- Microwave water-vapor profiler (SSM/T-2): A passive microwave sensor used to obtain water-vapor mass in seven layers and relative humidity at six levels. It provides data on contrail formation as well as location of weather systems with high water-vapor content with no associated clouds.[14]

- Microwave imager/sounder (SSMIS) (Block 5D-3 only): Also a passive microwave sensor. However, it combines the capabilities of the SSMI, SSM/T-1, and SSM/T-2 for the Block 5D-3 satellite. It is capable of scanning a swath width of 920 nm with resolutions ranging from 6.7 to 27 nm.[15]

- Ionospheric plasma drift and scintillation monitor (SSI/ES): A suite of four sensors that measures ion and electron temperatures, densities, and plasma irregularities characterizing the high-latitude space environment.[16]

- Enhanced ionospheric plasma drift and scintillation monitor (SSI/ES-2): This sensor is an upgrade to the SSI/ES. Data supports high frequency (HF) and ultrahigh frequency (UHF) communications and provides atmospheric drag calculations for low Earth orbit satellites.[17]

- Plasma monitor system (SSI/ES-3) (Block 5D-3 only): This sensor is an upgrade to the SSI/ES-2 and performs the same mission.

- Precipitating electron and ion spectrometer (SSJ/4): Detects and analyzes electrons and ions that precipitate into the ionosphere, producing the auroral displays. The sensor supports those missions which require knowledge of the state of the polar ionosphere such as communications, surveillance, and detection systems (for example, the over-the-horizon [OTH] radar) that propagate energy off or through the ionosphere.[18]

- Precipitating particle spectrometer (SSJ/5) (launched on *DMSP F16*): A follow-on to the SSJ/4 with a new detector design capable of providing a greater detailed analysis of the ionosphere.[19]

- Gamma ray detector (SSB/X): An array-based system that detects the location, intensity, and spectrum of x-rays emitted from the earth's atmosphere.[20]

- Gamma ray detector (SSB/X-2): An upgraded SSB/X with the additional capability to detect gamma ray bursts.

- Triaxial fluxgate magnetometer (SSM): Provides information on geomagnetic fluctuations that affect HF communications.[21]

- Ultraviolet limb imager (SSULI) (Block 5D-3 only): Uses the ultraviolet spectrum to provide additional data for users of HF communications, satellite drag and vehicle reentry issues, and OTH radar.[22]

- Ultraviolet spectrographic imager (SSUSI) (Block 5D-3 only): Gives the 5D-3 satellite the ability to obtain photometric observations of the nightglow and nightside aurora.[23]

- Laser threat warning sensor (SSF): An operational, static Earth-viewing, laser threat warning sensor.[24] Currently in prototype on the 5D-2 satellites, the operational version was launched on *DMSP F16* and *DMSP F17*.

The newer Block 5D-3 satellites include upgraded instruments, solid-state data recorders, and a UHF downlink which will enable data to be sent directly to tactical users sometime in the future.

Command, Control, and Communications Segment

The command, control, and communications (C3) segment (fig. 15-3) makes use of ground station sites to command and control DMSP satellites. The sites include the Fairchild Satellite Operations Center at Fairchild AFB, Washington; the Hawaii Tracking Station; the Thule Tracking Station in Greenland; and the New Hampshire Tracking Station. These sites collect environmental data collected by the DMSP constellation, which is then routed to the DMSP user community. Through its communications links, the control segment provides all functions necessary to maintain the state of health of the DMSP satellites and to recover the payload data acquired during satellite orbit. Although real-time, primary-sensor payload data are available to deployed tactical terminals worldwide, access to stored data is obtained only when the DMSP satellite is within the field of view (FOV) of a DMSP-compatible ground station. Once the stored data has been transmitted to one of the four ground stations (Thule, Fairbanks, Hawaii, and New Hampshire), that data is usually relayed to the Air Force Weather Agency (AFWA) and the Fleet Numerical Meteorological and Oceanographic Center (FNMOC) for processing via two domestic communications satellites (DOMSAT).[25]

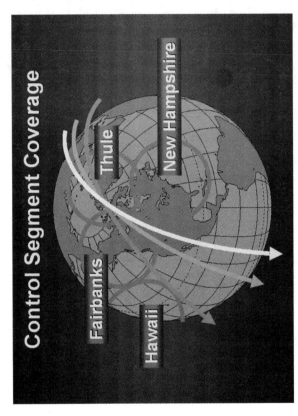

Figure 15-3. DMSP control segment coverage. (*Reprinted from* Air University, *Space Primer*, unpublished book, 2003, 13-5.)

The Multipurpose Satellite Operations Center (MPSOC), manned by the 6th Space Operations Squadron (6 SOPS) at Offutt AFB, Nebraska (colocated with the AFWA), was the primary center for DMSP operations. As part of the merger of the DMSP with its civilian counterpart, NOAA, the MPSOC was closed during May 1998. NOAA assumed all functions related to command and control of the DMSP constellation at their Satellite Operations Control Center at Suitland, Maryland, on 29 May 1998.[26] The Space and Missile Systems Center at Los Angeles AFB, California, is currently responsible for managing the actual Defense Meteorological Satellite Program.[27]

The 6 SOPS was officially inactivated on 11 June 1998 because its operational mission was assumed by NOAA. Subsequently, the 6 SOPS Air Force Reserve Unit was activated at Schriever AFB, Colorado, and provides a "hot backup" capability for the MPSOC and takes 10 to 15 percent of the satellite contacts per week.

The Air Force Satellite Control Network, using its Automated Remote Tracking Station (ARTS), can be used for routine telemetry, tracking, and commanding (TT&C) functions. Only three of the stations (Thule ARTS, New Hampshire ARTS, and Hawaii ARTS) currently have the necessary hardware and software enhancements to retrieve DMSP mission data. Additionally, the NOAA site at Fairbanks, Alaska, supports DMSP data retrieval.[28]

User Segment

While the C3 segment meets the ongoing needs of the DMSP satellites, the DMSP user community is serviced by centralized and tactical components of the user segment. The user segment consists of Earth-based processing and communications functions required to receive, process, and distribute global weather data to support Air Force, Army, Navy, and Marine Corps requirements. Vans and shipboard terminals, using direct readout of real-time infrared and visible spectrum images from the DMSP satellites, also form a part of this segment.

AFWA and FNMOC are the centralized components of the user segment. Products provided by AFWA include aviation, terminal, and target forecasts; weather warnings and advisories; automated flight plans; and exercise/special mission support. AFWA recovers the stored mission data from the DMSP satellites as well as data from other sources (GOES, POES, etc.), generates weather and space environmental products, and provides operational support to their respective customers. AFWA is the lead DOD organization for the overall processing and distribution of centralized meteorological mission sensor data in support of worldwide military activity.[29]

FNMOC, located in Monterey, California, receives DMSP data to provide operational products and forecasts to the Navy. Specifically, FNMOC provides naval forces with analyses and forecasts of oceanographic and marine weather parameters at any global location, to include ocean surface and subsurface temperatures and other meteorological conditions. AFWA and FNMOC also provide support to other elements of DOD and many government agencies.[30]

The tactical components of the DMSP user segment are the fixed and mobile land- and ship-based tactical terminals operated by the Air Force, Navy, and Marine Corps. These terminals recover direct readouts of real-time visible and infrared cloud-cover data from the DMSP satellites as well as SSMI data.[31]

Tactical terminals (TACTERM) have been a part of the DMSP since the early 1970s. These TACTERMs have the capability to receive, process, decrypt (when necessary), display, and distribute the data from any DOD or NOAA meteorological satellite. They also receive localized information from the satellite, with the satellite transmitting the information it is currently observing down to the tactical user. Soft-copy data (terminal display) is available in real time while hard-copy data is available within 10 minutes. Imagery resolution can be both fine (0.3 nm) and smooth (1.5 nm).

The Mark IV terminal is a transportable satellite terminal designed for worldwide tactical deployment in hostile environments. Mounted in a standard shelter, the Mark IV can be towed over virtually any terrain or transported on C-130 or larger aircraft. Once deployed, it can be set up and operational within eight to 10 hours.[32]

The DMSP satellite does not constantly transmit tactical data; it must be commanded to do so. Tactical users (shipboard or land-based) must make their requirements known to AFWA. AFWA coordinates with the NOAA Operations Center to command the satellite to transmit the tactical data during specific portions of its orbit. Not all mission sensor data is available to the tactical user, but information from the operational line-scan system and special sensor microwave imager is available.

Another TACTERM, the Mark IVB, increases the ability to process DMSP, POES, and GOES satellite data, allowing for processing and displaying OLS and mission sensor data by the tactical user. It provides timely environmental databases and images from remotely sensed satellite observations to users and external communications/

processing systems. The Mark IVB is a stand-alone system consisting of a tracking antenna for polar orbiting satellites (to include DMSP) and a pointing antenna for geostationary satellites such as GOES. The system also has a processing area containing a console for operator/maintenance personnel to control and monitor the system and to perform routine maintenance.[33]

The AN/SMQ-10 and AN/SMQ-11 shipboard receiving terminals are complete satellite meteorological terminals that receive, process, and display real-time DMSP data. The data retrieved from the DMSP include the following: (1) high-resolution visible and infrared images of clouds; (2) atmospheric moisture and temperature profiles; (3) high-resolution ice-edge mapping in polar regions; (4) ocean wind velocity; and (5) ionospheric data.[34] The system is designed to be used aboard aircraft carriers and designated capital ships. The SMQ-11, an upgrade to the SMQ-10, is capable of receiving full-resolution DMSP OLS and SSMI data as well as data from other civilian satellites.

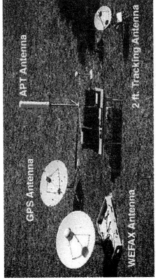

Figure 15-4. Small tactical terminal. (*Reprinted from* DMSP Overview, http://www.fas.org/spp/military/program/met/overview/dmsp35a.html [accessed 28 May 2009].)

A fully capable field system, the small tactical terminal (STT) is a lightweight, two-man portable, direct receiving, processing, and display system (fig. 15-4). The STT processes and stores data, generates meteorological soft- and hard-copy display products, and forwards imagery and data to other systems. It receives and automatically processes the DMSP real-time data smooth (RDS) and real-time data fine (RTD). (The basic terminal is only capable of processing smooth data [RDS].)[35]

The STT comes in four configurations: basic, enhanced, light-weight STT (LSTT), and the Joint Task Force Satellite Terminal (JTFST).[36] The basic STT can be upgraded to the enhanced configuration by adding an AN/TMQ-43 enhancement kit. The kit adds the capability to receive, process, and display RTD data from DMSP and high-resolution picture transmission (HRPT) data from NOAA satellites. The new LSTT can do everything the enhanced terminal can do but uses a smaller three-foot tracking dish. The four-foot dishes will be phased out as they need maintenance and replaced with three-foot dishes. The LSTT also has a smaller display system and can be carried in nine cases vice 12.

The STT receives data directly from the satellites in data streams consisting of visual and infrared imagery and mission sensor data. It receives and displays:

- Polar-orbiting automatic picture transmission (APT) imagery (basic configuration and above).

- HRPT imagery (enhanced, LSTT, JTFST).

- Weather facsimile (WEFAX) data (basic and above).

- High-resolution imagery transmitted by geostationary satellites (enhanced and above).[37]

The Army primarily uses the basic terminal, which receives only APT and WEFAX data, while the Air Force uses the enhanced, LSTT, and JTFST terminals.

DMSP Summary

The DMSP satisfies DOD's requirements for an enduring and survivable capability to collect and disseminate global visible and infrared cloud data to support worldwide DOD operations. Additionally, the DMSP collects and disseminates other specialized meteorological, terrestrial, oceanographic, and solar-geophysical data. The nominal two-satellite constellation provides worldwide data in a timely manner to the AFWA and FNMOC. Real-time regional data are also provided to deployed fixed and transportable (ground- or ship-based) tactical terminals. Figure 15-5 provides a graphical depiction of all three segments of DMSP.

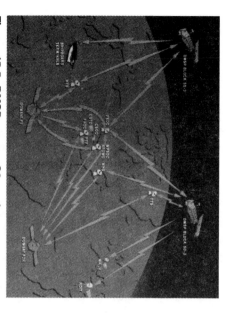

Figure 15-5. DMSP space, C3, and user segments. (*Reprinted from DMSP Overview,* http://www.fas.org/spp/military/program/met/overview/dmsp03.html [accessed 28 May 2009].)

NOAA Polar Operational Environmental Satellites

The POES satellite system is similar to the DMSP with regard to orbit type (sun-synchronous) and environmental monitoring capabilities. POES, however, is geared more toward civil applications, including weather analysis and forecasting, climate research and prediction, global sea surface temperature measurements, volcanic eruption monitoring, and forest fire detection, to name a few. These capabilities support aviation safety (i.e., volcanic ash detection and weather forecasting), support maritime and shipping safety through ice monitoring and prediction, and support search-and-rescue missions worldwide.[38]

The current NOAA POES constellation consists of four satellites: *NOAA-15*, launched 13 May 1998; *NOAA-16*, launched 21 September 2000; *NOAA-17*, launched 24 June 2002 (fig. 15-6); and *NOAA-18*, launched on 20 May 2005. All four of these satellites carry improved sensor suites, as compared to their predecessors, including the advanced microwave sounding units (AMSU-A), which provide more accurate temperature and water vapor profile information for weather forecasting.[39] They also carry the advanced very high resolution radiometer (AVHRR), which provides imagery data to scientific, commercial, and educational groups worldwide.[40] Finally, each of these satellites is equipped with the search and rescue satellite-aided tracking (SARSAT) system. The SARSAT system consists of the search and rescue repeater, which receives and retransmits position information from emergency beacons on three frequencies (121.5 MHz, 243 MHz, and 406 MHz) to ground stations. It also has a search and rescue processor which receives 406 MHz transmissions, provides measurements of the frequency and time, then retransmits the data in real time, and stores it aboard for later transmission.[41] It has the ability to store and continuously download received data for up to 48 hours to ensure that ground stations are able to pick up the signal and plan and conduct search and rescue missions. As of April 2008, 22,058 people worldwide have been rescued using this system.[42]

209

NOAA typically flies its satellites in pairs so that the two satellites are in complementary orbits. This means that the first satellite in the orbit would cross a certain point on the earth at a particular local time each day—mid-morning, for example. The second satellite would complement the first by crossing that same point on the earth at a later local time that same day, in this case mid-afternoon. This allows analysts to study the change in the weather pattern from the mid-morning to the mid-afternoon and facilitates among other things the creation of forecasts.

Figure 15-6. NOAA-17. (NASA image)

NASA Earth Observing System

The Earth observing system (EOS) of satellites was developed by NASA as part of the US Global Change Research Program to "monitor, understand, and ultimately predict the nature of global changes and the mechanisms that cause them."[43] The *Terra* satellite, formerly known as the *EOS AM-1*, was launched on 18 December 1999.[44] The *Terra* was the first in the EOS program series. It was launched from the US Air Force Western Space and Missile Center, Vandenberg AFB, into a 705 km (438-mile) sun-synchronous orbit with a morning (1030 local time) sun-shadow crossing time. *Terra* was designed with an operational lifetime of five years.[45]

The *Terra* spacecraft provides detailed measurements of clouds, aerosols, and the earth's radiative energy balance, together with measurements of the land surface and its interaction with the atmosphere through exchanges of energy, carbon, and water. These interactive processes present scientific questions of the highest priority in the understanding of global climate change.

The suite of instruments on the *Terra* spacecraft is highly synergistic, and measurements from each instrument directly address the primary mission objectives. For example, four of the five instruments will acquire simultaneous complementary observations of cloud properties and provide error-free Earth surface images. All instruments together will contribute to detecting environmental changes and thereby accelerate understanding of the total Earth system.[46]

The second EOS satellite, *Aqua* (formerly known as *EOS PM-1*), was launched on 4 May 2002. The primary mission of *Aqua* was to collect information about the earth's water cycle in all its forms (liquid, gaseous, and ice) as well as to measure the rate of flow of radiative energy, aerosols, vegetation cover on the land, oceanic organic matter, and air, land, and water temperatures.[47] It was designed for an operational life of six years.[48]

The *Aqua* satellite was the first mission in a six-satellite constellation of EOSs called the A-Train.[49] The purpose of the A-Train constellation was to provide near simultaneous measurements of aerosols, clouds, temperature, relative humidity, and other information by positioning the satellites such that each one passes over the same geographic area in succession (usually separated by a few minutes along the same orbit). This allows scientists to develop a clearer overall picture of the various elements affecting environmental conditions.[50] The other satellites comprising the A-Train constellation include the *Aura*, launched 15 July 2004, the French *PARASOL*, launched 18 December 2004, and the *CloudSat* and *Calipso*, both launched 28 April 2006.[51] The sixth satellite, the *Orbiting Carbon Observatory* (OCO), was launched 24 February 2009, but the fairing on the Taurus XL launch vehicle apparently failed to separate.[52]

Civil/Foreign Geostationary Weather Satellites

The average time it takes to get a DMSP product to its user is 15 to 45 minutes depending on satellite overpass and priority of the tasking. To help offset this time delay, civilian and foreign geostationary satellites are employed. Geostationary satellite systems such as NOAA's GOES and Europe's Meteorological Satellite (METEOSAT) offer a rapid refresh rate of cloud/weather data every 30 minutes. These satellites also offer a constant look angle resulting in high-quality "nightly news" pictures (fig. 15-7). Spatial resolution can be as good as 0.5 nm; however, resolution degrades the farther away you get from the nadir (center of the field of view).

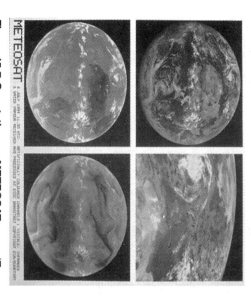

Figure 15-7. Geostationary METEOSAT scan. (European Space Agency photo)

Currently, NOAA operates two GOES satellites over the United States: (1) *GOES East* at 74.7° west longitude, and (2) *GOES West* at 134.9° west longitude.[53] The European Space Agency's METEOSAT series of satellites, which are similar to GOES, covers the Atlantic Ocean and European landmass. Spatial resolution of the METEOSAT is 2.5–5 km at nadir (located at 0° longitude).[54] An improved version called METEOSAT Second Generation (MSG) is capable of resolutions of 1 km. The most recent satellite, *MSG-2*, launched from Kourou, French Guiana, on 21 December 2005.[55]

Other international geostationary satellites include Japan's geostationary meteorological satellite (GMS) and the Indian National Satellite (INSAT) System. The GMS is based on an older GOES design and maintains similar capabilities. The GMS has since been replaced by Japan's Multifunctional Transport Satellite (MTSAT)-1R, which launched on 26 February 2005.[56] The MTSAT-1R is currently located in geostationary orbit at 140° east longitude.[57]

INSAT is operated by India; because of its imaging over the Indian landmass, India has chosen not to share INSAT data with the rest of the world. However, there is an agreement in place with the Indian government that allows INSAT data to be passed to the United States.[58] INSAT also provides a communications relay for India as a secondary mission. The most recent INSAT launch was *INSAT 4B*, which launched from Kourou, French Guiana, on 11 March 2007.[59]

The ability for weather satellites to image landmasses as well as clouds has opened the door for other types of civil/commercial imaging systems that further study the world environment. Primarily designed to aid in scientific studies of the earth's environment, such as rain forests, desert regions, and so forth, environmental satellites have also been used to gain wide-area imagery for military purposes.

National Polar-Orbiting Operational Environmental Satellite System

On 10 May 1994, the White House issued Presidential Decision Directive/National Science and Technology Council-2 (PDD/NSTC-2), "Convergence of U.S. Polar-Orbiting Operational Environmental Satellite Systems." The purpose of the PDD was to establish "a single, converged, operational system [that] can reduce duplication of efforts in meeting common requirements while satisfying the unique requirements of the civil and national security communities."[60] The program resulting from that directive was designated as the National Polar-Orbiting Operational Environmental Satellite System (NPOESS).[61]

The tri-agency NPOESS Integrated Program Office (IPO) was created on 3 October 1994 to develop, manage, and operate NPOESS.[62] The NPOESS IPO includes representation from the Department of Defense, NASA, and the Department of Commerce, more specifically NOAA. The NPOESS IPO is located organizationally within NOAA and is based in Silver Spring, Maryland. NOAA has overall responsibility for the program, including C3 operations of the satellites. DOD is responsible for the major systems acquisition and support of the NPOESS satellite systems. NASA is responsible for developing and fielding new technologies that meet the operational requirements of NPOESS.[63] The three objectives of NPOESS include the following: (1) provide a single, national, polar-orbiting, remote-sensing capability to acquire, receive, and disseminate global and regional environmental data; (2) incorporate new technologies from NASA's Office of Earth Science (OES) program; and (3) encourage international cooperation.[64]

In an effort to meet the first objective, DOD's Defense Meteorological Satellite Program and NOAA's polar operational environmental satellites have been merged to be operated jointly by the NPOESS Integrated Program Office. The original plan was to launch a constellation of six NPOESS satellites to provide accurate and timely atmospheric, oceanic, terrestrial, climatic, and solar-geophysical data products that met the operational requirements of both the civilian and military users.[65] While these new satellites were being developed, the remaining DMSP and POES satellites currently in the inventory would continue to be launched to provide weather and environmental data. This planned "evolution" of capabilities from DMSP/POES to NPOESS was supposed to begin with the launch of the first NPOESS satellite, *NPOESS C1*, in 2008.[66] However, due to massive cost overruns in the acquisition of the new NPOESS satellites, major changes had to be made to the program. These changes included a reduction in satellites from six to four, a reduction in sensors to be carried aboard the satellites (to reduce costs), and a new projected launch date for *NPOESS C1* of 2013.[67] The projected launch dates for *NPOESS C2, C3*, and *C4* are 2016, 2020, and 2022, respectively.[68]

To meet the second objective, NASA, in conjunction with the NPOESS IPO, is working on the NPOESS Preparatory Project (NPP). The purpose of the NPP is twofold. First, the NPP will serve as a "bridge" between NASA EOS satellites (*Terra* and *Aqua*) and NPOESS by providing a platform to calibrate, validate, and verify the next generation of operational sensors scheduled to be flown aboard the NPOESS. The NPP will enable continuity by providing weather/environmental data after *Terra* and *Aqua* have reached the end of their operational lifetimes.[69] Second, the NPP will provide risk reduction for NPOESS through pseudo-operational demonstration and validation of instruments and algorithms prior to the first NPOESS flight in 2013.[70] The NPP satellite is currently scheduled to launch in June 2010.[71]

The third and final objective of encouraging international cooperation is being met via the incorporation of the European Meteorological Operational (MetOp) Satellite Program as part of the NPOESS constellation.[72] MetOp-A launched on 19 October 2006. The MetOp-A satellite is equipped with an array of sophisticated instrumentation, thus enabling a "major advance in global weather forecasting and climate monitoring capabilities."[73] The MetOp-A program was established by the European Space Agency and European Organization for the Exploitation of Meteorological Satellites (EUMETSAT). EUMETSAT has partnered with NOAA to provide free meteorological data to users worldwide free of charge.[74] MetOp-A is currently flying in a complementary orbit to NOAA-18 (see previous section on NOAA POES for a description of complementary orbits). MetOp-A serves as the primary mid-morning weather-monitoring satellite, and NOAA-18 is the primary mid-afternoon weather-monitoring satellite.[75]

Although there have been some delays in the acquisition process for NPOESS, the program is well on its way to being fielded as a fully operational system. The motives and reasoning for initiating this program are still valid. With continued cooperation among the US agencies within the NPOESS IPO as well as our European counterparts, the National Polar-Orbiting Operational Environmental Satellite System will carry on the legacy established by DMSP and POES by providing improved forecasts and warnings and long-term data continuity for climate monitoring and assessment in support of military and civilian users.[76]

Notes

1. A. K. Sharma and Tony Reale, "Updates on Operational Processing for NOAA/NESDIS (National Environmental Satellite, Data, and Information Service) Sounding Data Products and Services," http://cimss.ssec.wisc.edu/itwg/itsc/itsc15/presentations/session11/11_2_sharma.pdf (accessed 16 April 2008).

2. Air Force, "Defense Meteorological Satellite Program," Fact Sheet, http://www.losangeles.af.mil/library/factsheets/factsheet.asp?id=5321 (accessed 23 February 2008).

3. NOAA NESDIS, "National Polar-Orbiting Operational Environmental Satellite System," http://www.ipo.noaa.gov/Science/why_polarTXT.html (accessed 19 April 2008).

4. Air Force, "Defense Meteorological Satellite Program."

5. National Snow and Ice Data Center, "Defense Meteorological Satellite Program (DMSP) Satellite F13," http://www.nsidc.com/data/docs/daac/f13_platform.gd.html (accessed 23 February 2008).

6. Gen Kevin Chilton, "AFSPC Wraps Up Busy 2006 Providing Spacepower," Astro News, 9 February 2007, http://www.aerotechnews.com/Astro/Astro_020907.pdf (accessed 16 April 2008).

7. NASA National Space Science Data Center, "DMSP 5D-3/F16," http://nssdc.gsfc.nasa.gov/nmc/master Catalog.do?sc=2003-048A (accessed 23 February 2008).

8. R. G. Isaacs and J. C. Barnes, "Intercomparison of Cloud Imagery from the DMSP OLS, NOAA AVHRR, GOES VISSR, and Landsat MSS," Journal of Atmospheric and Oceanic Technology 4 (December 1987), http://ams.allenpress.com/archive/1520-0426/4/4/pdf/i1520-0426-4-4-647.pdf (accessed 24 February 2008).

9. National Geophysical Data Center, "OLS—Operational Linescan System," http://www.ngdc.noaa.gov/dmsp/sensors/ols.html (accessed 23 February 2008).

10. NOAA DMSP Sensors Directorate, "DMSP Sensors," http://eic.ipo.noaa.gov/IPOarchive/SCI/sensors/doc88.pdf (accessed 24 February 2008).

11. Isaacs and Barnes, "Intercomparison of Cloud Imagery," 649.

12. National Geophysical Data Center, "SSM/I-Microwave Imager," http://www.ngdc.noaa.gov/dmsp/sensors/ssmi.html (accessed 23 February 2008).

13. National Geophysical Data Center, "SSM/T-Atmospheric Temperature Profiler," http://www.ngdc.noaa.gov/dmsp/sensors/ssmt.html (accessed 23 February 2008).

14. National Geophysical Data Center, "SSMT/2 Atmospheric Water Vapor Profiler," http://www.ngdc .noaa.gov/dmsp/sensors/ssmt2.html (accessed 23 February 2008).

15. NOAA DMSP Sensors Directorate, "DMSP Sensors," 41.

16. National Geophysical Data Center, "SSIES Ion Scintillation Monitor," http://www.ngdc.noaa.gov/ dmsp/sensors/ssies.html (accessed 23 February 2008).

17. Herbert J. Kramer, *Observation of the Earth and Its Environment: Survey of Missions and Sensors*, 4th ed. (New York: Springer, 2002), 669.

18. Ibid.

19. Ibid.

20. Ibid., 670.

21. Ibid.

22. Ibid., 670–72.

23. Ibid., 672–73.

24. Ibid., 670.

25. Air Force, "Defense Meteorological Satellite Program."

26. NOAA, "National Polar-Orbiting Operational Environmental Satellite System (NPOESS)," updated August 2002, http://www.publicaffairs.noaa.gov/grounders/npoess.html (accessed 24 February 2008).

27. Air Force, "Defense Meteorological Satellite Program."

28. Wiley J. Larson and James R. Wertz, eds., *Space Mission Analysis and Design*, 3rd ed. (El Segundo, CA: Microcosm Press, 1999).

29. Air Force, "Air Force Weather Agency," Fact Sheet, http://www.af.mil/factsheets/factsheet .asp?fsID=157 (accessed 24 February 2008).

30. FNMOC, "Fleet Numerical Meteorology & Oceanography Center," Command brief, https://www.fnmoc .navy.mil/public/welcome/cmd_brief.pdf (accessed 24 February 2008).

31. Air Force, "Defense Meteorological Satellite Program."

32. Air Force Qualification Training Package (AFQTP) 2EXXX-201LB, "Communications-Electronics (C-E) Manager's Handbook," http://www.armymars.net/ArmyMARS/MilInfo/cemgrs-handbook.pdf (accessed 24 February 2008).

33. Ibid., 40.

34. See chapter 4 in Gary Federici, *From the Sea to the Stars*, Naval Historical Center online publication, http://www.history.navy.mil/books/space/Chapter4.htm (accessed 24 February 2008).

35. National Security Space Road Map, "Small Tactical Terminal," http://www.fas.org/spp/military/ program/nssrm/initiatives/stt.htm (accessed 24 February 2008).

36. Ibid.

37. AFQTP 2EXXX-201LB, "C-E Manager's Handbook," 35.

38. NOAA NESDIS, "Polar Operational Environmental Satellite," http://www.oso.noaa.gov/poes/ (accessed 19 April 2008).

39. NASA Science Mission Directorate, "NOAA/POES," http://nasascience.nasa.gov/missions/noaa/ #amsu (accessed 19 April 2008).

40. NOAA, "NOAA-16 Environmental Satellite Successfully Completes Testing and Is Turned Over to NOAA," http://www.publicaffairs.noaa.gov/releases2000/nov00/noaa00r323.html (accessed 19 April 2008).

41. NOAA NESDIS, "Search and Rescue Satellites," http://www.sarsat.noaa.gov (accessed 19 April 2008).

42. Ibid.

43. Congress, Office of Technology Assessment, *Global Change Research and NASA's Earth Observing System, OTA-BP-ISC-122* (Washington, DC: Government Printing Office, November 1993), iii.

44. NASA, "NASA: TERRA (EOS AM-1)," http://terra.nasa.gov/Events/ (accessed 24 February 2008).

45. Congress, Office of Technology Assessment, *Global Change Research and NASA's Earth Observing System*, 26.

46. NASA, "NASA: TERRA (EOS AM-1)."

47. NASA Goddard Space Flight Center, "Aqua Project Science," http://aqua.nasa.gov/ (accessed 19 April 2008).

48. NASA Goddard Space Flight Center, "Aqua Project Science: Aqua's Instruments," http://aqua.nasa .gov/about/instruments.php (accessed 19 April 2008).

49. NASA, "Aqua," http://www.nasa.gov/mission_pages/aqua/ (accessed 19 April 2008).

50. NASA, "A-Train Constellation," http://www-calipso.larc.nasa.gov/about/atrain.php (accessed 19 April 2008).

51. NASA Goddard Space Flight Center, "Aqua Project Science."

52. NASA, "NASA's Launch of Carbon-Seeking Satellite Is Unsuccessful," press release, 24 February 2009, http://www.nasa.gov/home/hqnews/2009/feb/HQ_09-039_OCO_failure.html (accessed 27 May 2009).

53. NOAA Satellite and Information Service, "Geostationary Satellites," http://www.oso.noaa.gov/goes/ (accessed 24 February 2008).

54. David Baker, ed., *Jane's Space Directory, 2003-2004* (Alexandria, VA: Jane's Information Group, 2003), 414–15.

55. European Space Agency, "Meteosat Second Generation," http://www.esa.int/esaMI/MSG/SEM4BEULWFE_0.html (accessed 24 February 2008).

56. NASA GOES Project, "GEO-News around the World," http://goes.gsfc.nasa.gov/text/geonews.html#GMS (accessed 24 February 2008).

57. Japanese Meteorological Agency, "Meteorological Satellites," http://mscweb.kishou.go.jp/general/activities/gms/index.htm (accessed 24 February 2008).

58. NASA GOES Project, "GEO-News around the World."

59. Arianespace, "Launch Status," http://www.arianespace.com/site/search/search_sub_index.html (accessed 24 February 2008).

60. PDD NSTC-2, "Convergence of U.S. Polar-Orbiting Operation Environmental Satellite Systems," 10 May 1994.

61. US House, House Science Committee Hearing: *The Future of NPOESS—Results of the Nunn-McCurdy Review of NOAA's Weather Satellite Program*, 109th Cong., 2d sess., 2006.

62. NOAA, "National Polar-orbiting Operational Environmental Satellite System (NPOESS)."

63. NOAA NESDIS, "Directorate and Agency Contributions," http://npoess.noaa.gov/About/agencies.html (accessed 19 April 2008).

64. NOAA NESDIS, "NPOESS: National Polar-orbiting Operational Environmental Satellite System," http://eic.ipo.noaa.gov/IPOarchive/ED/Outreach_Materials/program-information/CoverPagesalnserts-092507.pdf (accessed 18 April 2008).

65. NOAA, "National Polar-orbiting Operational Environmental Satellite System (NPOESS)."

66. Ibid.

67. "House Science Committee Hearing Charter: The Future of NPOESS: Results of the Nunn-McCurdy Review of NOAA's Weather Satellite Program," SpaceRef.com, http://www.spaceref.com/news/viewsr.html?pid=20863 (accessed 19 April 2008).

68. NASA, "Mitigation Approaches to Address Impacts of NPOESS Nunn-McCurdy Certification on Joint NASA-NOAA Goals," White Paper, http://www7.nationalacademies.org/ssb/NPOESSWorkshop_Cramer_NRC_06_19_07_final.pdf (accessed 18 April 2008).

69. R. Taylor and M. Crison, "NPOESS Preparatory Project (NPP): Status Update for Interim Science Panel," 2 August 1999, http://jointmission.gsfc.nasa.gov/documents/powerpoint/RSDO_ISP8-2-99.ppt (accessed 19 April 2008).

70. NASA Goddard Space Flight Center, "Earth Observing System: NPP," http://eospso.gsfc.nasa.gov/eos_homepage/mission_profiles/show_mission.php?id=19 (accessed 19 April 2008).

71. NASA Science, "NPOESS Preparatory Project (NPP)," http://nasascience.nasa.gov/missions/npoess-preparatory-project-npp (accessed 19 April 2008).

72. Stephen A. Mango, "NPOESS/NPP Calibration/Validation/Verification Program: Its Role in Emerging Global Remote Sensing Systems and Its Potential for Improved Numerical Weather Prediction and Climate Monitoring," http://wgcv.ceos.org/docs/plenary/wgcv24/MangoWGCV24.pdf (accessed 19 April 2008).

73. European Space Agency, "MetOp: Meteorological Missions," http://www.esa.int/esaLP/SEMN1FAATME_LPmetop_0.html (accessed 19 April 2008).

74. Ibid.

75. NOAA NESDIS, "More Information on POES Satellites," http://www.nesdis.noaa.gov/POES.html (accessed 19 April 2008).

76. NOAA NESDIS, "IPO Information Center," http://eic.ipo.noaa.gov/IPOarchive/ED/Outreach_Materials/program-information/CoverPagesalnserts-092507.pdf (accessed 19 April 2008).

Chapter 16

Navstar Global Positioning System

Maj Jennifer Krolikowski, USAF

The global positioning system (GPS) is truly unique when compared to other Department of Defense space assets.[1] Although GPS was originally procured to aid in navigation, it has become a universal system used by both the civilian world and the military. GPS has become so integrated into our everyday lives that the Department of Homeland Security has declared it a part of the United States' critical infrastructure. Used by cell phones, computers, and cars, GPS can be found everywhere. This chapter will discuss the GPS missions; segments; limitations and vulnerabilities; tactics, techniques, and procedures; and modernization efforts.[2]

Missions

The GPS system is charged with three missions: navigation, time transfer, and nuclear detonation detection.

Navigation

The mission most commonly thought of is the navigation mission. GPS offers highly accurate position and velocity any time, any place. The required number of GPS signals needed for triangulation are guaranteed anywhere on the earth between the 70° north and 70° south latitudes—it is truly a global system. There is limited GPS capability at the poles due to poorer satellite visibility.

Another benefit of GPS is that it can perform in all weather conditions. The system is not affected by cloud cover. Unlike laser-guided munitions, GPS-aided bombs can be used at any time, 24/7. Some of the applications for navigation are determining position, targeting, and mapping.

Time Transfer

The second mission of GPS is time transfer. Ironically, this is probably the least-known mission, but it is now becoming the most used. The time standard used by DOD is Coordinated Universal Time, or UTC, which is the time maintained by the US Naval Observatory (USNO) and is considered the "world's time." Typically, it is not very practical to call the USNO every time a time hack is needed. Because GPS is widely available at all times and places, it has therefore become DOD's primary source for timing information. Since GPS time is within 20 nanoseconds (ns) of UTC time, GPS will likely be sufficient as a timing source for most purposes.

One of the applications of the time transfer mission is synchronizing digital communications. During frequency hopping, GPS timing is used to make sure each communication terminal moves to the new frequency at the same time. Another application is synching up networks, such as those used by computers, automated teller machines, or cell phones.

Nuclear Detonation Detection System

The GPS satellites carry an additional payload suite to support a Nuclear Detonation Detection System (NDS). The sensor array includes optical, x-ray, dosimeter, and electromagnetic pulse (EMP) sensors. The sensors detect and measure light, x-ray, subatomic particle, and EMP phenomenology to pinpoint the location and yield of a surface or airborne nuclear detonation. The information sensed on the GPS NDS system is relayed to the ground-based Integrated Correlation and Display System (ICADS) via a dedicated channel, L3 (1381.05 MHz). NDS supports several tasks, such as treaty monitoring and nuclear force management.

GPS Segments

The GPS system is made up of three parts: the space segment (or satellites), the control segment, and user equipment.

Space Segment

At a minimum, the GPS constellation needs 24 satellites in six orbital planes in order to ensure that at least four satellites are in view by the user at all times. The constellation flies in a semisynchronous orbit at approximately 20,000 km away from the earth. Another name for this orbit is middle Earth orbit (MEO). Although GPS has a semisynchronous orbit, its period is actually 11 hours and 58 minutes, vice 12 hours as the orbit implies. The two-minute differentiation is because the GPS period is based on a sidereal day and not the solar day.

The current constellation is around 30 satellites. The added redundancy offers improved accuracies and availability to users over the nominal 24-satellite constellation. Given how important GPS is to the world, constellation management is taken very seriously to avoid potential gaps in coverage or outages of service. Block IIR/IIR-M satellites are launched off of a Delta II rocket. The Block IIF will launch from the evolved expendable launch vehicle (EELV) boosters.

GPS offers two types of services to its user base—the standard positioning service (SPS) and the precise positioning service (PPS). The SPS is available for anyone's use—military or civil. SPS offers 3–5 meter accuracy. The PPS can only be accessed by authorized personnel—those with the correct decryption keys such as the US military or its allies. PPS accuracy is 2–4 meters. There are several signals and codes that make up each of the GPS services (fig. 16-1).

Today, GPS transmits on the frequencies L1 (1575.42 MHz) and L2 (1227.6 MHz), which are along the x-axis. The power levels for the signals are on the y-axis. The codes transmitted on these frequencies are the course acquisition (C/A) code (the green spike) and the pseudorandom (P[Y]) code (the yellow humps). Currently, the C/A code is transmitted on L1 and P(Y) is on both L1 and L2. The C/A code is what everyone receives—it is the code within the SPS. The P(Y) is an encrypted code and can only be received by those with the appropriate keys. This is the code that is obtained when a user is subscribed to the PPS.

Control Segment

While it is necessary to have satellites in the sky transmitting navigation signals, a control segment is needed to command them. This section discusses how that control segment works and what the GPS operations center (GPSOC) can provide the war fighter.

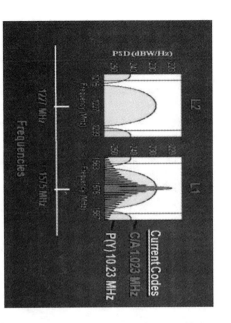

Figure 16-1. Signal/frequency/code relationship. (National Security Space Institute [NSSI] graphic prepared by the author)

The headquarters for the control segment is the master control station (MCS) at Schriever AFB, operated by the 2nd Space Operations Squadron

(2 SOPS). There is an unmanned backup master control station (BMCS) in Gaithersburg, Maryland, that is required to stand up within 24 hours in case something happens to the MCS. The alternate master control station (AMCS) is being built at Vandenberg AFB and is slated to replace the BMCS. The architecture evolution plan (AEP) must go online before the AMCS can go operational.

The GPSOC, part of the MCS team, is the one-stop shop for accuracy models, constellation health, and GPS service questions. It operates 24/7 and can provide assistance at any time. Not only does the GPSOC support the war fighter but also the civil community. The Federal Aviation Administration (FAA) or Coast Guard can use the GPSOC to answer civil-related GPS questions.

In addition to the master control station, there are six GPS monitoring stations and ground antennas, located at Colorado Springs, Kwajalein Atoll, Hawaii, Ascension Island, Diego Garcia, and Cape Canaveral. The Cape Canaveral site is primarily used for system checkout after launch, but it has transmit/receive capability that can act as a backup for the control segment, if necessary. Additionally, the Air Force Satellite Control Network has nondedicated resources that can provide ad hoc support to the GPS control segment. The National Geospatial-Intelligence Agency (NGA) also has a monitor station infrastructure used for its mapping missions. The Air Force is working with the NGA to incorporate the NGA's monitor stations with the GPS sites. This will allow 2 SOPS to observe the satellites more often and thus be able to discern more quickly if there is an issue or anomaly. As a result, the constellation accuracy performance will improve.

GPS satellites are commanded and controlled via the monitor stations, the MCS, and the ground antenna. Essentially, high-quality GPS receivers are placed at various precise locations throughout the world. These receivers track the satellites just like a normal receiver would—they obtain the satellites' ephemeris and any data. Information is then transferred to the MCS where it is put into the Kalman filter. The filter is an algorithm that can determine how the satellite has deviated from where it should actually be. The MCS takes that data and transmits back to the satellite via the ground antenna to update the satellite with its true location and time. For example, the monitor station is located at (0, 0), and the local time is 1700. This is known to be absolutely true. The GPS satellites are telling the monitor station it is at (1, 1), and the local time is 1705. The monitor station relays that information to the MCS. The MCS then builds an upload that will adjust the satellite transmissions. As a result, the monitor station's GPS-calculated position becomes more reflective of where the station truly is. These upload corrections occur at least once per day.

User Equipment

Millions of users, both civil and military, are employing GPS in thousands of ways. This is possible through the third GPS segment—the user equipment. Given that the GPS industry is around $1 billion a year, receivers come in many shapes and forms and are easily obtained. However, they all work essentially the same way.

Each receiver contains an almanac that tells it which satellites to start looking for in order to acquire their signals. For instance, if the receiver is in Colorado Springs at 0800, the almanac tells it to find space vehicle (SV) 4, 17, 23, and so forth. The receiver acquires the signal from the satellites and compares the receiver's internally generated code (specific for each satellite) to the code it is obtaining from the satellites. It also starts to look at each satellite's navigation data to see where the satellite thinks its position is and how far the clock has drifted and get information about atmospheric-delay corrections.

It takes some amount of time for the signal from the satellite to reach the receiver. This is known as the time offset. The receiver then shifts its internally generated code to line up with the code received from the satellite and record that time offset. Based on the time offset, the distance between the satellite and the receiver can be determined.

This process is followed for at least four satellites. The cumulative information is entered into the position equations and calculated. As a result, the user then knows his or her position in the world and can navigate from there. If the receiver were turned off in Colorado Springs and turned back on in Hawaii, it would initially try to acquire the satellites from its last known position—Colorado Springs. As the receiver does not find the appropriate satellites, it will begin searching the entire almanac until it acquires the satellites overhead and can determine its new position.

Timing is very important when establishing an accurate position. Typically, the time it takes for a GPS signal to reach the receiver is 0.07 seconds. If the time offset is errant by 1 ns, it equates to a foot of error when calculating the distance to the satellite. This, in turn, decreases accuracy when the receiver calculates the position solution. Only atomic clocks give the level of fidelity required to provide highly accurate locations.

Four satellites are needed to solve for latitude, longitude, altitude, and receiver clock bias. It is impractical to have atomic clocks in a receiver—they are too large and expensive. Therefore, most receivers have the same kind of timing source that is in a watch. As a result, the receiver is not perfectly synched up with the satellites and has a bias. Fortunately, that receiver has the same clock error with each of the satellites it talks to. So while the position is being calculated, the bias is solved for as well.

Limitations and Vulnerabilities

Even though GPS is an awesome system, it does have some limitations and vulnerabilities, specifically in accuracy and low signal power.

Accuracy

It is impossible for GPS to be 100 percent accurate because there are several sources that introduce errors into the navigation solution. These contributing factors—troposphere, ionosphere, multipath, satellite clock, satellite ephemeris, wrong datums/grids, dilution of precision—are the most common, and largest, sources of error.

Most signals are degraded as they pass through the atmosphere. The same is true for GPS. When the GPS signal goes through the troposphere, 90 percent of the error induced by this part of the atmosphere comes from the "dry atmosphere." This part of the error is really easy to model and can be calculated and accounted for. The remaining 10 percent of the error comes from the "wet atmosphere." This part of the error is very difficult to model, so these inaccuracies must just be accepted. Fortunately, this is not a significant source of error.

On the other hand, the ionosphere can produce large sources of error. For example, the triangle in figure 16-2 represents the true position of the user. The perceived position calculated by a single-frequency receiver is seen in figure 16-3. If a dual-frequency receiver is used, the result from the second signal portrays the position in figure 16-4. The dual-frequency receiver subtracts the two values and can determine the true position that is in figure 16-2. Remember that the C/A code, the one used by civil receivers, is only transmitted on one frequency. Therefore, civil receivers cannot currently correct for ionosphere-induced errors. Some of the GPS modernization efforts address this issue for civil users by adding a second civil frequency.

Figure 16-3. Error induced on L1 by the ionosphere. (NSSI graphic prepared by the author)

Figure 16-2. True position. (NSSI graphic prepared by the author)

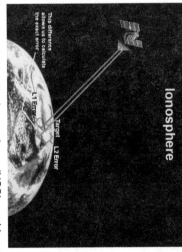

Figure 16-4. Error induced on L2 by the ionosphere. (NSSI graphic prepared by the author)

Multipath occurs when the signal bounces off objects before the user equipment receives it. This phenomenon is most prevalent in urban canyons. As the signal bounces around, it takes longer to reach the receiver, thereby increasing the time offset. As a result, the calculated distance to the satellite is longer, and the position is less accurate. There are a couple of ways to mitigate this. First, the signal structure is known as right-hand circularized. When it bounces off of a building, it becomes left-hand circularized. The receiver is programmed to disregard left-handed signals. Second, the receiver knows it should be obtaining the signal in a certain amount of time—around 0.07 seconds. If a signal breaks an established threshold, the receiver will disregard that signal.

One of the factors that 2 SOPS works to control is the errors generated by inaccurate satellite clocks and ephemeris data. Keeping the satellite information as precise as possible is done through the daily uploads discussed in the section on the control segment.

It should be noted that not all grids are the same. The difference between using a World Geodetic System (WGS) 84 or a Tokyo grid could lead to 1 km of error when talking about the same coordinate point. The best way to avoid this is by making sure everyone is using the same grid. While this may seem to be common sense, there are numerous cases in which a local population has used its mapping system, which was found to be incongruent with those used by standard GPS users.

The final source of error is generated through the geometry of the constellation with respect to the user. This is called the dilution of precision (DOP) (fig. 16-5). The solid line represents the actual ranging from the satellite to the receiver. The dashed line shows what the receiver thinks is the range to the satellite, or the pseudorange. Therefore, anywhere in the box is where the user could be.

If the geometry is a little more spread out, as in figure 16-6, the box becomes much smaller and provides much better accuracy. Therefore, the best configuration is one satellite overhead and the rest along the horizon.

Low Signal Strength

GPS is highly susceptible to jamming. Four parameters need to occur to be able to jam: a higher transmitted power, transmitting at the correct frequency, alignment with the antenna, and line of sight to the antenna.

First, the GPS signal is very weak and operates below the noise threshold. Basically, the GPS signal is equivalent to shining a 25-watt light bulb from 20,000 km away. In

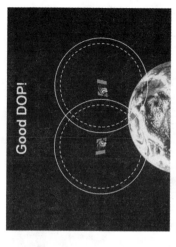

Figure 16-6. Good constellation geometry or DOP. (NSSI graphic prepared by the author)

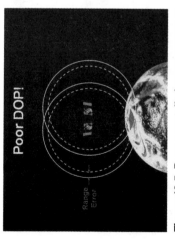

Figure 16-5. Poor constellation geometry or DOP. (NSSI graphic prepared by the author)

terms of power, the GPS signal is 10–16 watts. Because the signal does not have a lot of power and is traveling a long distance, it is remarkably easy to make a jammer that transmits higher power levels. Second, because the frequencies on which GPS transmits are common knowledge—L1 and L2—it is not hard to program a jammer to hone in on those frequencies. Third, since most receiver antennas are omnidirectional, alignment is not an issue for a jammer. Finally, the only thing that is mostly variable to a jammer is its line of sight. If a jammer cannot see the receiver, it will not be able to jam it.

Tactics, Techniques, and Procedures

There are a number of tactics, techniques, and procedures (TTP) that are used to overcome the limitations and vulnerabilities of GPS. The most common TTPs deal with accuracy prediction and jamming mitigation.

Accuracy Prediction

The GPS Interference and Navigation Tool (GIANT) is used to generate a variety of products. It can predict the accuracy for a given region over a 24-hour period. It can also provide a chart that depicts the DOP for an area of interest. This is useful when trying to determine if a GPS-aided munition will be effective or if mission planners should strike a target at another time or use a different platform if it is a time-sensitive target. It should be noted that DOP is unit-less and *not* the accuracy for that area. A DOP of two does not mean that the accuracy is two meters. It means that the constellation geometry is favorable. Typically, if the DOP is greater than six, the accuracies will not be good enough for most military missions.

GIANT can also map out what the jamming environment looks like. By inserting a known jammer location and the power it is emitting, GIANT relays how effective the jammer is to various platforms. It lets the user know where to acquire the C/A code and hand off to P(Y) before being adversely affected by the jammer. In addition, GIANT can aid in developing a flight plan that would avoid the jammers all together.

Jamming Mitigation

While GPS is relatively easy to jam, the GPS signal structure itself offers some anti-jam capability (fig. 16-7).

We can think of jamming these signals as trying to block a bridge. If the bridge is narrow, few rocks are needed to block it. If it is a fairly wide bridge, a lot of rocks are required. The same is true of signals. If the bandwidth of the signal is small (like C/A), the signal can be jammed by relatively low power. If it has a large bandwidth (like P(Y)), more power is needed. The more power that is used to jam a signal, the easier it is to locate the jammer. Also, if an adversary jams P(Y) on L1, the user could switch to L2 and still get GPS. Therefore, even more power is necessary to jam both frequencies. Unfortunately, most military receivers must acquire C/A first before getting handed off to P(Y). Given this requirement and the fact that it does not take a lot of power to jam C/A, it is very appealing to attack the C/A code.

As part of the modernization effort, one antijam capability being fielded is the M-code. The M-code is spread across two frequencies, has a large bandwidth, and is split. The

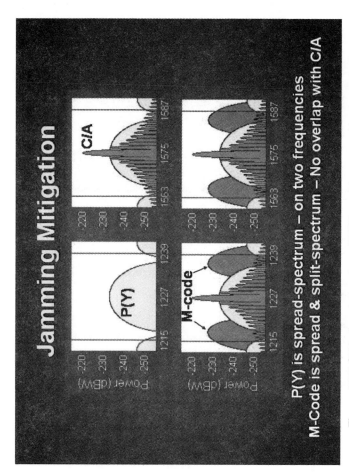

Figure 16-7. GPS signal structure. (NSSI graphic prepared by the author)

M-code also has a little more power associated with it. As a result, an inordinate amount of power will be needed to jam the entire M-code. Also, it will no longer be essential to acquire C/A before acquiring the M-code—the M-code will be direct access. Another benefit is that the M-code is spectrally separated from the C/A code, thereby reducing potential interference issues.

In addition to the signal structure, there are other ways to mitigate a jammer's effectiveness. By using directional antennas, the receiver will look only for satellites above the horizon, usually 10° or higher. This nullifies the jammers that are transmitting on the earth's surface. Another technique is antenna nulling. In this case, an antenna is made up of a number of elements. If one of the elements detects a jamming signal, that element is shut off, leaving the rest of the antenna to function normally to receive the GPS signal without interference. To prevent a jammer from having line of sight to the receiver, the user could go behind a mountain, dig a hole, or use his or her body to block the jamming signal.

Modernization

There are a number of efforts underway in each of the GPS segments to improve the system and address additional user needs. This section describes modernization efforts in the space, control, and user segments.

Satellite Evolution

The current GPS constellation contains Block IIA and IIR satellites. Both of these transmit only two signals and codes—C/A on L1 and P(Y) on both L1 and L2. Within the Block IIR-M, the M-code, a second civil signal (L2C), and flex power are added. L2C enables civil receivers to correct for the ionosphere. Flex power allows power to be transferred from one signal to another, thus providing some additional antijam capability. Block IIF will have everything that IIR-M offers but will add a third civil signal on L5. That signal will be used during "safety of life" applications. The final block being developed is GPS III. It will have all the same capabilities as IIF and many added capabilities. It will have increased power in the form of a spot beam. It will have slightly better accuracy, mostly due to crosslinks that will greatly reduce the age of data. Assured integrity is a major requirement desired by the civil community. With this precision, approach landings are possible with confidence that the GPS is available and working. Finally, as part of the negotiations with Galileo, GPS III will have a fourth civil signal on L1 (L1C) that will be compatible with the signals transmitted on Galileo. Table 16-1 summarizes the capabilities of each GPS block.

Table 16-1. Evolution of GPS capabilities

Block IIA/IIR	Block IR-M, IIF	Block III
• Basic GPS	IIR-M: IIA/IIR capabilities plus:	Incremental acquisition:
• Standard service (16–24 M SEP)	• 2nd civil signal (L2C)	• Increased AJ power
– Single frequency (L1)	• Earth-coverage military code	• Assured integrity
– C/A code navigation	IIF: IIR-M capability plus:	• Increased security
• Precise service (16 M SEP)	• 3rd civil signal on L5	• System survivability
– Two frequencies (L1 & L2)	• Flex-power upgrade adds ability to increase power on either P- or M-code signals to defeat low-level enemy jamming	• Increased accuracy
– P-code navigation		• 4th civil signal on L1C for Galileo compatibility

Control Segment Upgrades

A lot of work is being done to update the control segment as well. That effort is called the architecture evolution plan (AEP). AEP is required to command and control the Block IIF satellites and to operate the M-code signals in a test mode. By implementing AEP, the backup master control station can be replaced by the alternate master control station.

Recently deployed was the Launch, Anomaly Resolution, and Disposal Operations (LADO) software. LADO replaced the command and control structure used by the Air Force Satellite Control Network (AFSCN).

The final control segment upgrade is the Operational Control Segment of the Future (OCX). OCX will incorporate some of the functionality that was originally allocated to AEP and add GPS III–unique functions, like commanding the spot beam. In addition, the OCX architecture is designed to be very flexible so future upgrades will be easier to accomplish.

Receiver Modernization

On the user equipment side, the Defense Advanced GPS Receiver (DAGR) is being fielded to replace the existing precision lightweight GPS receivers (PLGR). The DAGR will be a dual-frequency receiver, unlike the PLGR, which can obtain only L1. Therefore, the DAGR will be able to correct for the ionosphere whereas the PLGR cannot. The DAGR will have a graphical display versus the numerical latitude/longitude the PLGR shows today. Although DAGR cannot receive the M-code, it is much better than the handhelds currently in the field.

The next generation of user equipment is called the Modernized User Equipment (MUE). Essentially, MUE will be a "common card" for all systems—like aircraft, handhelds, ships, and so forth—that can be easily integrated into the platform. These cards will be able to acquire all of the GPS codes—P(Y), M, and C/A codes (YMCA).

In the area of security, the Selective Availability Anti-Spoofing Module (SAASM) was developed. SAASM will allow compromised receivers to be "shut off" by denying the receiver new crypto keys. Key updates over the horizon will be possible so receivers will not have to be taken back to the depot for new keys. This greatly reduces logistics footprints. Also, SAASM chips have a special antitamper coating on them to prevent people from reverse engineering the processor.

Notes

1. This chapter is adapted from a lesson written by Maj Jennifer Krolikowski for the National Security Space Institute.

2. For additional reading on GPS and related topics, see Ahmed El-Rabbany, *Introduction to GPS: The Global Positioning System* (Norwood, MA: Artech House, 2002); Joint Requirements Oversight Council, *Joint Capabilities Document for Positioning, Navigation and Timing*, Version 7.1 Draft, April 2006; Steven Lazar, "Modernization and Move to GPS III," *Crosslink*, Summer 2002, http://www.aero.org/publications/crosslink/summer2002/07.html (accessed 12 March 2008); Keith D. McDonald, "The Modernization of GPS: Plans, New Capabilities and Future Relationship to Galileo," *Journal of Global Positioning System* 1, no. 1 (2002): 1–17; Michael Russell Rip and James M. Hasik, *The Precision Revolution* (Annapolis, MD: Naval Institute Press, 2002); and GPS Operations Center, *NAVSTAR GPS User Equipment Introduction: Public Release Version*, September 1996, http://gps.afspc.af.mil/gpsoc/gps_documentation.aspx (accessed 7 May 2009).

Chapter 17

Missile Warning Systems

Maj Edward P. Chatters IV, USAF; and Maj Bryan Eberhardt, USAF

This chapter addresses the missile warning systems controlled by US Strategic Command (USSTRATCOM) in support of the North American Aerospace Defense Command (NORAD) agreement to protect the continental United States and Canada from ballistic missile attack.[1] Also covered are systems developed for theater-level missile defense in accordance with the Missile Defense Act of 1991, as amended by Congress in 1992, for the protection of forward-deployed US forces and allies.[2]

Space-Based Warning Sensors

The earliest space-based missile warning system was the Missile Defense Alarm System (MIDAS) satellite, which was part of the Air Force missile warning program in the late 1950s.[3] It was designed to detect and track hot exhaust gases from intercontinental ballistic missiles (ICBM) during the boost phase. In 1963, MIDAS became the first space-based system to accurately detect a missile launch when it reported on both Minuteman and Polaris ICBM test launches, which were deliberately scheduled to coincide with the MIDAS orbit.[4] MIDAS was eventually phased out in the late 1960s in favor of the Defense Support Program (DSP), which has a more advanced sensor design and a more robust spacecraft platform. DSP has been the stalwart of missile warning since the 1970s, with a total of 23 satellites launched in the program. The early single-string, mainframe processors at the ground stations were replaced by the newer and more robust Space-Based Infrared System (SBIRS) in 2002, although that system will continue to incorporate DSP satellites until the launch of the first SBIRS geosynchronous satellites in 2010.

Space-Based Infrared System

The primary mission of SBIRS is to provide space-based surveillance for missile warning, missile defense, battlespace characterization, and technical intelligence. SBIRS contributes to missile warning by providing timely and accurate data to the president, geographic and functional combatant commanders (CCDR), and other users within the space community regarding detection, identification, and predicted impact-point location of ballistic missile launches. The missile defense mission is supported by SBIRS via the timely, accurate, and reliable transmission of ballistic missile launch and in-flight data to missile defense assets in-theater in order to allow those systems to respond to an enemy attack. The SBIRS technical intelligence mission is performed through the expeditious relaying of infrared target signatures and threat performance data to the intelligence community for analysis. The SBIRS battlespace characterization mission refers to the provision of data used to enhance the overall situational awareness of decision makers, support battle damage assessments, and aid in intelligence preparation of the operational environment.[5]

SBIRS is an integrated "system of systems" consisting of space and ground components.[6] The space component currently consists of a constellation of geosynchronous DSP satellites, a key part of North America's early warning system. The space component will eventually include SBIRS-High (fig. 17-1), originally designed to consist of four geosynchronous Earth orbit (GEO) and two highly elliptical orbit (HEO) satellites. However, due to massive cost overruns and schedule delays, only two or three GEO satellites are actually scheduled to be deployed.[7] The ground component consists of control stations such as the Mission Control Station located at Buckley AFB, Colorado, which is responsible for consolidating event data from dispersed legacy DSP ground systems.[8]

In geosynchronous orbits, DSP satellites (fig. 17-2) serve as the continent's first line of defense against ballistic missile attack and are normally the first systems to detect space and missile launches. In addition to launch detections, DSP satellites also have numerous sensors on board to detect nuclear detonations (NUDET).[9]

Remote ground stations receive missile warning data from the satellites and feed the data via secure communications links to ground stations for processing. These ground stations include both the fixed mission control station and mobile/deployable ground stations.[10] The ground stations assess system reliability, attempt to identify the type of launch occurring, and generate a launch report. Crews send these reports to the NORAD operations centers at Cheyenne Mountain AFS, Colorado; the Alternate Missile Warning Center at Offutt AFB, Nebraska; and other command centers.

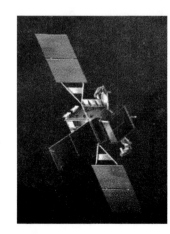

Figure 17-1. SBIRS artwork. (*Reprinted from* Lockheed Martin, "SBIRS Artwork," http://www.lockheedmartin.com/data/assets/8207.gif [accessed 7 April 2008]).

Figure 17-2. DSP satellite. (USAF image)

Defense Support Program

The Defense Support Program, comprised of both ground and satellite segments, began with the first DSP satellite launch in the early 1970s. Since that time, DSP satellites have provided uninterrupted early-warning capability. In 2001, the DSP ground system was replaced by the SBIRS ground system, though the DSP satellites continue to operate as part of the newer SBIRS architecture.[11]

DSP Satellite Evolution. Over the years, the DSP satellites have seen many improvements. Initially, there were phase-one and phase-two (first and second generation) satellites weighing approximately 2,000 pounds with solar panels generating about 400 watts of power. The third-generation satellite was called Multiple Orbit Satellite/Program Improvement Module (MOS/PIM). The MOS/PIM variant was designed to address emerging threats such as antisatellite systems and ground-based lasers.[12] Despite the multiple-orbit option available on this generation of satellites, it was never exercised. However, this generation of satellites did introduce an antijam command capability.

The major improvement in the fourth generation of satellites, known as Sensor Evolutionary Development (SED) satellites, was the increase in infrared detection cells from 2,000 to 6,000 cells, which enhanced the satellites' ability to discriminate between launch events.[13] Along with the increased cell count was the experimental medium-wave infrared (MWIR) package, also known as the second-color experiment.[14] This package was a proof of concept for implementation on the fifth and final generation of DSP satellites, DSP-1. We refer to this fifth generation as the final generation of DSP satellites because of the development of a new family of satellites as part of the SBIRS.

DSP satellites have routinely exceeded their design life by many years.[15] The design life of DSP-1-era birds was three to five years; however, many satellites have reached 10 to 15 years of service. By 2006, there were as many as 10 DSP satellites still operating.[16] In fact, "DSP satellites have exceeded their specified design life by some 30 percent through five upgrade programs."[17]

Current DSP Satellites. As the capabilities of DSP satellites have grown, so have their weight and power. Unlike the old lightweight, low-power satellites, the newest generation of DSP satellites weighs over 5,000 pounds, and the solar arrays generate 1,285 watts of power. The current DSP satellite is approximately 33 feet long and 22 feet in diameter.[18] The system is comprised of the satellite vehicle, also referred to as the bus, and the sensor (fig. 17-3). The satellites are placed in geosynchronous orbit. Global coverage can be efficiently achieved with three satellites. Additional satellites can provide dual or triple coverage, providing for more accurate and timely event reporting.

The DSP satellite spins around its Earth-pointing axis, which allows the infrared (IR) sensor to sweep across each point on the earth. While full-time global coverage by a sensor that stares at the entire earth is preferable, this method reduces the size of the IR sensor and limits the amount of data needing to be downlinked and processed.

DSP-1 Sensor Overview. The sensor (fig. 17-4) detects sources of IR radiation. A telescope/optical system and a photoelectric cell (PEC) detector array, comprised primarily of lead sulfide detectors and some Mercad-Telluride cells for the MWIR detection capability, are used to detect IR sources. IR energy enters the opening in the IR sunshade, passes through the corrector lens, travels past the PEC array, reflects off the mirror, and is focused onto the PEC array.

The PEC array contains more than 6,000 detector cells.[19] The cells are sensitive to energy in the infrared spectrum. As the satellite rotates, the earth's surface is scanned by this array. With the PEC array scanning the field of view, a cell passing across an IR source will develop a signal with an amplitude proportional to the source's intensity. The signal is then amplified, passed through an analog-to-digital converter, and placed on the downlink for transmission to the ground station.[20]

Theater Missile Warning

To meet the war fighter's growing demand for situational awareness of theater-class ballistic missiles, the theater event system (TES) was created.[21]

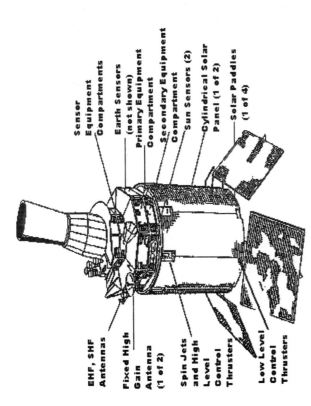

Figure 17-3. Defense Support Program satellite. *(Reprinted from Air University,* Space Primer, *unpublished book, 2003, 15-3.)*

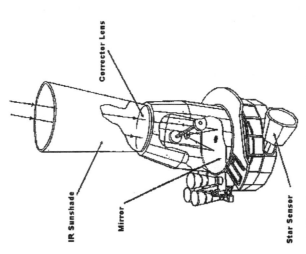

Figure 17-4. DSP sensor schematic. *(Reprinted from Air University,* Space Primer, *unpublished book, 2003, 15-4.)*

Theater Event System

The TES provides highly accurate tactical threat data through the use of stereo processing (or better) of the DSP satellite data. The TES is composed of three elements: SBIRS, the joint tactical ground station (JTAGS), and tactical detection and reporting (TACDAR). All three legs rely on IR detection for characterization and profiling of theater ballistic missile launches. An example of the TES architecture is shown in figure 17-5.

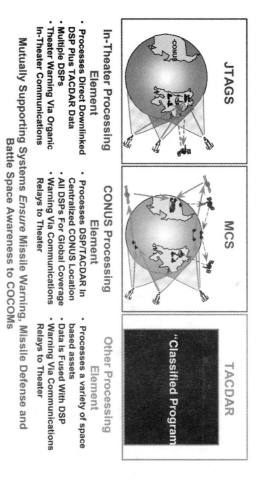

Mutually Supporting Systems *Ensure* Missile Warning, Missile Defense and
Battle Space Awareness to COCOMs

Figure 17-5. TES example. (*Reprinted from* Mike Nadler, Space and Missile Defense Future Warfare Center, "Early Warning," briefing, 21 August 2007.)

As discussed above, SBIRS accomplishes both the strategic and tactical missile warning function. JTAGS is the mobile, in-theater element of TES; it provides to the theater CCDR a direct downlink of DSP data for in-theater processing. The Army Space Command has operational control of the JTAGS.[22]

TACDAR is an additional sensor that can provide missile launch reports. The TACDAR sensor rides on a classified host satellite and therefore will not be discussed in this reference.[23] Inquiries on TACDAR may be forwarded through USSTRATCOM Global Operations (J3).

How Do I Get TES Data?

The TES has the primary mission of reporting theater/tactical threats. For theater warning, the TES (SBIRS, JTAGS, or TACDAR) reports the launch (voice and data) in-theater over two types of satellite broadcast networks: the Integrated Broadcast Service-Simplex (IBS-S), formerly the tactical related applications (TRAP) data dissemination system (TDDS), and/or the Integrated Broadcast Service-Interactive (IBS-I), formerly the tactical information broadcast service (TIBS). IBS-S transmits real-time data via the Secret Internet Protocol Router Network or tactical terminal to the Global Command and Control System.[24] IBS-I can provide timely intelligence information directly from collectors and associated ground processing facilities to the theater commanders for targeting, battle management, and overall situational awareness.[25] Theoretically, one event could be reported by all three TES elements, but the "first detect—first report" procedures help control and deconflict multiple reports of the same event. Regardless, tactical display processors in the field have coding that helps correlate missile tracks received over both networks to ensure that duplicate tracks from the same event do not appear as two separate launches in theater.

Warning data goes out over the theater satellite broadcast networks and can be incorporated in battle-management systems such as the Air Defense Systems Integrator (ADSI), the Constant Source Terminal, the Combat Intelligence Correlator (CIC), and the Airborne Warning and Control System (AWACS). See figure 17-6 for details.

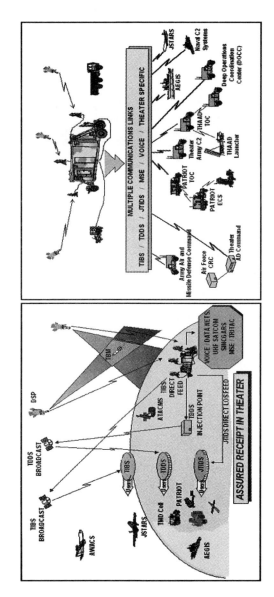

Figure 17-6. JTAGS communications and interoperability. (*Reprinted from* Army Field Manual 40-1, *Joint Tactical Ground Station Operations*, 9 September 1999.)

Ground-Based Warning Sensors

The ground-based warning sensors consist of three separate types of systems: Ballistic Missile Early Warning System (BMEWS), Perimeter Acquisition Vehicle Entry Phased-Array Weapons System (PAVE PAWS), and Perimeter Acquisition Radar Attack Characterization System (PARCS). The BMEWS sensor sites include Site I at Thule AB, Greenland; Site II at Royal Air Force Fylingdales, United Kingdom; and Site III at Clear AFS, Alaska. The PAVE PAWS sensor sites are located at Cape Cod AFS, Massachusetts, and Beale AFB, California. The PARCS sensor is located at Cavalier AFS, North Dakota.[26] A more detailed description of these sensor sites is provided in chapter 19.

Summary

Space-based infrared sensors and missile warning radar sites around the globe provide the world's most sophisticated missile warning system for the president, secretary of defense, geographic and functional CCDRs, and the entire joint military community. The robustness of the US missile warning systems and their inherent redundancy ensure that the United States will be able to promptly react and respond to any attack on its sovereignty or national interests. The US missile warning posture will continue to be enhanced as additional components of SBIRS and other missile warning follow-on systems attain full operational capability.

Notes

1. "Agreement between the Government of Canada and the Government of the United States of America on the North American Aerospace Defense Command," 28 April 2006, http://www.treaty-accord.gc.ca/ViewTreaty.asp?Treaty_ID=105060&bPrint=True&Language=0 (accessed 8 April 2008).

2. H. F. Cooper, *Summary of SDI Programs and Plans for Theater and National Ballistic Missile Defenses* (Washington, DC: Strategic Defense Initiative Organization, 4 January 1993).

3. Smithsonian National Air and Space Museum, "Sensor, Infrared, Series III, Missile Defense Alarm System," http://collections.nasm.si.edu/code/emuseum.asp?profile=objects&newstyle=single&quicksearch=A1 9700253000 (accessed 26 May 2009).

4. Jeffrey Richelson, "Space-Based Early Warning: From MIDAS to DSP to SBIRS," http://www .gwu.edu/~nsarchiv/nsaebb/nsaebb235/index.htm (accessed on 26 May 2009).

5. Maj Jay A. Moody, *Achieving Affordable Operational Requirements on the Space Based Infrared System (SBIRS) Program: A Model for Warfighter and Acquisition Success?* (Maxwell AFB, AL: Air Command and Staff College, 1997), 5.

6. Lori Reichert, "Lockheed Martin Team Passes SBIRS High System Critical Design Review," Lockheed Martin Press Release, http://www.lockheedmartin.com/news/press_releases/2001/LockheedMartinTeam PassesSBIRSHighSy.html (accessed 7 April 2008).

7. Marcia S. Smith, *Military Space Programs: Issues Concerning DOD's SBIRS and STSS Programs*, Congressional Research Service Report for Congress (Washington, DC: Library of Congress, January 2006).

8. Air Force Space Command (AFSPC), "Space Based Infrared Systems," Fact Sheet, http://www .afspc.af.mil/library/factsheets/factsheet.asp?id=3675 (accessed 7 April 2008); and Desmond Ball, *A Base for Debate: The US Satellite Station at Nurrungar* (North Sydney, Australia: Allen & Unwin, 1987, 36–65.

9. AFSPC, "Space Based Infrared Systems."

10. Ball, *A Base for Debate*, 49–51.

11. AFSPC, "Space Based Infrared Systems."

12. Maj James J. Rosolanka, *Defense Support Program (DSP): A Pictorial Chronology, 1970–1998* (Los Angeles AFB, CA: SBIRS System Program Office, 1998).

13. Paul B. Stares, *Space and National Security* (Washington, DC: Brookings Institution Press, 1987), 26.

14. Rosolanka, *Defense Support Program*, 17.

15. Northrop Grumman, "Defense Support Program," http://www.northropgrumman.com/capabilities/ missile_defense/defense_support.html (accessed 7 April 2008).

16. Austronautix, "DSP," http://www.astronautix.com/craft/dsp.htm (accessed 8 April 2008).

17. "Defense Support Program," Federation of American Scientists, http://www.fas.org/spp/military/ program/warning/dsp.htm (accessed 8 April 2008).

18. Tamar A. Mehuron, ed., *2002 Space Almanac*, *Air Force Magazine*, August 2002, 40.

19. Mohamed M. Abid, *Spacecraft Sensors* (Hoboken, NJ: John Wiley & Sons, 2005), 135–203.

20. NASA, "Space Shuttle STS-44 Press Kit," http://science.ksc.nasa.gov/shuttle/missions/sts-44/sts-44 -press-kit.txt (accessed 7 April 2008).

21. USSTRATCOM, "Theater Ballistic Missile Warning," http://www.stratcom.mil/fact_sheets/fact _tbmw.html (accessed 8 April 2008).

22. Mike Nadler, Space and Missile Defense Future Warfare Center, "Early Warning," briefing, 21 August 2007.

23. Ibid.

24. Joint Interoperability Test Command, "Tactical Data Dissemination System (TDDS)," http://jitc.fhu .disa.mil/gcsiop/interfaces/tdds.pdf (accessed 7 April 2008).

25. Col James W. McClendon, "Information Warfare: Impacts and Concerns," in *Battlefield of the Future: 21st Century Warfare Issues*, ed. Barry R. Schneider and Lawrence E. Grinter (Maxwell AFB, AL: Air University Press, 1995).

26. AFSPC, *Space Surveillance Network (SSN) Site Information Handbook* (24 October 2007), 70–90.

Chapter 18

Intercontinental Ballistic Missiles

Maj Jane Gibson, USAF, and MAJ Kenneth G. Kemmerly, USA

This chapter covers American nuclear ballistic missile systems: the land-based intercontinental ballistic missiles (ICBM) and the submarine-launched ballistic missiles (SLBM). These ballistic systems are designated space assets because the weapon system travels through space to its given target, though on a trajectory that does not achieve a full orbit. Air Force Space Command is responsible for the ICBM force but will soon be transferring that to Air Force Global Strike Command. The SLBMs are under the responsibility of the US Navy.

Origins of ICBMs

The first reference to the use of rockets dates back to 1232 when the Chinese defenders of K'aifung-fu used "fire arrows" against attacking Mongols. Progress in rocketry was slow, at best, for the next seven centuries.

The Germans began development of a missile arsenal during the 1930s at Kummersdorf and Peenemünde, with increased emphasis during World War II. These experiments resulted in the Vergeltsungswaffe Ein and Zwei (Revenge Weapons One and Two), or V-1 and V-2. While the V-1 was an early unmanned aircraft system, the V-2 was a 46-foot-long rocket that used alcohol and liquid oxygen as propellants. It reached an altitude of 50 to 60 miles, had a maximum range of 200 miles, and carried a one-ton warhead. The system's accuracy was 2.5 miles. The war ended before the results of research into longer-range (transatlantic) two-stage rockets, called the A-9 and A-10, could be used. These weapons might have been operational by 1948.[1]

ICBM Characteristics

The ballistic missile as a weapon is often compared to an artillery cannon and its ballistic projectile. Critical to the accuracy of an artillery projectile are its elevation and speed. Apart from atmospheric resistance, gravity is the only vital force operating on the projectile, causing a constant-acceleration fall to Earth. As the distance to the target increases, so must the elevation (angle of launch toward the target) or speed (muzzle velocity) of the projectile increase.

For the ballistic missile payload or reentry vehicle (RV) to reach the target, the missile must be aimed toward the desired impact point and given a specific speed and altitude. There is one point somewhere along the missile flight path at which a definite speed must be achieved. The flight control system is responsible for getting the missile to this point.

From the moment of liftoff, the missile must stabilize in its vertical climb. It must be rolled about its longitudinal axis to the target azimuth and pitched over toward the target. The missile must be accelerated and given any necessary corrections along its roll, pitch, and yaw axes, while various engines must be ignited and terminated at precise times. In addition, the reentry vehicle must be armed and separated from the missile. These operations are performed by the flight control system through two basic subsystems: (1) the autopilot subsystem (or attitude control) and (2) the inertial guidance subsystem or radio.

An inertial guidance system is completely independent of ground control. It is capable of measuring its position in space and computing a trajectory that takes the payload to the target. It also generates steering signals to properly orient the missile, signals the engines to cut off at the proper time, and signals the warhead to prearm.

When a ballistic missile is launched, it will pass through several phases of flight, beginning with the powered (boost) phase, proceeding through the mid-course (coasting) phase, and ending with the terminal (reentry) phase. A typical flight profile is shown in figure 18-1.

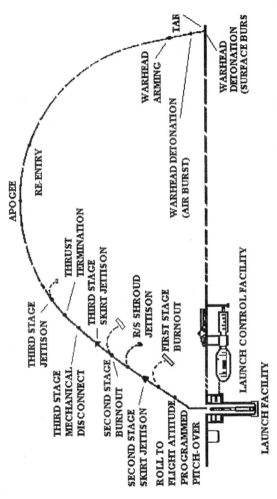

Figure 18-1. Typical ICBM flight profile. (*Reprinted from Air University,* Space Primer, *unpublished book, 2003, 17-3.*)

Reentry Vehicles

A ballistic missile is only powered for a short time during flight. The total flight time for an ICBM is about 30 minutes, but powered flight lasts only five to 10 minutes. The remainder of the time is spent "coasting" to the target. The velocity of powered flight may reach 15,000 mph, or Mach 20, but it really is gravity that does the work of getting the payload to the target. Once an ICBM-borne vehicle begins to encounter atmospheric drag during reentry, aerodynamic heating and braking begins. Induced drag and lift affect the reentry vehicle's trajectory. There are no control surfaces on a true ballistic reentry vehicle. It acts more like a bullet as it falls to the target.

Reentry vehicles have two means of dealing with the heat developed during reentry into the atmosphere: heat sink and ablative. Heat-sink vehicles disperse heat through a large volume of metal, while ablative surfaces are coverings that absorb heat and

236

slough off of the reentry vehicle, carrying away the heat. Continued use of heat-sink vehicles became impractical because of the tradeoff between RV weight, booster size, and range of the payload. The use of ablative materials helped reduce these problems.

Reentry is incredibly severe, with a necessary tradeoff between survivability and accuracy. In general, steeper reentry angles yield more accurate ballistic vehicles. However, the steeper the angle, the greater the temperature encountered and G-loading (stress caused by maneuvering during reentry) induced on the RV. The challenge is to design a reentry vehicle that will not vaporize from the heat or break up from the G-loading when reentering the earth's atmosphere and yet will maintain the needed accuracy. During development of reentry vehicles, an intense program, including shock tests, materials research, hypersonic wind-tunnel tests, ballistic research, nose-cone drop tests, and hypersonic flight, was used to optimize design of the reentry vehicles.

There are several design requirements for an RV. Foremost is the ability to survive the heat encountered during reentry; the internal temperature must be kept low enough to allow the warhead to survive reentry. A body reentering the atmosphere at speeds approaching Mach 20 experiences temperatures in excess of 15,000 degrees Fahrenheit (F). In practice, the RV never reaches this temperature because of a strong shock wave ahead of the blunt body that dissipates more than 90 percent of this energy to the atmosphere. As the RV reenters the atmosphere, it encounters tremendous deceleration forces—as high as 50 Gs, or 50 times the normal force of gravity. All internal operational components must function under these extreme conditions and additionally must withstand the high lateral loads and intense vibrations encountered.

An RV may be deflected from its calculated trajectory by aerodynamic lift forces. Stability, assisted by a form of attitude control and further augmented by some means of averaging deflection, must be designed into the RV. An arming and fusing mechanism must also be incorporated into the RV to prevent nonprogrammed weapon detonation. From a defensive standpoint, the higher the terminal velocity, the less likely an RV will be intercepted. Higher velocity also decreases the probability of missing the target due to atmospheric deflection. Further, an RV must have a sensing mechanism to indicate the proximity of the target and to arm the warhead. What must also be considered is that the weight of the vehicle must be kept to a minimum in order to maximize the range of the weapon.

Nuclear Weapons Effects

Nuclear weapons effects are normally divided into three types: residual, long-lived, and initial. Residual effects are those which begin about one minute after a nuclear detonation, and they continue for about two weeks. These effects include fallout and its associated radiation, discussed below. Long-lived effects include the subsequent damage to the environment and some radiation concerns, also discussed below. The initial effects are generally the most germane to military matters. There are six primary nuclear weapons effects:

1. Electromagnetic pulse (EMP)
2. Nuclear radiation
3. Air blast
4. Ground shock
5. Thermal radiation
6. Dust and debris

Each of these initial effects can be compared to naturally occurring phenomena. An electromagnetic pulse is similar to lightning bolts, which produce a tremendous surge of electrical current and generate huge magnetic fields—both of which affect electrical equipment. Depending on the altitude of the explosion, EMP effects can occur for thousands of miles around a nuclear detonation.

Nuclear radiation is similar to a powerful x-ray and varies depending on the weapon-burst option used (fig. 18-2). Radiation resulting from a nuclear detonation includes x-rays, gamma rays, neutrons, and ionizing radiation. These forms of radiation are emitted not only at the time of the detonation (initial radiation) but also for long periods of time afterward (residual radiation).[2]

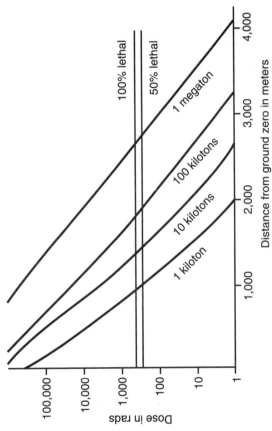

Figure 18-2. Nuclear weapons effects versus distance. (*Reprinted from Air University, Space Primer, unpublished book, 17-6.*)

An air blast is the wind generated by the detonation. These winds can be 10 times stronger than those found in the most powerful hurricane. They actually "slap" the earth hard enough to contribute to the ground shock at the detonation site. The ground shock is nearly 250 times worse than the greatest earthquake. The lateral accelerations are transmitted over large distances at very high speeds.

Heat is another product, with the sun's thermal radiation a useful comparison. The temperatures in the fireball reach upwards of 14,000° F. As a comparison, the sun's surface temperature is approximately 11,000°.

Finally, a ground burst will generate large amounts of dust and debris. The debris can bury undamaged structures while the dust clouds can act as sandblasting equipment on aircraft and missiles flying through them.

The most familiar phenomenon relating to both blast effects and target hardness is overpressure. This is measured in pounds per square inch (psi). A one-cubic-foot block of concrete exerts one psi on the ground beneath. Stacking a second block on the first

238

will increase the pressure to two psi and so forth. Five Washington Monuments placed atop of each other equate to 500 psi; a sonic boom registers a mere 0.3 psi.

Blast overpressure is heightened by the interaction of the primary shock wave and a reflected shock wave. The primary wave is radiated outward from ground zero and compresses the air in front of it. This wave will strike the earth and reflect upward and outward, creating the reflected wave. This wave moves faster than the primary wave because the air resistance has been decreased by the passage of the first wave. The primary wave will be reinforced by the reflected wave, forming a Mach front. A drawing of this phenomenon would resemble the letter Y, with the intersection of the Y termed the *triple point*. Below the triple point, the two blast waves will strike like a single powerful blow. Anything above the triple point is the overpressure. Table 18-1 shows the effects of overpressures on building materials.

Table 18-1. Overpressure sensitivities

Structural element	Failure	Approximate side-on peak overpressure in PSIs
Glass windows, large and small	Shattering, occasional frame failure	0.5–1.0
Corrugated asbestos siding	Shattering	1.0–2.0
Corrugated steel paneling	Connection failure followed by buckling	1.0–2.0
Wood-frame construction	Failure occurs at main connections, allowing a whole panel to be blown in	1.0–2.0
Concrete or cinder block wall panels, 8–12 inches thick (unreinforced)	Shattering	1.5–5.5
Brick wall panel, 8–12 inches thick (unreinforced)	Shearing and flexure	3.0–10.0

The power of a nuclear explosion is almost incomprehensible, but the following example may help to put it into perspective. Five million one-ton pickup trucks loaded with TNT would have the same explosive yield as a single five-megaton nuclear weapon. A surface burst of this weapon would yield the following results at a distance of 3,200 feet (0.6 miles) from ground zero:

- Fireball diameter: 2.8 miles
- 5.5 billion kW hours of x-rays
- 14,000 degrees
- 250 G lateral acceleration
- 500 psi
- 3,500 mph winds
- 20 inches of debris
- Debris weighing as much as 2,000 lb. impacting at 250 mph

The effects on people are shown in table 18-2. Doses of radiation are described in units of roentgen equivalent mammal (REM). REM is a standard measurement of radiation effects on humans. One REM is the equivalent of one roentgen of high-penetration x-rays.

Table 18-2. Nuclear radiation effects on people

Dose in REMs	Radius in feet from 20 kiloton air burst		Probable effects
	Unprotected persons	Troops in covered foxholes	
0–80	5,550	4,200	No obvious effects. Minor blood changes possible.
80–120	5,250	3,900	Vomiting and nausea for about one day in 5–10 percent of exposed persons. Fatigue, but no serious disability.
130–170	4,800	3,750	Vomiting and nausea for about one day followed by some symptoms of radiation sickness in about 25 percent of exposed persons. No deaths anticipated.
180–260	4,500	3,600	Vomiting and nausea for about one day followed by some symptoms of radiation sickness in about 50 percent of exposed persons. No deaths anticipated.
270–390	4,200	3,300	Vomiting and nausea in nearly all persons on first day, followed by other symptoms of radiation sickness. About 20 percent deaths within two to six weeks after exposure. Survivors convalescent for up to three months.
400–550	3,900	3,000	The midlethal dose. Vomiting, nausea, and radiation sickness symptoms. About 50 percent deaths within one month. Survivors convalescent for up to eight months.
550–750	3,750	2,850	Vomiting and nausea in all persons within a few hours, followed by other symptoms of radiation sickness. 90 to 100 percent deaths. The few survivors convalescent for six months.
1,000	3,600	2,550	Vomiting and nausea in all persons exposed. Probably no survivors.
5,000	3,000	2,250	Incapacitation almost immediately. All persons will die within one week.

ICBM Development in the United States

At the end of World War II, the United States and the Soviet Union recruited as many German scientists as possible to aid in the development of their respective missile programs. Each began their own research programs into the use of missiles as weapons. Funding and weight limitations prevented these programs from quickly advancing. It wasn't until 1954 that Air Force Secretary Talbott directed all necessary steps be taken to advance the Atlas ICBM project.

On 27 October 1955, a contract was awarded to produce another ICBM, the Titan I. The Thor and Jupiter intermediate-range ballistic missile (IRBM) programs also began in December of 1955, with the highest possible priority. The Army had responsibility for all short-range (under 200 miles) surface-to-surface missiles. The Navy had control of all ship-based missiles, and the Air Force got all other surface-to-surface missiles.

The first US IRBM was the Thor (fig. 18-3). It was deployed in the United Kingdom between 1959 and 1963. The Thor was housed horizontally in an above-ground shelter. It had to be raised to the vertical position and fueled before launch. Its propellants were RP-1 (a high-grade kerosene) and liquid oxygen. The Thor had a range of 1,500 nautical miles (nm) and could place a one-megaton warhead within 4,600 feet of the target. The Thor design would later be used as a satellite launch booster.

First-Generation ICBMs

The first Atlas D ICBM was launched 9 September 1959 at Vandenberg AFB, California. Gen Thomas D. Power, commander-in-chief of Strategic Air Command, then declared the Atlas operational. Only six days later, a Minuteman research and development tethered launch occurred at Edwards AFB, California. This was a model with inert second and third stages and a partially charged first stage. It had a 2,000-foot nylon tether to keep the missile from traveling too far. On 31 October 1959, the first nuclear-tipped Atlas was placed on alert at Vandenberg AFB. Deployment of the three D models were in soft, vertical gantries at Vandenberg AFB). For in-flight guidance, the Atlas used a combination of both radio and inertial systems (fig. 18-4).

The E model incorporated many improvements over the D model. Perhaps the most significant was the replacement of radio guidance with an all-inertial system, making the E model invulnerable to jamming. The E model was also housed horizontally, but it was in a semihard "coffin" launcher that was buried to reduce its vulnerability to blast and overpressure. The F model was kept in an underground, hardened silo and raised to the surface by an elevator for launch; this was called "hard silo-lift." The silo was nearly 180 feet deep.

The Titan I was also being developed and deployed in a configuration similar to the Atlas F. Both used the same propellants and the same silo lift technique. One primary difference was in the command and control. The Atlas F system had one launch control center connected with, and in command of, one silo and missile. The Titan I system had three silos connected to the underground launch control center. Another difference was that the Titan I used a radio-inertial guidance system similar to the Atlas D. The sixth and last Titan I squadron became operational at Mountain Home AFB,

Figure 18-3. A test Thor takes flight at Cape Canaveral, FL, on 5 December 1959. The small particles falling away from the rocket are ice formed from frozen condensation on the outside of the chilled liquid oxygen tank. (USAF photo)

Figure 18-4. Atlas, the Air Force's first ICBM, was a national priority and one of Gen Bernard Schriever's major achievements. (USAF photo)

Idaho, on 16 August 1962. Only four months later, on 20 December, the last Atlas F squadron at Plattsburgh AFB, New York, achieved operational status.

Even as these milestones were reached, the days of the first-generation ICBMs were numbered. The newer Titan II and Minuteman ICBMs were more survivable, quicker reacting, and more economical to operate and more reliable. On 24 May 1963, Gen Curtis E. LeMay, Air Force chief of staff, announced the phaseout of the Atlas D and E and the Titan I. By its completion, that phaseout also encompassed the Atlas F, with the last Atlas F being removed from alert at Lincoln AFB, Nebraska, on 12 April 1965 and subsequently shipped to Norton AFB, California, for storage.[3]

Second-Generation ICBMs

The second generation of ICBMs, the Titan II and the Minuteman, shared only one characteristic—they were housed and launched from hardened underground silos. The Titan II was a large, two-stage, liquid-fueled missile that carried a single warhead. Its range was about 5,500 nm. The missiles were deployed at three wings. Davis-Monthan AFB, Arizona, was the home of the first operational wing. McConnell AFB, Kansas, and Little Rock AFB, Arkansas, were the homes of the other two.[4]

The Titan II offered five distinct advantages over the Titan I. First, the Titan II's reaction time was reduced from 15 minutes to less than one minute because it used storable hypergolic propellants (fuel that, upon being mixed, ignites without external aid, i.e., a spark). Second, it used an all-inertial guidance system, a major improvement over its radio-controlled predecessor. Third, the missile carried the largest and most powerful warhead ever placed on a US missile. Fourth, each launch complex contained only one missile, instead of the cluster of three used in Titan I; this separation enhanced survivability. And last, the Titan II was designed to be launched from inside its silo, that is, without being elevated to an above-ground position. This limited the missile's vulnerability to damage except during the earliest stages of flight.

The Minuteman is a three-stage, solid-fueled missile housed in a remote launch facility. Its range is in excess of 5,500 nm. From the beginning, it was intended to be a simple, efficient, and survivable weapon system. Its main features are reliability and quick reaction.

The first Minuteman, the Minuteman IA, went on strategic alert during the Cuban missile crisis of October 1962. President Kennedy later referred to this missile as his "ace in the hole" during negotiations with the Soviets.

The Minuteman II became operational in 1964 and replaced many of the Minuteman I missiles. This system, known as the LGM30F or more simply the F model, was more than 57 feet long, weighed over 73,000 pounds, and, like the Minuteman I, carried a single warhead.

Whereas Titan crews consisted of two officers and two enlisted technicians, the Minuteman crews are composed of only two officers. A single Titan missile was controlled from its launch control center (LCC). The Minuteman is operated by a similar procedure, but the crew controls 10 to 50 missiles.

Because the Titan was increasingly expensive to operate and was hampered by a series of accidents, the Reagan administration announced its deactivation in October 1982. The system deactivation began in 1984, and the last Titan II wing was deactivated in August 1987. The Bush administration began deactivation of the Minuteman II to comply with Strategic Arms Reduction Treaty (START) requirements. The last Minuteman II was removed in 1994.[5]

Third-Generation ICBMs

While Titan II missiles were deployed in only one model, the Minuteman series spanned several models. The latest, and only operational version, is the Minuteman IIIG. The last Minuteman III was deployed in July 1975. It is almost 60 feet tall and weighs approximately 79,000 pounds.[6] The Minuteman III originally carried three reentry vehicles, each capable of striking a different target. The Minuteman force was downloaded to single reentry vehicles after 2002 based on the Moscow Treaty (or Strategic Offensive Reductions Treaty [SORT]).[7]

The Minuteman is hot-launched (ignition occurs in the silo), and the missile flies out through its own flame and exhaust. An Avcoat material protects the first stage from the extreme heat generated during this process.

The most recently deployed US ICBM was the Peacekeeper. However, the Peacekeeper was retired from duty in 2005, again following the Moscow Treaty.[8] The Peacekeeper was a four-stage, solid-fuel missile which originally replaced 50 Minuteman III missiles at F. E. Warren AFB, Wyoming. These missiles were deployed in converted Minuteman silos. The first 10 Peacekeeper missiles achieved operational alert status in December 1986 as part of the 400th Strategic Missile Squadron.

The Peacekeeper was 71 feet long and weighed 195,000 pounds—nearly three times the weight of a Minuteman III. This allowed it to carry up to 12 reentry vehicles, although 10 was the operational configuration. The missile was about 7.5 feet in diameter through all four of its stages.

Peacekeeper missiles were housed inside a reinforced steel canister within a silo. They were cold-launched using a technique similar to the system used by the SLBM submarines. At the bottom of the canister was a launch ejection gas generator (LEGG). A small rocket motor in the LEGG was fired into 130 gallons of water contained in a reservoir; this created steam pressure that pushed the Peacekeeper up and out of the canister prior to ignition of the first stage.

The Peacekeeper was protected during launch and in the missile's flight environment by an ethylene-acrylic rubber coating. No ablative material was needed because of the cold-launch. The Peacekeeper was further protected inside its canister by Teflon-coated urethane pads. Nine rows of pads were used to protect and guide the missile smoothly up and out of the canister during launch. The pads fell away when the missile cleared the canister.

In compliance with the Moscow Treaty, Peacekeeper deactivation began in 2002, and the final Peacekeeper was removed in September 2005.[9] The silos have been kept intact, a change from past deactivations. Adam Hebert reports that then-Maj Gen (sel) Mark D. Shackelford, director of requirements for Space Command, said that "the Air Force has decided that launch control centers and silos are 'not to be destroyed.' Instead, this infrastructure will go into indefinite 'mothball status' to ensure that the facilities will be available in case the need for them arises."[10] Also many parts of the Peacekeeper missiles will be reutilized. The reentry vehicles will be "transferred to the Minuteman III program to replace the aging warheads and the booster components will be recycled for space launches."[11]

Current ICBMs

The presently deployed ICBM force consists only of Minuteman IIIG missiles deployed as follows:

- 150 at Malmstrom AFB, Montana
- 150 at Minot AFB, North Dakota
- 150 at F. E. Warren AFB, Wyoming

The Minuteman III (LGM-30G) "G" model is a three-stage, solid-propellant, inertially guided ICBM with a range of more than 6,300 miles. It employs a multiple independently targetable reentry vehicle (MIRV) system with a maximum of three reentry vehicles. The post-boost control system (PBCS) provides maneuvering capability for deployment of the reentry vehicles and penetration aids. It is comprised of a missile guidance set (MGS) and a propulsion-system rocket engine (PSRE). The G model is maintained on alert in a hardened, underground, unmanned launch facility (LF) (fig. 18-5), just as the F model was. The LFs are situated at least three miles apart and are also at least three miles removed from the LCC. Each LF in the squadron is connected to other squadron resources by a buried cable system. When necessary, this allows one LCC to monitor, command, and launch its own 10 missiles (called a flight) and all 50 missiles in the squadron.

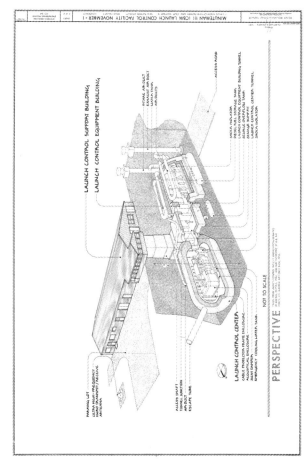

Figure 18-5. Minuteman launch facility. (*Reprinted from* Air University, *Space Primer,* unpublished book, 2003, 17-8.)

The Minuteman II missiles are currently being enhanced and modified to maintain the viability of the force until at least the year 2020. On the missile itself, the solid propellant of the first- and second-stage motors is being washed out and repoured while the third-stage motors are being remanufactured. Part of this endeavor is to find an environmentally acceptable propellant replacement. The rapid execution and combat targeting (REACT) service life extension program (SLEP) is designed to provide long-term supportability of the system's aging electronics components. It also modifies the LCC, allowing real-time status information on the weapons and communications nets to correct operability problems, improve responsiveness to launch directives, and provide a rapid retargeting capability. Peacekeeper ICBM reentry vehicles have been

Figure 18-6. Minuteman III. A maintainer looks over a Minuteman III in a silo about 60 miles from Grand Forks AFB, North Dakota, in 1989. (USAF photo)

modified under the safety-enhanced reentry vehicle (SERV) program and are replacing the current Minuteman MK12 reentry vehicles (RV) in phases; this modification is expected to be complete in 2012.

Three solid-propellant rocket motors make up the propulsion system of the Minuteman G model (fig. 18-6). The first stage uses a Thiokol M-55 solid-propellant motor that generates 200,400 pounds of thrust. The second-stage motor is built by Aerojet (SR19-AJ-1), and it develops 60,700 pounds of thrust. These stages are identical to those of the Minuteman F model. The third stage uses a single fixed exhaust nozzle with the liquid injection thrust vector control (LITVC) system and roll control ports for attitude control. The third stage is a Thiokol SR73-AJ-1 motor that delivers 34,500 pounds of thrust. For thrust termination, there are six thrust termination ports mounted at the forward end of the third stage. These "blow out" when the missile reaches the desired point in its trajectory, from which it will deploy the weapons payload. A shroud protects the payload during the early phases of the missile's flight. Deployment of the reentry vehicles and penetration aids (designed to confound enemy defenses) is accomplished by the PBCS, a "mini fourth stage." The PBCS fires periodically to provide maneuvering vectors during deployment of the payload and penetration aids. This process allows the G model to hit up to three separate targets at different ranges with great accuracy.

US Submarine-Launched Ballistic Missiles

In 1955, the National Security Council requested an intermediate-range ballistic missile for the defense of the United States. They further decided that part of the IRBM force should be sea-based. As a result, the Navy was directed to design a sea-based support system for the existing liquid-fueled Jupiter IRBM. This led to the development of the Special Projects Office (SPO) by the secretary of the Navy. The SPO was tasked with adapting the Jupiter IRBM for shipboard launch. Originally, the Jupiter was an Army missile designed for land-based launches. Because of the unique handling and storage requirements, there were numerous issues with the storage and safety of liquid propellants aboard submarines. As a result, the Navy began an effort parallel to the Air Force in the development of solid-fueled rocket motors.

Breakthroughs in solid fuels, which resulted in smaller and more powerful motors, occurred in 1956. Reductions in the size of missile guidance, reentry vehicles, and warheads further aided in smaller missile technology. The first solid-fueled missile incorporating this new technology was named Polaris. The first submarine launch of a Polaris occurred in July 1960 from the USS *George Washington*. Three hours later a second missile was successfully launched. These two shots marked the beginning of sea-based nuclear deterrence for the United States.

Since then, the Fleet Ballistic Missile (FBM) has progressed through Polaris and Poseidon to the Trident I and the only remaining SLBM in service, the Trident II. The Poseidon included MIRV capability, while both generations of Trident provided increases in range and accuracy. There have been other changes as well. The launcher system evolved from compressed air units to steam-gas generators, while the missile fire control system has developed through semiconductor and solid-state electronics to the present microchip technology. Missile guidance systems now use in-flight stellar updates, and navigation has matured from external fixes to onboard computers.

The first nuclear ballistic missile submarine was constructed by cutting a fast-attack submarine (USS *Scorpion*) into two pieces and inserting a 16-tube missile compartment section. Since then, several classes of submarines have been designed and built specifically for the FBM mission. The Ohio-class (726-class) submarine is the newest generation of fleet ballistic missile submarine (SSBN). The first submarine of this class was deployed in 1981. This is the same class of submarines that carry the Trident II strategic weapon system (SWS) and missile.

Polaris

The Polaris (A-1) program began in 1957; later versions were called A-2 and A-3. Its innovations included a two-stage solid propulsion system, an inertial navigation guidance system, and a miniaturized nuclear warhead. Production ended in 1968 after more than 1,400 missiles had been built. The last version, the A-3, had an increased range (2,900 miles compared with 1,700 miles for the A-2 model) and multiple warhead capability. The missile was replaced by the Poseidon SLBM and later by the Trident.

Poseidon

The Poseidon (C-3) weapon system was deployed on Poseidon (Lafayette- and Benjamin Franklin-class) submarines, carrying 16 missiles each. The Poseidon submarine was similar to the one that carried the Polaris. Now out of service, they were deployed from Charleston, South Carolina, and Holy Loch, Scotland.

Trident I

The Trident I (C-4) backfit weapon system was initially deployed on Poseidon submarines starting in 1979. The Trident I system consisted of the Trident I missile and updated launch and preparation equipment. The Trident I missile had increased range and accuracy over the Poseidon (C-3) and was deployed on early Ohio-class submarines in 1981. The updated weapon system included many improvements resulting from new technology. The Trident I missile was phased out of service following the Nuclear Posture Review.

Trident II

The Trident II (D-5) was deployed on the later Trident (Ohio-class) submarines, starting in March 1990. This weapon system consists of Trident II missiles and a combination of new and modified preparation and launch equipment. The Trident II missile is significantly larger than the Trident I because of the increased size of the first stage motor, giving it a greater payload capacity. The latest electronics give it improved reliability and maintainability. The launch platform is basically the same submarine that carries the Trident I, deployed from naval submarine bases at Bangor, Washington, and Kings Bay, Georgia. Trident II missiles are also provided to the United Kingdom, which operationalizes them with its own warheads on the missiles and deploys them on Vanguard-class submarines.

Current SLBM—Trident II D-5

The Trident II D-5 is a three-stage, solid-propellant, inertial- and stellar-guided SLBM. It has a range of over 4,000 nm (over 4,600 statute miles). It carries a MIRV reentry system and is deployed on Ohio-class submarines.

Figure 18-7. Trident II. First launch of a Trident missile on 18 January 1977 at Cape Canaveral, Florida. (USAF photo)

Three solid-propellant rocket motors make up the propulsion subsystem of the Trident II D-5 missile (fig. 18-7). Each stage of the D-5, like the C-4, contains nitroglycerin and nitrocellulose-based propellants in the motor casing. The motor casing for the first and second stages is constructed of graphite and epoxy, while the third stage of the D-5 consists of Kevlar/epoxy materials. These materials are lighter than those used in the Trident I. The first stage is approximately 26 feet long, almost seven feet wide, and weighs 65,000 pounds. Stage two is eight feet wide, and weighs approximately seven feet wide, and weighs approximately 19,000 pounds. The third stage is 10 feet tall, 2.5 feet in diameter, and weighs 4,200 pounds. A single movable nozzle, actuated by a gas generator, steers each stage. Like the C-4, the third stage of the D-5 is surrounded by the PBCS and the RV mounting platform, which operate much like those for ICBMs.

The Trident II D-5 is 44 feet in length, approximately seven feet in diameter, and weighs 130,000 pounds. Like the Trident I C-4, the D-5 employs an aerospike during first-stage burn. The nose fairing is constructed of Sitka spruce and jettisons during second-stage burn. All other airframe characteristics of the D-5 are the same as the Poseidon C-3 and the Trident I C-4.

Ohio-Class Submarine

Only 14 of the original 18 Ohio-class submarines remain in service. In the early 2000s, the first four ships were retired along with the missile they were designed to carry, the Trident C-4. Each is 560 feet long, 42 feet in beam, and has a submerged displacement of 18,750 tons (fig. 18-8). Although over two times larger than the

Figure 18-8. Ohio-class ballistic missile submarine. US Navy's Trident nuclear-powered submarine USS *Alaska* (SSBN 732) is guided into an explosives handling wharf at the Naval Station. (US Navy photo by Gene Royer)

Franklin-class in volume displacement, the Ohio-class requires only 16 officers and 148 enlisted crew members. The Ohio-class submarine carries up to 24 Trident II missiles.

Notes

1. V2ROCKET.COM, "A-4/V-2 Makeup—Tech Data & Markings," http://www.v2rocket.com/start/makeup/design.html (accessed 8 May 2009).

2. AtomicArchive.com, "Nuclear Radiation," http://www.atomicarchive.com/Effects/effects14.shtml (accessed 18 May 2009).

3. "SM-65 Atlas," Federation of American Scientists Web site, http://www.fas.org/nuke/guide/usa/icbm/sm-65.htm (accessed 8 May 2009).

4. "SM-68B Titan II," Federation of American Scientists Web site, http://www.fas.org/nuke/guide/usa/icbm/sm-68b.htm (accessed 8 May 2009).

5. National Park Service, "Strategic Arms Reduction Treaty and Disarmament of Minuteman II (1990s)," in *Minuteman Missile Historical Resource Study,* http://www.nps.gov/archive/mimi/history/srs/hrs3-2a.htm (accessed 8 May 2009).

6. Air Force, "LGM-30 Minuteman III," Fact Sheet, http://www.af.mil/factsheets/factsheet.asp?id=113 (accessed 8 May 2009).

7. DOD, Office of the Undersecretary of Defense for Acquisition, Technology, and Logistics, "Moscow Treaty: Article-by-Article Analysis," http://www.dod.mil/acq/acic/treaties/sort/sort_axa.htm (accessed 18 May 2009).

8. Ibid.

9. Ibid.

10. Adam J. Hebert, "The ICBM Makeover," *Air Force Magazine* 88, no. 10 (October 2005): 35.

11. Ibid.

Chapter 19

Space Surveillance Network

Maj Edward P. Chatters IV, USAF; and Maj Brian J. Crothers, USAF

The space surveillance network (SSN) is a combination of optical and radar sensors used to support the Joint Space Operations Center's (JSpOC) mission to detect, track, identify, and catalog all manmade objects orbiting the earth. This chapter looks at the various components of the SSN, its sites, and how they combine to support the space surveillance mission. This chapter also contains a description of the radar and optical sensors, which are the two primary technologies used by the SSN.

SSN Radar Sensor Systems

Radar sensors used by the SSN are divided into two categories: mechanical, the oldest type of radar used by the SSN, and the newer phased-array radars.

Mechanical Radars

Mechanical radars (fig. 19-1), or mechanical trackers, are employed to track a target throughout the radar's coverage. A single beam of radar energy is sent out toward the target. The energy is reflected off the target and returned to the radar receiver for measurement. The transmitter sends out another beam of radar energy, and the cycle repeats itself as the radar follows the target throughout its coverage. The mechanical tracker is a good system for tracking near-Earth objects because it can acquire a large number of data points. It directs the radar beam by reorienting the antenna and is very precise in predicting the trajectory of near-Earth objects. The main limitation of the mechanical tracker is that it can track only one object at a time. It cannot "search" for targets very efficiently because it sends out only a single beam of radar energy at a time. Some mechanical radars have the ability to move the radar beam in a pattern so that the radar can perform a search function.[1]

Phased-Array Radar

Phased-array radar (PAR) is the newest radar technology used within the SSN. Rather than the antenna being moved mechanically, the radar energy is steered electronically. In a PAR there are many thousands of small transmit/receive (T/R) antennas placed on the side or face of a large wedge-shaped structure. If the signals from the separate T/R antennas are released at the same time and in phase, they form a radar beam whose direction of travel is perpendicular to the array face.

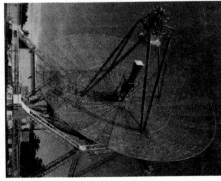

Figure 19-1. Kwajalein tracking radar. (US Army photo)

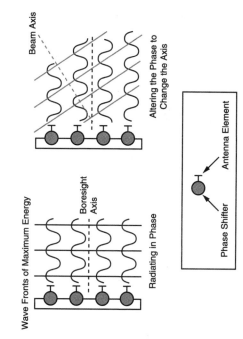

Wave Fronts of Maximum Energy

Beam Axis

Boresight Axis

Radiating in Phase

Altering the Phase to Change the Axis

Phase Shifter

Antenna Element

Figure 19-2. Changing direction of beam in phased-array radar. (*Adapted from* University of Wisconsin Naval ROTC, "Naval Weapons Systems Lesson 7: Electronic Scanning and Phased Array Radars," course files.)

To detect objects that do not lie directly in front of the array face, time-delay units, or phase shifters, are used. This phase-lag steering is a computer procedure in which the radiating elements are delayed sequentially across the array, causing the wave front to be at an angle to the perpendicular as shown in figure 19-2. This controls the direction of the beam. Since these radars have several thousand T/R antenna elements, multiple beams can be formed at the same time. A PAR is capable of simultaneously tracking numerous targets since a computer calculates the proper time delays of these beams.[2] The number of targets a PAR can track is most often limited by the amount of power available. However, there are two disadvantages of a PAR: the high cost of building it and complex maintenance.

Optical Sensor Systems

Optical sensors are very basic. They simply gather light waves reflected off of an object to form an image. This image can then be measured, reproduced, and analyzed. However, these sensors are limited due to their reliance on light; they cannot track during the day or under overcast sky conditions. The objects tracked must also be in sunlight and have some reflective qualities. Electro-optical sensors are the only optical sensors used operationally today to support the space surveillance mission.

Electro-optical refers to the way the sensor records the optical image. Instead of being imprinted on film, the image is changed into electrical impulses and recorded onto magnetic tape. This is similar to the process used by video recorders. The image can also be analyzed in real time. The primary electro-optical sensors used in the SSN are part of the Ground-Based Electro-Optical Deep Space Surveillance (GEODSS) System.

Space Object Identification

Space object identification (SOI) analyzes signature data to determine satellite characteristics such as size, shape, motion, and orientation. SOI information is used to determine the operational status of various payloads and may forecast maneuvers or deorbits. The process of using SOI data, in conjunction with other intelligence resources, to determine the nature of unidentified payloads is called mission payload assessment.

There are four categories of sensor SOI: wideband, narrowband, photometric, and optical imaging. Wideband SOI provides a detailed radar picture of the satellite. Two sensors [Haystack and the Advanced Research Projects Agency [ARPA] Lincoln C-Band Observable Radar [ALCOR]] have the capability of providing wideband SOI.[3] Narrowband SOI provides a two-dimensional depiction of the radar energy charted on a graph as amplitude versus time. Narrowband SOI sensors include Ascension, Beale, Cavalier, Clear, Cape Cod, Cobra Dane, Eglin, Fylingdales, and Millstone. Photometric SOI is the analysis of the intensity, luminance, and illuminance from systems like GEODSS and the Midcourse Space Experiment/Space-Based Vehicle (MSX/SBV). Finally, optical-imaging SOI refers to object identification obtained using optical telescopes that are augmented with Advanced Electro-Optical System (AEOS) long-wave infrared (LWIR) (AEOS-L) and AEOS adaptive optics sensors.[4]

Space Surveillance Network Sensor Missions

All sensors in the SSN are responsible for providing space surveillance and SOI to the JSpOC located at Vandenberg AFB, California, and to the Alternate Space Control Center (ASCC) at Dahlgren, Virginia. The sensors in the network are categorized primarily by their availability to support the JSpOC. This availability is based on the primary mission of each sensor. The SSN sensor missions are divided into three categories: dedicated, collateral, and contributing.

Dedicated Sensors

A dedicated sensor is a US Strategic Command (USSTRATCOM) operationally controlled sensor with a primary mission of space surveillance support. Dedicated sensors include GEODSS systems, the Air Force Space Surveillance System (AFSSS), and the Eglin AFB AN/FPS-85 phased-array radar.[5]

GEODSS. GEODSS has the mission to detect, track, and collect SOI on deep-space satellites in support of the JSpOC. Each GEODSS site (fig. 19-3) is controlled and operated by the 21st Space Operations Group, 21st Space Wing, Peterson AFB, Colorado. There are currently three detachments operating GEODSS sensors: Detachment 1, Socorro, New Mexico; Detachment 2, Diego Garcia, British Indian Ocean Territories; and Detachment 3, Maui, Hawaii.[6] The GEODSS sites provide near-real-time deep-space surveillance capability.

To perform its mission, GEODSS depends on three main elements: powerful telescopes, low-light television, and high-speed computers. Each site has three telescopes: two main and one auxiliary (with the exception of Diego Garcia, which has three main telescopes). The

Figure 19-3. GEODSS Diego Garcia. (USAF photo by SMSgt John Rohrer)

main telescopes have a 40-inch aperture and a two-degree field of view. The system operates only at night, when the telescopes are able to detect objects 10,000 times dimmer than the human eye can detect. Since it is an optical system, cloud cover and local weather conditions influence its effectiveness.[7]

The telescopes move across the sky at the same rate as the stars appear to move. This keeps the distant stars in the same positions in the field of view. As the telescopes slowly move, the GEODSS cameras take very rapid electronic snapshots of the field of view. Four computers then take these snapshots and overlay them on each other. Star images, which remain fixed, are electronically erased. However, manmade space objects do not remain fixed, and their movements show up as tiny streaks that can be viewed on a console screen. Computers measure these streaks and use the data to calculate the positions of objects, such as satellites in orbits from 3,000 to 22,000 miles. This information is used to update the list of orbiting objects and is sent nearly instantaneously from the sites to JSpOC.[8] The GEODSS system can track objects as small as a basketball more than 20,000 miles in space.

Moron Optical Space Surveillance. The Moron Optical Space Surveillance (MOSS) System was fielded at Moron AB, Spain, during the first quarter of fiscal year 1998. MOSS operates in conjunction with the existing GEODSS network. The GEODSS network called for an additional site in the Mediterranean to provide contiguous geosynchronous coverage. Air Force Space Command (AFSPC) fielded MOSS to provide this critical geosynchronous belt metric and SOI coverage.[9]

MOSS consists of one high-resolution electro-optical telescope and the MOSS Space Operations Center (MOSC) van. The telescope has a nominal aperture of 22 inches and a focal length of 51 inches (f 2.3). The camera houses a 1024 x 1024 MIT/LL charge-coupled device focal-plane array. Commercial power is conditioned by an uninterruptible power supply and backed up by a diesel generator.[10]

Air Force Space Surveillance System. Naval Space Command built the oldest sensor system in the SSN—Naval Space Surveillance (NAVSPASUR), also known as the Fence—whose mission was to maintain a constant surveillance of space and provide satellite data to the SSN. It reached initial operational capability in 1961. NAVSPASUR operations were transferred to Air Force control on 1 October 2004, and it was renamed the Air Force Space Surveillance System.[11]

AFSSS uses three transmit antennas and six receive antennas, all geographically located along the 33rd parallel of the United States. The transmitters send out a continuous wave of energy into space, forming a "detection fence" which covers 10 percent of the earth's circumference and extends 15,000 miles into space. When a satellite passes through the fence, the energy from the transmitter sites "illuminates" it, and a portion of the energy is reflected back to a receive station. When the reflected energy is acquired by at least two receive sites, an accurate position of the satellite can be determined through triangulation.[12]

AN/FPS 85 PAR. Located at Eglin AFB, Florida, the AN/FPS-85 PAR (fig. 19-4) is operated by AFSPC, 21st Space Wing, 20th Space Surveillance Squadron (SPSS). The 20 SPSS operates and maintains the only phased-array space surveillance system dedicated to tracking space objects. Built in the mid-1960s, it is one of the earliest phased-array radars. The Air Force assumed operational control of the site on 24 January 1969. The previous primary mission at Eglin was submarine-launched ballistic missile (SLBM) warning. Once the southeast radar at Robins AFB, Georgia, known as the Perimeter Acquisition Vehicle Entry Phased-Array Weapons System (PAVE PAWS), became operational, the SLBM warning coverage was redundant, and Eglin's mission changed in 1987 to dedicated space surveillance.[13]

Figure 19-4. AN/FPS-85 PAR at Eglin AFB. (USAF photo)

Collateral Sensors

A collateral sensor is a USSTRATCOM operationally controlled sensor with a primary mission other than space surveillance (usually, the site's secondary mission is to provide surveillance support). Collateral sensors include the Maui Optical Tracking and Identification Facility (MOTIF), Maui Space Surveillance System (MSSS), Ballistic Missile Surveillance System (BMEWS), PAVE PAWS, and Perimeter Acquisition Radar Attack Characterization System (PARCS), as well as the Antigua, Ascension, and Kaena Point radars.[14] MSSS was once part of the 18th SPSS Detachment 3, but AFSPC transitioned it to the Air Force Research Laboratory on 1 October 2000.[15]

Ballistic Missile Early Warning System. BMEWS is a key radar system developed to provide warning and attack assessment of an intercontinental ballistic missile (ICBM) attack on the continental United States (CONUS) and southern Canada from the Sino-Soviet land mass. BMEWS III also provides warning and attack assessment of an SLBM/ICBM attack against the United Kingdom and Europe. The tertiary mission of BMEWS is to conduct satellite tracking as collateral sensors in the space surveillance network. BMEWS consists of three sites: site 1 at Thule AFB, Greenland; site 2 at Clear AFS, Alaska; and site 3 at Royal Air Force Station Fylingdales, United Kingdom.

Site 1, Thule (fig. 19-5), is operated by the 12th Space Warning Squadron (SWS), a unit of AFSPC's 21st Space Wing. Initial operations at site 1 began in October 1960. Its original equipment consisted of four detection radars (DR) and a single tracking radar (TR). After more than 26 years of continuous operation, the DRs and TR were replaced with a phased-array radar. The upgraded radar became operational in June 1988.[16]

The 13 SWS at Clear AFS, Alaska, began operations in 1961 with three DRs (AN/FPS-50s), each 400 feet long and 165 feet high, and a TR (AN/FPS-92) that was 84 feet in diameter and weighed 100 tons (fig. 19-6). Clear has been upgraded with a dual-faced phased-array radar similar to Thule and the PAVE PAWS sites. The radar system has two faces, which together form a coverage area 240 degrees wide and 4,828 kilometers into space. The coverage extends from the Arctic Ocean all the way to the west coast of the lower 48 states.

The Royal Air Force at Fylingdales operates a three-faced phased-array radar. The original configuration consisted of three mechanical tracking radars that have since

Figure 19-5. PAR at Thule AFB. (USAF photo)

been dismantled. The Fylingdales PAR searches the sky for possible missile threats with full 360-degree coverage. Fylingdales' primary mission is to provide warning of an IRBM, medium-range ballistic missile (MRBM), or SLBM attack against the United Kingdom and Western Europe. Its secondary mission is to provide warning of an ICBM/SLBM attack against the CONUS. Fylingdales' tertiary mission is to provide space surveillance data on orbiting objects to the JSpOC Space Situational Awareness Operations Cell and Alternate Space Control Center.[17]

PAVE PAWS. Advancing technology provided the former Soviet Union the capability to launch ballistic missiles from submarines. Studies indicated the need for early warning facilities to detect such an attack. The PAVE PAWS mission is to provide warning and attack assessment of an SLBM attack against the CONUS and southern Canada. PAVE PAWS also provides limited warning and attack assessment of an ICBM attack against North America from the Sino-Soviet land mass. The secondary mission, like BMEWS, is to provide satellite tracking data as collateral sensors in the space surveillance network.[18]

PAVE PAWS currently consists of the initial two sites. Site 1 (fig. 19-8) is located at Cape Cod AFS, Massachusetts, and is operated by the 6 SWS. Site 2 is at Beale AFB, California, and is operated by the 7 SWS. Both sites operate a dual-faced phased-array radar (AN/FPS-115). The computer hardware and software were upgraded in the mid-1980s, when the other two sites were built.

The PAVE PAWS phased-array antenna, as with any other directional antenna, receives signals from space only in the direction in which the beam is aimed. The maximum practical deflection on either side of the antenna

Figure 19-6. Tracking radar at Clear AFS. (USAF photo)

Figure 19-7. Solid state PAR at Fylingdales. (Royal Air Force photo)

Figure 19-8. PAVE PAWS site. (DOD photo)

center of the phased-array beam is 60 degrees. This limits the coverage from a single antenna face to 120 degrees. To provide surveillance across the horizon, the building housing the entire system and supporting antenna arrays is constructed in the shape of a triangle. Two of the three sides have radar elements mounted on them. The two radiating faces, each with 1,792 active elements, are tilted back 20 degrees to allow for an elevation deflection from three to 85 degrees above the horizon. The lower limit provides receiver isolation from signals returned from ground clutter and for environmental microwave-radiation hazard protection of the local area. PAVE PAWS radar beams reach outward for nearly 5,556 kilometers in a 240-degree sweep. At its extreme range, it can detect an object the size of a small car. Smaller objects can be detected at closer range.[19]

The PAVE PAWS system is capable of detecting and monitoring a large number of targets that would be consistent with a massive SLBM attack. The system must rapidly discriminate between vehicle types, calculating their launch and impact points in addition to the scheduling, data processing, and communications requirements. The operation is entirely automatic, only requiring people for system monitoring and maintenance and as a final check on the validity of warnings. Three different computers communicating with each other form the heart of the system, which relays the information to JSpOC and Cheyenne Mountain AFS.

Perimeter Acquisition Radar Attack Characterization System. PARCS is operated by the 10 SWS, located just 15 miles south of the Canadian border at Cavalier AFS, North Dakota (fig. 19-9). The PARCS sensor was originally built as part of the Army's Safeguard antiballistic missile (ABM) system. It became operational on 1 October 1975 and was ordered deactivated the next day by Congress. It was modified by the Air Force in 1977 for use as a missile warning/space surveillance sensor.

The PARCS mission is to provide warning and attack characterization of an SLBM and ICBM attack against the CONUS and southern Canada. It is one of the workhorses of the SSN, along with Eglin, providing surveillance, tracking, reporting, and SOI data on highly inclined and polar-orbiting objects. Because of its unique origin, PARCS can track hundreds of objects simultaneously. PARCS uses a single-faced phased-array radar (AN/FPQ-16). The radar, computer, communications equipment, and operations rooms are housed in a reinforced concrete building, originally designed to ride out a missile attack as part of the Safeguard ABM system. The single-faced radar looks due north and slopes from the side of the building at a 35-degree angle.[20] This site is considered a "CONUS isolated" location due to its remote location.

Ascension Radar. The primary mission of the Ascension radar is to provide radar-tracking data to support test and evaluation of developmental and operational ICBMs, space launch vehicles, and aeronautical development programs for the Launch Test Range System (LTRS), formerly the Eastern Range (ER). When not supporting its

Figure 19-9. PARCS at Cavalier AFS. (USAF photo)

primary mission, the unit has the secondary mission of space surveillance in support of the USSTRATCOM space surveillance network.[21]

Kaena Point Radar. The Kaena Point radar became operational as a Western Range asset in 1978. It is located at the northwesternmost corner of the island of Oahu, Hawaii. In 1986 the site began supporting the SSN as a collateral SSN sensor. The Kaena Point radar ceased support to the space surveillance network on 31 December 2006.

Contributing Sensors

Contributing sensors are those owned and operated by other agencies that provide space surveillance support upon request from the JSpOC. They are Millstone/Haystack, the ARPA Long-Range Tracking and Identification Radar (ALTAIR), and Cobra Dane.

Millstone/Haystack. The Millstone/Haystack complex is owned and operated by Lincoln Laboratories of the Massachusetts Institute of Technology (MIT). Millstone/Haystack is part of the Lincoln Space Surveillance Complex (LSSC), which consists of four large-aperture high-power radars: the Millstone Hill Radar (MHR) L-Band, the MHR ultra-high frequency (UHF), Haystack Long-Range Imaging Radar (LRIR), and the Haystack Auxiliary (HAX) Radar. The LSSC sensors are contributing sensors. Millstone Hill Radar and Haystack LRIR are both located in Tyngsboro, Massachusetts.[22]

Millstone is a deep-space radar that contributes 80 hours of space surveillance per week to the JSpOC. Haystack is a deep-space imaging radar that provides wideband SOI data to the JSpOC. Haystack supports the JSpOC one week out of every six. USSTRATCOM has limited recall of the Haystack sensor outside of scheduled times.

ALTAIR. ALTAIR is located on Kwajalein Atoll in the western Pacific Ocean and is operated by the Army. Its primary mission is to support test and evaluation of developmental and operational ICBMs, space launch vehicles, and aeronautical development programs. ALTAIR also serves as a contributing sensor in support of the space surveillance mission. ALTAIR is a near-Earth and deep-space tracking radar. Due to its proximity to the equator, ALTAIR alone can track one-third of the geosynchronous belt.[23]

Space Surveillance

Because of the limited number of sensors and their geographical distribution (fig. 19-10), the SSN cannot track every satellite continuously. To maintain a database of all manmade objects in Earth orbit, the JSpOC uses a tracking cycle that starts with a prediction. The JSpOC makes an assumption as to where a newly launched object will be and then sends out this prediction in the form of a "nominal" element set (ELSET) to the space surveillance sensors. These sensors use this nominal ELSET to search for the object. If the assumption is close, the sensor will detect and track the object. The sensor then collects observations from the space track and transmits the observation data back to JSpOC for processing and analysis.

The JSpOC uses this information to compute an initial ELSET, or prediction, which is then sent to the other sensors in the SSN. Once an object's ELSET is established, the JSpOC will periodically update it to correct for maneuvers and orbital perturbations.[24] This cycle continuously repeats itself for new launches as well as for existing Earth-orbiting space objects. Refer to chapter 6 for more detailed information on ELSETs.

Figure 19-10. Space surveillance network. (DOD graphic)

Another tool used by JSpOC to efficiently distribute the limited tracking capabilities of the SSN is prioritized sensor tracking. A North American Aerospace Defense Command (NORAD)/USSTRATCOM regulation defines categories of priority and specific data-collection instructions, assigned according to each satellite's type and orbit. Generally, satellites with high-interest missions or unstable orbits (objects about to decay) will have higher priority and data-collection requirements than other satellites.

Summary

The space surveillance network is absolutely essential to the United States and its goal of maintaining space superiority and space situational awareness. The information provided by the SSN is used by the Joint Space Operations Center in operational and tactical planning for all Department of Defense space capabilities. The synergistic effects of the various sensor sites described above have allowed the Joint Space Operations Center to maintain a robust satellite catalog of over 11,000 objects that are currently orbiting the earth. This chapter discussed the different sensor technologies used to track satellites orbiting the earth. It also highlighted features of the various sensor sites that constitute the space surveillance network and provided a brief description of the JSpOC process of tasking sensor sites and analyzing space track data. It is important to understand that as the technology and capabilities of spaceborne platforms improve and the population of objects orbiting Earth increases, the sensor sites of the space surveillance network need to be modified and enhanced to keep pace with the evolving space environment.

Notes

1. AFSPC, *Space Surveillance Network (SSN) Site Information Handbook*, 24 October 2007, 96.

2. Ibid., 70.

3. William W. Camp, Joseph T. Mayhan, and Robert M. O'Donnell, "Wideband Radar for Ballistic Missile Defense and Range-Doppler Imaging of Satellites," *Lincoln Laboratory Journal* 12, no. 2 (2000): 267–80.

4. AFSPC, *SSN Site Information Handbook*, 57.

5. Jeffrey T. Richelson, *The U.S. Intelligence Community* (Boulder, CO: Westview Press, 1999), 243–46.

6. AFSPC, *SSN Site Information Handbook*, 121.

7. Ibid.

8. Ibid., 123.

9. Ibid., 139.

10. Ibid.

11. Air Force, "20th Space Control Squadron, Detachment 1," Fact Sheet, http://www.peterson.af.mil/library/factsheets/factsheet.asp?id=4729 (accessed 16 January 2008).

12. AFSPC, *SSN Site Information Handbook*, 143.

13. Ibid., 78.

14. Richelson, *U.S. Intelligence Community*, 246–47.

15. Air Force, "Det 3, 21st Operations Group," Fact Sheet, http://www.peterson.af.mil/library/factsheets/factsheet.asp?id=4741 (accessed 24 February 2008).

16. AFSPC, *SSN Site Information Handbook*, 73.

17. Ibid.

18. Ibid., 86.

19. Ibid.

20. Ibid., 82.

21. Ibid., 96.

22. Ibid., 103.

23. Ibid., 110.

24. Ibid., 40–41.

Chapter 20

Space-Lift Systems

*Maj Christopher J. King, USAF; LCDR Jeremy Powell, USN;
and Maj Edward P. Byrne, USAF*

Space-launch systems provide access to space—a key to any activity in space. Historically, access to space was primarily a function of national governments. Today, space launch is primarily a commercial enterprise. Historically, specific payloads flew on specific boosters. For example, global positioning system (GPS) satellites launched from Delta II launch vehicles.[1] Today, various payloads can fly on different boosters. This section describes only US launch vehicles. It describes the current inventory of unmanned boosters and manned systems and concludes with a look at future systems.

Unmanned Boosters

Unmanned systems in the current inventory include the Delta II rocket, evolved expendable launch vehicle (Delta IV and Atlas V), Pegasus, Minotaur, Taurus, and the Falcon launch vehicle.

Delta II

The Delta II rocket (fig. 20-1) is part of a family of medium-lift-class vehicles from which a variety of satellites has been launched as part of US and international space programs. It launches from Space Launch Complexes (SLC) 17A and 17B at Cape Canaveral AFS, Florida, and from SLC-2 at Vandenberg AFB, California. The original Delta launch vehicle consisted of a Thor intermediate range ballistic missile (IRBM) first stage and Vanguard second and third stages.[2] Continued improvements allow the Delta II to inject over 4,000 pounds into a geosynchronous transfer orbit (GTO).[3]

The National Aeronautics and Space Administration (NASA) placed the original contract with Douglas Aircraft Company in April 1959.[4] The early three-stage vehicle had a length of 85.4 feet, a first-stage diameter of eight feet, and a liftoff weight of 113,500 pounds.[5] The modified

Figure 20-1. Delta II launch. (NASA photo)

Thor first stage had a thrust of about 170,000 pounds. On 13 May 1960, the first Delta failed to achieve orbit, but subsequent vehicles proved to be highly reliable.[6]

In 1987, the Air Force entered into a contract with McDonnell Douglas (which merged with Boeing in August 1997) to build the first 18 Delta II rockets.[7] The vehicle was developed after the Air Force decided to return to a mixed fleet of expendable launch vehicles following the *Challenger* disaster and other launch failures.

The first Delta II successfully launched on 14 February 1989.[8] The Delta II 6925 carried nine GPS satellites into orbit. The Delta II 7925, the current version of this venerable launch vehicle, boosted the remainder of the original GPS constellation into orbit. It continues service in launching the current Block IIR version of GPS.

The Delta II's first stage is 12 feet longer than previous Deltas, bringing the total vehicle height to 130.6 feet.[9] The payload fairing (shroud covering the third stage and the satellite) was widened from eight to 9.5 feet to hold the GPS satellite.[10] The solid-rocket motors (3, 4, or 9, depending on the configuration) that ring the first stage contain a more powerful propellant mixture than previously used.

Delta 7925 began boosting GPS satellites in November 1990.[11] The Delta 7925 added new solid-rocket motors with cases made of a composite material called graphite-epoxy. The motor cases built by Hercules Aerospace are lighter than the steel cases they replaced, but just as strong. The new motors are six feet longer and provide much greater thrust. The main-engine nozzle on the first stage was also enlarged to give a greater expansion ratio for improved performance.[12]

The Delta program has a history of successful domestic/foreign military and commercial launches. The Delta has accomplished many firsts over its lifetime: it was the first vehicle to launch an international satellite (*Telstar I* in 1962), the first geosynchronous orbiting satellite (*Syncom II* in 1963), and the first commercial communication satellite (*COMSAT I* in 1965).[13]

The major elements of today's Delta II launch vehicle are the first stage, with its graphite-epoxy motor (GEM) solid strap-on rocket motors, the second stage, an optional third stage with spin table, and the payload fairing. The Delta II launch-vehicle series are the 7300, 7400, and 7900. The Delta II also has a "heavy" configuration that employs larger-diameter GEM-46 solid strap-on rocket motors on the 7900-series vehicle to increase the performance capability. The payload lift capabilities are listed in table 20-1.

Table 20-1. Delta II family

	732X-10	742X-10	792X-10	792XH-10
GTO	900 kg (1,980 lb.)	1,070 kg (2,370 lb.)	1,750 kg (3,850 lb.)	2,120 kg (4,680 lb.)
LEO	2,450 kg (5,410 lb.)	2,380 kg (6,230 lb.)	4,490 kg (9,910 lb.)	5,430 kg (11,970 lb.)

Adapted from United Launch Alliance, "Delta II," http://www.ulalaunch.com/docs/product_sheet/DeltaIIProductCardFinal.pdf (accessed 28 May 2009).

Evolved Expendable Launch Vehicle

The evolved expendable launch vehicle (EELV) is the Air Force's space-lift modernization program. EELV reduces the cost of launching by at least 25 percent over current

Delta, Atlas, and Titan launch systems.[14] Part of these savings results from the government now procuring commercial launch services and turning over responsibility for operations and maintenance of the launch complexes to the contractors. This new space-lift strategy reduced the government's traditional involvement in launch processing while saving a projected $6 billion in launch costs between the years 2002 and 2020. In addition, EELV improves space-launch operability and standardization.

The two primary launch contractors are Boeing (Delta IV) and Lockheed Martin (Atlas V). However, in May 2005 Lockheed Martin and Boeing announced their plans to form a joint venture called United Launch Alliance (ULA), which officially began operations in December 2006. ULA provides reliable and cost-efficient Delta and Atlas launch services solely in support of US government launch requirements.

Delta IV. Boeing's version of the EELV is the Delta IV family of boosters (fig. 20-2), consisting of five vehicle configurations: the Delta IV Medium (Delta IV M), three variants of Delta IV Medium-Plus (Delta IV M+), and the Delta IV Heavy (Delta IV H). Its first launch was in November 2002, when it lofted a European Telecommunications Satellite Organization (EUTELSAT) commercial communications satellite into a geosynchronous transfer orbit.[15] The Delta IV design is based on a modular common booster core using the liquid hydrogen–liquid oxygen RS-68 engine, which produces over 660,000 pounds of thrust.[16] A single common booster core is used for medium-lift applications, but the Delta IV can be configured with up to four strap-on solid-rocket boosters to lift from 9,200 to 14,500 pounds to a GTO.[17] The Delta IV launches from SLC-37 at Cape Canaveral AFS and from SLC-6 at Vandenberg AFB. The booster with its payload fairing stands from 200 to 225 feet tall. For heavy-lift applications, two full-sized common booster cores can be strapped onto a center common booster core to allow up to 29,000 pounds to GTO or 45,200 pounds to LEO.[18] Detailed Delta IV launch payload capabilities are listed in table 20-2.

Atlas V. Lockheed Martin's entry into the Air Force's EELV competition is the Atlas V (fig. 20-3). The Atlas V comes from a family of launch vehicles

Figure 20-2. Delta IV launch. (USAF photo)

Table 20-2. Delta IV family

	Delta IV M	Delta IV M+ (4, 2)	Delta IV M+ (5, 4)	Delta IV H
GTO	4,300 kg (9,840 lb.)	6,030 kg (13,290 lb.)	7,020 kg (15,470 lb.)	12,980 kg (28,620 lb.)
LEO	9,150 kg (20,170 lb.)	12,240 kg (26,980 lb.)	13,360 kg (29,450 lb.)	22,560 kg (49,740 lb.)

Adapted from United Launch Alliance, "Delta IV," http://www.ulalaunch.com/docs/product_sheet/DeltaVProductCardFinal.pdf (accessed 28 May 2009).

that made its debut in 1957 as America's first operational intercontinental ballistic missile (ICBM). The Atlas, Atlas II, and Atlas III launch vehicles have logged nearly 600 launches for US government and commercial missions. The decision by the Air Force to retain two EELV lines resulted in some launches for the Atlas V but not as many as the Delta IV model. The first Atlas V launch from SLC-41 at Cape Canaveral AFS was in August 2002, when it successfully boosted a new European commercial communications satellite into GTO.[19] Its first successful West Coast launch occurred in March 2008 from SLC-3E at Vandenberg AFB.

Like the Atlas III, the Atlas V 400 and 500 series share a core that uses Russian RD-180 engines and is augmented for heavy payloads with two strap-on boosters.[20] The RD-180 engine can produce 861,000 pounds of thrust at liftoff.[21] It also uses the common core booster with up to five strap-on solid-rocket boosters. The common core booster is 12.5 feet in diameter by 106.6 feet long and uses 627,105 pounds of liquid oxygen and RP-1 rocket fuel propellants.

Figure 20-3. Atlas V. (USAF photo)

Additionally, on Atlas V, Lockheed Martin introduced a 4.57-meter usable diameter Contraves payload fairing in addition to retaining the option to use the heritage Atlas payload fairings. The Contraves fairing is a composite design based on flight-proven hardware. Three configurations will be manufactured to support Atlas V. The short- and medium-length configurations are used on the Atlas V 500 series.

The Centaur upper stage uses a pressure-stabilized propellant tank design and cryogenic propellants. The Centaur stage for Atlas V is stretched 5.5 feet and is powered by either one or two Pratt & Whitney RL10A-4-2 engines, with each engine developing a thrust of 22,300 pounds. Operational and reliability upgrades are enabled with the RL10A-4-2 engine configuration. The inertial navigation unit located on the Centaur provides guidance and navigation for both the Atlas and Centaur and controls both Atlas and Centaur tank pressures and propellant use. The Centaur engines are capable of multiple in-space starts, making possible insertion into low Earth parking orbit, followed by a coast period and then insertion into GTO.

The Atlas V can lift 20,000 pounds to LEO or 10,900 pounds to GTO.[22] The booster stands 191 feet tall and is 12.5 feet in diameter.[23] Detailed payload lift capabilities are listed in table 20-3.

Pegasus. Orbital Sciences Corporation developed Pegasus (fig. 20-4) privately. Its first launch into orbit occurred on 5 April 1990 from a B-52 aircraft over the Pacific Ocean.[24]

The triangular-winged rocket is set free at an altitude of 40,000 feet and falls for five seconds.[25] The first-stage engine then ignites and flies like a missile in second- and third-stage burns. Pegasus is designed to carry light payloads weighing between 450 and 600 pounds into polar orbit or up to 900 pounds into equatorial orbit.[26] A nominal altitude would be around 280

Table 20-3. Atlas V family

	401	431	551	Heavy
GTO	4,950 kg (10,900 lb.)	7,800 kg (17,190 lb.)	8,700 kg (19,180 lb.)	13,000 kg (28,660 lb.)
LEO	9,750 kg (21,490 lb.)	13,620 kg (30,020 lb.)	18,500 kg (40,780 lb.)	29,420 kg (64,860 lb.)

Adapted from United Launch Alliance, "Atlas V," http://www.ulalaunch.com/docs/product_sheet/AtlasProductCardFinal.pdf (accessed 28 May 2009).

Figure 20-4. Pegasus launch vehicle. (NASA photo)

Figure 20-5. Orbital Sciences Corporation L-1011 Pegasus launcher. (NASA photo)

Figure 20-6. Minotaur I launch. (NASA photo)

miles. The vehicle has three graphite-epoxy composite-case Hercules motors, a fixed delta platform composite wing, and an aft skirt assembly that includes three control fins, an avionics section, and a payload fairing. A fourth stage can be added to increase payload weight.

Pegasus weighs about 41,000 pounds at launch and is 50 feet long and 50 inches in diameter.[27] The XL model uses stretched first and second stages, making it about five feet longer than the standard Pegasus. The first XL launch in July 1994 ended in failure.[28] However, it since has flown successfully over 30 times launching more than 70 satellites.[29]

A new launch platform for the Pegasus was also developed. A modified L-1011 (fig. 20-5), purchased from Air Canada, debuted in mid-1994.[30]

Minotaur. The Minotaur program was developed for the Air Force's Orbital/Suborbital Program (OSP) as a low-cost, four-stage space-launch vehicle (SLV). The Minotaur I SLV uses a combination of government-supplied surplus Minuteman II ICBM motors and proven Orbital space-launch technologies (fig. 20-6). The OSP has since expanded to include Minotaur IV and Minotaur V versions utilizing surplus Peacekeeper motor stages.

The Minuteman motors served as the first and second stages of the Minotaur I. Its third and fourth stages, structures, and payload fairing were taken directly from Orbital's existing Pegasus XL rocket. The addition of improved avionics systems, including modular avionics control hardware (MACH), already used on many of Orbital's suborbital launch vehicles, further enhanced the Minotaur I's capabilities.

Minotaur I made its inaugural flight in January 2000, successfully delivering a number of small military and university satellites into orbit and marking the first use of surplus Minuteman boosters in a space launch. Several derivatives of Minotaur were developed or proposed, but only four are in use today:

1. Minotaur I SLV (the original Minotaur) consists of an M55A1 first stage, SR19 second stage, Orion 50XL third stage, Orion 38 fourth stage, and optional hydrazine auxiliary propulsion system (HAPS) fifth stage for velocity trim and multiple payload deployment. The Minotaur I has the capability to launch a 580 kg payload to low Earth orbit (LEO).

2. Minotaur IV SLV uses surplus Peacekeeper motors for its first three stages. It consists of an SR118 first stage, an SR119 second stage, an SR120 third stage, an Orion 38 fourth stage, and an optional HAPS fifth stage. The Minotaur IV SLV has the capability to launch a 1,750 kg payload into LEO.

3. Minotaur IV+ SLV uses the same configuration as the standard Minotaur IV except it replaces the Orion 38 fourth stage with a Star 48V motor for additional performance.

4. Minotaur V uses the same configuration as the Minotaur IV+ with the addition of either a Star 37FM or FMV fifth stage. The Minotaur V can be used for placing small spacecraft on high-energy trajectories, such as GTO, highly elliptical orbit (HEO), and lunar.

Minotaur SLV launches can occur from the California Spaceport (SLC-8) on Vandenberg AFB, from Pad 0B at the Virginia Spaceflight Center on Wallops Island, from the Kodiak Launch Complex in Alaska, and from Spaceport Florida on Cape Canaveral AFS. To date, seven successful Minotaur launches (Minotaur I) have taken place. The first five launches took place from SLC-8 and the last two from Pad 0B. The first Minotaur IV launch is scheduled for late 2009 from the Kodiak Launch Complex.

Taurus. The Taurus rocket launches small satellites into LEO (fig. 20-7). Developed under the sponsorship of the Defense Advanced Research Projects Agency (DARPA), Taurus was designed for easy transportability and rapid setup and launch. Since its debut flight in 1994, Taurus has conducted seven of eight successful missions, launching 12 satellites for commercial, civil, military, and international customers.[31]

Taurus is a ground-based variant of the air-launched Pegasus rocket and is a four-stage, inertially guided, all-solid-propellant vehicle.[32] Two fairing sizes offer flexibility in designing a particular mission, and with the addition of a structural adapter, either can accommodate multiple payloads, resulting in lower launch costs for smaller satellites "sharing" a mission.[33]

A cornerstone of the Taurus program is a simplified integration and test capability that includes horizontal integration of the rocket's upper stages and off-line encapsulation of the payload within the fairing. The upper stages and the encapsulated cargo are delivered to the launch site, where they are mated. The whole assembly is then stacked on the first stage using a mobile crane.[34]

The Taurus launch system includes a complete set of ground support equipment to ensure the ability to operate from austere sites. Thus far, Taurus has launched from the US government's Western Range at Vandenberg AFB, but it is also approved for launch from Cape Canaveral AFS, Wallops Flight Facility in Virginia, and Kodiak Launch Complex, Alaska.[35]

The first Taurus launch occurred at Vandenberg AFB on 13 March 1994.[36] It is designed to respond rapidly to launch needs and can be ready for launch within eight days. The launch site is a concrete pad with a slim gantry based on its design to be a simple "mobile" launch platform.

The overall length of Taurus is 90 feet, and it weighs 150,000 pounds at launch.[37] Its maximum diameter (first stage) is 92 inches.[38] The vehicle, shown in figure 20-7, is designed to carry 3,000 pounds into a low polar orbit, up to 3,700 pounds for a due east launch, and up to 950 pounds to geosynchronous transfer orbit.[39]

Falcon Launch Vehicle. The Falcon family of launch vehicles is the newcomer to the launch industry and is produced by Space Exploration Technologies (SpaceX). SpaceX, established in 2002, set out with the goal of providing a more reliable, simpler, lower-cost, and more responsive option for meeting global launch requirements. Starting in March 2006, SpaceX conducted three launches of the Falcon 1, with the fourth flight completing its first successful operational mission in September 2008. Currently,

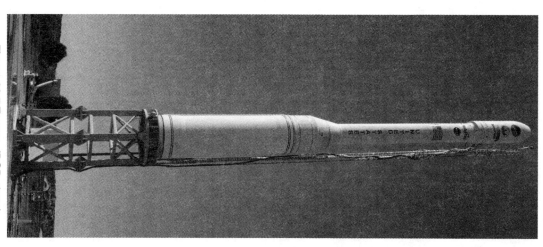

Figure 20-7. Taurus. (DOD photo)

SpaceX produces the Falcon 1 (fig. 20-8) and Falcon 9 series of launch vehicles.

The Falcon 1 launch vehicle is a two-stage rocket that uses liquid oxygen and rocket-grade kerosene (RP-1) as propellant. The first stage is reusable and uses a single Merlin 1C engine producing 94,000 pounds-force (lbf.) of thrust. The second stage uses a single SpaceX Kestrel engine with a multiple restart capability and produces 6,900 lbf. of thrust. The Falcon 1 can launch a 480 kg payload to LEO. In mid-2010, the Falcon 1 will be phased out and replaced by the more capable Falcon 1e.

The Falcon 1e is similar to the Falcon 1 but takes advantage of certain technological and weight-saving advances. The Falcon 1e measures over six meters longer and has a thrust of 128,000 lbf. in vacuum, giving it the capability to launch a 900 kg payload into LEO.

The Falcon 9 is also a two-stage rocket that uses liquid oxygen and RP-1 as propellant (fig. 20-9). The Falcon 9 first stage incorporates nine SpaceX Merlin 1C engines, producing a total of 1.1 million lbf. in vacuum. The second stage is a shorter version of the first stage and uses a single Merlin 1C engine. Depending on the launch site, the Falcon 9 can launch up to 10,450 kg to LEO and over 4,500 kg to GTO.

The Falcon 9 Heavy is similar to the standard Falcon 9, but it includes two additional Falcon 9 first-stage engines used as strap-on boosters. The Falcon 9 Heavy will produce over 3.3 million lbf. in vacuum and place over 29,600 kg into LEO and over 15,000 kg into GTO.

To date, SpaceX has conducted four Falcon 1 launches, all from the US Army's Kwajalein Atoll. The first Falcon 9 launch is currently scheduled for 2009 from SLC-40 at Cape Canaveral AFS.

Manned Boosters—The Space Transportation System

The Space Transportation System (STS), also known as the space shuttle (fig. 20-10), is a reusable spacecraft designed to be launched into orbit by a rocket and then return to the earth's surface by gliding down and landing on a runway.

Figure 20-8. Falcon 1. (Photo courtesy of SpaceX)

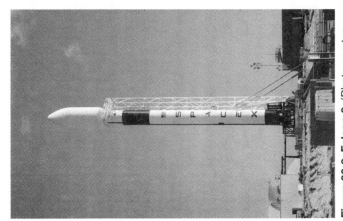

Figure 20-9. Falcon 9. (Photo courtesy of SpaceX)

The shuttle was selected in the early 1970s as the principal space launcher and carrier vehicle to be developed by NASA.[40] It was planned as a replacement for the more expensive, expendable booster rockets used since the late 1950s for launching major commercial and government satellites. Together with launch facilities, mission control and supporting centers, and a tracking and data relay satellite system, it would complete NASA's new Space Transportation System.

Although the shuttle launched several military payloads in its early days, such as the Defense Support Program satellite, the Air Force abandoned it as a primary launch vehicle after the *Challenger* disaster.[41] However, it is capable of military missions again if the decision were made to use it that way.

After numerous delays, the shuttle program started operations in the early 1980s. Despite several problems, the spacecraft demonstrated its versatility in a series of missions until the fatal disaster during the *Challenger* launch on 28 January 1986 forced a long delay.[42] The pro-

Figure 20-10. Space Transportation System. (NASA photo)

gram resumed in late 1988, and the modifications to the shuttle affected neither the basic design of the craft nor its overall dimensions. Again, disaster struck on 1 February 2003 with the loss of *Columbia* on reentry.[43] After the loss of *Columbia*, it was decided that the STS would fly long enough to complete the International Space Station and then be retired by 2010.

The three main components of the space shuttle are the orbiter, the external fuel tank, and the solid-rocket motors. The shuttle weighs 4.5 million pounds at launch, stands 184.2 feet tall, and can carry up to 63,500 pounds of cargo to LEO on one mission.[44] The orbiter, 78 feet across the wing tips and 122.2 feet long, is the portion resembling a delta-winged jet fighter.[45] It is a rocket stage during launch, a spaceship in orbit, and a hypersonic glider on reentry and landing. A three-deck crew compartment and an attitude thruster module are in the nose, the mid-body is the cargo hold or payload bay (15 ft wide and 60 ft long), and the tail holds the three main engines plus maneuvering engine pods.

Each engine, burning hydrogen and oxygen, produces up to 394,000 pounds of thrust.[46] The external tank, actually an oxygen tank and a hydrogen tank joined by a load-bearing intertank, is the structural backbone of the shuttle. Measuring 27.56 feet wide and 154.2 feet tall, it carries 1,520,000 pounds of liquefied propellants for the main engines.[47] The shuttle's main engines produce over 37 million horsepower and empty the external tank in about 8.5 minutes.[48]

Two solid-rocket boosters, each slightly over 12 feet wide and 149 feet tall, provide the shuttle with a lift to the upper atmosphere so the main engines can work more efficiently.[49] Each produces an average thrust of 3.3 million pounds.[50] The propellant in the solid-rocket motors consists of ammonium perchlorate, aluminum powder, iron oxide, and a binding agent. Total thrust of the vehicle at liftoff (two solid motors and three liquid engines) is 7.78 million pounds.[51]

The shuttle's main engines are ignited first, followed by ignition of the booster rockets about six seconds before liftoff. Then the hold-down bolts release the spacecraft to allow it to fly. The shuttle lifts off vertically about 2.5 seconds later with all five engines operating. As soon as it clears the gantry, it rolls and pitches to fly with the orbiter upside down, as the craft's design puts the thrust vector off-center.

At T+2 minutes 12 seconds, the boosters burn out and are jettisoned from the external tank at an altitude of approximately 24 statute miles.[52] The boosters then parachute into the sea for recovery, refurbishing, and reuse. Meanwhile, the shuttle continues under the power of the main engines. Just short of orbital velocity, the engines shut down (T+8 minutes 32 seconds), and the tank is jettisoned (T+8 minutes 50 seconds).[53] The tank burns up as it reenters the atmosphere.

Once the vehicle is in space, it maneuvers using two different systems: the orbital maneuvering system (OMS) and the reaction control system (RCS). The orbiter's own OMS engines act as the third stage that puts the craft into orbit.

The OMS uses two bipropellant, 6,000-pound-thrust rocket engines mounted in pods on the aft end of the orbiter fuselage.[54] The hypergolic propellants consist of monomethylhydrazine and nitrogen tetroxide, with about 21,600 pounds of propellant stored within the orbiter in titanium tanks.[55] The OMS is used for orbit insertion or transfer, orbit circulation, rendezvous, and deorbit.

The RCS uses 38 bipropellant liquid-rocket engines and six bipropellant liquid-rocket vernier thrusters.[56] Fourteen of the engines are on the orbiter's nose, together with two verniers. The remaining engines and verniers are split equally between the two OMS pods of the aft end of the orbiter fuselage. The RCS uses the same type of propellants as the OMS but carries the fuel in separate tanks. There is a system to transfer fuel to and from the RCS to the OMS. The RCS is used to maneuver in space during rendezvous and deorbit maneuvers.

A crew of four—commander, pilot, mission specialist, and payload specialist—normally operates the vehicle. A crew must have a minimum of two members and may have a maximum of eight except as noted. In an emergency, 10 people can fit in the orbiter. The interior of the orbiter is pressurized, allowing the astronauts to operate in a short-sleeve environment without spacesuits. Passengers can fly on the shuttle without extensive astronaut training because of the relatively light 3G acceleration during launch and the pressurized cabin. Four attachment points support the self-contained crew module within the fuselage; the entire module is welded to create the pressure-tight vessel. The module has a fuselage side hatch for access, a hatch into the airlock from the mid-section, and a hatch from the airlock into the payload bay. As previously mentioned, the crew module is divided into three levels. The upper flight deck has seats for the mission and payload specialists, the commander, and the pilot. The upper deck also contains dual flight controls and the controls for the remote manipulator system (RMS), which extracts payloads from the shuttle's cargo bay. The mid-level deck has additional seating, a galley, electronics bays, and crew sleeping and comfort facilities. The lowest level houses environmental equipment and storage.

At the end of the orbital mission, the orbiter is protected from the heat of reentry by heat-resistant ceramic tiles. As dynamic pressure from the air increases, control of the vehicle switches from the RCS to aerodynamic surfaces, and the orbiter glides to a landing.

Future Space Lift

The space shuttle program is at a turning point as it moves toward retirement in 2010. Meanwhile, as a result of the NASA Authorization Act of 2005, the United States is transitioning from a country that sends astronauts to orbit the earth to one that sends humans out into the solar system.

Constellation Program

NASA's Constellation Program is building the next generation of spacecraft for human exploration. The Orion crew exploration vehicle will launch on the Ares I rocket (fig. 20-11). The Ares V will launch cargo. Constellation will return humans to the moon by 2020 to set up a lunar outpost in preparation for journeys to Mars.

Orion will be similar in shape to the Apollo spacecraft, but significantly larger. The Apollo-style heat shield is understood to be the best shape for reentering Earth's atmosphere, especially when returning directly from the moon. Orion will be 16.5 feet in diameter and have a mass of about 25 tons. Inside, it will have more than 2.5 times the volume of an Apollo capsule. The larger size will allow Orion to accommodate four crew members on missions to the moon and six on missions to the International Space Station by 2014

Figure 20-11. Ares vehicle. (NASA photo)

tion or Mars. Orion is scheduled to fly its first missions to the moon by 2020 and carry out its first sortie to the moon by 2020.

A launch-abort system atop the Orion capsule will be capable of pulling the spacecraft and its crew to safety in the event of an emergency on the launch pad or any time during ascent. Orion's power and propulsion systems will be housed in a service module that will be mounted directly below the capsule, covering the entry heat shield during launch and in-space activities. A spacecraft adapter will connect the Orion capsule and service module to the launch systems.

Orion will be launched into LEO by the Ares I crew launch vehicle. To maximize the crew's safety, Orion and its abort system will be placed at the top of the Ares I rocket. The rest of the two-stage Ares I will be stacked vertically, below the crew vehicle. This design will virtually eliminate the possibility of debris from the booster striking Orion during ascent.

Orion will be able to remain docked to the space station for up to six months, providing a means for the crew to return to Earth at any time. The spacecraft will have the ability to stay in lunar orbit untended for the duration of a lunar visit that could last up to six months. Orion will be capable of carrying pressurized cargo to the space station on unpiloted missions.

For missions to the moon, NASA will use two separate launch vehicles, each derived from a mixture of systems with their heritage rooted in Apollo, space shuttle, and commercial launch-vehicle technology. An Ares V cargo launch vehicle will precede the launch of the crew vehicle, delivering to LEO the Earth departure stage and the lunar module that will carry explorers on the last leg of the journey to the moon's surface. Orion will dock with the lunar module in Earth orbit, and the Earth departure stage will propel both on their journey to the moon. Once in lunar orbit, all four astronauts will use the lunar landing craft to travel to the moon's surface, while the Orion spacecraft stays in lunar orbit. Once the astronauts' lunar mission is complete, they will return to the orbiting Orion vehicle using a lunar ascent module. The crew will use the service-module main engine to break out of lunar orbit and head to Earth. Orion and its crew will reenter the earth's atmosphere using a newly developed thermal protection system. Parachutes will further slow Orion's descent through the atmosphere.

Operationally Responsive Space-Lift Initiative

The Air Force began the operationally responsive space-lift initiative in 2003.[57] The goal of the program is to pave the way for reusable rockets that could be launched at a low cost on short notice. As part of a one-year analysis of alternatives study that began 1 March 2003, teams are investigating a variety of space planes, air-launched boosters, and fully reusable, as well as expendable or partly reusable, space lifters.[58] The study is closely linked to NASA's Next Generation Launch Technology Program, the follow-on to their recently scaled-back Space Launch Initiative. A multistaged system could be in place by 2014, depending on funding.[59] Also, a low-cost, expendable, upper-stage booster and an orbital transfer vehicle capable of handling spacecraft servicing are planned for development. The goal is to have a system that can launch within hours to days as opposed to the weeks to months of preparation required by current boosters. Payloads could include the common aero vehicle (CAV), a reentry vehicle that can deliver a variety of munitions to a ground target, or microsatellites.

Scorpius-Sprite Program

One possible contender for an operationally responsive space-lift solution is Microcosm's Sprite Mini-Lift launch vehicle. The Air Force, the Missile Defense Agency, and NASA, as well as Microcosm's own research and development funds, fund research for the ongoing Scorpius-Sprite program.[60]

Scorpius, the suborbital research vehicle, has already flown and will be scaled up to become the orbital Sprite. The Sprite will be 53 feet tall and consist of six 42-inch-diameter pods around a central core, giving it an overall diameter of 11.2 feet.[61] It will be a three-stage launcher with six 20,000-pound-thrust engines followed by a second-stage single 20,000-pound engine.[62] The third stage will produce 2,500 pounds of thrust and place a 700-pound payload in a 100-nautical-mile (nm) low Earth orbit for $1.8 million.[63] A primary goal is to simplify launch operations so that liftoff occurs within eight hours of bringing the vehicle to the pad.

Force Application and Launch from CONUS

The Force Application and Launch from CONUS (FALCON) program objectives are to develop and demonstrate technologies that will enable both near-term and far-term capabilities to execute time-critical, global-reach missions. A near-term capability will be accomplished via development of a rocket-boosted, expendable, munitions delivery

270

system that delivers its payload to the target by executing unpowered boost-glide maneuvers at hypersonic speed. This concept, called the common aero vehicle, will be capable of delivering up to 1,000 pounds of munitions to a target 3,000 nm downrange.[64] An operationally responsive space-lift booster vehicle will place the CAV at the required altitude and velocity. The FALCON program will develop a low-cost rocket booster to meet these requirements and demonstrate this capability in a series of flight tests culminating with the launch of an operable CAV-like payload.

The vision for a far-term capability entails a reusable, hypersonic aircraft capable of delivering 12,000 pounds of payload to a target 9,000 nm from CONUS in less than two hours.[65] Many of the technologies required by CAV are also applicable to this vehicle concept, such as high lift-to-drag technologies, high-temperature materials, thermal protection systems, and periodic guidance, navigation, and control. Initiated under the space-vehicle technologies program and leveraging technology developed under the hypersonics program, FALCON will build on these technologies to address the implications of powered hypersonic flight and the reusability required to enable this far-term capability. The FALCON program addresses many high-priority mission areas and applications such as global presence, space control, and space lift.

Notes

1. Justin Ray, "Delta Rocket Puts on Late-Night Show with GPS Launch," Spaceflight Now, http://www.spaceflightnow.com/delta/d308/ (accessed 10 February 2008).

2. Mike Gruntman, *Blazing the Trail: The Early History of Spacecraft and Rocketry* (Reston, VA: American Institute of Aeronautics and Astronautics, 2004), 253.

3. Genesis Mission, "Genesis Launch Vehicle: The Delta Rocket," http://www.genesismission.org/educate/scimodule/LaunchPropulsion/L&P_PDFs/C4_STdeltarocket.pdf (accessed 10 February 2008).

4. Ibid. 2.

5. Roger D. Launius and Dennis R. Jenkins, *To Reach the High Frontier: A History of U.S. Launch Vehicles* (Lexington, KY: University Press of Kentucky, 2002), 105–7.

6. Ibid., 11.

7. Air Force, "Delta II Launch Vehicle," Fact Sheet, http://www.af.mil/factsheets/factsheet.asp?fsID=97 (accessed 10 February 2008).

8. David Baker, ed., *Jane's Space Directory, 2002–2003* (Alexandria, VA: Jane's Information Group, 2002), 264.

9. Ibid., 265–66.

10. Ibid., 266–67.

11. Launius and Jenkins, *To Reach the High Frontier*, 132.

12. Ibid.

13. Ibid., 116–23.

14. Air Force Space Command, "Evolved Expendable Launch Vehicle," Fact Sheet, http://www.afspc.af.mil/library/factsheets/factsheet.asp?id=3643 (accessed 18 February 2008).

15. Ibid.

16. Ibid.

17. Baker, ed., *Jane's Space Directory*, 269.

18. Ibid.

19. Astronautix, "Atlas V," http://www.astronautix.com/lvs/atlasv.htm (accessed 18 February 2008).

20. Ibid.

21. Ibid.

22. Baker, ed., *Jane's Space Directory*, 258–59.

23. Astronautix, "Atlas V."

24. Baker, ed., *Jane's Space Directory*, 275.

25. Orbital Sciences Corporation, "Pegasus," http://www.orbital.com/SpaceLaunch/Pegasus/ (accessed 14 February 2008).

26. Baker, ed., *Jane's Space Directory*, 274–75.

27. Ibid., 274.

28. Orbital Sciences Corporation, "Pegasus Mission History," http://www.orbital.com/SpaceLaunch/Pegasus/pegasus_history.shtml (accessed 14 February 2008).

29. Ibid.

30. Baker, ed., *Jane's Space Directory*, 274.

31. Astronautix, "Taurus," http://www.astronautix.com/lvs/taurus.htm (accessed 16 February 2008).

32. Ibid.

33. Ibid.

34. Baker, ed., *Jane's Space Directory*, 279.

35. Astronautix, "Taurus."

36. Baker, ed., *Jane's Space Directory*, 278.

37. Ibid.

38. Ibid.

39. Astronautix, "Taurus."

40. NASA, "The Shuttle: Background and Status," http://spaceflight.nasa.gov/shuttle/reference/shutref/sts/background.html (accessed 18 February 2008).

41. Baker, ed., *Jane's Space Directory*, 500.

42. Launius and Jenkins, *To Reach the High Frontier*, 399–400.

43. NASA, "Columbia Mission Overview," http://www.nasa.gov/columbia/mission/index.html (accessed 18 February 2008).

44. NASA, "Space Shuttle Basics," http://www.spaceflight.nasa.gov/shuttle/reference/basics/index.html (accessed 18 February 2008).

45. Ibid.

46. Baker, ed., *Jane's Space Directory*, 503.

47. NASA, "Space Shuttle Basics."

48. Ibid.

49. Baker, ed., *Jane's Space Directory*, 503.

50. Ibid.

51. Ibid.

52. NASA, "Space Shuttle Basics."

53. Ibid.

54. Dennis R. Jenkins, *Space Shuttle: The History of Developing the National Space Transportation System* (Marceline, MO: Walsworth Publishing, 1992), 213.

55. Ibid.

56. Ibid., 214.

57. "Operationally Responsive Spacelift Initiative," GlobalSecurity.org, http://www.globalsecurity.org/space/systems/ors.htm (accessed 19 February 2008).

58. Ibid.

59. Ibid.

60. "Microcosm's Scorpius/Sprite," GlobalSecurity.org, http://www.globalsecurity.org/space/systems/sprite.htm (accessed 19 February 2008).

61. Ibid.

62. Ibid.

63. Ibid.

64. "Hypersonic Cruise Vehicle Force Application and Launch from CONUS," GlobalSecurity.org, http://www.globalsecurity.org/space/systems/hcv.htm (accessed 21 February 2008).

65. Ibid.

Space System Threats

Maj Brian Garino, USAF, and Maj Jane Gibson, USAF

Most US military operations are touched in one way or another by space—we are more dependent on space than any other nation.[1] This dependency has opened up critical vulnerabilities that must be addressed. Aircrews, mission planners, director of space forces (DIRSPACEFOR) staff members, and all personnel involved with combined air operations center (CAOC) planning and air tasking order (ATO) development should understand the threats to space operations and space support functions, as well as the intelligence, surveillance, and reconnaissance (ISR) threat from other nations' space-based systems. Regarding threats to space systems and associated links and nodes, the presented threat will more than likely influence the effectiveness and/or efficiency of other friendly-force operations. This effect will not only affect planning timelines but could also result in the loss of valuable military assets and human life. Space threats include, but are not limited to, (1) tracking and monitoring satellites and their transmissions; (2) electronic attack (EA) against space-based services at the transmission site, the satellite, and the user's equipment; (3) physical attacks against actual satellites and spacecraft; and (4) the use of space for adversary force enhancement and adversary intelligence preparation of the battlefield. These threats could cause communication problems in disseminating and executing the ATO, impact the successful guiding of weapons and aircraft to the target, cause the loss of national overhead and air-breathing ISR systems, compromise operations security (OPSEC) and information security (INFOSEC), and impact force protection posture.

Vulnerabilities can be exploited by focusing attacks on any one of the three segments that make up our space capability—ground, communication (link), and space. The ground segment includes fixed and mobile land, sea, or airborne equipment used to interact with the space segment. The link segment is the data transmitted between the ground and space segments. The space segment includes satellites, space stations, or reusable space-transportation systems. The ability of our space systems to fulfill their missions can be augmented through various methods including redundancy, hardening, maneuverability, denial, and passive defense.

Ground Segment Threats

One of the easiest ways to disrupt, deny, degrade, or destroy the utility of space systems is to attack or sabotage the associated ground segments. The ground segment is defined by ground station operations to include telemetry, tracking, and commanding (TT&C) of the space nodes and space-launch mission functions. DOD satellites are network-controlled at Schriever AFB, Colorado, via the Air Force Satellite Control Network (AFSCN). The ground segment includes satellite communications (SATCOM) transmission and reception devices, such as GPS receivers. These specialized facilities are critical to the continued operation and effective use of satellites. At the same time, these facilities often represent the most vulnerable segment of most space systems because they are subject to attack by a variety of means, ranging from physical attack to computer network intrusion.[2]

These nodes are the most vulnerable to direct attack, network attack, or jamming. Many satellite tracking and control stations are lightly guarded, but their remote locations provide some measure of protection. Many of our satellite communications, launch, data reception, and control facilities are described in open-source materials. With the proliferation of bomb-making techniques and explosive materials, our continental United States (CONUS)-based facilities are at an increased risk. This includes domestic and international terrorists, as well as traditional state actors. An attack on a fixed ground facility can stop data transmission, kill skilled analysts and technicians, render launch facilities unusable, and prevent control of satellites. A single incident or a small number of incidents could significantly impact our space systems for years.[3]

Research, sustainment, integration, and test facilities are also vulnerable. The life-cycle of a space system is processed through commercial facilities that are well-known and are susceptible to physical attack. For example, on 10 May 1992, two individuals scaled the fence surrounding the Rockwell facility in Seal Beach, California. Using false identifications, the individuals penetrated a clean room where a GPS satellite was being assembled and attacked it with axes. They caused several million dollars worth of damage before being subdued.[4]

Network attack against ground nodes is a growing threat, as many countries have developed dedicated cyber-attack or hacking capabilities. Hackers routinely probe DOD networks and computers. Detected probes and scans are increasing, access to hacking tools is becoming easier, and hacking techniques are growing more sophisticated.[5]

Communications (Link) Segment Threats

Both the ground-segment and the space-segment nodes are tied together by information conduits called links. These links are identified as control or mission links. Control links command the satellite and its sensors. Mission links describe the operational data transmitted to or from the satellite. These links are vulnerable to multiple types of electronic attack.

Electronic Attack

Electronic attack is defined as any action involving the use of electromagnetic energy and directed energy to control the electromagnetic spectrum or to attack an adversary.[6] US space systems could be functionally neutralized by jamming and/or spoofing.

Jammers usually emit noise-like signals in an effort to mask or prevent the reception of desired signals. All military and commercial satellite systems are susceptible to uplink and downlink jamming. In either case, the jammer must operate in the same radio band as the system being jammed. Uplink jammers on the ground must be roughly as powerful as the ground-based emitter associated with the link being jammed. However, ground-based downlink jammers can often be much less powerful and still be effective. Since most satellites rely on uplinked command and control information from the ground for station keeping, payload management, and satellite health and status, attacking a satellite's uplink during critical commanding periods could seriously degrade mission performance. The effectiveness of electronic jamming, however, is limited because of line-of-sight restrictions and increased satellite autonomy. Therefore, attacking the downlink is usually easier and more reliable.[7]

Uplink Jamming

There are two types of satellite uplink signals: signals for retransmission (payload signals such as TV and communications) and the command uplinks to the satellite. Uplink jamming against a payload signal is an attractive EA strategy because all recipients of the target transmission are affected. The jamming uplink signal is a radio frequency (RF) signal of approximately the same frequency as the target uplink signal. It is transmitted up to the satellite onto the same transponder as the target signal and affects the transponder's ability to distinguish the true signal from the jamming signal. Note that the target uplink source and signal are not affected; the inability of the satellite's transponder to distinguish between the signals results in a loss of downlink or corrupted downlink. The effectiveness of uplink jamming is extremely dependent on obtaining detailed information on the target signal. This can be done through formal signals intelligence (SIGINT) processes or (in some cases) open-source intelligence (OSINT) research. Once this is gathered and analyzed, the uplink jamming source must be able to acquire the proper satellite and transponder, as well as produce a signal with the correct characteristics and power necessary to overcome the signal to be jammed.

Targets of uplink jammers are the satellites' radio receivers, including their sensors and command receivers. Uplink jamming is more difficult, since considerable jammer transmitter power is required. However, its effects may be global, since the satellite or space system could be impaired for all users.

Downlink Jamming

There are two main targets for downlink jamming: SATCOM broadcasts and navigation satellite (NAVSAT) broadcasts. In a downlink jamming scenario, the objective of the EA is to disrupt or temporarily keep the spacecraft's transmission (communication or navigation signal) from being received by select ground users. A downlink jamming system accomplishes this by broadcasting an RF signal of approximately the same frequency as the targeted downlink signal but with more power. This jamming signal is transmitted toward a terrestrial (ground-based) or airborne satellite downlink reception antenna where it overpowers the satellite's signal. With smart jamming (vice brute-force jamming), the jamming signal attempts to emulate the satellite's signal and, if successful, can provide the targeted user with false data or information. The effectiveness of downlink jamming is dependent upon the jammer being able to operate within line of sight (LOS) of the ground site and within the field of view of the ground site's antenna; effectiveness is also dependent upon the jamming signal being processed by the SATCOM receiver. LOS restrictions can be overcome to a degree by utilizing an airborne platform; the altitude gained by the airborne platform expands the coverage and aids in overcoming ground-based obstacles. It is difficult to assess the effectiveness of downlink jamming as this normally requires monitoring the output of the targeted receiver (often not possible).

The targets of downlink jammers are ground-based satellite data receivers, ranging from large, fixed ground sites to handheld GPS user sets. Downlink jamming only requires a very low-power jammer, though its effects are local (from tens to hundreds of miles, depending on the power of both the jammer and downlink signal). Since downlink telemetry contains the mission information and health and status information, successfully attacking the downlink directly attacks information flow and, therefore, has a more immediate effect on denying or disrupting the satellite's mission.[8]

Sophisticated technologies for jamming satellite signals are emerging. For example, Russia markets a handheld GPS jamming system (fig. 21-1). A one-watt version of that system, the size of a cigarette pack, can deny access to GPS out to 50 miles; a slightly larger version can jam up to 120 miles.[9]

Spoofing

Spoofing is the ability to capture, alter, and retransmit a communication stream in a way that misleads the recipient.[10] Attacking the communication segment via spoofing involves taking over the space system by appearing as an authorized user. Once established as a trusted user, false commands can be inserted into a satellite's command receiver, causing the spacecraft to malfunction or fail its mission. Spoofing is one of the most discreet and deniable forms of attacking our space systems.[11]

Figure 21-1. Russian GPS jammer. (National Air and Space Intelligence Center photo)

Space Segment Threats

Spacecraft themselves are complex, expensive, and relatively fragile. They are susceptible to a variety of lethal attacks, including kinetic energy and directed energy (laser and high-powered RF). From the attacker's perspective, destroying a spacecraft using an antisatellite weapon (ASAT) may be preferable because target destruction can be complete and easily verified, although the political ramifications could be significant. Execution of most ASAT options requires detailed and complex information about the weapon system, the satellite, the ground infrastructure, and the command and control (C2) network. Such efforts are extremely expensive and easily detectable by dedicated intelligence organizations. As a result, ASAT development worldwide has been limited.

Kinetic-Energy Weapons

Kinetic-impact weapons cause structural damage by impacting the target with one or more high-speed masses. Small pieces of debris can inflict substantial damage or destroy a satellite. On 11 January 2007, China successfully tested a direct-ascent, kinetic-kill ASAT vehicle, destroying an inactive Chinese *Feng Yun 1C (FY-1C)* weather satellite (launched in 1999). The satellite was in a polar orbit at an altitude of 865 km (537 miles) and was attacked when it passed over the Xichang Space Centre in Sichuan Province. The satellite broke into more than 900 pieces, generating more debris than any previous space event and threatening many operational spacecraft. The launch vehicle was probably a mobile, solid-fuel KT-1 missile, a version of the DF-21 medium-range ballistic missile (MRBM), with a range of 1,700 km to 2,500 km, although according to some accounts it was a KT-2, also mobile and solid fuel, based on DF-31 intermediate-range ballistic missile (IRBM)/intercontinental ballistic missile (ICBM) technology, with a range of more than 6,000 km. The launch vehicle and warhead were guided to the target by ground-based radars.[12]

The threat of hostile actions involving microsatellites (microsats) that can target US commercial space systems is of growing concern. Microsats offer the opportunity for a broad range of countries to enter space using off-the-shelf hardware to build inexpensive satellites and very affordable launch options to place them into orbit. Currently at least 40 countries have demonstrated some ability to design, build, launch, and operate microsats. Used offensively, maneuvering microsats can inspect and interfere with operations of orbiting assets. India, Russia, China, and Japan all have the ability to launch microsats as secondary payloads to low Earth orbit (LEO) and geosynchronous Earth orbit (GEO). "Parasitic" microsats/nanosatellites could also be launched inside the structure of primary payloads without the knowledge of the launch provider and deployed at GEO without detection.

Directed-Energy Weapons

Directed-energy weapons include laser, RF, and particle-beam weapons. Directed-energy weapons are considered "standoff" weapons because they are primarily either ground- or air-based systems that never get very close to their target. Most of these concepts are technically sophisticated and attack the target from longer ranges than most kinetic interceptors. In addition, these technologies are capable of engaging multiple targets, whereas interceptors tend to be single-shot systems. Additionally, if the geometric conditions are right, directed-energy weapons can acquire and attack their targets in seconds, whereas kinetic-interceptor engagement times tend to be much longer. Finally, standoff directed-energy weapons provide the enemy with a degree of deniability. This is because the attack is relatively quick—probably no intelligence indicators associated with it—and because the degradation of the target spacecraft may not be immediately apparent, making it difficult to figure out when and where the attack actually occurred.[13]

Laser Weapons. Laser systems, including coherent radiation, aligned waveform, and other devices operating at or near the optical wavelengths, operate by delivering energy onto the surface of the target. The gradual or rapid absorption of this energy leads to several forms of thermal damage. Generally, an antisensor laser weapon could be used against satellites at any altitude. This leads to the requirement for the laser beam to propagate over very long ranges (tens to hundreds or even thousands of kilometers) and still deliver lethal power to the target. This results in demanding weapon-system requirements: high laser power (megawatt class lasers are required for most long-range, nonsensor blinding missions), high beam quality, large-aperture beam director, extremely stable beam pointing system, and so forth. These factors make laser weapons extremely complex.[14]

The effectiveness of a given laser system is dependent upon the specific operational elements of the laser. Due to the complexity of conditioning the beam to compensate for atmospheric effects, space-based laser weapons have been studied for years, as alternatives to ground- and air-based laser weapons.[15]

Radio Frequency Weapons. RF weapons concepts include ground- and space-based RF emitters that fire an intense burst of radio energy at a satellite, disabling electronic components. RF weapons are usually divided into two categories: high-power micro-wave (HPM) weapons and ultrawideband (UWB), or video pulse, weapons.[16]

UWB weapons generate RF radiation covering a wide frequency spectrum—nominally from about 100 MHz to more than 1 GHz—with limited directivity. Because of the UWB weapon's low-energy spectral density and directivity, permanent damage to electronic components would be very difficult to achieve, except at very short ranges. The UWB enters through the satellite's antenna at its receive frequency, as well as through openings in the system's shielding. If enough power is applied, the received radiation may cause major damage to the satellite's internal communications hardware. However, in many cases, UWB weapons will simply cause system upset, which may persist only while the target is being irradiated or may require operator intervention to return the satellite to its normal state.[17]

HPM weapons generate an RF beam at a very narrow frequency band, in the 100 MHz to 100 GHz range, with higher directivity. The HPM devices operate by penetrating through antennas or into the interior of the target through cracks, apertures, or seams with longer wavelength radiation. The penetrating radiation causes damage or disruption as it is absorbed by internal electronic components.[18]

Unlike traditional electronic warfare, the induced electrical energy does not need to be collected by a receiver in-band and made to look precisely like a train of specific input signals. Rather, UWB and HPM can produce so-called backdoor effects from overwhelming circuits with induced signals and high-power transients that penetrate the system's openings or cracks. It is difficult to close off these paths, since features such as openings and electrical wiring are essential to system operation. Because disruption and upset require only a few volts at extremely low current levels, the power levels needed to achieve these effects can be fairly small, and the matching of signal waveforms can be quite imprecise.[19]

Particle-Beam Weapons. Particle-beam weapon concepts are space-based systems that fire an intense beam of elementary particles at a satellite, disabling electronic components. These weapons accelerate atomic particles, such as negative hydrogen or deuterium ions, to relativistic velocities (significant fractions of the speed of light) toward their target. They can cause permanent damage by radiating enough energy to overload the satellite's internal electronics. Since these accelerated particles cannot penetrate the atmosphere, weapons using this technology against satellites must be based in space. Particle-beam weapons include both charged particle-beam (CPB) weapons and neutral particle-beam (NPB) weapons. Charged particle beams do not propagate in straight lines in outer space because of the earth's magnetic field. Because of this, their utility in the counterspace role appears limited. However, neutral particles can propagate long, linear distances in outer space.[20]

Interceptor Types

Interceptor systems and system concepts can be divided into a number of distinct categories: low-altitude, direct-ascent interceptors; low-altitude, short-duration orbital interceptors; high-altitude, short-duration orbital interceptors; and long-duration

278

orbital interceptors. These weapons are typically ground- or air-launched into intercept trajectories or orbits that are nearly the same as the intended target satellite. Radar or optical systems on board the satellite guide it to close proximity of the target satellite.[21]

Low-Altitude, Direct-Ascent Interceptors. Low-altitude, direct-ascent interceptors are launched on a booster from the ground or from an aircraft into a suborbital trajectory that is designed to intersect that of an LEO satellite. Because these interceptor systems are on a direct suborbital trajectory, the on-orbit lifespan of these systems is measured in minutes, making them the simplest type of interceptor weapons to design, build, and test.[22] The US Navy's intercept of a failed US intelligence satellite in February 2008 is an example of a low-altitude, direct-ascent interceptor.

Low- and High-Altitude, Short-Duration Orbital Interceptors. A low-altitude, short-duration orbital system is an interceptor that is launched from the ground into a temporary parking orbit from which it maneuvers to engage and attack the target satellite. A high-altitude, short-duration weapon is an interceptor that is launched from the ground into a temporary parking orbit from which it maneuvers to attack a high-altitude satellite. Because these interceptor systems enter a temporary parking orbit, the on-orbit lifespan of these systems is measured in hours, which makes them slightly more complex than direct-ascent weapons.[23]

Long-Duration Orbital Interceptors. The long-duration orbital system is an orbital interceptor that is launched into a storage orbit for an extended period of time, possibly months to years, before it maneuvers to engage and attack the target satellite. The weapon may be stand-alone or covertly placed on or in a "mothership" satellite. Feasible concepts, in order of increasing sophistication, include the farsat, nearsat, space mine, fragmentation or pellet ring, and space-to-space missile. Farsats are parked in a storage orbit away from their targets and maneuver to engage them on command. Nearsats are deployed and stay near their targets to inspect and attack on command. Space mines are parked in orbits that intersect the target's orbit and are detonated during a periodic close encounter. Fragmentation or pellet rings are vast quantities of small, nonmaneuvering objects that are dispersed from one or more satellites in such a way that an artificial Earth-orbiting ring is created. Satellites flying through the ring are damaged or destroyed. Space-to-space missiles are rocket-propelled interceptors launched from an orbiting carrier platform into an orbit that intercepts the intended target.[24]

Nuclear Threat

A nuclear explosion can affect all three segments that make up the US architecture at the same time. Since the effects of nuclear detonation move out rapidly and permeate all space, no satellites have to be targeted directly. The aggressor can simply aim the weapon at an empty point in space, reducing the requirement for a highly accurate missile-guidance system. The environmental effects of a nuclear explosion have been divided into three categories: electromagnetic pulse (EMP), transient nuclear radiation, and thermal radiation. As for the success of a nuclear strike, it depends on three basic factors: the type of warhead (e.g., thermal nuclear, enhanced radiation, and yield), the altitude of the detonation, and the distance of the burst from its intended target.[25]

Electromagnetic Pulse

EMP affects the ground, communication, and space segments of our systems. The EMP threat is unique in two respects. First, its peak field amplitude and rise rate are high. These features of EMP will induce potentially damaging voltages and currents in unprotected electronic circuits and components. Second, the area covered by an EMP signal can be immense. As a consequence, large portions of extended power and communications networks, for example, can be simultaneously put at risk. Such far-reaching effects are peculiar to EMP. Neither natural phenomena nor any other nuclear weapon effects are so widespread.[26]

Within nanoseconds (billionths of a second) of a nuclear detonation, any electrical system is threatened by EMP. One significant factor in EMP effects is the amount of coverage desired. The area of exposure will depend on the size of the yield and the altitude of the burst. Based on the line-of-sight factor, the higher the burst altitude, the greater its coverage. Because of this factor, high-altitude electromagnetic pulse (HEMP) is the highest concern, as the entire electronic spectrum could be affected.[27]

Military systems must survive all aspects of the EMP, from the rapid spike of the early-time events to the longer-duration heave signal. One of the principal problems in assuring such survival is the lack of test data from actual high-altitude nuclear explosions. Only a few such experiments were carried out, and at that time the theoretical understanding of the phenomenon of HEMP was relatively poor. No high-altitude tests have been conducted by the United States since 1963. In addition to the more familiar high-yield tests mentioned above, three small devices were exploded in the Van Allen belts as part of Project Argus. That experiment was intended to explore the methods by which electrons were trapped and traveled along magnetic field lines.[28]

Effects on Space Assets

Perhaps the most devastating threat could come from a low-yield nuclear device, on the order of 50 kilotons, detonated a few hundred kilometers above the atmosphere. A nuclear detonation would increase ambient radiation to a level sufficient to severely damage nearby satellites and reduce the lifetime of satellites in LEO from years to months or less. The lingering effects of radiation could make satellite operations futile for many months. Even nuclear detonations in the 10-kiloton range could have significant effects on satellites for many months. To execute this mission, all that is needed is a rocket and a simple nuclear device. Countries such as Iran, North Korea, Iraq, and Pakistan possess missiles that could carry warheads to the necessary altitudes and either have, or are believed to be developing, nuclear weapons.[29]

Conclusion

Although we have historically considered our CONUS space facilities safe, the events of 11 September 2001 demonstrate that enemy tactics can affect us anywhere. As a result, we must consider the vulnerability of our ground segment throughout the spectrum of conflict—from peace to war. Easy access by anyone with hostile intent makes our ground segment more vulnerable—attacking the ground segment can be as easy as planting an improvised explosive device. Moreover, denying or deceiving the communications link segment is technologically achievable for any adversary we might face. On the other hand, attack against the space segment requires money, know-how, and access, which limits the potential adversaries to a few countries. Increasingly, we are relying on commercial systems for our space operations, which are usually not "hardened" against potential threats as our military systems are. This further complicates the issue of insuring survivability of our space capabilities. In conclusion, our space systems must be regarded as a system made up of multiple parts—ground segment, link segment, and space segment. All of these are essential to the accomplishment of the space mission, and all must be survivable.

Notes

1. Commission to Assess US National Security Space Management and Organization, *Report of the Commission*, 11 January 2001, http://space.au.af.mil/space_commission/index.htm (accessed 11 May 2009), 13.

2. Tom Wilson, "Threats to United States Space Capabilities," prepared for the Commission to Assess US National Security Space Management and Organization, http://www.fas.org/spp/eprint/article05.html#10 (accessed 11 May 2009).

3. Ibid.

4. Ibid.

5. Ibid.

6. Ibid.

7. Col James G. Lee, "Counterspace Operations for Information Dominance," in *Beyond the Paths of Heaven: The Emergence of Space Power Thought*, ed. Col Bruce M. DeBlois (Maxwell AFB, AL: Air University Press, 1999), 281.

8. Ibid., 281–82.

9. Wilson, "Threats to United States Space Capabilities."

10. Dennis Howe, ed., *FOLDOC: Free On-Line Dictionary of Computing*, http://www.foldoc.org (accessed 11 May 2009).

11. Lee, "Counterspace Operations," 284.

12. Desmond Ball, "Assessing China's ASAT Program," *Austral Special Report 07-14S*, 14 June 2007, http://www.nautilus.org/~rmit/forum-reports/0714s-ball/fig1-schematic.html (accessed 11 May 2009).

13. Wilson, "Threats to United States Space Capabilities."

14. Ibid.

15. Ibid.

16. Ibid.

17. Ibid.

18. Ibid.

19. Ibid.

20. Ibid.

21. Ibid.

22. Ibid.

23. Ibid.

24. Ibid.

25. Ibid.

26. "Nuclear Weapon EMP Effects," Federation of American Scientists, http://www.fas.org/nuke/intro/nuke/emp.htm (accessed 11 May 2009).

27. Ibid.

28. Ibid.

29. Commission to Assess US National Security Space Management and Organization, *Report*, 21.

Chapter 22

Spacecraft Design, Structure, and Operations

Maj Brian W. Garino, USAF; and Maj Jeffrey D. Lanphear, USAF

Spacecraft are fairly complex vehicles by nature. Thousands of parts and pieces are combined and packed into the nose cone of a rocket and blasted into the cold vacuum of space. Once in orbit, the spacecraft must supply the payload with electrical power, keeping it not-too-hot and not-too-cold, pointing its sensors in the right direction, and processing its data. This chapter will attempt to explain how these functions are accomplished.

A typical spacecraft consists of a mission payload and the bus (or platform). The bus is made up of five supporting subsystems: structures, thermal control, electrical power, attitude control, and telemetry, tracking, and commanding (TT&C).

Structures Subsystem

The functions of the structures subsystem are to enclose, protect, and support the other spacecraft subsystems and to provide a mechanical interface with the launch vehicle. Structural members provide the mating and attachment points for subsystem components such as batteries, propellant tanks, electronics modules, and so on. The structure must also sustain the stresses and loads experienced during environmental testing, launch, perigee and apogee firings, and deployment of booms, solar arrays, and antennas.

Noises, high g-forces, and vibrations can be especially severe on the spacecraft during launch. Acoustic noise is at its highest in the early stages of the launch and is transmitted from the rocket motors by the air through the fairings or housing and into the spacecraft. Steady loads are transmitted through the structure as the rockets accelerate the spacecraft to the velocities required for injection into orbit.[1] A wide range of vibration frequencies is transmitted through the spacecraft supports from the rocket motors. Pyrotechnic devices and springs send sudden shocks through the structure as the spacecraft separates from the booster and various components are deployed into their operational configurations.

When the spacecraft reaches its final orbital position, the loads on the spacecraft are greatly reduced in the zero-gravity environment, but the alignment requirements of sensitive instruments can be very rigorous. In addition, there are many environmental protection factors that exist in space that must also be considered. The designer must satisfy all these requirements while minimizing the structure's mass and cost.[2]

Structure Types

There are two main types of satellite structure: open truss and body mounted. An open truss structure has a specific shape to it (fig. 22-1), usually a box or a cylinder.

Inside the body of the spacecraft is a honeycomb structure where the equipment boxes are attached. In a body-mounted structure, equipment is attached directly to the structural elements. These satellites do not have a specific shape to them. There are also combinations of these two structure types in which part of the satellite has a shape such as a box, with some equipment attached to the exterior.[3]

Inflatable structures are the latest trend in spacecraft structures. Inflatable structures have the advantage of low mass and low volume during launch, but following deployment, they can expand to volumes not achievable in rigid structures (fig. 22-2).

Figure 22-1. Space-based infrared telescope facility. (NASA image)

Materials

When designing a component for structural use in a spacecraft, the engineer must at some point in the analysis decide what materials to use (fig. 22-3). Thousands of different materials are used in making a spacecraft. Many of them serve dual or triple roles to save weight and avoid complexity. For example, the frame of a spacecraft could be a heat sink and electrical ground as well as the main structure.

During its lifetime, the spacecraft will be subjected to severe conditions. These may include various mechanical loads, vibrations, thermal shocks, electrical charges, radiation, or a chemical and particulate environment. The material selected must meet various standards for strength, stiffness, weight, thermal expansion, and melting point. Other properties must also be examined since structural materials often serve multiple roles.

Figure 22-2. Spartan 207 inflatable antenna. (NASA photo)

Finally, the availability, formability, and ease with which parts can be machined out of a particular material will influence the selection process. Some materials are scarce and expensive. Others are extremely brittle or soft. Some are hard to cast, forge, or machine. Almost every material presents some type of fabrication problem.

Aluminum, magnesium, titanium, and beryllium are the elements that make up the major lightweight alloys used in space vehicles. They are all much lighter than steel and are nonmagnetic. Aluminum alloys are the most widely used struc-

Figure 22-3. Various materials evident in a spacecraft. (NASA photo)

284

tural materials. Their strength-to-weight ratio exceeds steel, which, combined with their availability and ease of manufacture, makes them very desirable.

Magnesium is lighter than aluminum, but not as strong. It is useful for lower-strength, lightweight applications at temperatures up to 400° Fahrenheit (F). Fabrication is similar to that of aluminum in that parts can be made and joined together in much the same way. Corrosion in the presence of moisture is a problem with magnesium and its alloys; coatings and finishes are needed for protection.

Titanium can replace aluminum in higher-temperature environments, as it has the ability to remain strong at temperatures up to 1,200° F. In situations where a structure must be lightweight and strong when subjected to 400–1,200° F, aluminum cannot be used. Unfortunately, titanium is not as light or durable as aluminum. It has a tendency to become brittle at low temperatures and when placed under repeated loads. It is also more difficult to weld.

Beryllium is used to make phenomenally light alloys. Its strength is close to that of steel, and its density is comparable to aluminum. This makes for extremely stiff, lightweight structures. An added plus is beryllium's ability to retain its properties at temperatures up to 1,000° F. However, beryllium is more difficult to fabricate than aluminum and is susceptible to surface damage while it is being machined due to its brittle properties. An additional consideration is beryllium's toxicity. It presents a serious health hazard to unprotected workers. Finally, beryllium is more costly than many other metals.

Graphite, plastics, nylon, and ceramics comprise the nonmetallic materials used in spacecraft. Graphite is not usually thought of as a structural material. It is weak and brittle at room temperature, but it is widely used as a thermal protection material. Since the strength of graphite improves with higher temperature up to about 4,500° F, it is very possible that vehicles which must enter Jupiter's atmosphere or orbit very close to the sun may have some structural parts made of graphite.

Plastic has many desirable qualities as a spacecraft component material. It is very inexpensive, readily available, and easy to fabricate into intricate shapes. It is also durable and is a good electrical and thermal insulator. For spacecraft interiors, where temperatures are relatively low, plastic may be a good replacement for light alloys. Nylon has a unique advantage in that mechanisms made of it may not need lubrication. Nylon may be the optimal material for low-power gear trains in space.

The general property of ceramics is that they are extremely weak in tension and very brittle. They can, however, withstand very high temperatures, protecting themselves by gradual erosion. Hence, ceramics are useful in some radomes, jet vanes, leading edges, and solid-rocket nozzles.

In the future, aerospace fabrication will make greater use of composites. Composites are two or more materials manufactured together to form a single piece that can have almost any property an engineer specifies. Uni- or omni-directional strength, resistance to high temperatures, and resistance to corrosives are a few of these properties. Examples of composites are fiberglass and carbon epoxy, both structural materials, and carbon composite, a thermal protection material used on leading edges of the space shuttle.[4]

Thermal Control Subsystem

The sources of thermal energy in a spacecraft include people (in manned missions), electronic equipment, frictional heat generated as the vehicle leaves or reenters the atmosphere, the sun, heat reflected from the earth (altitude dependent), and Earth thermal radiation (altitude dependent).

The purpose of the spacecraft thermal-control subsystem is to control the temperature of individual components, which ensures proper operation through the life of the mission. Some components must be maintained below a critical temperature. For example, high temperature limits the reliability and lifetime of transistors due to increased electromigration effects. Optical sensors require that the temperature stay within a critical range to minimize lens distortion, and hydrazine propellant must be maintained above a critical temperature (10^9 Celsius [C]), or it will freeze.[5] The thermal control process has to meet the requirements of all subsystems. Balance between structural and thermal requirements is necessary to achieve the best spacecraft configuration to permit proper thermal balance.

The thermal control subsystem uses every practical means available to regulate the temperature on board a satellite. Selection of the proper thermal control system requires knowledge of mission requirements as well as the operational environment. Temperatures within space vehicles are affected by both internal and external heat sources.[6] Thermal control techniques can be divided into two classes: passive thermal control and active thermal control.[7]

Passive Thermal Control

A passive thermal-control system maintains temperatures within the desired temperature range by control of the conductive and radiative heat paths. This is accomplished through the selection of the geometrical configuration and thermo-optical properties of the surfaces. Such a system does not have moving parts or moving fluids and does not require electrical power. Passive systems offer the advantages of high reliability due to the absence of moving parts or fluid, effectiveness over wide temperature ranges, and light weight. A disadvantage is low thermal capacity. Passive thermal-control techniques include thermal coatings, thermal insulations, heat sinks, and phase-change materials.

Spacecraft external surfaces radiate energy to space. Because these surfaces are also exposed to external sources of energy, their radiative properties must be selected to achieve a balance between internally dissipated energy, external sources of energy, and the heat rejected into space. The two properties of primary importance are the emittance of the surface and solar absorbency. Paints and coatings can be used to reduce reflection and to increase or decrease absorption of heat or light energy. Two or more coatings can be combined in an appropriate pattern to obtain a desired average value of solar absorbance and emittance (i.e., a checkerboard pattern of white paint and polished metal).[8]

On radiators, low absorbance and high emittance are desirable to minimize solar input and maximize heat rejection to space. The initial values of a radiator coating are important because of degradation over the lifetime of the mission. Degradation can be significant for all white paints. For this reason, the use of a second surface mirror-coating system is preferred. An example of such a coating is vapor-deposited silver on 0.2 millimeter (mm)-thick fused silica, creating an optical solar reflector. Degradation of thermal coatings in the space environment results from the combined effects of high-vacuum, charged particles and ultraviolet radiation from the sun.[9]

286

Thermal insulation is designed to reduce the rate of heat flow per unit of area between two boundary surfaces at specified temperatures. Insulation may be a single, homogeneous material such as low-thermal-conductivity foam or an evacuated multilayer insulation in which each layer acts as a low-emittance radiation shield and is separated by low-conductance spacers.

Multilayer insulation consists of several layers of closely spaced radiation-reflecting shields, which are placed perpendicular to the heat-flow direction. The aim of the radiation shields is to reflect a large percentage of the radiation the layer receives from warmer surfaces.[10] Multilayer insulations are widely used in the thermal control of spacecraft and components in order to accomplish the following:

- Minimize heat flow to or from the component.

- Reduce the amplitude of temperature fluctuations in components due to time-varying external radiative heat flux.

- Minimize the temperature gradients in components caused by varying directions of incoming external radiative heat.

Heat sinks are materials of large thermal capacity, placed in thermal contact with the components whose temperature is to be controlled. When heat is generated by the components, the temperature rise is restricted because the heat is conducted into the sink. The sink will then dispose of this heat to adjacent locations through conduction or radiation. Heat sinks are commonly used to control the temperature of those items of electronic equipment that have high dissipation or a cyclical variation in power dissipation.

Solid liquid phase-change materials (PCM) present an attractive approach to spacecraft passive thermal control when the incident orbital heat fluxes, or onboard equipment dissipation, change widely for short periods. The PCM thermal control system consists primarily of a container filled with a material capable of undergoing a chemical phase change. When the temperature of spacecraft surfaces increases, the PCM will absorb excess heat through melting. When the temperature decreases, the PCM gives heat back and solidifies. Phase-change materials used for temperature control are those with melting points close to the desired temperature of the equipment. Then the latent heat associated with the phase change provides a large thermal inertia as the temperature of the equipment passes through the melting point. However, the phase-change material cannot prevent a further temperature rise when all the material is melted.

One of the more common methods of rejecting heat generated from onboard electronics is to mount the electronics just inside the spacecraft bus structure. Thus, the energy is conducted over a short path to an external spacecraft thermal-control surface (frequently referred to as a radiator and sometimes as a shearplate). This surface is usually coated with a low-solar-absorbance/high-infrared-emittance coating (usually a white paint). Such surfaces are usually positioned by spacecraft orientation to point to deep space. Thus, the natural environment is minimized or eliminated, and maximum heat rejection occurs.[11]

Active Thermal Control

Passive thermal control may not be adequate and efficient for the applications where the equipment has a narrowly specified temperature range or where there is great

287

variation in equipment power dissipation and solar flux during the mission. In such cases, temperature sensors may be placed at critical equipment locations. When critical temperatures are reached, mechanical devices are actuated to modify the thermo-optical properties of surfaces, or electrical power heaters turn on or off to compensate for variations in the equipment power dissipation. Active thermal-control techniques include louvers, electrical heaters, and cooling systems.

For a spacecraft in which the changes in internal power dissipation or external heat fluxes are severe, it is not possible to maintain the spacecraft equipment temperatures within the allowable design temperature limits unless the ratio of absorbance to emissivity can be varied. A very popular and reliable method that effectively gives a variable ratio is through the use of louvers. When the louver blades are open, the effective ratio is low (low absorbtivity, high emissivity); when the blades are closed, the effective ratio is high (high absorbtivity, low emissivity). The louvers also reduce the dependence of spacecraft temperatures on the variation of the thermo-optical properties of the radiator.[12]

Electrical heaters (resistance elements) are used to maintain temperatures above minimum allowable levels. Electrical heaters can be turned on or off from the ground, thermostatically controlled, or continuously on. In most cases, satellites have redundant sets of heaters and thermostats to increase reliability.

Some sensors, especially infrared sensors, require constant cold temperatures. These types of sensors must be isolated from heat-producing system components and may need a further cooling system to function properly. Depending on mission length, the cooling system can be either an open- or closed-loop system. On shorter missions, an open-loop system using an expendable coolant may be selected for its simplicity and higher reliability. Expendable systems commonly depend on the cooling effects of materials undergoing phase change from a solid or liquid to a gaseous form. The gas is then vented out into space after use. For longer missions, closed-loop systems are needed. These systems normally depend on a cryogenic cooler using a liquid such as nitrogen, which is recirculated between the sensor and the cooler.

Radiators are another type of closed-loop system used in cooling. They are active due to the circulation of fluid through the system. Radiator systems require large surface areas to dissipate heat into space, a major disadvantage of this type of system.[13]

Electrical Power Subsystem

A successful mission is dependent on the reliable functioning of the power subsystem. The stringent demands on performance, weight, volume, reliability, and cost make the design of the spacecraft power subsystem a challenging endeavor. Significant advances have been made in this area, resulting in the development of more reliable and lightweight power systems. At the same time, research continues to develop new and novel designs that will maximize reliability while further lowering weight.

Elements of a Spacecraft Power Subsystem

The amount of electrical power a spacecraft requires is dictated by the mission. Uninterrupted power must often be supplied for up to 10 years or more. The generation of electrical power on board a spacecraft generally involves four basic elements:

1. A source of energy, such as direct solar radiation, nuclear power, or chemical reactions.

2. A device for converting the energy into electricity.

3. A device for storing the electrical energy to meet peak and/or eclipse demands.

4. A system for conditioning, charging, discharging, regulating, and distributing the generated electrical energy at specified voltage levels.

Figure 22-4. Solar panels provide energy for Earth-orbiting satellites. (NASA photo)

The most favorable energy source for Earth-orbiting satellites is solar radiation (fig. 22-4). Because Earth-orbiting satellites pass into and out of Earth's shadow, solar radiation must normally be augmented by another source. Chemical sources such as rechargeable storage batteries serve this purpose. These batteries employ electrochemical processes and have typical efficiencies of 75 percent.[14] When a satellite is in Earth's shadow, it often switches over to battery power, and when it is in the sunlight, the solar arrays power the spacecraft (as well as recharge the batteries).

As an alternative to solar energy, nuclear-powered radioactive isotope generators have also been used. This power source is especially practical for exploration missions to the outer planets, where solar radiation levels are low. For example, the solar radiation reduces from about 54 watts per square foot in the vicinity of Mars to about 4.6 watts per square foot near Jupiter. It therefore becomes necessary to use other primary sources of energy for spacecraft missions to Jupiter and beyond.[15]

Photovoltaic and solar thermionic devices both harness energy from the sun. The photovoltaic energy source uses potential differences created by electromagnetic radiation illuminating semiconductors to provide power. The solar thermionic system uses a temperature gradient set up across different types of semiconductors to create a flow of current. This method is seldom used.

Choosing a spacecraft power source for a particular mission may be difficult. Continuous power requirements, solar eclipse conditions, and power subsystem weight are all major factors in the final decision. Sometimes a combination of energy sources may be required.[16]

Solar Arrays

Solar arrays are mounted on the satellite in various forms. They may be body mounted, stationary, or on directional, steerable wings. A solar array consists of solar cells that convert solar energy into electric power by the photovoltaic effect (fig. 22-5).

The power output of a single cell is quite low, so the individual cells are arranged in series to provide the desired voltage and in parallel to achieve the desired current requirements. In addition, solar array modules are constructed to minimize power loss resulting from individual solar cell failures. Without this precaution, the loss of a single cell would create an open circuit for that entire string, and the output from that string would be totally lost.[17]

Some satellites cannot use deployable solar arrays because of the type of attitude control system they employ. Spin-stabilized satellites cannot support large deployable solar arrays because of the stresses placed on the panels while the satellite rotates. For this reason, spin-stabilized satellites require body-mounted solar arrays (fig. 22-6). Body mounting is a very simple approach that utilizes available space on the satellite surface.

Some solar arrays are directional. A solar array drive is employed to control the angle of the arrays so they are always perpendicular to the sun's rays. In contrast, stationary arrays are deployable arrays locked into position relative to the spacecraft body once deployed.

The power of a solar array varies with time due to:

- The variation in solar intensity.
- Variation in the angle between the solar array surface and solar rays.
- Radiation degradation in solar-cell power characteristics.
- Array contamination by thruster propellants and so forth.
- Temperature of the solar array.

Figure 22-5. International Space Station with large deployable solar arrays. (NASA photo)

Figure 22-6. Spacecraft with body-mounted solar array. (Air Force photo)

When designers select the proper size of the solar arrays, it is important that they consider these factors so that the satellite will have enough power to remain mission effective to the end of its life.[18]

Solar array size is driven by a combination of satellite power requirements and the efficiency of the solar cells to convert solar energy to electrical energy. Thermal control of the solar array panels is achieved by the absorption of solar radiation by the solar cells on the front surfaces of the panels and reemission of infrared energy from the front and back of the panels.

The power from the solar cell is maximized when the angle of incidence of illuminating light is zero (i.e., it is perpendicular to the solar cell surface). The power decreases as the angle of incidence deviates from zero. The primary reason for the increased loss of power at greater angles of incidence is the change in reflection coefficients at large angles.[19]

Storage Batteries

In most spacecraft power systems that use solar radiation, the storage battery is the main source of continuous power. Batteries must provide continuous power to the spacecraft during peak power cycles and eclipse periods. The frequency and duration of eclipse periods depend on the spacecraft orbit.

The eclipse seasons in geostationary orbits occur twice per year, during spring and autumn. These eclipse seasons are 45 days long and are centered on the vernal and autumnal equinoxes. There is one eclipse period per 24 hours with the maximum period being 72 minutes. The batteries discharge during an eclipse and are charged during the sunlight period. So the charge-discharge cycles for any storage battery on board a spacecraft in geosynchronous orbit will be about 90 per year.

In the case of low-orbiting satellites, the number of eclipses increases as the altitude of the satellite decreases. For a 550 km circular orbit, there will be about 15 eclipses per day. The maximum shadow duration is about 36 minutes during each 96-minute orbit. There will be about 5,500 charge-discharge cycles per year in this orbit. Depending on the orbit inclination, the spacecraft may be in continuous sunlight for long periods several times a year.

As mentioned above, batteries are necessary to maintain steady, reliable spacecraft power. A battery is an electrochemical device that stores energy in the chemical form and then converts it into electrical energy during discharge. Chemical reactions taking place inside the battery produce electrical energy whose magnitude is dependent upon various cell characteristics (i.e., individual cell voltage, efficiency of the electro-chemical reaction, size of the cell, etc.).[20]

Batteries are classified as either primary or secondary. Primary batteries are used on spacecraft in which the battery is the only source of electrical power and cannot be recharged. Thus, primary batteries are used for short-duration missions usually of less than a week. Primary batteries have the advantages of being cheap, reliable, and able to deliver relatively large amounts of energy per pound of battery (20–100 watt-hours/lb.).

Secondary batteries are rechargeable. They convert chemical energy into electrical energy during discharge and convert electrical back to chemical during recharge. This process can be repeated many times. Secondary batteries are used for longer-duration missions, such as those of the Defense Meteorological Satellite Program (DMSP), Defense Satellite Communications System (DSCS), and many others, in which solar arrays are the primary source of power. The advantages of secondary batteries are:

- Capability of accepting and delivering power at high rates (eclipse operations and peak power demands).
- Large number of charge-discharge cycles or long charge-discharge cycle life under a wide range of conditions.
- Long operational lifespan.
- Low volume.
- Low cost.
- High, proven reliability.

The disadvantages of secondary batteries are:

- The memory-effect process.
- The complexity and expense of charge-discharge monitoring equipment.
- Low energy-storage capability per pound of battery (6–45 watt-hours/lb.).

There are many types of secondary batteries available. However, only some are considered suitable for space applications. The nickel-cadmium (Ni-Cad) battery is probably one of the most common batteries used in spacecraft today. The primary factors affecting the useful life of a Ni-Cad battery are temperature, depth of discharge, and overcharging. Prolonged exposure of a Ni-Cad battery to high temperature will hasten the breakdown of the battery's internal components, while repeated overcharging at low temperatures can result in pressure buildup within the battery. Therefore, battery temperature is an extremely critical parameter. It is common practice to use radiators and heaters to keep battery temperature between $4°$ and $24°$ C ($39–75°$ F).[21]

Repeated deep battery discharges tend to damage the internal structure, causing cracks. These cracks absorb electrolyte and gradually dry out the battery. For a synchronous orbit application of seven to 10 years, a battery will encounter approximately 1,000 charge-discharge cycles over its lifetime. For this number of cycles, Ni-Cad battery depth of discharge is generally limited to between 50 and 60 percent of maximum capacity.

The batteries exhibit a gradual decay of terminal voltage during successive discharge periods. This effect is most pronounced when the charge-discharge cycle is repetitive and is referred to as the memory effect. When the battery is cycled to a fixed depth of discharge, the active material that is not being used gradually becomes unavailable, resulting in an effective increase in depth of discharge. In addition to the gradual decay of discharge voltage, the batteries also exhibit a tendency toward the divergence of the individual cell voltages during charge and discharge. Battery performance can be restored to a certain extent by reconditioning. A typical reconditioning process for a rechargeable battery consists of effecting a deep discharge and then recharging at a high rate. Reconditioning is a process regularly begun before eclipse season on many spacecraft. Procedures to enhance battery life include maintaining batteries within a small temperature range, proper reconditioning, and trickle charging between eclipse seasons to prevent cadmium migration from negative electrodes to positive electrodes.[22]

Another type of secondary battery is the nickel-hydrogen battery (Ni-H$_2$). This battery is actually a hybrid battery–fuel cell device. It has a positive electrode, much like a conventional battery, and a fuel-cell negative electrode. Hydrogen gas is diffused onto a catalyst, usually platinum, at the negative electrode where the reaction occurs. High-pressure vessels (500 pounds per square inch [psi]) are required to store the hydrogen gas.

Nickel-hydrogen batteries are increasingly being used on newer spacecraft such as military strategic and tactical relay (Milstar) and replacement GPS satellites. Compared to Ni-Cad batteries, Ni-H$_2$ batteries have higher specific energy, can tolerate a higher number of discharge-recharge cycles, and operate at near-optimum output over a wider range of temperatures.[23]

The newest technology is the lithium-ion battery. Lithium-ion batteries offer a 300 to 400 percent increase in specific energy over older Ni-Cad batteries. For the satellite designer, this means reduced weight and volume (fig. 22-7).[23]

Nuclear Power

Most spacecraft nuclear-power generators are capable of delivering a range of power from a few watts up to several hundred. They have been

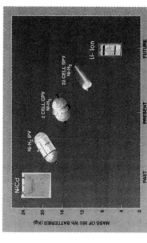

Figure 22-7. Advances in battery technology for space applications. (NASA graphic)

292

used very successfully on many deep space missions when solar flux levels were too low for photovoltaic solar cells to be effective.

Political and environmental issues with nuclear-powered satellites were underscored in 1978 after the Soviet Union's *COSMOS 954* plunged to Earth, scattering nuclear material over a large part of northwest Canada. From the beginning of the US space nuclear-power program, great emphasis has been placed on the safety of people and the protection of the environment. The operational philosophy adopted for orbital missions requires that the normal lifetime in space be long enough to permit radioactive decay of the radioisotope fuel to a safe level prior to reentry into the earth's biosphere. Stringent design and operational measures are used to minimize the potential interactions of the radioactive materials with the global populace and to keep any such exposure levels within limits established by international standards.

Like fuel cells, nuclear power generators have a major role in space exploration. There are two basic types of nuclear-powered generators. Radioisotope thermoelectric generators (RTG) rely on the decay of radioisotopes to produce electricity (fig. 22-8). The second type uses the heat from a nuclear fission reactor, much like nuclear generators on Earth, to produce electricity on the spacecraft.[24]

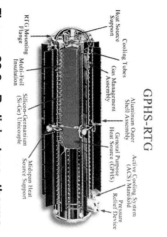

Figure 22-8. Radioisotope thermoelectric generator. (NASA graphic)

With an RTG, the radioactive material is encased in a special container from which the decay particles cannot escape. As the container absorbs energy produced by the alpha and beta particles, it is heated to a high temperature. This heat, in conjunction with a thermoelectric couple, produces electricity.

For the fission reactor, electricity is generated utilizing one of two basic reactor designs, either static or dynamic. The static system uses no moving parts and is usually preferred for this reason. The dynamic system uses the heat to perform mechanical work on a turboalternator assembly, which generates the electricity.

The advantages of nuclear energy include its ability to provide power for long-duration missions without reliance on solar illumination, high system reliability, and high power output versus low mass. Among the primary disadvantages of nuclear power systems are their high cost, shielding requirements (for fission reactors), the need for cooling systems to prevent thermal damage (fission reactors), and relatively low efficiencies (less than 18 percent efficiency). The high level of environmental concern and corresponding political ramifications are also factors that must be addressed with nuclear systems.[25]

Attitude Control Subsystem

Attitude control can be defined as the process of achieving and maintaining a desired orientation in space. An attitude control system is both the process and hardware by which the attitude is controlled. In general, an attitude control system consists of three components: navigation sensors, guidance section, and control section. An attitude maneuver is the process of reorienting the spacecraft from one attitude to another.

When conducting an attitude maneuver, a navigation sensor locates known reference targets such as the earth or sun to determine the spacecraft attitude. The guidance section determines when control is required, what torques are needed, and how to generate them. The control section includes hardware and actuators that supply the control torques.[26]

Active and Passive Control Systems

There are two categories of attitude control systems: active and passive. Active systems use continuous decision making and hardware (closed loop) to maintain the attitude. The most common sources of torque actuators for active control systems are thrusters, electromagnets, and reaction wheels. In contrast, passive attitude control makes use of environmental torques (open loop) to maintain the spacecraft orientation.[27] Gravity gradient and solar sails are common passive attitude-control methods.

Attitude control systems are highly mission dependent. The decision to use a passive or active control system or a combination of the two depends on mission pointing and stability requirements, mission orbital characteristics, and the control system's stability and response time. For example, a near-Earth, spin-stabilized spacecraft could use magnetic coils for attitude maneuvers and for periodic adjustment of the spin rate and attitude. Above synchronous altitudes, thrusters would be required for these functions because the earth's magnetic field is generally too weak at this altitude for effective magnetic maneuvers.

Any satellite orbit requires stabilization to increase its usefulness and effectiveness. For instance, when a satellite is not stabilized, it must use omni-directional antennas so that ground stations can receive its downlink information regardless of the satellite's orientation. This necessitates a high-power transmitter, and only a small portion of the total power is radiated to Earth. On the other hand, if there are means to stabilize the satellite so its directional antennas can be pointed at the earth, then lower power may be used to transmit information to the ground.

Spacecraft attitude-control systems incorporate four functions: satellite pointing, orbital transfer maneuvers, stabilization against torques, and satellite despin.[28] Solar arrays generate maximum power when they are perpendicular to the sun. In addition, some satellites carry scientific payloads which must observe a celestial body. In order to observe it, the spacecraft must be able to accurately find the object, track it, and point applicable sensors at it. Sensors must be accurately pointed at Earth to detect intercontinental ballistic missile (ICBM) launches as well as movement of troops, ships, aircraft, and so forth.

During orbital transfer maneuvers, it is necessary to be as precise as possible. Therefore, before firing, the attitude control system must meet stringent requirements on the accuracy of the spacecraft orientation. Aligning the spacecraft for perigee and apogee motor firing requires knowledge of the orbital characteristics at the time at which the motors are fired. This knowledge optimizes the transfer maneuver by ensuring the thruster firings are aligned with the desired orbital plane, minimizing both time and propellant requirements. If the spacecraft relies on solar energy for electrical power generation during the transfer maneuver, then the spacecraft must be optimized for maximum solar-cell illumination during the transfer. The spacecraft must be reoriented again after the completion of the transfer maneuver.[29]

Disturbance torques are environmental torques (i.e., drag, solar wind, magnetic field, gravity, and micrometeoroid impacts) or unintentional internal torques (i.e., liquid propellant slosh and center of gravity changes). Because these can never be totally eliminated, some form of attitude control system is required. Control torques, such as those produced by thrusters, are generated intentionally to control spacecraft attitude.[30]

Traditionally, spacecraft employing solid-propellant apogee motors have adopted spin stabilization during the parking and transfer phases. Even spacecraft that have active attitude control systems in their operational orbits are frequently spin stabilized in an initial (transfer orbit) phase of their mission. Spin stabilization during transfer orbit allows thermal control to be distributed evenly throughout the spacecraft. If the spacecraft is required to be three-axis stabilized, it must be despun before being injected into the appropriate attitude. If the spacecraft is to be spin stabilized, then the spin rate must be increased or decreased, depending on the final spin rate required.

Navigation Sensors

As mentioned before, sensors are required to determine the orientation of the spacecraft and its current state. The types of sensors used on a particular vehicle depend on several factors, including the type of spacecraft stabilization, orbital parameters, operational procedures, and required accuracy.[31]

Sun sensors are the most widely used sensor type. The sun is sufficiently bright to permit the use of simple, reliable sensors without discriminating among sources and with minimal power requirements. Many missions have solar experiments, most with sun-related thermal constraints, and nearly all require the sun for power. Consequently, many missions are concerned with the orientation of the spacecraft with respect to the sun. Attitude control systems are frequently based on the use of a sun reference pulse for thruster firings. Sun sensors are also used to protect sensitive equipment, such as star trackers, from harmful particle bombardment as well as to position solar arrays to achieve maximum power-conversion efficiency.

The orientation of the spacecraft to the earth is of obvious importance to navigation, communications, weather, and Earth-resources satellites. To a near-Earth satellite, the earth is the second brightest object and covers up to 40 percent of the sky. The earth presents an extended target to a sensor, compared with point source approximations used for sun and star detectors. Consequently, detecting only the presence of the earth is normally insufficient for even crude attitude determination, and nearly all sensors are designed to locate the earth's horizon.[32]

Unfortunately, the location of the earth's horizon is difficult to define because its atmosphere causes a gradual decrease in radiated intensity away from the true or hard horizon of the solid surface. Earth-resources satellites, such as LANDSAT (fig. 22-9), communications, and weather satellites, typically require a pointing accuracy of 0.05 degrees to less than a minute of arc, which is typically beyond the state of the art for horizon sensors.

Earth emanates infrared radiation. The infrared intensity in the 15-micron spectral band is relatively constant. Most horizon sensors now use the narrow 14- to 16-micron band. Use of the infrared spectral band avoids large attitude errors caused by visible light off high-altitude clouds. In addition, the operation of an infrared horizon sensor is unaffected when looking at the shadowed side of the earth. Infrared detectors are less susceptible to sunlight reflected by the spacecraft than are visible-light detectors and, therefore, avoid reflective problems. Sun interference problems are also reduced in the infrared band where the solar intensity is only 400 times that of the earth, compared with 30,000 in the visible spectrum.[33]

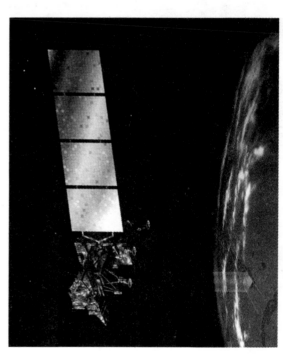

Figure 22-9. LANDSAT with Earth and star sensors. (NASA image)

Star sensors measure star coordinates and provide attitude information when these observed coordinates are compared with known star positions and magnitudes obtained from a star catalog. In general, star sensors are the most accurate of navigation sensors, achieving accuracy to the arc-second range. However, this capability is not achieved without considerable cost. Star sensors are heavy, expensive, and require more power than most other navigation sensors. In addition, computer software requirements are extensive because measurements must be preprocessed and identified before attitudes can be calculated. Because of their sensitivity, star sensors are subject to interference from the sun, earth, and other bright objects. In spite of these disadvantages, the accuracy and versatility of star sensors have led to applications in a variety of different spacecraft attitude control systems.

Star sensing and tracking devices can be divided into three major categories: star scanners, which use the spacecraft rotation to provide the searching and sensing function; gimbaled star trackers, which search out and acquire stars using mechanical action; and fixed-head star trackers, which have electronic searching and tracking capabilities over a limited field of view.

Stray light is a major problem for star sensors. Therefore, an effective sun shade is critical to star-sensor performance. Carefully designed light baffles are usually employed to minimize exposure of the optical system to sunlight and light scattering caused by dust particles, clouds, and portions of the spacecraft itself. Even with a well-designed sun shade, star sensors are typically inoperable within 30 to 60 degrees of the sun.

Star scanners used on spinning spacecraft are the simplest of all star scanners because they have no moving parts. Gimbaled star trackers are commonly used when the spacecraft must operate at a variety of attitudes. This type of tracker has a very small optical field of view (usually less than one degree). Gimbaled star trackers normally operate on a relatively small number of target stars. A major disadvantage of gimbaled star trackers is that the mechanical action of the gimbal reduces their long-term reliability. Fixed-head trackers use an electronic scan to search their field of view and acquire stars. They are generally smaller and lighter than gimbaled star trackers and have no moving parts.[34]

Magnetometers can be used to measure both the direction and magnitude of the earth's magnetic field to the milligauss accuracy. They are reliable, lightweight, and have low power requirements. They operate over a wide temperature range and have no moving parts. However, magnetometers are not accurate inertial navigation sensors because the earth's magnetic field is not completely known, and the models used to predict the magnetic field direction and magnitude at the spacecraft's position are subject to substantial errors. Furthermore, because the earth's magnetic field strength decreases with distance from the earth, residual spacecraft magnetic biases eventually dominate the total magnetic field measurement. Magnetometers are generally limited to spacecraft with altitudes below 1,000 km.[35]

A gyroscope is any instrument which uses a rapidly spinning mass to sense and respond to changes in the inertial orientation or its spin axis. There are three basic types of gyroscopes used on spacecraft: rate gyros, rate-integrating gyros, and control-moment gyros. The first two types are attitude sensors used to measure changes in the spacecraft orientation. Rate gyros measure spacecraft angular rates and are frequently part of a feedback system for spin-rate control or attitude stabilization. Rate-integrating gyros measure spacecraft angular displacement directly. Control-moment gyros generate control torques to change and maintain the spacecraft's orientation.[36]

Notes

1. Jerry Jon Sellers, *Understanding Space: An Introduction to Astronautics* (Boston: McGraw Hill, 2004), 501.
2. Ibid., 504.
3. Sellers, *Understanding Space*, 499.
4. Wiley J. Larson and James R. Wertz, *Space Mission Analysis and Design*, 3rd ed. (El Segundo, CA: Microcosm Press, 1999), 459–62.
5. Ibid., 428.
6. Ibid.
7. Sellers, *Understanding Space*, 481.
8. Wiley and Wertz, *Space Mission Analysis*, 431.
9. Ibid., 435–36.
10. Ibid., 4
11. Ibid., 440–46.
12. Ibid., 442.
13. Ibid., 439–42.
14. Sellers, *Understanding Space*, 465.
15. Ibid., 470.
16. Ibid.
17. Larson and Wertz, *Space Mission Analysis*, 411–18.
18. Ibid.
19. Ibid.
20. Ibid., 418–22.
21. Ibid.
22. Ibid.
23. NASA, "Advances in Battery Technology for Space Application," http://sbir.gsfc.nasa.gov/SBIR/successes/ss/7-015text.html (accessed 5 April 2008).
24. Sellers, *Understanding Space*, 470.

25. Ibid., 470–71.
26. Wiley and Wertz, *Space Mission Analysis*, 354–55.
27. Sellers, *Understanding Space*, 422.
28. Ibid., 407.
29. Ibid., 412.
30. Ibid., 413.
31. Wiley and Wertz, *Space Mission Analysis*, 371.
32. Sellers, *Understanding Space*, 418.
33. Ibid.
34. Ibid., 419.
35. Ibid., 421.
36. Ibid., 419.

Acronyms and Abbreviations

Δυ   delta-v
ω   argument of perigee
Ω   ascending node
2 SOPS   2nd Space Operations Squadron
3 SOPS   3rd Space Operations Squadron
4 SOPS   4th Space Operations Squadron
6 SOPS   6th Space Operations Squadron

A

a   semimajor axis
AA   attack assessment
AADC   area air defense commander
AB   air base
ABM   antiballistic missile
ACC   Air Combat Command
ACCE   air component coordination element
ACS   attitude control subsystem
ACSC   Air Command and Staff College
ADEOS   Advanced Earth Observation Satellite
ADRG   Arch Digitized Raster Graphics
ADSI   Air Defense Systems Integrator
AEHF   Advanced Extremely High Frequency
AEOS   Advanced Electro-Optical System
AEOS-L   Advanced Electro-Optical System long-wave infrared
AEP   architecture evolution plan
AEPDS   Advanced Electronic Processing and Dissemination System
AETF   air and space expeditionary task force
AFB   Air Force Base
AFCC   Air Force Communications Command
AFDD   Air Force doctrine document
AFGSC   Air Force Global Strike Command
AFM   Air Force manual
AFQTP   Air Force qualification training package
AFRL   Air Force Research Laboratory
AFS   Air Force station
AFSATCOM   Air Force satellite communications
AFSCN   Air Force Satellite Control Network
AFSOC   Air Force Special Operations Command
AFSPC   Air Force Space Command
AFSPC/CC   commander, Air Force Space Command
AFSPCPAM   Air Force Space Command pamphlet
AFSSS   Air Force Space Surveillance System
AFSST   Air Force space support team
AFTTP   Air Force tactics, techniques, and procedures

AFWA	Air Force Weather Agency
AIRS	Advanced Inertial Reference Sphere
Al	aluminum
ALCM	air-launched cruise missile
ALCOR	ARPA Lincoln C-Band Observable Radar
ALERT	attack and launch early reporting to theater
ALTAIR	ARPA Long-Range Tracking and Identification Radar
AMCS	alternate master control station
AMOS	Affordable Modular Optimized Satellite; Army Research Projects Agency (ARPA) Maui Optical Site
AMSU	advanced microwave sounding unit
AMWC	Alternate Missile Warning Center
AO	area of operations
AOC	air operations center (JP 1-02); air and space operations center (USAF); auxiliary output chip
AOI	area of interest
AOR	area of responsibility
APStar	Asia Pacific Telecommunications Satellite Company
APT	automatic picture transmission
ARFOR	Army forces
ARNS	aeronautical radio navigation service
ARPA	Advanced Research Projects Agency
ARSPACE	Army Space Command
ARSST	Army space support team
ARSTRAT	Army Strategic Command
ARTS	automated remote tracking station
A-S	antispoofing
ASARS-2	Advanced Synthetic Aperture Radar System-2
ASAT	antisatellite
ASCC	Alternate Space Control Center; Army service component command
ASCO	Arab Satellite Communications Organization
ASEDP	Army Space Exploitation Demonstration Program
AsiaSat	Asia Satellite Telecommunications Company
ASIS	Army Space Initiatives Study
ASPADOC	alternate space defense operations center
ASPO	Army Space Program Office
ATACMS	Army Tactical Missile System
ATO	air tasking order
ATV	automated transfer vehicle
AU	distance of Earth from the sun
AUST-T	Advanced Universal System Test Terminal
AUTONAV	autonomous navigation
AVHRR	advanced very high resolution radiometer
AWACS	Airborne Warning and Control System
AWC	Air War College
AWN	Automated Weather Network
AZA	auroral zone absorption

300

B

BDA — battle damage assessment
BIOT — British Indian Ocean Territory
BMD — ballistic missile defense
BMEWS — Ballistic Missile Early Warning System
BOA — battlefield ordnance awareness
BOC — binary offset carrier
bps — bits per second
BPSK — binary phase-shift keying
BSAT — Broadcasting Satellite System

C

c — linear eccentricity
C2 — command and control
C3 — command, control, and communications
C4 — command, control, communications, and computers
C4I — command, control, communications, and computers, and intelligence

C/A — course acquisition
CACS — command and control squadron
CALCM — conventional air-launched cruise missile
CANR — Canadian NORAD Region
CAOC — combined air operations center
CAP — Civil Air Patrol
CAV — common aero vehicle
CBERS — China-Brazil Earth Resources Satellite
CCD — camouflage, concealment, and deception
CCDR — combatant commander
CCIS — civil/commercial imagery system
CCS — constellation control station; Counter Communications System

CDF — commercial demonstration flight
CDR JFCC Space — commander, Joint Functional Component Command for Space
CDRUSSTRATCOM — commander, US Strategic Command
CEP — circular error probability
CERES — Central European Regional Satellite
CFACC — combined force air component commander (JP 1-02); combined force air and space component commander (USAF)

CGGE — CONUS Ground Gateway Element
CGS — CONUS ground station
ChinaSat — China Broadcast and Communications Satellite Corporation
CIA — Central Intelligence Agency
CIC — Combat Intelligence Correlator; Combined Intelligence Center

CINC	commander in chief
CIO	Central Imagery Office
CIR	color infrared
CIRA	Cospar International Reference Atmosphere
CJCS	chairman of the Joint Chiefs of Staff
CM	cruise missile
CMAS	Cheyenne Mountain Air Station
CME	coronal mass ejection
CMOC	Cheyenne Mountain Operations Center
CMR	Communication by Moon Relay
cm/s	centimeters per second
CNA	computer network attack
CND	computer network defense
CNES	Centre National d'Etudes Spatiales
CNO	chief of naval operations
CO_2	carbon dioxide
COA	course of action
COCOM	combatant command
COF	Columbus Orbital Facility
COMAFFOR	commander, Air Force forces
COMINT	communications intelligence
COMSATCOM	commercial satellite communications
CONOPS	concept of operations
CONUS	continental United States
COTS	commercial off-the-shelf
CPB	charged particle beam
CRT	cathode ray tube
CSA	Canadian Space Agency
CSEL	combat survivor evader locator
CSIL	Commercial Satellite Imagery Library
CSPE	communications systems planning element

D

D	distance
DAGR	Defense Advanced Global Positioning System (GPS) Receiver
DAMA	demand assigned multiple access
DARO	Defense Airborne Reconnaissance Office
DARPA	Defense Advanced Research Projects Agency
dB	decibel
dBW	decibel watt
DC	direct current
DCSOPS	Deputy Chief of Staff for Operations and Plans, US Army
DDC	data distribution center
DEFSMAC	Defense Special Missile and Aerospace Center
DEM	digital elevation model
DEW	distant early warning
DF	direction finding; Dong Feng

302

DGPS — differential global positioning system
DIA — Defense Intelligence Agency
DIOCC — Defense Intelligence Operations Coordination Center
DIRSPACEFOR — director of space forces (USAF)
DISA — Defense Information Systems Agency
DISN — Defense Information Systems Network
DMA — Defense Mapping Agency
DMS — defense message system
DMSP — Defense Meteorological Satellite Program
DOD — Department of Defense
DODI — Department of Defense instruction
DOMSAT — domestic communications satellite
DON — Department of the Navy
DOP — dilution of precision
DR — detection radar
DRC — data reduction center
DSC — defensive space control
DSCS — Defense Satellite Communications System
DSN — Defense Switched Network
DSP — Defense Satellite Program; Defense Support Program
DSTS — deep space tracking system
DTED — digital terrain elevation data
DTRA — Defense Threat Reduction Agency
DTS — Diplomatic Telecommunications Service
DWSW — Deployable Weather Satellite Workstation

E

e — eccentricity
EA — electronic attack
EAC — echelons above corps (Army)
EAM — emergency action message
EC — Earth coverage
ECI — Earth-centered inertial
EDGE — exploitation of differential GPS (DGPS) for guidance enhancement
EELV — evolved expendable launch vehicle
EGS — European ground station
EHF — extremely high frequency
EIRP — effective isotropic radiated power
ELINT — electronic intelligence
ELSET — element set
EM — electromagnetic
EMD — engineering and manufacturing development
EMP — electromagnetic pulse
EMSS — Enhanced Mobile Satellite Services
ENEC — extendable nozzle exit cone
EORSAT — Electronic Intelligence (ELINT) Ocean Reconnaissance Satellite
EOS — earth observing system

EOSAT	earth observation satellite
EPDS	Electronic Processing and Dissemination System
ER	Eastern Range; extended range
ERS	European remote sensing
ERTS	Earth Resources Technology Satellite
ESA	European Space Agency
ESSA	Environmental Science Service Administration
ET	external tank; extraterrestrial
ETM+	enhanced thematic mapper plus
ETRAC	enhanced tactical radar correlator
ETUT	enhanced tactical user terminal
EUMETSAT	European Organization for the Exploitation of Meteorological Satellites
EUTELSAT	European Telecommunications Satellite Organization
EUV	extreme ultraviolet
EVA	extravehicular activity

F

F	Fahrenheit
FAA	Federal Aviation Administration
FAB-T	Family of Advanced Beyond Line-of-Sight Terminals
FALCON	Force Application and Launch from CONUS
FAST	forward area support terminal
FBM	fleet ballistic missile
FDMA	frequency division multiple access
FEC	forward error correction
FEP	Fleet Satellite (FLTSAT) Extremely High Frequency (EHF) Package
FH	frequency-hopped
FISINT	foreign instrumentation signals intelligence
FLTFORCOM	Fleet Forces Command
FLTSAT	fleet satellite
FLTSATCOM	fleet satellite communications
FM	field manual (Army)
FNMOC	Fleet Numerical Meteorological and Oceanographic Center
FOSIC	Fleet Ocean Surveillance Information Center
FOV	field of view
FSSC	Fleet Surveillance Support Command
FSST	forward space support to theater
FSU	former Soviet Union
FSW	Fanhuishi Shiyan Weixing
ft.	foot
FY	Feng Yun

G

G2	intelligence (staff division)
G3	operations and plans (staff division)

304

G6	communications (staff division)
GAO	General Accounting Office
GATS	GPS-Aided Targeting System
Gbps	gigabits per second
GBS	Global Broadcast Service
GCC	geographic combatant commander
GCCS	Global Command and Control System
GCN	ground communications network
GCNU	ground communications network upgrade
GCSS	Global Combat Support System
GDA	gimbaled dish antenna
GDOP	geometric dilution of precision
GEM	graphite-epoxy motor
GEO	geosynchronous Earth orbit
GEODSS	Ground-Based Electro-Optical Deep Space Surveillance
GEOSAT	Geodetic/Geophysical Satellite
GHz	gigahertz
GIANT	Global Positioning System (GPS) Interference and Navigation Tool
GIG	Global Information Grid
GLONASS	Globalnaya Navigatsionnaya Sputnikovaya Sistema
GMF	ground mobile forces
GMS	geostationary meteorological satellite
GOES	geostationary operational environmental satellite
GOTS	government off-the-shelf
GPS	global positioning system
GPS MCS	Global Positioning System (GPS) Master Control Station
GPS/NDS	Global Positioning System (GPS) Nuclear Detection System
GPSOC	GPS Operations Center
GRAB	Galactic Radiation and Background
GSD	ground sampling distance
GSSC	Global SATCOM Support Center
GSU	geographically separated unit
GTO	geosynchronous transfer orbit

H

H_2O	hydrogen dioxide (water)
HAARP	High-Frequency Active Auroral Research Program
HAE	height above ellipsoid
HAPS	hydrazine auxiliary propulsion system
HAX	Haystack Auxiliary
H-bomb	hydrogen bomb
HDOP	horizontal dilution of precision
HELSTF	High-Energy Laser System Test Facility
HEMP	high-altitude electromagnetic pulse
HEO	highly elliptical orbit
HF	high frequency

HPM	high-power microwave
HQ	headquarters
HRPT	high-resolution picture transmission
HRV	high-resolution visible
HSD	high-speed data
HSI	hyperspectral imagery
HSMP	high-speed message processor
HSS	high-speed stream
HST	Hubble Space Telescope
HUMINT	human intelligence
Hz	hertz

I

i	inclination
IBS-I	Integrated Broadcast Service-Interactive
IBS-S	Integrated Broadcast Service-Simplex
ICADS	Integrated Correlation and Display System
ICBM	intercontinental ballistic missile
ICDB	integrated communications database
ICRF	International Celestial Reference Frame
IDCSP	Initial Defense Communications Satellite Program
IFOV	instantaneous field of view
IG	intelligence group
IGMDP	integrated guided missile development program
IGY	International Geophysical Year
IMF	interplanetary magnetic field
IMINT	imagery intelligence
IMO	International Meteor Organization
INFOSEC	information security
INMARSAT	international maritime satellite
INS	inertial navigation system
INSAT	Indian National Satellite
INTELSAT	international telecommunications satellite
IO	information operations
IOC	initial operating capability
IP	internet protocol
IPL	integrated priority list
IPO	integrated program office
IR	infrared
IRBM	intermediate-range ballistic missile
IRIS	Internet Routing in Space
IRS	Indian Remote Sensing (Satellite)
I_{sp}	specific impulse
ISR	intelligence, surveillance, and reconnaissance
ISRO	Indian Space Research Organization
ISS	International Space Station
ITAC	Intelligence and Threat Analysis Center

ITOS   Improved TIROS Operational Satellite
ITW   integrated tactical warning
ITW/AA   integrated tactical warning and attack assessment
IUS   inertial upper stage

J

JAOC   joint air operations center (JP 1-02); joint air and space operations center (USAF)
JAOP   joint air operations plan (JP 1-02); joint air and space operations plan (USAF)
JASSM   Joint Air-to-Surface Standoff Missile
JAXA   Japan Aerospace Exploration Agency
JBS   Joint Broadcast Service
JCS   Joint Chiefs of Staff
JDAM   Joint Direct Attack Munition
JEM   Japanese Experiment Module
JERS   Japanese Earth Resources Satellite
JFACC   joint force air component commander (JP 1-02); joint air and space component commander (USAF)
JFC   joint force commander
JFCC   joint functional component command
JFCC-GS   Joint Functional Component Command for Global Strike
JFCC-IMD   Joint Functional Component Command for Integrated Missile Defense
JFCC-ISR   Joint Functional Component Command for Intelligence, Surveillance, and Reconnaissance
JFCC NW   Joint Functional Component Command for Network Warfare
JFCC Space Joint Functional Component Command for Space
JFLCC   joint force land component commander
JIEDDO   Joint Improvised Explosive Device Defeat Organization
JIOC   joint information operations center
JITI   joint in-theater injection
JNTF   Joint National Test Facility
JOA   joint operations area
JOPES   Joint Operation Planning and Execution System
JOPP   joint operation planning process
JP   joint publication
JRSC   jam-resistant secure communications
JSAT   Japan Satellite System
JSCP   Joint Strategic Capabilities Plan
JSIPS   Joint Services Imagery Processing System
JSOP   joint space operations plan
JSOW   joint stand-off weapon
JSpOC   Joint Space Operations Center
JSTARS/GSM Joint Surveillance Target Attack Radar System/Ground Station Module
JTAGS   joint tactical ground station

JTF	joint task force
JTF-CND	Joint Task Force-Computer Network Defense
JTF-GNO	Joint Task Force-Global Network Operations
JTFST	Joint Task Force Satellite Terminal
JTRS	Joint Tactical Radio System

K

K	Kelvin
Ka	Kurtz-above band
kbps	kilobits per second
KE	kinetic energy
kg	kilogram
kHz	kilohertz
km	kilometer
km/sec	kilometers per second
Ku	Kurtz-under band
kW	kilowatt
kW/s	kilowatts per steradian

L

LAAS	Local Area Augmentation System
LADGPS	local-area differential GPS
LADO	Launch, Anomaly Resolution, and Disposal Operations
LANDSAT	land satellite
LASS	low-altitude space surveillance
lb.	pound
lbf.	pound-force
LCC	launch control center
LDR	low data rate
LEGG	launch ejection gas generator
LEO	low Earth orbit
LF	launch facility; low frequency
LH	liquid hydrogen
LISS	linear imaging self-scanning
LITVC	liquid injection thrust vector control
LLV	Lockheed Launch Vehicle
LMLV	Lockheed-Martin Launch Vehicle
LOC	line of communication
LORAN	long-range aid to navigation
LOS	line of sight
LPD	low probability of detection
LPI	low probability of intercept
LPS	large processing station
LPSU	large processing station upgrade
LRIR	Long-Range Imaging Radar
LS	light smooth
LSD	low-speed data

LSMP	low-speed message processor
LSSC	Lincoln Space Surveillance Complex
LSTT	light-weight small tactical terminal
LTRS	Launch Test Range System
LUF	lowest usable frequency
LWIR	long-wave infrared

M

m	mass; meter
MACH	modular avionics control hardware
MAGR	miniaturized aircraft GPS receiver
MAJCOM	major command
MARFORSTRAT	Marine Corps Forces, US Strategic Command
MASINT	measurement and signature intelligence
MB	megabyte
MBA	multiple beam antenna
Mbps	megabits per second
MC&G	mapping, charting, and geodesy
MCC	mission control center
MCS	master control station; mission control segment; mission control station
MDM	mission data message
MDR	medium data rate
MECA	missile electronics and computer assembly
MEO	medium Earth orbit
METEOSAT	Meteorological Satellite
METOC	meteorological and oceanographic
MetOp	Meteorological Operational (European satellite program)
MGS	missile guidance set; mobile ground system
MHR	Millstone Hill Radar
MHz	megahertz
mi	mile
MI	military intelligence
microsat	microsatellite
MIDAS	Missile Defense Alarm System
MIES	Modernized Imagery Exploitation System
MILSATCOM	military satellite communications
Milstar	military strategic and tactical relay
MIRV	multiple independently targetable reentry vehicle
MIT	Massachusetts Institute of Technology
MITT	mobile integrated tactical terminal
MLRS	Multiple Launch Rocket System
mm	millimeter
MMOAS	master of military operational art and science
MNAV	M-code navigation
MOC	Milstar Operations Center
MOD	Ministry of Defense

MOL	Manned Orbiting Laboratory
MOS	Marine Observation Satellite; modular optoelectronic scanner
MOSC	Moron Optical Space Surveillance (MOSS) Space Operations Center
MOS/PIM	Multiple Orbit Satellite/Program Improvement Module
MOSS	Moron Optical Space Surveillance
MOTIF	Maui Optical Tracking and Identification Facility
mph	miles per hour
MPSOC	Multipurpose Satellite Operations Center
M_R	mass ratio
MRBM	medium-range ballistic missile
m/s	meters per second
MSAT	Mobile Satellite
MSF	Milstar Support Facility
MSG	Meteorological Satellite (METEOSAT) Second Generation
MSI	multispectral imagery
MSIC	Missile and Space Intelligence Center
MSIP	multispectral imagery (MSI) processor
MSMR	multifrequency scanning microwave radiometer
MSOC	Milstar Satellite Operations Center
MSS	mobile service system; multispectral scanner
MSSS	Maui Space Surveillance System
MSTS	multisource tactical system
MSX/SBV	Midcourse Space Experiment/Space-Based Vehicle
MT	megaton
MTCR	Missile Technology Control Regime
MTSAT	Multifunctional Transport Satellite
MUE	Modernized User Equipment
MUF	maximum usable frequency
MUOS	Mobile User Objective System
MWIR	medium-wave infrared

N

NACA	National Advisory Committee on Aeronautics
NAS	naval air station
NASA	National Aeronautics and Space Administration
NASDA	National Space Development Agency
NASIC	National Air and Space Intelligence Center
NATO	North Atlantic Treaty Organization
NAV	navigation
NAVASTROGRU	Navy Astronautics Group
NAVSAT	navigation satellite
NAVSOC	Naval Satellite Operations Center
NAVSPASUR	Naval Space Surveillance
NAVSPOC	Naval Space Operations Center
NAVWAR	navigation warfare
NCA	National Command Authorities

NDI	nondevelopmental item
NDS	Nuclear Detonation Detection System
NESDIS	National Environmental Satellite, Data, and Information Service
NETWARCOM	Naval Network Warfare Command
NFL	new foreign launch
NGA	National Geospatial-Intelligence Agency
NHK	Nike-Hercules Korea
Ni-Cad	nickel-cadmium
Ni-H$_2$	nickel-hydrogen
NIPC	National Infrastructure Protection Center
NIR	near infrared
NITF	national imagery transmission format
nm	nautical mile
NMCC	National Military Command Center
NNSS	Navy Navigation Satellite System
NOAA	National Oceanic and Atmospheric Administration
NORAD	North American Aerospace Defense Command
NPB	neutral particle-beam
NPIC	National Photographic Interpretation Center
NPOESS	National Polar-Orbiting Operational Environmental Satellite System
NPP	National Polar-Orbiting Operational Environmental Satellite System (NPOESS) Preparatory Project
NRL	Naval Research Laboratory
NRO	National Reconnaissance Office
ns	nanosecond
NS	naval station
NSA/CSS	National Security Agency/Central Security Service
NSD	national security directive
NSDD	national security decision directive
NSPC	National Space Council
NSPD	national space policy directive
NSSA	National Security Space Architect
NSSI	National Security Space Institute
NSSO	National Security Space Office
NSST	naval space support team
NSTC	National Science and Technology Council
NSWCDD	Naval Surface Warfare Center, Dahlgren Division
NTR	nuclear thermal rocket
NUDET	nuclear detonation
NWS	North Warning System

O

O	oxygen molecule
O&M	operations and maintenance
O$_2$	oxygen (gas)
OAF	Operation Allied Force

OC	operations center
OCC	operations control center
OCM	ocean color monitor
OCO	Orbiting Carbon Observatory
OCS	offensive counterspace; operational control system
OCX	Operational Control Segment of the Future
OEF	Operation Enduring Freedom
OGA	other government agency
OGS	overseas ground station
OIF	Operation Iraqi Freedom
OLS	operational linescan system
OMS	orbital maneuvering system
OPCON	operational control
OPLAN	operation plan
OPORD	operation order
OPSEC	operations security
OSC	offensive space control; Orbital Sciences Corporation
OSEI	Operational Significant Event Imagery
OSINT	open-source intelligence
OSP	Orbital/Suborbital Program
OTH	over the horizon
OTH-B	over-the-horizon backscatter
OTS	Officer Training School
OUSD (A&T)	Office of the Undersecretary of Defense for Acquisition and Technology

P

PA	puncture acquisition
PAN	panchromatic
PAR	phased-array radar
PARCS	Perimeter Acquisition Radar Attack Characterization System
PAVE PAWS	Perimeter Acquisition Vehicle Entry Phased-Array Weapons System
PBCS	post-boost control system
PBV	post-boost vehicle
PCA	polar cap absorption
PCM	phase-change material
P-code	precision code
PD	presidential directive
PDD	presidential decision directive
PDOP	position dilution of precision
PE	potential energy
PEC	photoelectric cell
PLGR	precision lightweight global positioning system (GPS) receiver
PMT	photo multiplier tube
PNT	position, navigation, and timing
POES	polar operational environmental satellite;

PPL	polar-orbiting environmental satellite
PPS	preplanned launch
PPSE	precise positioning service
	Perimeter Acquisition Vehicle Entry Phased-Array
PPSW	Weapons System (PAVE PAWS) Southeast
	Perimeter Acquisition Vehicle Entry Phased-Array Weapons
	System (PAVE PAWS) Southwest
PR	production requirement
PRD	presidential review directive
PRN	pseudorandom noise
PSAD	Procurement and Systems Acquisition Division
psi	pounds per square inch
PSLV	polar satellite launch vehicle
PSRE	propulsion-system rocket engine
PUP	peripheral upgrade program
PVT	position, velocity, and timing
P(Y)	pseudorandom code

Q

QDR	Quadrennial Defense Review
QPSK	quadrature phase shift keying

R

R&D	research and development
RAF	Royal Air Force
RAOC	regional air operations center
RCMP	Royal Canadian Mounted Police
RCS	reaction control system
RDS	real-time data smooth
REACT	rapid execution and combat targeting
revs	revolutions
RF	radio frequency
RFI	radio frequency interference
RGS	relay ground station
RISTA	reconnaissance, intelligence, surveillance, and target acquisition
RMS	remote manipulator system
ROCC	regional operations control center
RORSAT	Radar Ocean Reconnaissance Satellite
ROTHR	relocatable over-the-horizon radar
ROW	rest-of-world
RPO	rendezvous and proximity operations
RSC	reaction control system
RSSC	regional satellite communications (SATCOM) support center
RTC	real-time command
RTD	real-time data fine
RTG	radioisotope thermoelectric generator
RV	reentry vehicle

S

S&T	science and technology
SA	selective availability
SAA	satellite access authorization
SAASM	Selective Availability Anti-Spoofing Module
SAGE	semiautomatic ground environment
SAM	surface-to-air missile
SAMT	state-of-the-art medium terminal
SAOC	sector air operations center
SAR	satellite access request; search and rescue; special access required; support assistance request; synthetic aperture radar
SARSAT	search and rescue satellite-aided tracking
SATCOM	satellite communications
SATCON	satellite control
SATRAN	satellite reconnaissance advance notice
SBIRS	Space-Based Infrared System
SC	space control
SCA	space coordinating authority
SCC	Space Communications Corp; space control center
SCG	security classification guide
SCI	sensitive compartmented information
SCIS	Survivable Communications Integration System
SCORE	Signal Communications by Orbiting Relay Equipment
SCT	single channel transponder
SDC	Satellite Data Collectors
SDIO	Strategic Defense Initiative Organization
SDS	satellite data system
SEC	Space Environmental Center
SECNAV	Secretary of the Navy
SED	Sensor Evolutionary Development
SEON	Solar Electro-Optical Network
SEP	spherical error probable
SERV	safety-enhanced reentry vehicle
SEU	single-event upset
SFA	space force application
SG	space group
SGP	Simplified General Perturbations (satellite)
SGS	Soviet Geocentric System
SHF	super-high frequency
SID	sudden ionospheric disturbance
SIDC	Space Innovation and Development Center
SIDEARM	Secondary Imagery Dissemination Environment and Resource Manager
SIGINT	signals intelligence
SINCGARS	single channel ground and air radio system
SIOP	Single Integrated Operational Plan
SLBM	submarine-launched ballistic missile

314

SLC — Space Launch Complex
SLCM — sea-launched cruise missile; submarine-launched cruise missile
SLEP — service life extension program
SLGR — small lightweight global positioning system (GPS) receiver
SLS — space launch squadron
SLV — space launch vehicle
SMABC — Space and Missile Applications Basic Course
SMART-T — Secure Mobile Anti-Jam Reliable Tactical Terminal
SMC — Space and Missile Systems Center
SMDBL — Space and Missile Defense Command (SMDC) Battle Lab
SMDC — Space and Missile Defense Command
SMDCOC — Space and Missile Defense Command Operations Center
SOC — satellite operations center; space operations center
SOCC — satellite operations control center
SOH — state of health
SOI — space object identification
SOM — satellite operations manager
SOP — standard operating procedure
SOPS — satellite operations squadron; space operations squadron
SORT — Strategic Offensive Reductions Treaty
SOS — Squadron Officer School
SPACEAF — Space Air Forces
SpaceX — Space Exploration Technologies
SPAWAR — Space and Naval Warfare (Systems Command)
SPC — stored programs command
SPIN — Satellite Communications (SATCOM) Planning Information Network
SPO — special projects office; system programs office
SPOT — Satellite Pour L'Observation de la Terre
SPS — simplified processing station; standard positioning service
SPSS — space surveillance squadron
SRBM — short-range ballistic missile
SRMU — solid rocket motor upgrade
SRS — satellite readout station
SRSU — satellite readout station (SRS) upgrade
SS — space support
SSA — space situational awareness
SSA OPS — space situational awareness operations
SSB — solar sector boundary
SSBN — fleet ballistic missile submarine
SSB/X — gamma ray detector
SSB/X-2 — upgraded gamma ray detector
SSC — space surveillance center
SSDC — Space and Strategic Defense Command
SSE — satellite communications (SATCOM) system expert
SSF — laser threat warning sensor
SSI/ES — ionospheric plasma drift and scintillation monitor
SSI/ES-2 — enhanced ionospheric plasma drift and scintillation monitor

SSI/ES-3	plasma monitor system
SSJ/4	precipitating electron and ion spectrometer
SSJ/5	precipitating particle spectrometer
SSM	triaxial fluxgate magnetometer
SSMA	spread spectrum multiple access
SSMI	special sensor microwave imager
SSMIS	microwave imager/sounder
SSM/T-1	microwave temperature sounder
SSM/T-2	microwave water vapor profiler
SSN	space surveillance network
SST	space support team
SSULI	ultraviolet limb imager
SSUSI	ultraviolet spectrographic imager
START	Strategic Arms Reduction Treaty
STO	space tasking order
STS	space transport system; Space Transportation System (space shuttle)
STT	small tactical terminal
SUNSAT	Stellenbosch University Satellite
SV	space vehicle
SWC	Space Warfare Center
SWF	shortwave fade
SWIR	shortwave infrared
SWO	space weapons officer; space weather officer; space weather operations
SWPC	Space Weather Prediction Center
SWS	space warning squadron; strategic weapon system

T

T	thrust
TACDAR	tactical detection and reporting
TACON	tactical control
TACSAT	tactical satellite
TACSATCOM	tactical satellite communications
TACTERM	tactical terminal
TAOS	Technology for Autonomous Operational Survivability
TASR	Tactical Automated Situational Receiver
TAT-1	transatlantic telephone (first cable)
TBM	tactical ballistic missile
TCF	technical control facility
TDDM	time-division data multiplexing
TDDS	tactical related applications (TRAP) data dissemination system
TDOA	time difference of arrival
TDOP	time dilution of precision
TEC	Topographic Engineering Center; total electron content
TEL	transporter erector launcher
TENCAP	tactical exploitation of national capabilities
TERCAT	terrain categorization

316

TERCOM	terrain contour matching
TES	theater event system
TIBS	tactical information broadcast service
TIROS	television infrared operational satellite
TLAM	Tomahawk Land Attack Missile
TLE	two-line element
TM	thematic mapper
TMD	theater missile defense
TMOS	Transformational Satellite Mission Operations System
TOMS-EP	Total Ozone Mapping Spectrometer-Earth Probe
TOS	Television Infrared Operational Satellite (TIROS) Operational System
TPFDD	time-phased force and deployment data
TR	tracking radar
T/R	transmit/receive
TRADOC	Training and Doctrine Command
TRAP	tactical related applications
TS	thermal smooth
TSAT	Transformational Satellite
TSS	Tri-band SATCOM Subsystem
TT&C	telemetry, tracking, and commanding
TTFF	time to first fix
TTP	tactics, techniques, and procedures
TVC	thrust vector control

U

UAV	unmanned aerial vehicle
UDMH	unsymmetrical dimethyldrazine
UE	user equipment
UEE	user equipment error
UERE	user-equivalent range error
UFO	ultra-high frequency follow-on
UHF	ultra-high frequency
ULA	United Launch Alliance
UN	United Nations
UNOOSA	United Nations Office for Outer Space Affairs
URE	user range error
USA	US Army
USAF	US Air Force
USASMDC	US Army Space and Missile Defense Command
USASMDC/ARSTRAT	US Army Space and Missile Defense Command/Army Forces Strategic Command
USCENTCOM	US Central Command
USMC	US Marine Corps
USNO	US Naval Observatory
USSPACECOM	US Space Command
USSTRATCOM	US Strategic Command

UTC	Coordinated Universal Time
UV	ultraviolet
UWB	ultrawideband

V

VDOP	vertical dilution of precision
VHF	very high frequency
VLF	very low frequency

W

WAAS	Wide Area Augmentation System
WADGPS	wide-area differential global positioning system (GPS)
WAGE	wide-area global positioning system (GPS) enhancement
WEFAX	weather facsimile
WGS	Wideband Global Satellite Communications (SATCOM)
WGS 84	World Geodetic System 1984
WIFS	wide field sensor
WIN-T	War-fighter Information Network Tactical Terminal
WOC	wideband operations center
WSMR	White Sands Missile Range
WSOC	wideband satellite operations center

X

XDOP	X or north-south dilution of precision
XDR	extended data rate
XIPS	xenon-ion propulsion system

Y

| YDOP | Y or east-west dilution of precision |
| YMCA | P(Y), M, and C/A codes (for global positioning system) |

Z

| ZY | Zi Yuan |

Abid, Mohamed M. *Spacecraft Sensors.* Hoboken, NJ: John Wiley & Sons, 2005.

"Agreement between the Government of Canada and the Government of the United States of America on the North American Aerospace Defense Command," 28 April 2006. http://www.treaty-accord.gc.ca/ViewTreaty.asp?Treaty_ID=105060&bPrint=True&Language=0 (accessed 8 April 2008).

Air Force Doctrine Document (AFDD) 1. *Air Force Basic Doctrine,* 17 November 2003.

AFDD 2-2. *Space Operations,* 27 November 2006.

AFDD 2-2.1. *Counterspace Operations,* 2 August 2004.

Air Force Institute of Technology Center for MASINT Studies and Research. "Intelligence: Toward a Better Definition." http://www.afit.edu/cmsr/Intelligence2.cfm (accessed 18 March 2008).

Air Force Qualification Training Package (AFQTP) 2EXXX-201LB. "Communications-Electronics (C-E) Manager's Handbook." http://www.armymars.net/ArmyMARS/MilInfo/cemgrs-handbook.pdf (accessed 24 February 2008).

Air Force Space Command (AFSPC). "Advanced Extremely High Frequency System." Fact Sheet. http://www.afspc.af.mil/library/factsheets/factsheet.asp?id=7758 (accessed 1 May 2009)

———. "AFSPC." Fact Sheet. http://www.af.mil/information/factsheets/factsheet.asp?id=155 (accessed 1 March 2008).

———. "Evolved Expendable Launch Vehicle." Fact Sheet. http://www.afspc.af.mil/library/factsheets/factsheet.asp?id=3643 (accessed 18 February 2008).

———. "Global Positioning System Constellation Status." http://gps.afspc.af.mil/gps/ (accessed 17 April 2009).

———. "MILSTAR Satellite Communications System." Fact Sheet. http://www.af.mil/information/factsheets/factsheet.asp?fsID=118 (accessed 12 February 2008).

———. "Space Based Infrared Systems." Fact Sheet. http://www.afspc.af.mil/library/factsheets/factsheet.asp?id=3675 (accessed 7 April 2008).

———. "Space Innovation and Development Center." Fact Sheet. http://www.afspc.af.mil/library/factsheets/factsheet.asp?id=3651 (accessed 1 March 2008).

———. *Space Surveillance Network (SSN) Site Information Handbook,* 24 October 2007.

———. "Wideband Global SATCOM Satellite." http://www.afspc.af.mil/library/factsheets/factsheet.asp?id=5582 (accessed 14 February 2008).

AFSPC Pamphlet (AFSPCPAM)15-2. *Space Environmental Impacts on DOD Operations,* 1 October 2003, certified current 7 December 2007.

Air Force Weather Agency (AFWA). "AFWA Space Weather Flight." http://www.afweather.af.mil/library/factsheets/factsheet.asp?id=5090 (accessed 16 April 2009).

Amateur Radio Satellite Corporation. "Keplerian Elements Formats." http://www.amsat.org/amsat/keps/formats.html (accessed 18 April 2008).

Arianespace. "Launch Status." http://www.arianespace.com/site/search/search_sub_index.html (accessed 24 February 2008).

Army Field Manual (FM) 3-14. *Space Support to Army Operations,* 18 May 2005.

Army Space and Missile Defense Command (SMDC). "About USASMDC." http://www.smdc.army.mil/SMDC/About.html (accessed 1 March 2008).

Arnold, H. J. P., ed. *Man in Space: An Illustrated History of Spaceflight*. New York: CLB Smithmark Publishing, 1993.

Associated Press. "Iran Launches Research Rocket, Unveils Space Center." *FOXNews.com*. http://www.foxnews.com/story/0,2933,327977,00.html (accessed 6 February 2008).

Astronautix. "Advanced Tiros N." http://www.astronautix.com/craft/advirosn.htm (accessed 24 January 2008).

———. "Atlas V." http://www.astronautix.com/lvs/atlasv.htm (accessed 18 February 2008).

———. "DSP." http://www.astronautix.com/craft/dsp.htm (accessed 8 April 2008).

———. "Milstar." http://www.astronautix.com/craft/milstar.htm (accessed 19 February 2008).

———. "Taurus." http://www.astronautix.com/lvs/taurus.htm (accessed 16 February 2008).

AtomicArchive.com. "Nuclear Radiation." http://www.atomicarchive.com/Effects/effects14.shtml (accessed 18 May 2009).

Baar, James, and William E. Howard. *Polaris!* New York: Harcourt, Brace, 1960.

Baker, David, ed. *Jane's Space Directory, 2002–2003*. Alexandria, VA: Jane's Information Group, 2002.

———. *Jane's Space Directory, 2003–2004*. Alexandria, VA: Jane's Information Group, 2003.

Ball, Desmond. *A Base for Debate: The US Satellite Station at Nurrungar*. North Sydney, Australia: Allen & Unwin, 1987.

———. "Assessing China's ASAT Program." Austral Special Report 07-14S, 14 June 2007. http://www.nautilus.org/~rmit/forum-reports/0714s-ball/fig1-schematic.html (accessed 11 May 2009).

Bergaust, Erik. *Rocket City, U.S.A.: From Huntsville, Alabama to the Moon*. New York: Macmillan, 1963.

Bertell, Rosalie. "Background of the HAARP Project." http://www.earthpulse.com/src/subcategory.asp?catid=1&subcatid=1 (accessed 2 April 2009).

Beyda, William J. *Data Communications: From Basics to Broadband*. 3rd ed. Boston, MA: Pearson Custom Publishing, 2002.

Bloomfield, Lincoln P. "The Prospects for Law and Order." In *Outer Space: New Challenge to Law and Policy*, edited by J. E. S. Fawcett. Oxford: Clarendon Press, 1984.

Boeing. "Boeing Satellites: Milstar II." http://www.boeing.com/defense-space/space/bss/factsheets/government/milstar_ii/milstar_ii.html (accessed 19 February 2008).

———. "Integrated Defense Systems: Boeing 702 Fleet." http://www.boeing.com/defense-space/space/bss/factsheets/702/702fleet.html (accessed 20 March 2008).

———. "Successful Launch Orbits the 11th Boeing-Built UHF Follow-On Naval Satellite." http://www.boeing.com/news/releases/2003/q4/nr_031217o.html (accessed 7 April 2008).

———. "Transformational Wideband Communication Capabilities for the Warfighter." http://www.boeing.com/defense-space/space/bss/factsheets/702/wgs/wgs_factsheet.html (accessed 14 February 2008).

———. "Wideband Global SATCOM Backgrounder." http://www.boeing.com/defensespace/space/bss/factsheets/702/wgs/docs/WGS_overview.pdf (accessed 14 February 2008).

"Boeing Completes On-Orbit Handover of Wideband Global SATCOM Satellite to USAF," Space War, http://www.spacewar.com/reports/Boeing_Completes_On_Orbit_Handover_Of_Wideband_Global_SATCOM_Satellite_To_USAF_999.html (accessed 14 February 2008).

Bond, Peter. *The Continuing Story of the International Space Station.* Chichester, UK: Praxis Publishing, 2002.

Briefing. 1st Space Control Squadron. 614th Space Operations Group. Subject: Welcome to the 1st Space Control Squadron, 4 June 2007.

Brinton, Turner. "Longer Life Expected for First WGS Satellite." *Space News.* https://halfway.peterson.af.mil/NSSI/NSSISpaceNewsArchives/20080201_NSSISpaceNews.doc (accessed 14 February 2008).

Broussely, Michel. *Industrial Applications of Batteries: From Cars to Aerospace and Energy,* edited by Gianfranco Pistoia. Cambridge, MA: Elsevier Science, 2007.

Brown, Lt Col Kendall K., ed. *Space Power Integration: Perspectives from Space Weapons Officers.* Maxwell AFB, AL: Air University Press, 2006.

Bush, Pres. George W. "Remarks at a Memorial Service for the STS-107 Crew of the Space Shuttle *Columbia* in Houston, Texas," 4 February 2003. Washington, DC: Government Printing Office, 2003. http://fdsys.gpo.gov/fdsys/pkg/WCPD-2003-02-10/pdf/WCPD-2003-02-10-Pg156.pdf (accessed 27 March 2009).

———. "A Renewed Spirit of Discovery." Program announcement, 14 January 2004. http://georgewbush-whitehouse.archives.gov/space/renewed_spirit.html (accessed 30 March 2009).

Butler, Amy. "Fourth Satellite Busts Budget." *Aviation Week,* 4 March 2008. http://www.aviationweek.com/aw/generic/story_channel.jsp?channel=space&id=news/AEHF03048.xml (accessed 15 March 2008).

Buxbaum, Peter A. "Wideband Comms: Change Is in the Air." *Defense Systems,* December 2007.

Camp, William W., Joseph T. Mayhan, and Robert M. O'Donnell. "Wideband Radar for Ballistic Missile Defense and Range-Doppler Imaging of Satellites." *Lincoln Laboratory Journal* 12, no. 2 (2000): 267–80.

Chairman of the Joint Chiefs of Staff (CJCS) Instruction 6250.01. *Satellite Communications,* 30 April 2007.

CJCS Manual 3122.03. *Joint Operation Planning and Execution System.* Vol. 2, *Planning Formats and Guidance,* 17 August 2007.

Chaisson, Eric, and Steve McMillan. *Astronomy Today.* Englewood Cliffs, NJ: Prentice Hall, 1993.

Chartrand, Mark R. *Satellite Communications for the Nonspecialist.* Bellingham, WA: SPIE: The International Society for Optical Engineering, 2004.

Chilton, Gen Kevin. "AFSPC Wraps up Busy 2006 Providing Spacepower." *Astro News,* 9 February 2007. http://www.aerotechnews.com/Astro/Astro_020907.pdf (accessed 16 April 2008).

Chobotov, Vladimir A., ed. *Orbital Mechanics.* 3rd ed. Reston, VA: American Institute of Aeronautics and Astronautics, Inc., 2002.

Civil Air Patrol (CAP) Advanced Technology Group. "Satellite Tool Kit Lesson Plans: Orbital Mechanics Power Point Slides Day 2." http://atg.cap.gov/ (accessed 23 March 2008).

Commercial Space Act of 1998. Public Law 105-303. HR 1702 (28 October 1998). http://www.nasa.gov/offices/ogc/commercial/CommercialSpaceActof1998.html (accessed 2 April 2009).

Commission to Assess US National Security Space Management and Organization. *Report of the Commission.* 11 January 2001. http://space.au.af.mil/space_commission/index.htm (accessed 11 May 2009).

Communications Act of 1934 as Amended by the Telecommunications Act of 1996. http://www.fcc.gov/Reports/1934new.pdf (accessed 22 May 2009).

Congress, Office of Technology Assessment. *Global Change Research and NASA's Earth Observing System, OTA-BP-ISC-122.* Washington, DC: Government Printing Office, November 1993.

Cooper, H. F. *Summary of SDI Programs and Plans for Theater and National Ballistic Missile Defenses.* Washington, DC: Strategic Defense Initiative Organization, 4 January 1993.

Cooper, John Cobb. *Explorations in Aerospace Law: Selected Essays by John Cobb Cooper,* edited by Ivan Vlasic. Montreal: McGill University Press, 1968.

Corbett, Julian S. *Some Principles of Maritime Strategy,* introduction and notes by Eric J. Grove. Annapolis, MD: Naval Institute Press, 1988.

Defense Information Systems Agency (DISA). "Enhanced Mobile Satellite Services (EMSS)." http://www.disa.mil/services/emss.html (accessed 2 April 2008).

"Defense Support Program." Federation of American Scientists. http://www.fas.org/spp/military/program/warning/dsp.htm (accessed 8 April 2008).

Department of Defense (DOD). "Military Strategic and Tactical Relay (MILSTAR) Satellite System." FY99 Annual Report. http://www.globalsecurity.org/military/library/budget/fy1999/dot-e/airforce/99milstar.html (accessed 29 February 2008).

———. *Unmanned Aerial Vehicles Roadmap 2002–2027.* Washington, DC: Office of the Secretary of Defense, December 2002.

DOD Directive 3100.10. *Space Policy,* 9 July 1999. http://www.dtic.mil/whs/directives/corres/pdf/310010p.pdf (accessed 15 May 2009).

DOD, Office of the Undersecretary of Defense for Acquisition, Technology, and Logistics. "Moscow Treaty: Article-by-Article Analysis." http://www.dod.mil/acq/acic/treaties/sort/sort_axa.htm (accessed 18 May 2009).

Dicerto, J. J. *Missile Base beneath the Sea: The Story of Polaris.* New York: St. Martin's Press, 1967.

DiNunzio, Mario R. *Theodore Roosevelt: An American Mind.* New York: Penguin, 1994.

Dolman, Everett C. *Astropolitik: Classical Geopolitics in the Space Age.* New York: Frank Cass Publishers, 2002.

"DSCS-3." GlobalSecurity.org. http://www.globalsecurity.org/space/systems/dscs_3.htm (accessed 11 February 2008).

el-Hasan, Muhammed. "Northrop Hopes for Satellite Bid." *Daily Breeze.com,* 26 October 2007.

el-Rabbany, Ahmed. *Introduction to GPS: The Global Positioning System.* Norwood, MA: Artech House, 2002.

Erwin, Sandra I. "High Frequency: Navy Upbeat about Communications Spacecraft, Despite Radio Troubles." *National Defense,* July 2007.

322

European Space Agency (ESA). "Aurora Exploration Programme." http://www.esa.int/SPECIALS/Aurora/SEMZOS39ZAD_0.html (accessed 6 February 2008).

———. "Meteosat Second Generation." http://www.esa.int/esaMI/MSG/SEM4BEULWFE_0.html (accessed 24 February 2008).

———. "MetOp: Meteorological Missions." http://www.esa.int/esaLP/SEMN1FAATME_LPmetop_0.html (accessed 19 April 2008).

ESA Science and Technology. "Plasma Regions: The Magnetotail." http://sci.esa.int/science-e/www/object/index.cfm?fobjectid=33272&fbodylongid=1171 (accessed 16 April 2009).

Federici, Gary. *From the Sea to the Stars*. Naval Historical Center online publication. http://www.history.navy.mil/books/space/Chapter4.htm (accessed 24 February 2008).

Fleet Numerical Meteorology and Oceanography Center (FNMOC). "Fleet Numerical Meteorology & Oceanography Center." Command brief. https://www.fnmoc.navy.mil/public/welcome/cmd_brief.pdf (accessed 24 February 2008).

Fought, Bonnie E. "Legal Aspects of the Commercialization of Space Transportation Systems." *Berkeley Technology Law Journal* 3, no. 2 (Spring 1988). http://www.law.berkeley.edu/journals/btlj/articles/vol3/fought.html (accessed 19 May 2009).

"Ft. Detrick Base Guide: 53rd Signal Battalion." dcmilitary.com. http://www.dcmilitary.com/special_sections/sw/082807_Detrick/ss_140741_31958.shtml (accessed 13 February 2008).

General Accounting Office (GAO). *Improvements Needed in Military Space Systems' Planning and Education*. Washington, DC: GAO, May 2000.

———. *Seasat Project*. PSAD-76-76 (Procurement and Systems Acquisition Division). Washington, DC: GAO, 25 February 1976.

Genesis Mission. "Genesis Launch Vehicle: The Delta Rocket." http://www.genesismission.org/educate/scimodule/LaunchPropulsion/L&P_PDFs/C4_STdeltarocket.pdf (accessed 10 February 2008).

GeoEye Satellite Constellation. "IKONOS." http://www.geoeye.com/corporate/constellation.htm#IKONOS.

Giancoli, Douglas C. *Physics for Scientists and Engineers with Modern Physics*. Englewood Cliffs, NJ: Prentice Hall, 1989.

Google Lunar X Prize. Web site. http://www.googlelunarxprize.org/lunar/competition/guidelines (accessed 5 February 2008).

GPS Operations Center. *NAVSTAR GPS User Equipment Introduction: Public Release Version*, September 1996. http://gps.afspc.af.mil/gpsoc/gps_documentation.aspx (accessed 7 May 2009).

Grant, August E., and Jennifer H. Meadows, eds. *Community Technology Update*. 8th ed. St. Louis, MO: Focal Press, 2002.

Green, Constance, and Milton Lomask. *Vanguard: A History*. NASA History Series. Washington, DC: NASA, 1970.

Gruntman, Mike. *Blazing the Trail: The Early History of Spacecraft and Rocketry*. Reston, VA: American Institute of Aeronautics and Astronautics, 2004.

Hahn, CW2 Garth R., CW2 Anthony Kellar, and CW2 Steven Stubblefield. "Satellite Communications: Operating Together for National Defense." *Army Space Journal* 3, no. 1 (Winter/Spring 2004): 24–27.

Hardesty, Von, and Gene Eisman. *Epic Rivalry: The Inside Story of the Soviet and American Space Race*. Washington, DC: National Geographic Society, 2007.

BIBLIOGRAPHY

Harland, David M. *The Story of the Space Shuttle.* Chichester, UK: Praxis Publishing, 2004.

Harvey, Brian. *Russia in Space: The Failed Frontier?* Chichester, UK: Praxis Publishing, 2001.

Hattendorf, John B. "The Uses of Maritime History in and for the Navy." *Naval War College Review* 56, no. 2 (Spring 2003): 13–38.

Hays, Peter L., James M. Smith, Alan R. Van Tassel, and Guy M. Walsh, eds. *Spacepower for a New Millennium: Space and U.S. National Security.* New York: McGraw-Hill, 2000.

Hebert, Adam J. "The ICBM Makeover." *Air Force Magazine* 88, no. 10 (October 2005): 34–39.

Hollinger, Keith. "Narrowband SATCOM Support—Current/Future." Presentation. 2006 LandWarNet Conference, 23 August 2006.

"House Science Committee Hearing Charter: The Future of NPOESS: Results of the Nunn-McCurdy Review of NOAA's Weather Satellite Program." SpaceRef.com. http://www.spaceref.com/news/viewsr.html?pid=20863 (accessed 19 April 2008).

Howe, Dennis, ed. *FOLDOC: Free On-Line Dictionary of Computing.* http://www.foldoc.org (accessed 11 May 2009).

Howes, Kelly King. *War of 1812.* Detroit, MI: UXL, 2002.

"Hypersonic Cruise Vehicle Force Application and Launch from CONUS." GlobalSecurity.org. http://www.globalsecurity.org/space/systems/hcv.htm (accessed 21 February 2008).

Indian Space Research Organization. Web site. http://www.isro.org/ (accessed 6 February 2008).

Interagency Operations Security (OPSEC) Support Staff. *Operations Security Intelligence Threat Handbook,* April 1996, revised May 1996. http://www.fas.org/irp/nsa/ioss/threat96/part02.htm (accessed 18 March 2008).

———. "OPSEC Glossary of Terms." http://www.ioss.gov/docs/definitions.html (accessed 27 April 2009).

International Meteor Organization (IMO). "IMO Meteor Shower Calendar 2007." http://www.imo.net/calendar/2007 (accessed 16 April 2009).

Isaacs, R. G., and J. C. Barnes. "Intercomparison of Cloud Imagery from the DMSP OLS, NOAA AVHRR, GOES VISSR, and Landsat MSS." *Journal of Atmospheric and Oceanic Technology* 4 (December 1987): 647–667. http://ams.allenpress.com/archive/1520-0426/4/4/pdf/i1520-0426-4-4-647.pdf (accessed 24 February 2008).

Japanese Meteorological Agency. "Meteorological Satellites." http://mscweb.kishou.go.jp/general/activities/gms/index.htm (accessed 24 February 2008).

Jenkins, Dennis R. *Space Shuttle: The History of Developing the National Space Transportation System.* Marceline, MO: Walsworth Publishing, 1992.

———. *Space Shuttle: The History of the National Space Transportation System: The First 100 Missions.* Cape Canaveral, FL: Dennis Jenkins Publishing, 2001.

Joint Forces Command. "Joint Forces Command Glossary." www.jfcom.mil/about/glossary.htm.

Joint Interoperability Test Command. "Tactical Data Dissemination System (TDDS)." http://jitc.fhu.disa.mil/gccsiop/interfaces/tdds.pdf (accessed 7 April 2008).

Joint Publication (JP) 1-02. *Department of Defense Dictionary of Military and Associated Terms,* 12 April 2001 (as amended through 17 October 2008).

JP 2-0. *Joint Intelligence,* 22 June 2007.

324

JP 3-14. *Space Operations*, 6 January 2009.

JP 5-0. *Joint Operation Planning*, 26 December 2006.

Joint Requirements Oversight Council. *Joint Capabilities Document for Positioning, Navigation and Timing*, Version 7.1 Draft, April 2006.

Jussel, Judson J. *Space Power Theory: A Rising Star*. Maxwell AFB, AL: Air University Press, 1998.

Kish, George. *A Source Book in Geography*. Cambridge, MA: Harvard University Press, 1978.

Klein, Lt Cdr John J. "Corbett in Orbit: A Maritime Model for Strategic Space Theory." *Naval War College Review* 57, no. 1 (Winter 2004): 59–74.

Kramer, Herbert J. *Observation of the Earth and Its Environment: Survey of Missions and Sensors*. 4th ed. New York: Springer, 2002.

Labrador, Virgil. "Military Satellite Market: Opportunities and Challenges." *MilsatMagazine* 1, no. 1 (First Quarter 2007): 16.

Lambakis, Steven. *On the Edge of the Earth: The Future of American Space Power*. Lexington, KY: University Press of Kentucky, 2001.

Larson, Wiley J., and James R. Wertz, eds. *Space Mission Analysis and Design*. 3rd ed. El Segundo, CA: Microcosm Press, 1999.

Launius, Roger D. *Frontiers of Space Exploration*. Westport, CT: Greenwood Press, 1998.

———. "The Satellite and Rocket Research Panel." NASA History Office home page. http://www.hq.nasa.gov/office/pao/history/index.html (accessed 16 January 2008).

———. *Space Stations: Base Camps to the Stars*. Washington, DC: Smithsonian Books, 2003.

Launius, Roger D., and Dennis R. Jenkins. *To Reach the High Frontier: A History of U.S. Launch Vehicles*. Lexington, KY: University Press of Kentucky, 2002.

Lazar, Steven. "Modernization and Move to GPS III." *Crosslink*, Summer 2002. http://www.aero.org/publications/crosslink/summer2002/07.html (accessed 12 March 2008).

Lee, Col James G. "Counterspace Operations for Information Dominance." In *Beyond the Paths of Heaven: The Emergence of Space Power Thought*, edited by Col Bruce M. DeBlois. Maxwell AFB, AL: Air University Press, 1999.

Leland, Joe, and Isaac Porche. *Future Army Bandwidth Needs and Capabilities*. Santa Monica, CA: RAND Corporation, 2004.

Ley, Willy. *Rockets, Missiles, and Men in Space*. New York: Viking Press, 1968.

Liopiros, Kostas, and Edward Lam. "Extremely High Frequency Satellites Offer Flexibility." *Signal* 44, no. 11 (July 1990): 77.

Lockheed Martin. "MILSTAR." http://www.lockheedmartin.com/products/Milstar/index.html (accessed 19 February 2008).

Lunar and Planetary Institute. "About Comets." http://www.lpi.usra.edu/education/explore/comets/ (accessed 16 April 2009).

Lupton, Lt Col David E. *On Space Warfare: A Space Power Doctrine*. Maxwell AFB, AL: Air University Press, 1988.

Mahan, Alfred Thayer. *The Influence of Sea Power upon History, 1660–1783*. New York: Hill and Wang, 1963.

Mango, Stephen A. "NPOESS/NPP Calibration/Validation/Verification Program: Its Role in Emerging Global Remote Sensing Systems and Its Potential for Improved Numerical Weather Prediction and Climate Monitoring." http://wgcv.ceos.org/docs/plenary/wgcv24/MangoWGCV24.pdf (accessed 19 April 2008).

Martin, Donald H. *Communications Satellites, 1958–1995*. El Segundo, CA: Aerospace Press, 1996.

———. "A History of U.S. Military Satellite Communication Systems." *Crosslink* 3, no. 1 (Winter 2001/2002): 8–13.

McClendon, Col James W. "Information Warfare: Impacts and Concerns." In *Battlefield of the Future: 21st Century Warfare Issues*, edited by Barry R. Schneider and Lawrence E. Grinter. Maxwell AFB, AL: Air University Press, 1995.

McDonald, Keith D. "The Modernization of GPS: Plans, New Capabilities and Future Relationship to Galileo." *Journal of Global Positioning System* 1, no. 1 (2002): 1–17.

McDonald, Robert A., and Sharon K. Moreno. *Raising the Periscope: Grab and Poppy: America's Early ELINT Satellites*. Chantilly, VA: NRO, 2005.

McLaughlin, William I. "Walter Hohmann's Roads in Space." *Journal of Space Mission Architecture*, issue 2 (Fall 2000): 1–14. http://www2.jpl.nasa.gov/csmad/journal/issue2/toc.pdf (accessed 10 January 2008).

Mehuron, Tamar A., ed. *2002 Space Almanac*. *Air Force Magazine*, August 2002.

"Microcosm's Scorpius/Sprite." GlobalSecurity.org. http://www.globalsecurity.org/space/systems/sprite.htm (accessed 19 February 2008).

Moody, Maj Jay A. *Achieving Affordable Operational Requirements on the Space Based Infrared System (SBIRS) Program: A Model for Warfighter and Acquisition Success?* Maxwell AFB, AL: Air Command and Staff College, 1997.

Moore, William K. "MASINT: New Eyes in the Battlespace." *Military Intelligence Professional Bulletin*, January–March 2003. http://findarticles.com/p/articles/mi_mOIBS/is_1_29/ai_97822088 (accessed 18 March 2008).

Muolo, Maj Michael J., ed. *Space Handbook: A War Fighter's Guide to Space*. Vol. 2, *An Analyst's Guide*. Maxwell AFB, AL: Air University Press, 1993.

Nadler, Mike. Space and Missile Defense Future Warfare Center. "Early Warning." Briefing, 21 August 2007.

National Aeronautics and Space Act. Public Law 85-568. 72 Stat. 426 (29 July 1958). http://www.nasa.gov/offices/ogc/about/space_act1.html (accessed 3 April 2009).

National Aeronautics and Space Administration (NASA). "About NASA." http://www.nasa.gov/about/highlights/what_does_nasa_do.html (accessed 1 March 2008).

———. "Advances in Battery Technology for Space Application." http://sbir.gsfc.nasa.gov/SBIR/successes/ss/7-015text.html (accessed 5 April 2008).

———. "Aqua." http://www.nasa.gov/mission_pages/aqua/ (accessed 19 April 2008).

———. "A-Train Constellation." http://www-calipso.larc.nasa.gov/about/atrain.php (accessed 19 April 2008).

———. "Columbia Mission Overview." http://www.nasa.gov/columbia/mission/index.html (accessed 18 February 2008).

———. "Constellation: America's Fleet of Next-Generation Launch Vehicles." NASA Fact Sheet. http://www.nasa.gov/mission_pages/constellation/ares/aresI.html (accessed 5 February 2008).

———. "Coronal Mass Ejections." Solar Physics Web site at Marshall Space Flight Center. http://solarscience.msfc.nasa.gov/CMEs.shtml (accessed 16 April 2009).

———. "Data Properties." In *Landsat 7 Science Data Users Handbook*. http://landsathandbook.gsfc.nasa.gov/handbook/handbook_htmls/chapter6/chapter6.html (accessed 5 April 2008).

———. "Definition of Two-line Element Set Coordinate System." Human Space Flight Web site. http://spaceflight.nasa.gov/realdata/sightings/SSapplications/Post/JavaSSOP/SSOP_Help/tle_def.html (accessed 18 April 2008).

———. "Electromagnetic Spectrum." Imagine the Universe Web site at Goddard Space Flight Center. http://imagine.gsfc.nasa.gov/docs/science/know_l1/emspectrum.html (accessed 16 April 2009).

———. "The Electromagnetic Spectrum." http://science.hq.nasa.gov/kids/imagers/ems/infrared.html (accessed 9 March 2008).

———. "Explanation of Executive Branch Policy Directives." http://www.au.af.mil/au/awc/awcgate/explain.htm (accessed 15 May 2009).

———. "Mitigation Approaches to Address Impacts of NPOESS Nunn-McCurdy Certification on Joint NASA-NOAA Goals." White Paper. http://ww7.nationalacademies.org/ssb/NPOESSWorkshop_Cramer_NRC_06_19_07_final.pdf (accessed 18 April 2008).

———. "NASA's Launch of Carbon-Seeking Satellite Is Unsuccessful." Press release, 24 February 2009. http://www.nasa.gov/home/hqnews/2009/feb/HQ_09-039_OCO_failure.html (accessed 27 May 2009).

———. "The Shuttle: Background and Status." http://spaceflight.nasa.gov/shuttle/reference/shutref/sts/background.html (accessed 18 February 2008).

———. "Shuttle-Mir: The U.S. And Russia Share History's Highest Stage." http://history.nasa.gov/SP-4225/multimedia/deorbit.htm (accessed 18 April 2008).

———. "Solar Flares." Solar Physics Web site at Marshall Space Flight Center. http://solarscience.msfc.nasa.gov/flares.shtml (accessed 16 April 2009).

———. "Solar Minimum Has Arrived." NASA Web site. http://www.nasa.gov/vision/universe/solarsystem/06mar_solarminimum.html (accessed 16 April 2009).

———. "The Solar Wind." Solar Physics Web site at Marshall Space Flight Center. http://solarscience.msfc.nasa.gov/SolarWind.shtml (accessed 16 April 2009).

———. "Space Shuttle Basics." http://www.spaceflight.nasa.gov/shuttle/reference/basics/index.html (accessed 18 February 2008).

———. "Space Shuttle STS-44 Press Kit." http://science.ksc.nasa.gov/shuttle/missions/sts-44/sts-44-press-kit.txt (accessed 7 April 2008).

———. "What Is the Magnetosphere?" Marshall Space Flight Center Space Plasma Physics Web site. http://science.nasa.gov/ssl/pad/sppb/edu/magnetosphere/ (accessed 16 April 2009).

———. "What Is SAR, Anyway?" http://southport.jpl.nasa.gov/polar/sar.html (accessed 5 March 2008).

NASA Ames Conference Center. "NASA Mission Statement." http://naccenter.arc.nasa.gov/NASAMission.html (accessed 1 March 2008).

NASA Education Working Group. Rockets: A Teacher's Guide with Activities in Science, Mathematics, and Technology. http://store.aiaa.org/kidsplace/kidsplacepdfs/Rockets.pdf (accessed 10 January 2008).

NASA Geostationary Operational Environmental Satellite (GOES) Project. "GEO-News around the World." http://goes.gsfc.nasa.gov/text/geonews.html#GMS (accessed 24 February 2008).

NASA Global Change Master Directory. "Ancillary Description Writer's Guide, 2008." http://gcmd.nasa.gov/User/suppguide/platforms/orbit.html (accessed 18 April 2008).

NASA Goddard Space Flight Center. "Aqua Project Science." http://aqua.nasa.gov/ (accessed 19 April 2008).

———. "Aqua Project Science: Aqua's Instruments." http://aqua.nasa.gov/about/instruments.php (accessed 19 April 2008).

———. "Earth Observing System: NPP." http://eospso.gsfc.nasa.gov/eos_homepage/mission_profiles/show_mission.php?id=19 (accessed 19 April 2008).

NASA Historical Staff. *Historical Sketch of NASA.* Washington, DC: NASA, 1965.

NASA Jet Propulsion Laboratory. "Voyager Mission Operations Status Report #2009-01-02." Week ending 2 January 2009. http://voyager.jpl.nasa.gov/mission/weekly-reports/index.htm (accessed 10 February 2009).

NASA Kennedy Space Center. "Project Skylab." http://science.ksc.nasa.gov/history/skylab/skylab-operations.txt (accessed 18 April 2008).

NASA National Space Science Data Center. "DMSP 5D-3/F16." http://nssdc.gsfc.nasa.gov/nmc/masterCatalog.do?sc=2003-048A (accessed 23 February 2008).

———. "Syncom 2." http://nssdc.gsfc.nasa.gov/nmc/masterCatalog.do?sc=1963-031A (accessed 18 April 2008).

NASA Science. "NPOESS Preparatory Project (NPP)." http://nasascience.nasa.gov/missions/npoess-preparatory-project-npp (accessed 19 April 2008).

NASA Science Mission Directorate. "NOAA/POES." http://nasascience.nasa.gov/missions/noaa/#amsu (accessed 19 April 2008).

National Geophysical Data Center. "Definition of the Ionospheric Regions (Structures)." http://www.ngdc.noaa.gov/stp/IONO/ionostru.html (accessed 16 April 2009).

———. "OLS—Operational Linescan System." http://www.ngdc.noaa.gov/dmsp/sensors/ols.html (accessed 23 February 2008).

———. "SSIES Ion Scintillation Monitor." http://www.ngdc.noaa.gov/dmsp/sensors/ssies.html (accessed 23 February 2008).

———. "SSM/I-Microwave Imager." http://www.ngdc.noaa.gov/dmsp/sensors/ssmi.html (accessed 23 February 2008).

———. "SSM/T-Atmospheric Temperature Profiler." http://www.ngdc.noaa.gov/dmsp/sensors/ssmt.html (accessed 23 February 2008).

———. "SSMT/2 Atmospheric Water Vapor Profiler." http://www.ngdc.noaa.gov/dmsp/sensors/ssmt2.html (accessed 23 February 2008).

National Geospatial-Intelligence Agency (NGA). "NGA Fact Sheet." http://www.nga.mil/NGASiteContent/StaticFiles/OCR/nga_fact.pdf (accessed 1 March 2008).

National Oceanic and Atmospheric Administration (NOAA). "About NOAA." http://www.noaa.gov/about-noaa.html (accessed 1 March 2008).

———. "National Polar-Orbiting Operational Environment Satellite System (NPOESS)," updated August 2002. http://www.publicaffairs.noaa.gov/grounders/npoess.html (accessed 15 May 2009).

———. "NOAA-16 Environmental Satellite Successfully Completes Testing and Is Turned Over to NOAA." http://www.publicaffairs.noaa.gov/releases2000/nov00/noaa00r323.html (accessed 19 April 2008).

NOAA DMSP Sensors Directorate. "DMSP Sensors." http://eic.ipo.noaa.gov/IPOarchive/SCI/sensors/doc88.pdf (accessed 24 February 2008).

NOAA National Environmental Satellite, Data, and Information Service (NESDIS). "Directorate and Agency Contributions." http://npoess.noaa.gov/About/agencies.html (accessed 19 April 2008).

———. "IPO Information Center." http://eic.ipo.noaa.gov/IPOarchive/ED/Outreach_Materials/program-information/CoverPagesaInserts-092507.pdf (accessed 19 April 2008).

———. "More Information on POES Satellites." http://www.nesdis.noaa.gov/POES.html (accessed 19 April 2008).

———. "National Polar-Orbiting Operational Environmental Satellite System." http://www.ipo.noaa.gov/Science/why_polarTXT.html (accessed 19 April 2008).

———. "NPOESS: National Polar-orbiting Operational Environmental Satellite System." http://eic.ipo.noaa.gov/IPOarchive/ED/Outreach_Materials/program-information/CoverPagesaInserts-092507.pdf (accessed 18 April 2008).

———. "Polar Operational Environmental Satellite." http://www.oso.noaa.gov/poes/ (accessed 19 April 2008).

———. "Search and Rescue Satellites." http://www.sarsat.noaa.gov (accessed 19 April 2008).

NOAA Satellite and Information Service. "About NESDIS." http://www.nesdis.noaa.gov/About/about.html (accessed 1 March 2008).

———. "Geostationary Satellites." http://www.oso.noaa.gov/goes/ (accessed 24 February 2008).

National Park Service. "Strategic Arms Reduction Treaty and Disarmament of Minuteman II (1990s)." In *Minuteman Missile Historical Resource Study*, http://www.nps.gov/archive/mimi/history/srs/hrs3-2a.htm (accessed 8 May 2009).

National Reconnaissance Organization (NRO). "Corona Facts." http://www.nro.gov/corona/facts.html (accessed 1 March 2008).

———. "Corona System Information." http://www.nro.gov/corona/sysinfo2.html (accessed 5 March 2008).

———. "Welcome to the NRO." http://www.nro.gov/index.html (accessed 1 March 2008).

National Security Space Architect (NSSA). "National Security Space Roadmap." http://www.fas.org/spp/military/program/nssrm/initiatives/usnds.htm (accessed 18 March 2008).

National Security Space Office (NSSO). Web site. http://www.acq.osd.mil/nsso/index.htm (accessed 2 April 2008).

National Security Space Road Map. "Small Tactical Terminal." http://www.fas.org/spp/military/program/nssrm/initiatives/stt.htm (accessed 24 February 2008).

National Snow and Ice Data Center. "Defense Meteorological Satellite Program (DMSP) Satellite F13." http://www.nsidc.com/data/docs/daac/f13_platform.gd.html (accessed 23 February 2008).

National System for Geospatial Intelligence Publication 1-0. *Geospatial Intelligence (GEOINT) Basic Doctrine*, September 2006. http://www.nga.mil/NGASiteContent/StaticFiles/OCR/geopub1.pdf (accessed 5 March 2008).

Naval Network Warfare Command (NETWARCOM). "Space." http://www.netwarcom.navy.mil/space.htm (accessed 1 March 2008).

Neal, Valerie. *Exploring the Universe with the Hubble Space Telescope*. Washington, DC: NASA, 1990.

Neufeld, Jacob. *Development of Ballistic Missiles in the United States Air Force, 1945–1960*. Washington, DC: Office of Air Force History, USAF, 1990.

Neufeld, Michael J. *Von Braun: Dreamer of Space, Engineer of War*. New York: Alfred A. Knopf, 2007.

Nixon, Pres. Richard M. "Statement about the Future of the United States Space Program," 7 March 1970. http://www.nixonlibraryfoundation.org/index.php?src=gendocs&link=papers_1970 (accessed 2 April 2009).

Northrop Grumman. "Defense Support Program." http://www.st.northropgrumman.com/capabilities/missile_defense/defense_support.html (accessed 7 April 2008).

"Northrop Grumman Demonstrates Compatibility of AEHF Satellite Interface with Terminals Using Extended-Data-Rate Waveform." *SpaceDaily*, 4 February 2008. http://www.spacedaily.com/reports/Northrop_Grumman_Demonstrates_Compatibility_Of_AEHF_Satellite_Interface_With_Terminals_Using_Extended_Data_Rate_Waveform_999.html (accessed 2 March 2008).

"Nuclear Weapon EMP Effects." Federation of American Scientists. http://www.fas.org/nuke/intro/nuke/emp.htm (accessed 11 May 2009).

Oberg, James E. *Space Power Theory.* Washington, DC: Government Printing Office, 1999.

———. "Toward a Theory of Space Power: Defining Principles for U.S. Space Policy." Lecture. Army & Navy Club, Washington DC, 20 May 2003. www.marshall.org/pdf/materials/140.pdf (accessed 2 June 2009).

Olsen, Jim, and Bill Small. "NGA Transforms Dissemination While Improving CENTCOM Support." *Pathfinder: The Geospatial Intelligence Magazine* 6, no. 1 (January/February 2008). http://www.nga.mil/NGASiteContent/StaticFiles/OCR/pf_janfeb08.pdf (accessed 5 March 2008).

"Operationally Responsive Spacelift Initiative." GlobalSecurity.org. http://www.globalsecurity.org/space/systems/ors.htm (accessed 19 February 2008).

"OPLAN 1002 Defense of the Arabian Peninsula." GlobalSecurity.org. http://www.globalsecurity.org/military/ops/oplan-1002.htm (accessed 24 February 2008).

Orbital Sciences Corporation. "Pegasus." http://www.orbital.com/SpaceLaunch/Pegasus/ (accessed 14 February 2008).

Parsons, Zoe. "Lunar Perturbations of a Supersynchronous Geo Transfer Orbit in the Early Orbit Phase." https://dspace.lib.cranfield.ac.uk/bitstream/1826/1767/1/ZParsons_Thesis%20MSc.pdf (accessed 18 April 2008).

Potter, E. R., and Chester W. Nimitz, eds. *Sea Power.* Englewood Cliffs, NJ: Prentice Hall, 1960.

Prasad, K. V. *Principles of Digital Communication Systems and Computer Networks.* Boston, MA: Charles River Books, 2004.

Presidential Commission on the Space Shuttle Challenger Accident. *Report of the Presidential Commission.* http://history.nasa.gov/rogersrep/v1ch4.htm (accessed 12 February 2009).

Presidential Decision Directive/National Science and Technology Council-2. "Convergence of U.S. Polar-Orbiting Operation Environmental Satellite Systems," 10 May 1994.

President's Science Advisory Committee. "Introduction to Outer Space." NASA Historical Reference Collection. 26 March 1958. http://history.nasa.gov/sputnik/16.html (accessed 3 April 2009).

Price, Maj J. Dave. "Life in the Joint Side of Space." *Army Space Journal* 6, no. 1 (Winter 2007): 22–23.

Prussing, John E., and Bruce A. Conway. *Orbital Mechanics.* New York: Oxford University Press, 1993.

Ray, Justin. "Delta Rocket Puts on Late-Night Show with GPS Launch." Spaceflight Now. http://www.spaceflightnow.com/delta/d308/ (accessed 10 February 2008).

Reichert, Lori. "Lockheed Martin Team Passes SBIRS High System Critical Design Review." Lockheed Martin Press Release. http://www.lockheedmartin.com/news/

press_releases/2001/LockheedMartinTeamPassesSBIRSHighSy.html (accessed 7 April 2008).

Richelson, Jeffrey. "Space-Based Early Warning: From MIDAS to DSP to SBIRS." http://www.gwu.edu/~nsarchiv/nsaebb/nsaebb235/index.htm (accessed on 26 May 2009).

———. *The U.S. Intelligence Community*, Boulder, CO: Westview Press, 1999.

Rip, Michael Russell, and James M. Hasik. *The Precision Revolution*. Annapolis, MD: Naval Institute Press, 2002.

Rosen, Milton W. *The Viking Rocket Story*. New York: Harper, 1955.

Rosolanka, Maj James J. *Defense Support Program (DSP): A Pictorial Chronology 1970–1998*. Los Angeles AFB, CA: SBIRS System Program Office, 1998.

RussianSpaceWeb.com. "Back to Basics: Another Apollo Clone." http://www.russian spaceweb.com/soyuz_acts_origin.html#2008 (accessed 6 February 2008).

Schuler, Maj Mark A. "It Isn't Space, It's Warfare!" In *Space Power Integration: Perspectives from Space Weapons Officers*, edited by Lt Col Kendall K. Brown. Maxwell AFB, AL: Air University Press, 2006.

Secretary of the Navy (SECNAV) Instruction 5400.39c. *Department of the Navy Space Policy*, 6 April 2004.

Sellers, Jerry Jon. *Understanding Space: An Introduction to Astronautics*. 2nd ed. Boston: McGraw Hill, 2004.

———. *Understanding Space: An Introduction to Astronautics*. 3rd ed. Boston: McGraw Hill, 2005.

Sharma, A. K., and Tony Reale. "Updates on Operational Processing for NOAA/NESDIS [National Environmental Satellite, Data, and Information Service] Sounding Data Products and Services." http://cimss.ssec.wisc.edu/itwg/itsc/itsc15/presentations/session11/11_2_sharma.pdf (accessed 16 April 2008).

Shelton, William. *Soviet Space Exploration: The First Decade*. New York: Washington Square Press, 1968.

Sherman, Ron. "MUOS: Milsatcom's Cutting Edge." *Avionics Magazine*, 1 June 2005. http://www.avtoday.com/av/categories/military/936.html (accessed 4 April 2008).

Siddiqi, Asif A. *Challenge to Apollo: The Soviet Union and the Space Race, 1945–1974*. NASA History Series. Washington, DC: NASA, 2000.

"SM-65 Atlas." Federation of American Scientists. http://www.fas.org/nuke/guide/usa/icbm/sm-65.htm (accessed 8 May 2009).

"SM-68B Titan II." Federation of American Scientists. http://www.fas.org/nuke/guide/usa/icbm/sm-68b.htm (accessed 8 May 2009).

Smith, M. V. "Ten Propositions Regarding Space Power." Thesis, Air University, Maxwell AFB, AL, June 2001.

Smith, Marcia S. *Military Space Programs: Issues Concerning DOD's SBIRS and STSS Programs*. Congressional Research Service Report for Congress. Washington, DC: Library of Congress, January 2006.

Smithsonian National Air and Space Museum. "Military Origins of the Space Race." http://www.nasm.si.edu/exhibitions/gal114/spacerace/sec200/sec231.htm (accessed 21 January 2008).

———. "Sensor, Infrared, Series III, Missile Defense Alarm System." http://collections.nasm.si.edu/code/emuseum.asp?profile=objects&newstyle=single&quicksearch=A19700253000 (accessed 26 May 2009).

Smolders, Peter. *Soviets in Space*. New York: Taplinger Publishing Company, 1974.

Snodgrass, Lt Col Roy. "Commercial SATCOM Support—Current/Future." Presentation. LandWarNet 2007, Annual Armed Forces Communications and Electronics Association Conference, Ft. Lauderdale, FL, 21 August 2007.

Space and Missile Systems Center (SMC). *The SMC Story*. http://www.losangeles.af .mil/shared/media/document/AFD-080606-049.pdf (accessed 20 May 2009).

———. Web site. http://www.losangelesafb.com/smc/smc.html (accessed 20 May 2009).

"Space Environment and Orbital Mechanics." Federation of American Scientists. http://www.fas.org/spp/military/docops/army/ref_text/chap5im.htm (accessed 18 April 2008).

Space Today Online. "China's Moon Flights." http://www.spacetoday.org/China/ ChinaMoonflight.html (accessed 5 February 2008).

Space.com. "Japan Announces Manned Moon Flight by 2025." http://www.space.com/ missionlaunches/ap_050406_japan_moon.html (accessed 5 February 2008).

Spiegel, Herbert J., and Arnold Gruber. *From Weather Vanes to Satellites: An Introduction to Meteorology*. New York: John Wiley and Sons, 1983.

Stares, Paul B. *Space and National Security*. Washington, DC: Brookings Institution Press, 1987.

———. *Space Weapons and US Strategy*. London: Croom Helm, 1985.

Sullivan, Walter. *Assault on the Unknown: The International Geophysical Year*. New York: McGraw-Hill, 1961.

Sweetman, Bill, and Kimberley Ebner, eds. *Jane's Space Systems and Industry: 2007– 2008*. Alexandria, VA: Jane's Information Group, 2007.

Szebehely, Victor G. *Adventures in Celestial Mechanics: A First Course in the Theory of Orbits*. Austin, TX: University of Texas Press, 1989.

Tatum, Steve. "Lockheed Martin Delivers Key Hardware for Third Advanced EHF Military Communication Satellite." Lockheed Martin press release. 22 December 2006.

Taylor, R., and M. Crison. "NPOESS Preparatory Project (NPP): Status Update for Interim Science Panel," 2 August 1999. http://jointmission.gsfc.nasa.gov/documents/ powerpoint/RSDO_ISP8-2-99.ppt (accessed 19 April 2008).

Terril, Delbert R., Jr. *Air Force Role in Developing International Outer Space Law*. Maxwell AFB, AL: Air University Press, 1999.

"Tier One: Private Manned Space Program." Scaled Composites. Web site. http://www .scaled.com/projects/tierone/ (accessed 5 February 2008).

"Treaty on Principles Governing the Activities of States in the Exploration and Use of Outer Space, Including the Moon and Other Celestial Bodies." 27 January 1967. Available in United Nations (UN) Publication ST/SPACE/11. New York: UN, 2002. http://www.unoosa.org/oosa/SpaceLaw/outerspt.html (accessed 2 April 2009).

United Nations Office for Outer Space Affairs (UNOOSA). "Space Law: Frequently Asked Questions." http://www.unoosa.org/oosa/en/FAQ/splawfaq.html (accessed 1 April 2009).

US Air Force. "3rd Space Operations Squadron." Fact Sheet. http://www.schriever .af.mil/library/factsheets/factsheet.asp?id=3914 (accessed 13 February 2008).

———. "4th Space Operations Squadron." Fact Sheet. http://www.schriever.af.mil/ library/factsheets/factsheet.asp?id=3915 (accessed 29 February 2008).

———. "20th Air Force." Fact Sheet. http://www.warren.af.mil/library/factsheets/ factsheet.asp?id=4697 (accessed 1 March 2008).

———. "20th Space Control Squadron, Detachment 1." Fact Sheet. http://www.peterson.af.mil/library/factsheets/factsheet.asp?id=4729 (accessed 16 January 2008).

———. "Advanced Extremely High Frequency (AEHF) System." Fact Sheet. http://www.losangeles.af.mil/library/factsheets/factsheet.asp?id=5319 (accessed 25 November 2007).

———. "Air Force Weather Agency." Fact Sheet. http://www.af.mil/factsheets/factsheet.asp?fsID=157 (accessed 24 February 2008).

———. "Defense Meteorological Satellite Program." Fact Sheet. http://www.losangeles.af.mil/library/factsheets/factsheet.asp?id=5321 (accessed 23 February 2008).

———. "Defense Satellite Communications System." Fact Sheet. http://www.losangeles.af.mil/library/factsheets/factsheet.asp?id=5322 (accessed 21 January 2007).

———. "Delta II Launch Vehicle." Fact Sheet. http://www.af.mil/information/factsheets/factsheet.asp?fsID=97 (accessed 10 February 2008).

———. "Det 3, 21st Operations Group." Fact Sheet. http://www.peterson.af.mil/library/factsheets/factsheet.asp?id=4741 (accessed 24 February 2008).

———. "LGM-30 Minuteman III." Fact Sheet. http://www.af.mil/information/factsheets/factsheet.asp?id=113 (accessed 8 May 2009).

———. "MILSTAR." Fact Sheet. http://www.losangeles.af.mil/library/factsheets/factsheet.asp?id=5328 (accessed 25 November 2007).

US Army. Army Space Reference Text. July 1993.

US Centennial of Flight Commission. "Sun Synchronous Orbit." http://www.centennialofflight.gov/essay/Dictionary/SUN_SYNCH_ORBIT/DI155.htm (accessed 18 April 2008).

US House. House Science Committee Hearing: The Future of NPOESS—Results of the Nunn-McCurdy Review of NOAA's Weather Satellite Program. 109th Cong. 2d sess., 2006.

US Navy. "Aerographer's Mate Non-Resident Training Course, April 1999." http://www.combatindex.com/store/NRTC/Sample/AEROGRAPHERS_MATE/Aerographers_Mate_Module_3.pdf (accessed 18 April 2008).

———. "UHF Follow-On Program." Navy Fact Sheet. http://www.spaceflightnow.com/atlas/ac203/03121uhfprogram.html (accessed 2 April 2008).

US Senate. Ambassador Goldberg: Hearings before the Committee on Foreign Relations. 90th Cong., 1st sess., 7 March 1967.

"U.S. Stealth Bombers to Use EHF SatCom from Northrop Grumman." MilsatMagazine 1, no. 1 (First Quarter 2007): 7–8.

US Strategic Command (USSTRATCOM). "Functional Components." http://www.stratcom.mil/organization-fnc_comp.html (accessed 16 January 2008).

———. "Joint Functional Component Command for Space." Fact Sheet. http://www.stratcom.mil/fact_sheets/fact_space.html (accessed 17 March 2008).

———. "Theater Ballistic Missile Warning." Fact Sheet. http://www.stratcom.mil/fact_sheets/fact_tbmw.html (accessed 8 April 2008).

———. "U.S. Strategic Command History." http://www.stratcom.mil/about-ch.html (accessed 16 January 2008).

V2ROCKET.COM. "A-4/V-2 Makeup—Tech Data & Markings." http://www.v2rocket.com/start/makeup/design.html (accessed 8 May 2009).

Wallace, Lane E. Dreams, Hopes, Realities: NASA's Goddard Space Flight Center: The First Forty Years. Washington, DC: NASA History Office, 1999.

Walters, Hellen B. Herman Oberth: Father of Space Travel. New York: Macmillan, 1962.

Watts, Barry D. "The Military Use of Space: A Diagnostic Assessment." Center for Strategic Budget Assessment. http://www.csbaonline.org/4Publications/PubLibrary/R.20010201.The_Military_Use_o/R.20010201.The_Military_Use_o.pdf (accessed 18 April 2008).

Weisbrot, Robert. *Maximum Danger: Kennedy, the Missiles, and the Crisis of American Confidence.* Chicago: Ivan R. Dee, 2001.

White, Gen Thomas D. "Air and Space Are Indivisible." *Air Force Magazine,* March 1958, 40–41.

White House. National Security Presidential Directive (NSPD) 23. *Missile Defense Policy,* 17 December 2002.

———. *National Space Policy Directives and Executive Charter,* 2 November 1989.

———. *US Commercial Remote Sensing Policy,* 25 April 2003.

———. *US National Space Policy,* 31 August 2006.

White, Irvin. *Decision-Making for Space: Law and Politics in Air, Sea and Outer Space.* West Lafayette, IN: Purdue University Press, 1971.

"Wideband Gapfiller System: Satellite Design." GlobalSecurity.org. http://www.globalsecurity.org/space/systems/wgs-satdesign.htm (accessed 14 February 2008).

Wilson, Tom. "Threats to United States Space Capabilities." Prepared for the Commission to Assess US National Security Space Management and Organization. http://www.fas.org/spp/eprint/article05.html#10 (accessed 11 May 2009).

Woodbury, David O. *Outward Bound for Space.* Boston: Little, Brown & Co., 1961.

Wright, David, Laura Grego, and Lisbeth Gronlund. *The Physics of Space Security: A Reference Manual.* http://www.amacad.org/publications/Physics_of_Space_Security.pdf (accessed 23 January 2008).

X Prize Foundation. "Ansari X Prize." http://www.xprize.org/x-prizes/ansari-x-prize (accessed 5 February 2008).

Xinhua News Agency. "China Launches First Manned Spacecraft." China View/View China. http://news.xinhuanet.com/english/2003-10/15/content_1123817.htm (accessed 5 February 2008).